THE ⟨THIEF OF⟩
VIRTUE

BY EDEN PHILLPOTTS

Author of "The Haven," "Children of the Mist,"
"The Three Brothers," etc.

NEW YORK
JOHN LANE COMPANY
MCMX

PUBLISHERS PRINTING COMPANY, NEW YORK

THE THIEF OF VIRTUE

BOOK I

CHAPTER I

CLOUD-SHADOWS swept a desert, and beneath their stains
the bosom of the waste appeared to rise and fall, as
though, not earth, but some enormous, animate creature
of earth, panted here, and stretched its rugged immensity
upon the midst of that wider world outspread around it.
Dartmoor, beheld from a height above her central plains,
sprang to a crown of tors, and rounded mightily on many
a hog-backed hill. Within this amphitheatre twinkled
the eastern arm of Dart, straggled a wood, and clustered
a few cottages beside the river; while at distances remote
from the central dwellings, sunk humbly beside this
streamlet or beneath that steep, there shone out roof-
trees of little farms.

The Moor encircled them in billowy plains of pallid
yellow and dim green. Its faces rolled upon each other;
they fell here to water-side; they ascended and broke
where the granite burst through them in peaks and ra-
vines; they brightened where the ling bloom spattered
their leagues with light. A lesser fret of inherent colour
was manifest under that mightier robe where sunshine
blazed and shadows sped. One garment covered all things
in permanent mosaic of herbage and stone, stark peat
and sparkling water—the intrinsic raiment of the Moor,

1

that altered only to the call of the seasons, vanished only at the fall of the snow. But the other, cast down by medley of light and cloud, spread, moved, and flowed along in a pattern more vast and grand.

At midday in summer, shadows, very purple under the ambient splendour of the hour, roamed over Dartmoor, sometimes in thronging companies and sometimes alone. They leapt the rivers, raced the level heaths, and climbed the hills. Upon the sky there worked two separate winds, and each drove its own flock. At lower level advanced the cumuli and threw their shades upon the earth; and above them great lines of transparent but visible vapour, filmy against the blue, sailed in upper zones, and by their direction marked another stream of air. The cirri, like fingers that rose out of a palm beneath the horizon, spread fanwise from a point unseen. Then to the zenith, in majestic and unfolding perspective they ascended. Beneath the sun these cloud-lances of the height, flying arrowy, burnt like flame, and by contrast dimmed the round, golden heads of the greater clouds beneath them. Most delicate and dazzling bright were they—mere flakes of fire upon the solar face that no way dimmed the downbeat of his glory; but that they, too, flung shadows and spread invisible gauze of shade among the darker umbrage might not be doubted, though the unseen passing of them cooled no cheek. Upon their aerial way they went, and closed their ranks again and narrowed as they sank to the farther horizon.

In the sunlit, lower strata the full sky pageant culminated. Here cloud-billows like bergs first floated along the edge of earth in level lines, wind-steered. Then they approached; their magnitude increased and they bulked enormous. Now, like volcanic isles, they loomed—like isles all built of mountains—and though light glowed upon their peaks and precipices, darkness and storm dwelt in the caverns beneath them. Concavities of gloom receded depth upon depth within their toppling and burning cornices; and many a convexity of light spread molten upon the inner darkness and set its neighbour cloud on fire. Out of the surges spired new pinnacles and spread new tides of vapour, now shadowed by other masses that whirled between them and the sun, now open to the ray, leaping and splashing in feathers and foam of fire against the blue. A thousand transient passages of waxing and waning splendour modified these fierce exchanges of light and shadow. Ever and anon they clashed indeed in fleeting battles, but more often each melted into the other; the radiance was overlaid with tender colours that pervaded and qualified; the gloom was shot and arched with bannerets and streamers of pure light. The breasts of the rolling legions blazed and faded, blazed and faded again; and their heaviest murk was apparent only, not real. For the least cloud-shadows racing over earth were darker far than the deepest, stormiest stains upon the cloud-cliffs ascending above them. There the darkness was light—the whole sky a relation of great and lesser light; and clouds that lowered sombre against some glory of fire-steeped vapour round about, or upon the azure of the firmament, sailed lustrous and luminous contrasted with the bosom of the earth-mother that bore them.

The intricate movements of these tangled and wind-tormented multitudes passed all telling. The staple of them furnished a loom for light direct and reflected, their substance also displayed violent and rapid motion. Only the remoteness of the clouds made it possible even to calculate the terrific turmoil of the flying masses, or guess at the extent of their furlings and unfurlings, their totterings and fallings, their uprisings and accumulations and their downfalls, dislimnings and destructions wrought by the hurricane aloft. They huddled together, ascended, collapsed; and before one might chronicle the overthrow of some cloud-palace a mile high, the levelled ruins spread for fresh elevations to lift upon. Above vaporous marshes arose castles, with silver flags flying from their towers and battlements; and ere the last pinnacle soared to its place, all burnt away again and shot in tattered wisps aloft or sank in radiant wreckage below. The pageant unrolled, hung three miles above the earth, and swept onward in ruin and renascence—a symbol of the suspected principle that all things shall for ever be coming but never be come.

The wonder of the clouds diminished, the cumuli humped and dwarfed; there grew increase of density and dimness along their faces and a lessened splendour upon their retreating heads. They shrank and dwindled. They departed, and distance at length hid all the wonder of their hearts until, mildly, gently, as ships on a summer sea, they sailed down to the distant earth-line. The snowy alps and tortured cloud-crests vanished; all detail died out of them; the glory and passion of them and their storms and strivings were merged into long, still lakes of pearl, that outlined uttermost earth and stretched above one faint thread, where sea met sky afar off in the south.

So they passed, to the shepherding of herald Hermes; and in their procession and recession they offered an image of that mightier duty trusted to the plume-footed son of Maia. For his the task, not only to lead the clouds from on high to their dissolving places in the deep; but also to guard those other vapours—the shades and shadows of mankind—upon their last pilgrimage from light into darkness, from the upper world to that nether kingdom where no sun shines.

CHAPTER II

A MAN who loved well enough to watch clouds now
beheld them. His face was tilted to the sky, for he lay
supine in the heath on Hartland Tor, and gazed upward.
But for once he perceived nothing; and though the turmoil above was miniatured on his blue eyes, mind had
drawn a shutter between the image of these things and
Philip Ouldsbroom's brain. Therein clouds of another
pattern ran together, but a sudden incident aroused him
out of his thoughts. There was a rush and hurtle of
wings overhead and a frightened scutter of lesser wings.
A great bird recovered itself after a futile stroke, and
soared away gleaming; a lesser bird sped by and dashed
with trembling speed into the heart of a furze brake. A
kestrel had struck at a linnet and missed her.

The man laughed.

"Ah! my bold hero, you must hawk better than that
if you want a dinner," he said.

Then his eyes followed the quarry.

"Good luck to the little un!" he added.

The man's heart was accurately revealed in this attitude to pursuer and pursued. He could find it in him to
view both with friendliness and sympathy.

His thoughts turned inward again, lighted by the incident.

Again he laughed to himself, drew a pipe from his
pocket and wiped his head, which was hot from long
basking in the sun.

"Hope I shan't strike and miss, like thicky criss-
hawk!" he thought.

He smoked, and his mind mirrored a fellow creature.
He saw a sturdy, strongly built girl of two-and-twenty,

5

clad in earth-colours—a Moor woman whose features were regular, whose dark grey eyes were bright, whose hair was black, whose bosom was deep and large. She had no great beauty in his opinion; but she possessed what he lacked, and he had thought of her as a wife.

"Unity!" he said out loud, and stretched in the hot heather and felt the sun burn. "A brave name that. 'Unity Crymes'; but 'Unity Ouldsbroom' come she takes me."

His thoughts rambled backward; he looked at a black band on his coat and remembered a hawk that had struck and not missed.

"Too old, some might say—too old for a wench in her early twenties; but none who knows me. Forty—what's forty to the likes of me? Forty years wise and twenty years old—that's what I be."

This man's widowed father had recently died and left him lonely. He dwelt at Hartland Farm above the hamlet of Postbridge, and upon his parent's passing became the owner of that tenement.

"The old chap was seventy-eight, barring two days, when he dropped," thought Philip—"and he died a boy. At least, that's how Barbara put it. And me—why, she'd say I wasn't old enough to marry!"

After a gap in his thoughts, he rose suddenly.

"Talking of Barbara—I'll go and see her. 'Tis the middle time of day, and the shop's like to be empty."

He shook himself and strode off down the ferny slope above his home, where it stood at the foot of the tor. To the valley he went, passed beside Dart, crossed the bridge and entered a low, slate-roofed and whitewashed house close at hand.

Here a department of the State had local habitation, and the business of the Post Office was pursued through that strange odour only to be smelled in such little general shops as Barbara Hext controlled at Postbridge.

At one end of the counter, behind an open wire grille, was the postal apparatus of ink-bottles, pens, red blotting-paper and the rest. Advertisements and announcements hung here, and an unusual air of neatness and briskness characterised the place. Even to the telegraphic forms and the pencil fastened to a string beside them, all was tidy and trim.

The shop counter spread from this sanctity, and here, too, there lacked the usual confusion of mingled goods. Everything proper to such a place appeared; but everything was orderly. Tubs of lard and butter, sides of bacon, sections of cheese, tins of sugar, raisins and tea, boxes of chocolates and bottles of sweets came in the first department. With them other comestibles were ranged, and then a barrier separated the next division, and one turned to china, ornamental and useful, saucepans, mouse-traps, oil cans, tools, string, knives, ditchers' gloves and sickles, various contrivances such as corkscrews and beer-taps on cards, wire nails, and countless other practical matters. Beyond again were woollen and cotton goods, men's braces and women's sun-bonnets, together with children's garments and the rough raiment in demand on Dartmoor.

The mingled odours of these things hung in the air; but even that was modified by their skilful distribution. A suggestion of ample accommodation implied by so much variety, in reality did not embrace it. The shop was very small, yet so perfect and systematic were the arrangements, that the mistress of it was never in a hurry and never at a loss. On a large card that extended half the length of the shop, were these words, '*If you don't see what you want, ask for it.*'

The mistress of this establishment was called Barbara Hext. She came of old Postbridge stock, but had lived a part of her life in London and elsewhere. Scandals were rumoured concerning her past, but her wits none questioned, and when she returned to her native village as a peace-loving, still handsome woman of fifty-five; when she succeeded the retiring postmaster and opened a little shop, she was well received and no questions asked concerning her career. Many liked and a few disliked her, but none doubted her sense or the value of her opinions, even though they ran counter to the accepted, seasoned wisdom of the village.

She sat now eating a sandwich of bread-and-cheese behind her counter, and casting figures in a long narrow
ledger. Her face was furrowed somewhat at the cheeks,
but her eyes were beautiful; her mouth possessed the firm,
full lines and fine colour of a young woman's; her hair
was only streaked with grey, and she wore a plain stuff
dress over a neat and bird-like figure. The fascination of
sex still strongly marked her, and many a man of middle
age had begged her to share his life.

There entered now Philip Ouldsbroom, a jovial and
Dionysian spirit He was fair and flaxen, with crisp,
sand-coloured hair. He shaved his ruddy face clean and
displayed a full throat, that went without a collar as
often as possible. His teeth were white and perfect; his
mouth was large and easy, and readier to expand than
tighten. His fine limbs were clad carelessly in worn garments. Though forty years old, the man's heart was
younger, and his trust was fuller than often happens at
that turning-point. He was the only son of parents who
had not married until somewhat late in life An untrou-
bled, prosperous existence had fallen to him, and he seldom looked ahead of the passing hour. But now, his aged
father dying suddenly, he was turned from his revels and
playthings to the reality of mastership. He liked women
well, but with a regard very general until now. They too
were fond of him and spoiled him. He was often on their
tongues. At present not a few wondered where his choice
of a wife would fall; for the time was come. Ouldsbroom indeed wanted a wife, and he knew the girl most
likely to please him.

"Can I have a tell, Barbara?" he asked. "I thought
I'd very likely catch you alone."

"And welcome. But put your pipe out first—I won't
have smoking here—not when I can prevent it."

He obeyed her, took a chair, turned its back to the
counter and straddled his legs across it A dog came up
and greeted him with effusion. It was a liver-coloured
spaniel and belonged to Miss Hext.

Philip helped himself to biscuits from an open tin and
began to talk with his mouth full.

" 'Tis like this—I never was fond of putting all my eggs in one basket.''

"So I've heard the women say,'' she answered drily.

"Bless 'em! But here I am—husband old; and I want a wife.''

She looked at him and took off a pair of spectacles.

With her glasses Miss Hext appeared to cast aside not a few years also.

"A wife, Philip?''

"And why not? I must have somebody to leave my farm to. And 'tis time I set about thinking on him. I talk plain to you, because you're the sensiblest female in these parts.''

"Might be that and not very witty. Well, who's the poor woman?''

Miss Hext's spaniel was sitting up with her eyes on Ouldsbroom—the image of patience but determined mendicity.

"You beauty!'' he said, and stooped down and rubbed his cheek against her muzzle. Then he gave her a biscuit.

"The very dogs see through you.''

He shrugged his shoulders.

"Let 'em. Well, what d'you say to Unity Crymes?''

Barbara did not answer, and he helped himself again.

"Those biscuits are for sale,'' she said.

"You're a dear woman, and the loveliest eyes on Dartmoor still,'' he declared irrelevantly. "But Unity?''

"You say Unity; I say Henry Birdwood.''

"Damn Henry Birdwood! 'Tis idle talk, for I asked her brother a week ago and he knew nought of it. At least he only said there might be something in it. They'm all Methodies together; and Unity and young Birdwood meet in that psalm-smiting hole up the village and shout from the same hymn-book—that's all.''

"You know you're lying.''

He grew hot and his face turned a shade redder. He clenched his fist and banged it on the counter.

"There's nothing in it, I tell you; and if there is? Him a shepherd and nought to hope for and nought saved; and me—a solid man with a farm of my own.''

"And forty to his twenty-five."

"What then? 'Tis fair fighting, Barbara; and if she's the woman I think, she'll know which side her bread's buttered."

Miss Hext did not speak, and he went on again.

"D'you like Birdwood?—honest now."

"That's neither here nor there."

"You know you hate all Methodies. And Unity—I'll soon stop that tomfoolery when I've got her."

"Think twice," she said; "though I'm a fool to tell a man to think twice who so seldom thinks at all. Don't you offer to marry Unity Crymes."

"Why d'you say that?"

"Because she's the sort will throw over the other and take you; and he's the sort——"

"Stop!" he shouted out. "You're all wrong and out of bias every way. How can she throw over the man afore they'm tokened? Don't I tell you he's nought to her?"

"Yes, you tell me so, you silly chap; but what do you know about it? Do the men and maidens give you all their secrets? If they are tokened, does it follow they've let all the world know it? They are the silent, sly sort— both of 'em; and they'll doubtless agree to wait a bit till his prospects better——"

He was tramping up and down with his blue eyes sulked over by yellow eyebrows.

"You're wrong; you're wrong," he said. Then a thought struck him. "Anyway, if I offer and she's tokened to t'other, she'll have to tell me so."

"And then what? Then, because you can't have her, you'll raise heaven and earth and fall out with Birdwood and make a lot of silly trouble."

"I *will* have her if I'm minded to it!"

"If you could have her for the asking—and I dare say you can, whether she's promised the other man or not— still, I'd say you were terrible mistaken."

"Why—why? What folly to talk to a grown man as if he was a boy."

" 'Tis worse to talk to a boy as if he was a man. But

I'm thinking of her, not you. You're not the husband
for her."

There came an interruption; a pony clattered to the
door and a man dismounted. The beast was rough, its
rider was rougher. He wore scanty, sun-tanned clothes
fretted to holes and rags; his hat was green with age and
battered, his shirt was also tattered and scarcely covered
his bosom. Upon one boot he carried a spur.

"Talk of the devil and you'll see his man," said Philip.
"Here's Ned Sleep, from Teign Head."

The newcomer entered, pushed back his hat, and without speech brought out a red handkerchief and began to
untie a knot in the corner of it. He was grizzled and thin
as a winter hedge. His teeth were broken; his cheek-
bones thrust forth above the bush of his black beard,
and his small eyes were also obscured by the long hairs
that hung over from his eyebrows. Forehead he had
scarcely any, and black hair descended to within an inch
of his brows.

"And how is it with you, Sleep?" asked Ouldsbroom.
But the man made no answer. He untied the knot in his
handkerchief and produced a coin.

"What can I do for you, Mr. Sleep?" inquired the
postmistress.

The customer debated the question with a certain
furtive caution. It was half a minute before he answered; and then in a hoarse voice he spoke.

"Penny stamp," he said, and put down his penny.

Philip laughed.

"And have 'e ridden all the ways from Teign Head
for that?" he asked.

Again Mr. Sleep weighed his answer with prolonged
caution, but at length replied.

"For that," he said, like an echo.

"And how's Henry Birdwood?" asked the master of
Hartland.

Mr. Sleep took his stamp, tied it up in the handkerchief, and prepared to depart.

"Give the man a drink of cider, Barbara," directed
Ouldsbroom. "Wilt have a drink, Ned?"

Sleep reflected, but the answer was long in coming.

"Thank you—'tis drowthy weather," he answered.

"And draw me a mug too; there's a dear soul. I've ate your biscuits till I be so dry as an old bone."

While Miss Hext obeyed, Philip asked another question.

"And what for do you want a stamp, Ned? I didn't know writing was in your line."

The Moor-man looked round doubtfully, and, after private consideration, drew a newspaper from his pocket.

"One of they fishing gentlemen left it on the river," he said very slowly. "And I come by it. And I read it."

He stopped, weary of words, and called Ouldsbroom's attention to an advertisement.

"'Shepherd wanted — no incumbrances,'" began Philip. Then he read on to himself.

Miss Hext returned with two pint mugs of cider upon a tray.

"Ned here's going to leave Teign Head," began the farmer; but Mr. Sleep put up his hand in deprecation.

"I don't say that—only—well—there 'tis: eighteen shillings a week."

"And don't Gregory Twigg give you that?"

The other shook his head.

"Be damned if I'd stop an hour," swore Ouldsbroom.

"Does he know you think to leave him, Ned?"

Sleep drank half his cider and the others talked together. Then, when the postmistress had forgotten her question, he answered it.

"I showed him the paper."

"And what did he say?"

"He said—he said 'twas a free country—no more."

"Free!" scoffed Miss Hext. "Even Twigg knows that's a lie. Show me a free man."

Mr. Sleep shook his head.

"Freedom's a very dangerous thing, ma'am," he said. "For my part I wouldn't trust it. I ban't wishful to feel what 'tis like, I'm sure. Still, I've a right to lift my eye to eighteen shillings."

"This paper's three weeks old, however," said Philip.

Sleep drank the rest of his cider and nodded while he

did so. Then, when he had wiped his mouth on his neck-kerchief, he replied:

" 'Twas but two days old when I comed by it; but a man doesn't change his state of life without a power of thought."

"Bah! You ought to have been a toad in a hole," said the farmer. "Get along with you!"

Ned without more words put his paper back in his pocket and prepared to depart, but when he had reached the door, he returned, lifted his boot on a box and removed his solitary spur. Then he put it upon the other boot.

"I kicked pony on left side coming down," he explained; "but I'll kick un 'pon right side going back"

"A fair-minded fool," laughed Ouldsbroom. "And you can tell Birdwood——" he broke off while Ned stood still. " 'Tis no odds," concluded Philip "I'll tell him myself."

"And what were you going to tell him?" asked Barbara when the horseman had ridden away.

"Why—just to keep his paws off Unity Crymes; but then I thought I'd do wiser to see her first."

"A very clever thought for certain."

"And what was you going to tell me against her?" he asked suddenly. "You'd got something to say when that zany come in and threw it out of your head."

"As well he did belike. You mind your own business, Philip, and I'll mind mine."

"Mine's simple. I'm going up to Stannon this instant moment"

"Mine's simple too. You owe me twopence for cider."

He paid her and then challenged her

"Look here now: I'll bet you a side of bacon to three of them big boxes of chocolate that Unity Crymes will be tokened to me this time to-morrow. And, if I win, she shall have the sweeties to-morrow night, and if I lose, you shall have the bacon afore Michaelmas."

She declined the wager

"I'm more like to lose than win," she answered

"Ha-ha!" he crowed; "that's a pretty good compliment to me, Barbara."

"It may be; but 'tis a pretty poor one to the woman. Just think of that. If she refuses you, then she's a better piece than I take her for, and if she don't—the Lord help you!"

"The stuff even a wise creature can talk! D'you think I don't know all about her and her sense and cleverness?"

"*You* know all about a woman!" she answered. "That bitch knows more about 'em than you do—or ever will."

The spaniel wagged her tail and cringed to his hand.

"Will you dance at the wedding, whether or no?" asked Philip.

Some children entered the shop, and the farmer, diving in his pocket, found three halfpence for them, called them by their names, picked up a very small boy, set him high aloft on an empty shelf and then went off. The children shouted with laughter, and Miss Hext had to fetch a pair of steps before she could rescue the baby from his perch.

CHAPTER III

CERTAIN tenement farms of Dartmoor lie in the rich
regions about East Dart, and save where the Duchy of
Cornwall has acquired them, they continue to be free-
holds independent of the surrounding Forest.

Hartland's most ancient walls still rise under the tor
that names them, and beneath, as the vale opens south-
ward, stand the snug and clustered homesteads of Lower
Merripit; Runnage, risen from its ashes with fine, dawn-
facing front; the ruin of Walna; Dury in the mire—
black and white behind its oaken grove; Peshull's three
massive dwellings, their mediæval walls in places five feet
thick. With this venerable abode and Hartland, the adjacent Bellaford's deep-eaved homesteads vie in age, and
lower yet, where Dart approaches her sister stream from
the west, stand the old mill of Babenay, Redden, not far
distant, and Brimpts upon the river's western bank

Under ancient laws the heirs of these old-time tenements, or those who might purchase the inheritance of
them, were at liberty to enclose eight further acres of the
waste upon payment of an annual shilling for the use of
the reigning monarch. These additional acres were called
'the newtake', and as a result of the privilege, there
sprang up an order of enclosed lands with dwelling-
houses upon them. Such extensions have in process of
time become farms on their own account, and we find
now, in addition to the homesteads mentioned above, not
a few centres of husbandry sprung from them. Of these
may be named Higher Merripit and Stannon, near Postbridge; Bellaford Combe and Laughtor Hole in the great
valley below.

15

Another group of tenements shall be found nigh West Dart, but our concern is with a few of those already mentioned.

To Stannon farm, beneath the hill of that name, Philip Ouldsbroom now turned his steps, tramped the modern thoroughfare of the Moor for a space, then left it half way up Merripit Hill and struck out northerly over the heather.

Presently, far beneath him, appeared the little farm

Seen from these lofty slopes, where they extend and form a giant easel for sunset to paint upon, little Stannon lay under its parent hill amid small crofts. The homestead looked like a grey hen with wings outspread above her chickens, for the walls sloped to right and left of the main mass in a manner simple and symmetrical Dwarfed to a spot appeared the farm under the tor that swept to the sky above it. A brook wound beneath and descended from its cradle of rushes upon White Ridge Its fountains glittered in a lace of silver that, crossing and recrossing, wove patterns upon the hill, then tumbled into one channel and began their work by carrying sweet water to Stannon.

To the south, below the farm, the valley opened and wound toward Postbridge through marshy bottoms of mire and scrub. But the birch and alder that aforetime flourished here are gone, though often a turf-cutter digs their ghostly limbs, still cased in silvery bark, from guardianship of the prophylactic peat.

Ouldsbroom descended the hill, fell into a rutted road that wound to the farm, crossed the brook and opened the wicket He made no ado at the door, but entered to find the folk of Stannon at their dinner Four people sat beside the table and consumed the second course of their meal—suet pudding with treacle

Quinton Crymes was a thin, brown man of thirty; but the robust and ruddy Gertrude, his wife, numbered several years less. They had been married a year, and she was with child Unity Crymes, the farmer's sister, and his labourer, one James Coaker, completed the household. The girl was clad in colours that had once been bright, but were now faded into dingy harmony. Green, blue and grey were felt as tones of her raiment; yet so modified and stained had they become, that she might have passed unperceived among the stones, dead heath, and fading brake fern of the waste Her dark hair was rough, her skirt was short, and her legs sturdy. Her full figure suggested maternity; her face was not unhandsome, largely modelled, and strong. She was a creature indigenous to the Moor as rock or fern. She could read and write, she possessed great decision of character and a secretive mind. Will power had run through the woman-mould in her family. The men were feebler and their wives generally ruled them Two elder brothers and two elder sisters she had; but none save Quinton offered her a home. One of her sisters was married to a huckster at Chagford; the other was in service at Exeter. The head of the family, John Crymes, worked in the granite quarries nigh Princetown and lived there with his wife and children, while to Quinton the farm of Stannon had descended from his grandfather. Unity abode here for the present, but Mrs. Crymes indicated that space at Stannon would be precious anon 'When my third comes,' she said with prophetic assurance, 'her'll have to go.'

It seemed probable, however, that Unity might find a home of her own before that event. The shepherd, Henry Birdwood, was courting her, and albeit she kept her own counsel in a manner very steadfast, Quinton and his wife both guessed that their neighbour from Teign Head would be the man. The farmer marvelled that such a good-looking youth as Birdwood could think twice of a woman in whom his fraternal eyes saw nothing, but he was none the less glad; and he and his wife did what they could to further the match

"Pick a bit with us, Ouldsbroom," said Quinton. " 'Tis a longful time since you was over here."

"I'll drink, if Unity will fetch me a mug," said the visitor. "Then, if she's done her meat, I want to speak to her "

Everybody was well used to Philip's direct and abrupt methods. Though a man who hated business, he was,

by this accident of impatience, not a bad business man.
His nature took him to the root of things   In love, in
work, in pleasure, in pain, he went to the point by the
shortest road he could find.   Nevertheless, this attitude
to life did not prevent him from wasting the greater part
of his time, but when something was to do, he did it with
the utmost expedition; delay was suffocation to him and
patience a virtue beyond his temperamental powers to
practise.

His demand to speak with Unity surprised nobody,
therefore.   The families were old friends and had inter-
married in a past generation.

Philip drank, uttered a few vague speeches, hoped that
all was well with his neighbours, and exhibited uncon-
cealed impatience   But Unity made no haste.   She
smiled out of her dark grey eyes at her sister-in-law when
the visitor arose and strode to the window; then she took
some more of the pudding.

Ouldsbroom ceased to speak, but gave off a vigorous
puff or two and, at last, sitting down again, began striking his leathern leggings with his stick

Quinton whispered under his breath to his sister.

"Get on! Don't keep the man waiting!"

Still she took no notice.

Then the master of Stannon strove to make conversation.

"Foxes be plenty for the hunters this autumn, Ouldsbroom "

"Ess fay—and geese will be few," said his wife
feelingly.   "Another of my fine goslings gone.   The
bowldacious varmints come down over in broad daylight.
Unity seed one lying watchin 'em, like a rich man watches
his money; didn't you, Unity?"

"Yes, I did," said the girl.   Then she drank some water,
wiped her mouth on the fall of the table-cloth, and rose.

"I'm ready now, Mr. Philip," she said

"Come on then," he answered, starting up.   "Best to
get your sun-bonnet."

"No, I don't want it. The sun can't come through my
hair."

He looked at her admiringly—her heavy locks curled neatly up, her clean-turned brown face, her firm mouth, and her big bosom.

They went out together, and Gertrude wondered what fancy was got into Ouldsbroom's head

"He've always been friendly enough to her—and to everything personable in a petticoat, for that matter. It surely can't be that he cares a jot about her?" she asked.

Quinton shook his head.

" 'Tis beyond reason I can't picture the man married. And yet like enough now his father's gone—— Of course 'twould be a terrible fine thing," he mused.

"Don't fancy such nonsense," answered the woman. " 'Twould be terrible fine, as you say, but terrible fine things don't happen in your family. Besides, we know very well she's so good as promised to Henry Birdwood."

Meantime Philip and the girl left Stannon.

"Come as far as the sheepfold," he said. " 'Tis out of the way and a nice bit of shade in the ruin."

She laughed and did not guess his purpose

"Lord love it!" she cried; "don't travel so fast, I've just had my dinner."

He stayed his speed.

"To think—to—think——" he began "How old are you—twenty-two—eh?"

"Twenty-two last month."

"And I never gived you a gift."

"Why should you?"

"I'm forty."

"Never!"

"Well, 'tis so, unless the front leaf of our old Bible's a liar. Forty; but don't feel it, or anything near it."

"Nor look it, I'm sure."

"Glad to hear you say that."

"You've worn well."

"Ess, I have—along of being in the open air and keeping an open mind I often go at this time of year and sleep up in the hills—just for love of the wakening. I've got holts like the foxes up-along. I'll show 'em to you some day."

He rambled on and she still wondered.

"D'you know what I'd like to happen best in the world?" he asked suddenly.

"How should I?"

"Why!" he burst out, "for me and you to sleep all night together in my den up under Cut Hill!"

"Be you out of your mind?"

"Not I. My mind's made up firm as a rock, and, look here, damn it, I can't wait till we get to the fold——"

He cast a glance round about the empty Moor, then turned to her.

"Sit down 'pon this stone and listen to me I want a wife, and there's only one woman will do Only one And you're the woman—you—you! Don't stare as if 'twas a thunderbolt. I will have it so, Unity. I've thought of it time and again since father died. I love you—every bit of you. I'm well to do. You shall have a servant Somehow it's come over me with a rush these late days It must be I'm not half good enough for such a rare fine girl, but all the same it must be. It shall, I tell you."

He sat down, and she felt his heavy hand on her shoulder, pulling her beside him. Her frame grew suddenly weak and limp from head to heel at this amazing proposal. She sank near the man, then wriggled farther off as he made to put his arm round her. But her nerve steadied quickly.

"This be too awful sudden," she said, and he saw that though her voice was steady her breast was not, and her colour was not She panted and she glowed. Then she grew pale and put her hand to her bosom, where these sudden emotions had raised an oppression.

"Everything with any taste to it comes sudden—good or bad I'm always sudden. But I'm a good laster You won't repent it. Proud I'll be to fetch and carry for you, Unity, and make you the first woman in Postbridge"

She did not answer, but her mind moved with swift calculation and she weighed all that this must mean Here was a man very eligible in her eyes and a man easy to be ruled. She had known him for five years and appraised his temper very accurately. He only needed the right hand and the light one But the other man—the man she loved—would try to rule her. She had always realised this, and had fancied that to be ruled was easier than to rule, and probably in the long run pleasanter; yet now the new prospect thrust so fiercely before her suggested that to reign over a rich man might be a finer thing than to be ruled by a poor one. Roughly that was the problem cast before her; but her knowledge of Philip Ouldsbroom and Henry Birdwood complicated it

Characteristic of the woman's devious spirit was the fact that one paramount condition in this problem she ignored She had promised to marry Birdwood

"Speak"! cried Philip at length. "I can't stand this. I'm burning alive! 'Tis the first time, mind—the first and the last, for 'yes' I will have. Who be you—a pretty, dinky chit of a cheel like you—to know better what's good for you than a grown man like me? You're the first—the very, very first, Unity. God strike me down this minute if you ban't the only woman that I've ever axed to marry me And d'you think I've waited forty year to hear 'no'? Not I! There's only one answer for me, and the quicker said the sooner comes my peace again. 'Tis a bargain—quick!'"

"What's the bargain then?" she asked—to gain time.

"That you come to Hartland and take all I've got to give you, and love me evermore through thick and thin till the end of us."

"You'll want somebody to look after your money?"

"The money looks after itself I want somebody to look after me I want you—only you. Will you come? I wish you could come now this minute "

Her self-contained nature withstood these shocks A mile off in the valley she saw a man slowly pushing forward on a pony Before him drifted half a hundred sheep. Philip's back was turned to the rider.

"You must give me time," she said.

"Why—why—what d'you want time for? Time was made for slaves. 'Tis only to waste it, if you take it The answer's got to be 'yes.' I will have you, I tell you."

"Go your ways and leave me," she said. "I won't keep you waiting long—I promise that; but a maiden can't decide the whole of her life in a moment. 'Tisn't true love to want to make her."

He flogged his legs and stamped his heels into the earth.

"What a nuisance that you can't see it and feel it like me. A toad under a harrow I shall be till you say 'yes.'"

"I'll make up my mind so swift as I can."

"I'll come over to-night then."

"That's too soon, Mr Philip."

"Drop that 'Mister.' I won't have it—as if I was a stranger instead of your husband. To-morrow morning then? I don't wait an hour longer. Why, what the hell d'you want to keep me on tenterhooks all these hours for? And loving me all the time, I'll swear."

"Go now," she said "And come back to me to-morrow, if you must. And think terrible serious about it. Belike you're making a fool of yourself so well as me "

"Kiss me then!" he said "You shall—you shall, or I'll give you no peace. I swore when I woke this morn that I'd kiss you afore night."

"There's a man in the valley."

"Let him rot there! What's any other man in the world to you but me?"

Before she could stop him he put his arms round her, held her tight to him and kissed her all over her face.

"To-morrow!" he said. "And now I be going to ride hell for leather to Tavistock for to buy you a proper ring with a proper jool in it!"

He went off to the west, and Unity remained sitting on the stone where he had left her. She put up a lock of hair from her face and considered the situation. Ouldsbroom was soon out of sight on his direct road to Hartland, but the man behind the sheep began to get nearer He could not see her where she sat, yet she marked him clearly, and noted that he hesitated at a point where two tracks met and ran into each other on the way to Postbridge.

One road would have taken Henry Birdwood by Stannon and given his sheep an additional journey before he reached their destined pasture; the other road was more direct and led onward into the Moor past the ruined sheepfold a few hundred yards from Unity's present position.

Birdwood took the shorter way and denied himself a possible glimpse of the woman he loved. She watched him and, in her mind's eye, saw him.

Her bent of spirit rather sought than evaded him at this crisis. The prospect of becoming Ouldsbroom's wife was far too splendid to ignore, even before the possibility of treachery to a man she liked better. But for the moment it struck her that some hint of events, some shadow of doubt, had better be thrown as quickly as she could throw it over her betrothed's life.

The opportunity had been thrust upon her, and opportunity she was not made to miss.

In her heart she knew already that she meant to marry Ouldsbroom. She recognised no moral side to this abrupt defection. She did not love Birdwood any the less. She left the details to look after themselves. Her present purpose was to tackle a painful and trying necessity before she had leisure to think any more about it. She was a sort of spirit who hated time to pass between her and execution of things difficult or unpleasant, and in this trait she resembled the man who had just offered to marry her.

Unity waited until the elder man was out of sight, then she went down to the sheepfold and surprised Henry Birdwood as he passed it on his way homeward

CHAPTER IV

THE ruined sheepfold stood four-square on the western slope of Stannon Hill Built nearly a hundred years ago, at the time when many enthusiastic spirits discovered Dartmoor and dreamed dreams of prosperity to be dug from her bowels or garnered on her breast, it adds one to a long list of futile enterprises and lies forlorn among the hills—historic evidence that even the toil of a Scot may miscarry. Down the midst run parallel rows of great stones, and at the eastern extremity still stand the roofless remains of a dwelling-house. The place was burned down long ago, a little girl perished in the fire; and her harmless, small, sad spectre still haunts her home, according to the fable of the folk.

Hither now came Henry Birdwood, and as he passed, Unity stepped from the ruin and called him

"Good luck!" he cried, "and vartue rewarded too; for I was in a mind to call at Stannon to win a sight of 'e; then I held on my shortest way for the sake of the sheep."

He shouted a direction to his two dogs, waved his arm and indicated his purpose They understood it, and with hasty excursions to right and left, with barking and riot and occasional further messages from their master, they gathered the sheep into the ancient fold. Here grew plenty of grass, and the flock, footsore and hot, was well content to rest Many among them crept into the shadow of the broken walls and panted themselves cool; others began immediately to graze; the dogs took station of vantage on a knap, and there sat down and kept watch with lolling tongues

24

Henry Birdwood was a slim, wiry man of five-and-twenty. No special distinction marked his features. He wore a close brown beard and whiskers; his nose was straight and rather finely modelled. His eyes were slate-grey and his forehead high. A general, lifeless, rectitude marked his days. He was the son of a wandering preacher and, albeit separated by many years from parental control, had preserved the lessons of youth, lived a self-respecting life and practised the precepts of his father. He was alone in the world, save for his parent, and now worked under one of the Duchy Moormen—Mr. Gregory Twigg—in the Eastern Quarter of the Forest.

The cot of Teign Head at midmost Moor was his home, and there he dwelt, alone save for the company of his underling, Ned Sleep. But Henry had sociable instincts. He knew the folk of Postbridge, and thither he rode twice or thrice weekly. On Sunday he never failed to attend at the whitewashed meeting-house of the Little Baptists. He was young in heart, very ignorant of life, and ardent under a reticent exterior. He had fallen in love with Unity, and hoped that he might be able to marry her after two years. For the present they had agreed to keep their betrothal a secret; but it was an open secret in more directions than one. Henry generally sat with the people from Stannon at Sunday service, and shared Unity's hymn-book.

In the light of his love the forms of religion had taken on more colour for him; and with his betrothed beside him he felt exalted in the act of praise.

Now broke a storm that was to test the strength of this youth and prove whether the roots of his faith were nourished on any enduring stuff or but loosely twined through conventional traditions imparted in childhood. Henry had promised his father to remain a steady chapel member; and he had found the promise easy enough to keep. He was a methodical man and fell naturally into a regular mode of living. Thus life had so far hidden the realities of himself from him.

He dismounted, kissed Unity, held her with one hand and stroked her cheek with the other. These endearments appeared indecent to her spirit at that moment; but the indecency lay in her own heart, not his actions.

She separated herself from him and took a plunge into the facts.

"Did you see Philip Ouldsbroom?" she asked.

"No—what of him?"

"He left me twenty minutes ago. Like a whirlwind the man came, and went. He's just asked me to be his wife, Henry."

"There!" he exclaimed. "That comes of keeping secrets I felt, somehow, 'twould have been better to let everybody know the truth when we were tokened."

"No," she answered. "'Twas I felt that I wanted it to be kept quiet, till we could get a little nearer to marriage."

"Be it as 'twill, 'tis no secret really," he declared. "Everybody knows it well enough—everybody but that great rattle-pate. He chatters so that he's got no time to listen, and so he's gone without this bit of news. He didn't like taking 'No' for answer, I'll warrant."

She spoke, then set her teeth for the battle.

"As to that, Henry, the man didn't get 'No' for answer."

"What d'you mean?" he asked in blank astonishment.

"Be reasonable. Try to look at it all round—all round A surprise like this—I'm a woman, not an angel."

He stared at her, and she did not drop her eyes.

"You mean——? You *can't*—you can't, Unity! That man—all top and no root—a blusterous, silly soul born with a silver spoon in his mouth—never known to work—never known to pray—never known to think And your word—your solemn word—given to me. Oh, Unity, what are you saying?"

"Look at my side and understand. I love you and I always shall; but 'tis no good thinking that a farm of my own and such great advantages as he offers to me, are nought 'Twould be selfishness to stand between me and them."

"'Selfishness!' 'Selfishness' betwixt me and you! You've promised, Unity."

"And because I've promised, I didn't say 'Yes' to the man. I love you—mind that. Whatever betide I always shall. But I want you to let me off marrying you."

"You barefaced wretch!" he cried out. "You can look me cool and calm in the face and say that?"

"That I can. Truth's truth, ugly as it may look to you. I swear afore God this minute that I care for you. All the same, I want to marry Philip Ouldsbroom. That's how 'tis, and I dare say 'tis terrible strange; but it's true."

Henry walked from her and took a turn up and down the sheepfold with his hands behind him and his eyes on the earth. She sat and watched him. She had spoken truth as it appeared to her at that moment. She had weighed the aspects of Birdwood on the one side and Hartland on the other. There lay the choice: between a man and a farm, not between one man and another. The slight passion in her went out to the shepherd; the foresight in her yearned for Hartland and comfort and power. Philip Ouldsbroom himself did not much affect the argument.

Birdwood came slowly back to her. He had grown calm. He even smiled.

"I'm sorry I used coarse words," he said. "After all that we've been to each other, 'tis a pity to have done it. Even such a clever girl as my Unity can get bewitched, it seems. And who can't when money's the matter? Of course 'twas a natural thing. To have Hartland flung in your lap—a startler. But I know you better than you know yourself. Yes, I do, Unity. Cool down, and you'll find that the farm will soon look very small against the love we have got for each other."

"No," she said stubbornly. " 'Tis not a bit of good talking like that, Henry, and I won't leave it there. I want you to let me be free. I must be free. I'm in earnest, and I'm cruel cool. Call me all the names you can lay your tongue to. I wish you would. I ask you to free me once for all."

"And you'll blush to think you've asked such a thing, when night comes and you go on your knees."

"I blush to think it now," she said. "But I don't go back on it. , I shan't change."

Silence fell for a moment between them Then he spoke again.

"I won't release you. Because you're mad—that's no reason why I should be We're to be wed in the sight of God I've promised, and I won't change. You don't know what you're doing or dreaming about. I'll go—to Ouldsbroom—this moment."

"You'll be too late He's riding to Tavistock."

"I shall catch him if I gallop for it"

Then he mounted and turned to his dogs.

"Bide there—watch!" he shouted to them, and they obeyed.

Without speaking to Unity again he trotted off, and such was his speed that he reached Ouldsbroom's home but a few moments after the master had arrived.

Hartland's ancient fabric stood with white front and roof of thatch among the high-climbing hills by Dart A squat chimney rose at each end, and the thatch was drawn down over the deep porch The small windows glimmered from heavy embrasures: the farmyard extended before the door; and at the entrance was a thick, clean mat of red fern. From within came the chirrup of chickens that had run through the opeway and were pecking up crumbs on the blue stone floor of the kitchen A few garden plants—ribes and a wind-worn lilac—made shift to live under the windows of Hartland, and the beds that contained them were separated from the rough pavement of the yard by a wall. Behind the homestead sloped a furze-clad hill to granite peaks and ledges, while beneath twinkled Dart, winding through Postbridge and onward under Lakehead Hill.

Ouldsbroom heard the shepherd arrive and, as Henry dismounted, came out to meet him He carried a hunk of bread-and-cheese in his hand, and his mouth was full

"The very man I wanted to see," he declared "Come in and have a drop of beer"

Birdwood refused, nor did he take the hand offered to him.

"I've just left my sweetheart, Unity Crymes," he answered.

"Have you? So much the better! Well, 'tis in a nutshell—a free world and I mean to marry her "

"You don't see what you're saying, Ouldsbroom. Can't you understand English? We're tokened "

"Then let's come to it hammer and tongs! 'Tokening' —what's that? Ban't mind of man or woman free to change? Marriage is different. I'm honest as any man, and marriage is marriage But 'tokening'—'tis no more than a word To-morrow I'll be tokened to her—yes, by God! I will The battle's to the strong, Henry. I'm no enemy to you or another; but I want that woman, and I'll have her if fighting can get her."

"You ought to have come to it sooner. Too late now."

"Don't you say that. 'Tis never too late this side 'o marriage. When you're at your fighting best, *do* your fighting best and gather to you all you can out of the world with both hands. That's my motto. When we go down and get old, then others will come along and take from us in their turn, like enough But now's my time. I'm strong, and I'm up top for the minute; and I want that woman, and I'm going to get her—fair fighting and all above board "

"You call it fair!"

"Yes, I do then. And where's your fairness in trying to keep her away if she likes me best?"

"*You!* She's just this moment told me she loves me Told me since she saw you."

"I'll not hear that," declared Philip. "The news have come on her a trifle sudden I don't ax her to do what's not possible. I'm a reasonable creature. She's larned in secret to be fond of you. Well, now she'll larn openly to be fond of me. As a man I'm so good as you, though no chapel member, and I'm a long sight better than you as a husband, because I've more to offer than you. Mind this: there's nothing against you I like you well enough and your master—that peacock, Gregory Twigg—can testify that I do. But, in a word, we've run on to the same hare, and I shall bring her down and win the course as sure as death.''

''Don't you see the right and wrong side of using your riches against a poor man to steal the only treasure in the world he's managed to get?''

''Right or wrong don't come in I'm hunger-starved for a woman—for that woman, and only that woman. I'm like a lion I seed in the beast show to Plymouth— running up and down dribbling at the mouth because he knowed the hour for his food was come. What's right and wrong to the hungry and thirsty? They make their own. They must drink and eat at any cost, and you can talk of how they came by their victuals after. I don't care a curse about right and wrong—dirty little silly words, both of 'em My right is to marry Unity Crymes, and I'm going to do it.''

''And I say you shall not!''

''That's better! Now we're on solid ground. I tell you again that I've nought against you, more than the wheel have against the stone it rolls over But don't come in the way. Your servant, Birdwood—your servant in everything but that. but I'll fight a thousand men your size for her;—fight 'em and beat 'em all. So now you know.''

''You couldn't if she was against you.''

''She's not against me I defy her to be against me. And if she's my side—that ends it.''

''She's got a soul and knows right from wrong, if you don't.''

''Right and wrong won't help you—preaching won't help you—no more than it ever helped anybody when they was after a female. The thing's got to be.'' He moved toward his stable, and Birdwood followed him.

''This won't come to good, Ouldsbroom. I urge you to think again. Don't influence a young girl by dangling your home and your money afore her eyes. Think of t'other side Even if she's weak enough to fling over justice and truth to her word for what you can offer— don't you see—don't you see you'll never be happy on such terms?''

"Hold off psalm-smiting, I tell you! I've got no use for it. Comfort yourself, if you please, by cursing money and the power of it. 'Tis good enough for me; and when you come to have two hundred pound a year like me, you'll tell different. I'm going to Tavistock now, to buy the woman a ring for her wedding finger."

"You'll mourn this day's work to your dying hour. Stamp and bluster as you will, you must mourn it; and you know you must. Laugh at right and wrong—call 'em dirty little words. Perhaps they are But wait and see what's bred out of 'em. Suffering and torture ban't dirty little words, anyway; and that you'll live to know so sure as you take that woman from her right and lawful man. Torture—torture—that's what you're breeding for yourself, and the last sting of it will be to know that you deserved it all "

Ouldsbroom had brought a big horse out of the stable, and now he saddled it and laughed at the other's words.

"You'm thrown away at Teign Head, Henry. You ought to have followed your father and gone preaching. Words come out of you like feathers off a goose. But I'll take all the future can do, very well content for the good of the present. Only a fool's 'feared of the future. 'Tis a hollow turnip with a light in it to fright childer. The future be the present before it gets to us; and what strong man ban't ever ready for the passing hour? I'm bursting with life, I tell you—such a fullness of it as you, though you're boy to my man, very likely will never know. Enough said. I'm sorry to the heart that I come between you and that girl. 'Tis damned bad luck for you; but I can't help it—no more than the cart can help running over the mouse in the dark. None's to blame."

"You're a liar, and you know you're a liar," answered the other. He spoke quietly and it was Philip, not the wronged man, who first showed anger in this conversation.

"Steady there! No man calls me liar to my face, young chap You're the liar to say it You snivelling chapel members ban't the only honest people in the world. I warn you And now I'm off. And fight fair—

mind that. Fight fair, or you'll find me an ugly customer."

He prepared to start; entered his house, changed his
coat, put on a collar and turned his purse out of a locked
desk at a corner of the kitchen.

"Shall be back afore supper," he said to an old woman
who was busy within; and then he took a round hat from
a peg in the hall and went back to his horse.

Henry Birdwood had gone, and with his departure the
elder become instantly amiable.

"Poor old Henry. Us must hit on something good to
take the sting out of this for the man," he thought. And
not a small part of his reflections upon the ride to Tavistock centred in the shepherd and how best to improve his
lot. But this he did not do from feeble-minded desire to
meet his conscience in the way and compound therewith.
He felt no more uneasiness than the victorious hart feels
when a defeated rival falls or flies.

As for the younger man, he returned dazed and bewildered to his flock. As yet he failed to grasp the significance of the last hour Experience had never shown him
any such nature as this—riding, as it seemed, on a whirlwind above right and justice For the moment Birdwood
suffered neither rage nor grief, but only amazement.

CHAPTER V

On the evening of this day Barbara Hext sat alone in her
kitchen. The hour was late; the girl who worked for her
had gone home; her sole companion was the liver-coloured
spaniel called 'Sarah.'

Miss Hext was fallen into a reverie—an accident rare
in her life. Things had happened in the morning to
throw her back upon the past. A man in the storm
of love had done it; and when her private hours were
come, instead of planning purchases for the shop, consult-
ing dealers' catalogues, or mending clothes, she read old
letters.

None knew certainly concerning her youth save that
she was the daughter of a dead and gone and godless
water-bailiff. She had lived in London with a well-born
man for three years; then he married, and she left him
and returned to the Moor. Lovers came—some for her
little fortune and some for herself. And once she loved
and promised to marry. But when she told him the truth
in the hour that she accepted him, he made it a condition
that she should give away her money to the last farthing. She declined to do so; the match was broken off,
and Barbara, who had no mind to the other suitors, disappeared again.

For ten years she worked in London as forewoman in a
department of a large general store. She had no more
lovers, and became studious and contemplative. Then, on
the edge of middle age, she returned to the home of her
childhood and set up her little shop there. The folk
believed that she was rich, and they knew that she was
kind. But her goodness had always been a matter of
debate. None understood her; Nonconformists and those

of the Establishment alike feared her, and feared for her. Herself she was fearless and was reported to believe in nothing.

Barbara read the letters, and emotion shone in her eyes. She spoke aloud in a gentle, murmuring voice that none at Postbridge had heard

"No lovers like that now," she said. "No men like that now neither. How wise he was, and how straight with me! Never hid the truth—never told me a lie. 'Take me or leave me,' was his word. 'Marry you I can't; love you I will, and make your life wiser and happier I will.' 'Cold-blooded,' my old father called it. What then? Better be cold afore than after. I got more than I gave—sense and knowledge, and the power to look all round things, and patience with the fools. You can lie down again, 'Sarah.' You've heard all this afore—and only you."

The dog at sound of her voice had risen and, 'with reverential eyes and pendant paws,' sat up beside Barbara's feet. Miss Hext had taught the creature thus to attend when she spoke aloud, and its semblance of understanding was startling and entertaining to chance spectators. As the postmistress sometimes said, fifty years earlier such an accomplishment would have earned her the horse-pond and her dog the halter—for a pair of witches.

She tied up the letters and put them away; then she went into the shop and fetched herself a dozen raisins and a biscuit. Her supper done, she was about to retire and leave 'Sarah' as usual to run free in the premises, when there came the sudden thunder of a knock at the shop door.

Miss Hext opened it to find a man of rather less than middle height before her. His hat was off, and he was mopping his head

"Why, Mr. Twigg!" she cried.

"Yes; no wonder you're a bit surprised to see one that goes by clockwork down here at this hour. Ten 'tis—in fact, a bit after ten "

"Lucky I wasn't to bed."

"Very; and if you had been, I should have roused you up. I want some linseed for a poultice. My daughter Millicent—or Millicent Mary, as we call her—is took ill."

"Poor little maid! You're sure linseed is right?"

"Have no fear on that score," answered Mr. Twigg. "I'm a scholar, as you know, and a reader and a thinker also The 'Mother's Guide' is perfectly clear. In a word, Millicent Mary has got the croup. My wife's working at her; but a linseed poultice I've ordered, and as by chance all my staff's away for the minute, I had to come and fetch it myself."

Gregory Twigg was inclined to be stout He had a pugnacious nose, an assertive manner, and a ridiculous conceit of himself. He had gathered together some long words from the newspapers and enjoyed to use them. He patronised all men, and some he angered and some he entertained. Vanity was the mainspring of Mr. Twigg; his religion, his possessions, his importance, his wife, his children, and his mental endowments were the subjects on which he preferred to discourse. He conducted a small public-house and kept three horses. He farmed the East Quarter of the Moor from the Duchy, and employed upon it a few humble men He had come to regard himself as a sort of adjunct of the overlord, and believed that not a little of the prosperity of Dartmoor depended upon him. He gave advice generously, but took none. He resented criticism, and a joke against himself was the highest offence in his eyes He pitied the people and did not regard himself as one of them. His inn, 'The Warren House,' a mile from Postbridge, was not very prosperous, but he set the fact down to his own superior parts and high level of conversation Money was very scarce with him, but he believed that none knew the fact His ostler, however, had made no secret of delayed settlements, and few were deceived by Gregory's affectation of prosperity.

He was a Nonconformist, and a tower of strength in the local circle of the Little Baptists

Miss Hext quickly produced the linseed, but she advised other treatment also.

"Have no fear," he answered. "As the father of four I am always prepared. And don't hesitate to send in your account, Miss Hext. I never like bills to run 'Ready money' is my motto, and you'll not find a better."

"My little bill went to you last month."

"You surprise me," he said. "But in financial operations on the scale—on my scale—a trifle will often get overlooked "

"There's no hurry."

"Don't say that The labourer is worthy of his hire Why should you be kept waiting? Because you don't go to church or chapel—eh? No, no; I'm not that sort We must each make our peace with God in our own hearts —eh?"

"Better be gone," she said, "or you'll have to make your peace with Mrs. Twigg."

"I never hurry It shortens life."

"But your child's life."

"You're wrong there," he answered "I can't leave you under that mistaken idea. There is not a shadow of danger. Had I seen the symptoms were dangerous, I should have brought out the gig Hullo! who is this?"

A galloping horse sped over the bridge and stopped beside them. It had come fast; and as it was pulled up and stretched its legs and put down its head, the sweating sides of it steamed in the light from Miss Hext's open door.

"Good-evening!" cried the rider "Surprised you together, have I! Here's fine news for your wife, Greg!"

He shouted with laughter, and proclaimed himself to be Philip Ouldsbroom.

Of all men Philip was the one that Mr. Twigg liked least, so he took a swift departure.

"I shall let it be known how the patient is to-morrow," he said. "Good-night; good-night, Ouldsbroom. Try and not make loose jokes at your age Your horse is over-ridden. It will be ill to-morrow, or I know nothing of the subject."

"You don't!" replied the farmer. "Horses! You drive 'em like a lady."

Twigg departed into the darkness, and Ouldsbroom got down.

"Can't you find nought better than that pious peacock to——?"

"Be off!" she said. "And he's right for once, and you're wrong. Have you been trying to ride away from your stupid self? You oughtn't to push your horse like that."

"The hoss be unharmed. He knows my ways. He'll have good payment for his trouble afore I turn in. Look here, Barbara—I've got it—the ring." He took a little box out of his pocket and handed it to her.

She opened it, examined the ring, and gave it back to him.

"You silly madman!" she said. "And so she took you?"

"All but the word. To-morrow morning she's to say 'Yes.' Eight hours—eight mortal hours more have I got to wait. At six I'll be over at Stannon, if I can bide that long. Now 'tis ten. Let me come in and have a tell along with you, Barbara, to shorten the time."

"Get home," she said, "and have a tell with your God, and steady your mind a bit."

"God—who's he? I didn't know you believed in that party."

"Yes, I do. Everybody does. I larned that long ago. Thinking people make their own pattern of God. We've all got one, even them that pretend loudest they haven't. You're the sort I like, Philip—a pet of mine, with all your stupid follies; and you know it very well. But never a man stood in need of a God more. You take my advice and set about finding one."

"Wonders never cease. Us will have you going to church or along with the Little Baptists next."

"No, you won't. Their Gods are not mine. Jehovah's too hard and Christ's too soft for me. Get home and read the Book of Job. Read it through, and if it don't send you to sleep, 'twill do you good mayhap. That's my

Biblebook—the only one I read They are live people in it—all of 'em, down to that busy rascal, Satan. You can match 'em in Postbridge. Now be off, and walk your horse back."

"I'll do as you say. 'Tis a day of wonders. To think of Barbara Hext preaching!"

She laughed, and shut the door upon him, while he went off and led his horse by the bridle rein.

Arrived at Hartland, he tended the weary animal, then went into his house and found his two labourers had retired; but the old woman who looked to his dwelling was waiting up for him. He sent her to bed, supped heavily, then lighted his pipe and went into the parlour for the family Bible.

He read a few chapters of Job, but comprehended them not. The mighty poem bored him and made him drowsy. Soon after midnight he fell asleep and did not wake until four o'clock, to find kitchen lamp and kitchen fire both out. Then he lighted a candle, ascended to his room, made a toilet there, and, at the first glimmer of dawn, went out of doors

He climbed Hartland Tor and, hidden to windward of them, watched a brace of fox cubs playing together.

"You'll be standing afore the puppies in a month, my brave heroes!" he thought And then he scared them, laughed to see them run, felt in his pocket to prove the ring was safe, and went his way to Stannon Grey light soaked the air and earth as he reached Unity's home before half-past five o'clock No life stirred, but he knew the girl's bedroom window It faced alone over the Moor on the northern side of the farmhouse Philip now walked beneath it and flung stones at the window. She was sleeping heavily after a sleepless night, and presently, in his efforts to waken her, he broke the glass with a crash A dog barked at the sound and came galloping from the front of the house. It knew Philip, and greeted him effusively. At the same moment the white blind above was moved and Unity's eyes appeared Ouldsbroom kissed his hand to her and she vanished. In ten minutes she stood beside him.

"Well? Well? Say it, for God's sake!" he burst out " 'Tis ages ago since I saw 'e!"

"Yes."

He shouted like a boy loosed from school, and embraced her.

"I knew it!" he cried; "I knew it from the first moment I loved you. I knew it in my bones!"

"But mark this, afore 'tis too late," she said, pushing him from her "Mark this, Philip, I know too little of you—too little by far. And what do you know of me? Still less. Leave it open; I pray you leave it——"

"Stop," he interrupted her "Stop there; not another word will I hear of that nonsense. I love you, and I'll very soon larn you what love is. Ban't no slow-growing, patient thing; it comes full-grown, wi' no more patience than the lightning. And so 'twill be with you afore you're a month older. Don't I understand? Didn't I tell Birdwood yesterday how 'twas? Yesterday—yesterday—I say 'yesterday'; but what's time? 'Tis a hundred years agone that I sent the man about his business Think no more of him. Leave him to me. He shall bless my name afore I've done with him. Ban't the strongest the justest?"

"Take time, Philip. Get to know me better. I'm far off what you think."

"Leave all that. Haven't I seen through and through you for a month? Here—here's your ring That'll show you! Does your brother know?"

"There's no hurry, I keep telling you"

"Ban't there, by God! A man on fire's generally like to be in a hurry; and you'll be a woman on fire afore many hours are over your head. Love! There—but I'll soon show you what love be like!"

He broke off and shouted to Quinton Crymes, who was just passing into his plot of cabbage beside the farm.

"Here—come here and hear the news, boy! Great news, I warn 'e!"

"Hullo!" cried the farmer. "What's fetched you over so early?"

"This here minx—who else should? And she will

be obeyed, of course. Wants to marry me—*will* do it.
What d'you say to that?"

Crymes stared

"Then what about Birdwood?"

"Let be," said Philip. "Leave him to me. He's out
of it and never was in it worth mentioning. Can't a
woman make a mistake? A very understanding young
chap. Well, then, let him use his understanding and larn
that the battle's to the strong."

Crymes regarded his sister with suspicion. Then his
slow mind moved and suspicion changed into respect
From being nothing, she promised to become a power.
Gradually he found himself rejoicing.

"This is big news," he said. "Come in and take a bit
o' breaksis along with us, Ouldsbroom."

"So I will then; and let me tell her—let me tell your
wife. I like to startle a person."

"No," said Quinton firmly. "She ban't in a case to
be startled. Her babby's due in a month. I'll break it
gently."

But the breakfast was not successful, because Gertrude
Crymes liked Birdwood She had as frank a nature as
Philip himself, and roundly told him that he was doing
wrong He blustered and argued, but heard the other
side from one who felt no sympathy with his untutored
spirit. He lost his temper.

"The sooner my wife gets beyond reach of your frosty
tongue, the better for her," he declared, and rose from
the table.

"Be at sheepfold towards evening, Unity," he said,
with the air of one commanding

Then he was gone, and upon his departure a very vigorous argument broke out behind him. Gertrude and her
husband took opposite sides; Unity said nothing, Mr.
Coaker, who was a bachelor, entirely agreed with his
master that the rich and prosperous Ouldsbroom was a
better match for any woman than a poor shepherd, no
matter how high his principles or good his character
might be. Jimmy Coaker was a cynic and spoke accordingly.

"You've got to reckon up Hartland and two hundred a year and a silly man against a very proper young chapel-going chap—and nought," he said. "If you was one sort of woman, I should say, 'Take the Little Baptist and nothing'; but being as you are—a pretty strong-minded fashion of female—I say, 'Go for the money, with Ouldsbroom thrown in.' He isn't bad—only weak-minded. If you're worth your salt, you soon will have him under your thumb, and then you're the better every way, and he's none the worse for a clever wife who'll help to keep his money in his pocket and hide his folly from the sight of the neighbours."

"You speak like the sour old carmudgeon you are," retorted Mrs. Crymes hotly. "Good powers! Can two men think so mean and small? Haven't she *promised* Henry? 'Tis horrid to know that any girl, worth calling herself a girl, can sink to such a nasty deed. Speak!" she continued, turning almost fiercely on her sister-in-law. "Haven't you got nought to say to throw light on this dark thing?"

Unity shook her head.

"I'm myself, and I've got nought to say, and I care nought what any think. I see it from my own point of view; and I know this: love of man ban't the only thing to guide a woman's life. 'Tisn't everything to a woman like me, any more than it is everything to most men. I ban't going to live or die for anybody but myself. I'm very fond of Henry, and always shall be fond of him, because he's a fine chap, though he've nothing to look to And Ouldsbroom's a fine chap; and whether I love him or no, be his business, not yours I told him square that I knew nought about him, and that us must wait a bit; and he shut my mouth. So I've nought on my conscience with him. And life's life, not love-making."

"You cold-blooded snake!" burst out the hot-blooded Mrs. Crymes.

But here her husband interposed, and the argument waxed high.

Gertrude exhausted herself, spoke of the disparity of age; the futility of linking life with such a man as Ouldsbroom; the wickedness of breaking a troth; the shame that must attach to a jilt's family at such a deed. Then Crymes denied all the disabilities, and his sister left him still arguing with his wife. Unity craved peace and silence. She did her work of washing up and attending to the poultry; then she explained to her angry sister-in-law that she would not be back before night, and took herself off into the Moor.

Until noon she tramped the lonely places, and once climbed the heights so that Teign Head cot under Manger Hill, in the very heart of the central waste, appeared beneath her eyes. Smoke rose above the dwelling, and she knew that Henry Birdwood and Mr Sleep were eating their dinner together. The thought 'for some reason served to comfort her, but she did not suffer her mind long to dwell on Birdwood.

"I may be a hard woman," she said to herself; "but that's like most of us; and that won't stop me from being a prosperous one anyhow. 'Tis better to be of some account than only happy like a sheep And why for shouldn't I be happy, come a child or two?"

She ate blackberries in the deep gorge of East Dart, and then, having dawdled through many hours, set out for the sheepfold.

Philip was there before her He kissed her and caressed her like a lover; then he made her sit on his lap.

"Where d'you think I went to when I left Stannon this morning?" he asked.

She shook her head.

"To parson Banns be going up Sunday Don't you break away! Too late now. Us'll be married in the Church Little did I think when I was there and heard 'em read the burial service over faither that next time I was in their shop 'twould be to hear 'em tell the marriage service over me! But so 'tis. I won't be married by they Little Baptists. I doubt if they can do it according to law."

"Of course they can."

"Well, I'm against 'em Your parson, with his game leg and his right-hand man, that puffed-out frog, Gregory

Twigg—— No; give me the Church for my job. You don't care?''

"It's all one to me."

"To-morrow Hartland will be ready for you to have a look round. I've set my old woman and Tommy Webber to work with soap and water, and I be going to make a bonfire of my father's clothes and his old bed and his old dog-eared chair. I couldn't sell 'em—haven't got the heart to—and I can't use them, so I'll burn 'em You come after noon to-morrow and I'll show you over the place. And I told parson that the first week in October would be the time."

She pleaded for a little delay, but he would none of it.

" 'Tis too sudden—who could face such a thing staring at one, with less than five weeks to go?''

"Five weeks, you call it. 'Twill be fifty years to me; and you knew this morning, when you looked at your ring——''

She put her hand to her pocket

"There!" she cried; "in all the storm and trouble of it, I've never even oped the packet."

"Do so then—'twill show you a bit more of my ways than you know, seemingly."

She opened the box and found a wedding-ring.

"That's the sort I am," he said. "Be life so long that a month more or less don't count in it? Let's live together every moment we can, and not throw away a chance, nor yet an hour. The people that wait, when they ban't bound to wait, don't know what love means. I ain't got no use for betrothals and tokenings, and all that. I want you, and I will have you inside five weeks from to-day.''

He rattled on in this strain; he laid the future before her painted in his own sanguine colours. She spoke a little at first, but he overbore her with his noise and exuberance, so that presently she simply sat on his lap, stared before her, and listened. Now and then he took breath and kissed her.

Two hours passed very swiftly; then he was reminded of another labour designed for that day.

"I'm going to see Henry Birdwood to-night," he said.
"A fine chap is Birdwood, and I'll be a friend to him if
he'll let me. Yesterday, afore you took me, I was a
bit touchy in temper. And who shall blame me? But
now 'tis all done, I can breathe again and look round
at the world in general. You know him better than me.
What does he want in life? What's the ruling passion
of the man?"

"I was."

"You, and the moon, and a few other things, be out
of reach for him. We'll leave that and talk about what's
possible. He's a bit pious, I'm told, along of having a
preacher for parent. Well, that sort are dull; but he's
young yet, and may take life more cheerful later on.
We'll see. Anyway, I might find him better money than
he gets from Gregory Twigg."

"You don't surely mean——?"

"To offer him a job? Why not? He's no fool. Not
just now, of course—plenty of time when he's got used
to things and we're married and settled."

"He'll never take anything from your hand."

"Won't he? Then let him go to hell for all I care,
if he's that sort. But perhaps he han't. Anyway, I'm
going up to see him to-night and ax his pardon if I said
anything to hurt him an hour after 'twas spoken. And
I'll bid him to the wedding presently."

He put the wedding-ring on and found it fitted well.
She took it off, however, immediately.

" 'Tis unlucky," she said.

Whereupon he laughed.

"We make our own luck by the sweat of our brow most
times," he answered. "Ban't I in luck this minute, and
won't the world know it Sunday when the banns be
called?"

"No," she replied. "Once for all, don't fool yourself
to think that. My brother's wife have a tongue in her
head, and very strong opinions about what I'm doing.
As like as not, the rest of Postbridge will be of the same
mind; so you may count upon sour looks for me, if not
for yourself."

He frowned.

"Them as look sourly at you over this job shall mighty soon look sour on their own account," he declared. "I'm not the quarrelsome sort, and will go a mile round to avoid a row any day of the week; but this be different. There'll soon be bloody heads about if any man says a word against you to me; and you can tell your sister-in-law that same. Let her mind her own business and bring a brave babby into the world. And now I'm off!"

He was soon gone, and she watched him strike away along the slope of the hill, breast it, and disappear beyond. She thought of what would happen between Henry and Philip; and then she took off the wedding-ring and dreamed of being a married woman.

A sort of savage satisfaction got hold upon her. For the first time she felt a sudden, fiery regard for this headlong man who was hastening her destiny at such a violent pace. She admired him for it. There was something big about him. He was a ship worth steering. She pictured herself cutting a brave figure at the helm of him.

Day sank into night without one cloud. After hours of hurrying vapour and high wind, the bustle and business of the sky was over, and a great, burning zone of orange-red now mantled above the vanished sun. It faded upward, through paler orange, by passages of waning splendour to the dark blue of the zenith; it deepened downward to pure mauve stretched in a veil above the purple of earth. Ghostly upon this light, yet trembling into gold as the sunset faded from about her, there hung the crescent of the young, cusped moon.

CHAPTER VI

THE folk streamed from their little meeting-house on a
Sunday evening of stars Autumn had already touched
a grove that marks the year at Postbridge and signals the
first pinch of early frosts when September comes; but
this night was mild and still A gentle haze hung in the
air, and through the windows of the chapel, sheaves of
light from oil lamps within struck the atmosphere and
lit it to mellow radiance

The ritual of the Little Baptists was severe, and orna-
ment they eschewed A rostrum at one end of the hall
and a large map of Palestine in a black frame at the
other, were the sole objects that arrested attention The
meeting-house was a converted barn, the gift of a pious
Little Baptist in the past. Its lines were lofty and
simple; the great beams of the roof stretched across a
whitewashed ceiling, and the glass windows, shaded by
red blinds, opened square and plain in the whitewashed
walls

Quinton Crymes and his wife were among the first to
emerge from service, and not far behind them there
followed Ned Sleep of Teign Head They stopped him
with a question. The evening had been marked by an
event most unusual, for Henry Birdwood was not in his
place.

"What's wrong with him?" asked Gertrude Crymes.
"Surely something uncommon bad have catched him
and struck him down, to keep him away from the Lord's
House?"

Sleep stood still and considered

"Well, when the time comed and I offered for to saddle

46

his pony along with my own—there 'twas. 'No,' he answered, 'I ban't going. I ban't going to pretend no more.' Those were his very words.''

Quinton looked at his wife and shrugged his shoulders.

"And thinking of it in my cautious fashion all the way to chapel," continued Sleep, "it struck me, all of a sudden, that perhaps it might be along of your sister that's jilted him."

Then he went down the hill to where his pony was tethered in the yard of a friend's house.

A man coming the other way stopped Quinton

"I didn't think you'd be let loose so soon," he said. "Be your old minister too dog-tired to give you his full dose to-night?"

"It may interest you to know that Henry wasn't there, Philip," said Mrs. Crymes. "That's your bad work Mark me, the young man will break away from all that he was taught now. And the sin will be yours."

" 'Tis an ill wind blows nobody any good; and if losing Unity be going to keep the man out of that den, so much the better for him," retorted Ouldsbroom. "I'd like to see the shutters up in your prayer-shop, Gertrude, and I'd say it to your minister so soon as you. A lot of sniffing, narrow zanies you be, and think yourselves the fat of the earth. By the same token, where's the peacock? I suppose he puffed out the lessons in his usual style?"

"He was there. He's gone up the hill with his family —if you mean Gregory Twigg."

"Who should I mean? I'll come back along by way of Stannon presently and pick a bit of supper, if 'tis all the same to you. I stuck my head round the door at church this morning and heard 'For the third and last time of asking.' I'd have called for three cheers if I'd had cheek enough; but instead of that I slipped away and give the first beggar I met a tanner for luck. So long till supper. I be going to send a cartload of good eating over from Tavistock for the wedding feast."

"That's my job—you didn't ought to do that," said Quinton Crymes in a voice somewhat half-hearted.

"Nonsense—nonsense! You with a family coming

and plenty to do with your money. I'm off to talk to Twigg about the drinks this minute.''

He strode up the hill and caught Mr. Twigg, his wife, and their elder children, before he reached the top of it.

Mr. Twigg was, as usual, in a mood of placid self-esteem. The sermon had pleased him, and, according to his custom, he preached it over again with his own improvements as he passed along.

"The starry 'osts,'' said Mr. Twigg; "the starry 'osts are as nothing; the moon is as nothing; and the sun is as nothing before the True Light. Remember, children, when they teach you about the stars and such like vain items, that they are as dust in the balance. There is only one True Light which lighteth every man that cometh into the world, and we have it. Who have it? The Little Baptists have it. How humble is that word 'little'—the 'Little Baptists.' We may call ourselves 'little,' but our Master knows better. I say that we have climbed the true, narrow road, and stand on the giddy peak at the Footstool of Grace; and we look down—we look down—not with pride but with thanksgiving—at the others struggling upward by roads that all lead on to precipices.''

"You put it a lot better than him,'' said Mrs. Twigg.

"Perhaps I do. Is that to be wondered at? Look at our heads. Mine is pretty near as big again as his. I suppose if I had been a minister of the Gospel I should have——''

Here Philip Ouldsbroom reached the speaker.

"Twigg—isn't it? Can you give me five minutes, Gregory?''

"Yes—if it's nothing that doesn't misbecome the Day.''

"To do a man a good turn don't misbecome the day, or the night either, I suppose?''

"Certainly not. I think I can boast my share of that sort of work. A tithe, Ouldsbroom—a tithe is my general rule. I do not mention it for self-glory, but as a statement of fact—and an example.''

"That's all right then; we'll trot on a bit if your missis don't mind."

"Let my wife and my daughters trot on," said Gregory Twigg "I've a fine physic, thank God, and make nothing of the hill; but I can't think and walk fast all to once. You go ahead, Mrs Twigg, along with Millicent Mary and Ethel"

"Now look here—about your man, Birdwood," began the farmer as soon as the publican's wife and children were out of earshot

"He is my man, as you say—a member of my staff."

"What a joker you are—but yet can't see a joke or take a joke. Your 'staff' would make a cat laugh—one old woman and a crack-brained boy and they two at Teign Head cot."

"Remember the Day, please, Ouldsbroom, and don't laugh at me, because I'll stand that from no man living. What about Henry Birdwood? You've done him a bad wrong—a very bad wrong. As a man of wide knowledge, of course nothing ever surprises me—still, it was wrong, and you know it."

"Wrong? Stuff and nonsense. 'Might's right' where the women are concerned, or any other sort of fighting, and your blessed God's always on the side of the strong. Look at yourself. Ban't you one of His pets and always have been?"

"I hope so, and I believe so," answered Mr Twigg. "And if so, there's a very good reason. David never saw the righteous man begging his bread. However, you're not in the fold, and though I should be glad to see you there——"

"Your fold! I'd sooner go partner with a pack of good sporting wolves than bleat along with your sheep. But Birdwood's the matter. What money does he get?"

"If I could be astonished, you'd astonish me," retorted Gregory, "and yet, again, you never would; for to be astonished at a fool is to be a fool. And whatever I am, in the course of nature and according to my skill and gifts, fool is not the word. You ask me what wages I give to Henry Birdwood. In anybody but you 'twould be a

great impertinence, and perhaps at any time but this I'd
refuse to answer. But we took bread at the Lord's Table
to-night, and I am at peace with all men, including myself. It may be over-generous, or it may not be, but, be
it as it will, Henry gets eighteen shillings."

"Don't you worry about being over-generous, Twigg.
Your best friend won't blame you there. Well, 'tis this
way: I've beaten the poor devil out of the field—smothered him; and now I've got my girl, I just begin to see,
in a sort of dim way, what he must feel to have lost her."

"If your conscience speaks, listen to it."

" 'Tisn't conscience—I've got no conscience, and don't
want none. But I've got a fellow-feeling for every sort
of man down in his marrow-bones, and, in a word, I want
to do Birdwood a good turn."

"Well, that's your business, not mine. Many is the
good turn have been put into my heart to do, Ouldsbroom; and I never turn a deaf ear to the prompting."

"If, now, Henry was to hear you'd raised his money to
a pound, 'twould be gert news for him."

"This is not the still small voice, and don't pretend it
is," said Mr. Twigg. "You deceive yourself. Anything
more sly and mean I never did hear. You want *me* to
spend two more shillings a week on one of my staff, and
you get the credit. You godless fellow—and the cheek
of it to a man in my position!"

Philip laughed.

" 'Tis just the other way," he answered; "and none
but a blockhead like you would have thought I meant
that. For the minute he's cruel sore because I've bested
him, and I can't do him any sort of a good turn openly
till he's calmed down a bit. In fact, I rode over last week
with an idea, and he behaved in a very manly way and
told me to go to blue, blazing hell. I could have shaken
hands with him at hearing those fine words in the mouth
of a Little Baptist."

"Don't say that, and don't think it," interrupted Mr.
Twigg warmly. "He's left us. Satan's led him into the
wilderness. We're all praying that he'll come back; but
for the moment he's broke loose."

"Well, anyway, I can't do nought for him at present, because 'tis poison to him to hear my name. He'd lie behind a hedge for me, I do believe. So, until he gets over the stroke of losing Unity Crymes, I can only help him in secret. Therefore I ax you to put two bob a week to his money and let me pay you privately. 'Twill cheer the poor beggar up a little these dark days."

"I'm well used to financial operations large and small," replied the other. "At the last Duchy dinner the bailiff said out before the throng that my accounts were a marvel. Just a gift, and I thank the Lord for my power of figures with my other possessions. To take two shillings from you and add them to Henry's wages can easily be done, of course."

"Then do it," said Philip; "and here's a florin, so begin this week. It must go on till I find him a better job, which I easily shall do come presently."

"If you're going to meddle with my staff——" began Gregory, but the other cut him short.

"Chuck that. Now there's another thing that hits you much closer. I'm going to be married Thursday, and 'tis a toss up whether I go down to Two Bridges for the drinks, or come to you for 'em."

"I wish it wasn't the Lord's Day," answered Twigg. "I suppose you couldn't walk home and have some supper with me and talk about other things till midnight? After the clock's struck, I'll go into drink in a manner that will surprise you; for I've a knowledge of the higher drinks—wine, in fact—that you won't match this side of Exeter."

"Right, my old bird! But I've got to eat to Stannon first and cuddle my girl for an hour. Then I'll come over to Warren House, and I shall expect you to open a bottle the minute your blessed Lord's Day be over."

"Not, of course, to go into figures till after midnight—still I should like to know, in quite a general way, what you propose to spend, Ouldsbroom? 'Twill work at the back of my mind unconsciously, and so the Sabbath won't be broken; yet, after midnight, I shall have it all ready and be able to tell you what can be done."

"Three pound on the drink I shall spend, and ten shilling on the tobacco."

"Not another word then! Leave it at that. I'll expect you between eleven and twelve. We'll open a bottle, too, since you command it, and drink to your good fortune in the married state."

"Right; and mind you remember Birdwood and his extra money," answered Philip "Take the credit yourself. That won't be difficult to a man with such large ideas as you. But of course my name musn't come into it."

They parted, and Ouldsbroom went northerly to Stannon while the publican overtook his wife.

CHAPTER VII

Two nights before his marriage-day Ouldsbroom went to see Barbara Hext. He had planned a little jollity for the Postbridge children, and Barbara was well content to assist him. ·Others also lent their aid. A tea was to be given in the village schoolroom, and all the local boys and girls were invited.

"I want for the little toads to remember the spread for many a day," declared Philip. "Be the sweeties and fruit got for 'em?"

" 'Twill all arrive to-morrow by carrier, and it's going to cost you two pounds ten shillings, my man."

"More—surely? 1 thought 'twas to run to three?"

"No," she said. "I'm doing my share. The children are all very good customers of mine, and 1'm glad of the chance to help make 'em happy."

"I'm terrible fond of 'em, and so's Unity. A quiver-full is what I want. Will you be gossip to the first?" he asked.

She shook her head at him.

"Don't meet troubles half way. How's the girl bearing up?"

He looked uneasy.

"She's all right. But a bit dazed, I think. Not too good company for the moment. Full of her own thoughts, no doubt, and what she's going to do at Hartland. A terrible tidy woman, I fancy. Goeth long walks 'pon the Moor alone, and won't let me come. I catched her crying, if you'll believe it—'twas a pitiful sight, and I didn't know what the mischief to do."

"Tears are new to you—eh? Got to forty years old and never learned the truth about women's tears! *Her* tears needn't trouble you, I reckon. No—nor any other female's. Don't I know their worth that have shed my share? You might so soon pity a goose going barefoot as a crying woman. Remember that.''

''All the same she ban't the crying sort, and it didn't ought to be a crying time. What's she got to cry for?''

''Plenty, for that matter. She's done a dirty thing, and—you needn't bounce and bluster here, Philip—you know it—none better.''

He flushed and snorted.

''I thought you, at least, had more sense. If she likes me better than t'other, what law's to prevent her being true to herself and to me?''

''True to herself very like; there's some who are only true to themselves when they are being untrue to others. Perhaps she's that sort, but I hope not, I'm sure. 'Tis your strength is to blame. She was that man's ewe lamb—his all.''

''What rot you people talk!'' he burst out; ''why, good God Almighty, I'm so friendly to Birdwood as any chap living. I've got no quarrel with him. I couldn't *make* the woman marry me. She's chose me, and if she'd chose me first instead of second, and then gone over to another man, should I have made such a dickens of a row? If the girl likes me better than him, why the mischief shouldn't she change her mind? Isn't life full of it? Don't we change our minds every hour about little things; then why for shouldn't we change about big things?''

''Talk won't better it.''

''I'm sorry for the man, and I shan't forget him. I'm strong; he ban't. Well, come presently, when his sore heart be whole again, I'm going to make it up to him.''

''Take care he don't make it up to you.''

''I'll take care. He's got no more to say since I talked to him.''

An irrational attitude flashed out in Barbara. She also had her prejudices.

''He's a Methody.'' she said; ''a Methody and the son of a Methody. Don't you forget that.''

"He's thrown 'em over. This thing have let a bit of light and air into his mind. He've got that much to thank me for already. I've larned him to take large views, and he's chucked his chapel for a start. He'll thank me yet. There's so good fish in the sea as ever come out. He'll live to thank me, I tell you, for teaching him a lot o' things. You'll see us stout friends afore the spring comes round."

"Once a Methody, always a Methody," repeated Miss Hext. "I know 'em. Don't you think that five years hence—or fifty years hence—that man will be any friend to you. Some men might take it, and swallow it, and look back after and even think that 'twas all for their good; but not Henry. If your wife turns out the worst wife that ever came out of Postbridge, he'll still feel that he has lost his all in her. He's a young man with a narrow upbringing and a narrow way of looking at life. This is his first facer, and that he's given up going to chapel on it don't mean any good to you. Did you read Job a bit ago when I advised you to?"

"I started, but mighty soon went to sleep."

"You're the sort—however, you don't want my sense, and I'm not built to croak, I hope. But make that man your friend at your peril. It can't be in nature; and if you try to break nature, she'll turn round and break you. I've seen the like in my life, and I've seen the sequel to it. Don't try to win round him. Keep clear of him."

"There!—There's charity! You'm enough to make me turn church-goer," he said. "But you're wrong for once, though not often wrong. I'll win him over; and if he won't be won—then let him go to heel, and bide at heel, for a cross-bred cur dog."

Other customers came in—a washerwoman and sick nurse known as Betty Dury, and a tall, hunchbacked, grizzly headed man called Peter Culme, a water-keeper.

"Give me a pound of tea and half a dozen dips, if you please, Miss," said the man. "And I do wish as you'd marry somebody and take out a licence to sell beer and baccy. 'Tis cruel that us can't get such common needs in Postbridge, and I shan't be able to stand thicky blown-

up fool at the 'Warren House' much longer. He talks
to the people as if they was all school-children at a
revel.''

"He've got his points though, Peter," argued Ouldsbroom. "I was laying in liquor against my marriage
feed back-along, and the larning of the man where wine's
the matter be a wonder. I will grant him that, though
a stuck-up peacock in most other ways.''

Miss Hext laughed.

"You silly creature!" she said. "D'you believe him?
Any rascal with a big voice and a lot o' bottles could
hoodwink you. 'Tisn't what he knows about wines; 'tis
what you don't know. He's sold you a lot of poison so
like as not.''

" 'Tis old, however, and age do build up a poor wine
into valiant drinking—so Twigg swears.''

"Just a thing a Methody would swear," she answered
"He never had no wine that would stand getting old.
I've drunk wine in my time, and I know.''

"Well, o' Thursday you'll be able to judge," declared
Philip. "He wanted to put me off with French wine,
and let me taste it. There! I thought 'twas a bottle
of ink he'd opened by mistake. 'Give me brown sherry
wine, as I can see through and know nought's hid in it,'
I said to Gregory. I'll have none of this bewitched mess.
Ban't going to begin my married life poisoning my
friends and future relations.' So brown sherry 'twill be,
and a bottle of champagne. I would have it, though
'twill cost five shilling.''

"What can I do for you, Betty?" asked the postmistress. "If you expect another telegram, I'm afraid
'tis too late.''

"He's dead," said the woman; "died last night. A
good job too, poor soul; and my husband went over for
to hear the will this morning. We'm down for ten
pounds, so Robert says that I must get a shadow o'
black.''

"I hope it won't keep you from the wedding, or your
childer from the party?" asked Philip.

The woman was lean and wrinkled, but younger by

many years than she appeared. Bad teeth and a mole under her eye spoiled a face that had been agreeable but for these blemishes.

"We'm coming," she said. "Robert's brother wasn't much to him. And he had a hundred and fifty to leave, and no family, and only left us ten. For twenty-five Robert said as he'd have mourned and took us all to the funeral; but not for less. So we shall be at Stannon and the children to the schoolroom; and thank you for it, I'm sure."

"I do hope, for the peace of your party, as you haven't asked Twigg," said Mr. Culme. "Dash that man! he puts me in a cool sweat o' fury every time I meet him. 'Neighbour Culme,' he calls me; and I won't have it—I won't take 'neighbour' from the man."

"What is there in that 'neighbour' that lowers a chap in his own conceit?" asked Ouldsbroom. "I know just how you feel, and 'tis only a saucy gas-bag like Twigg, or the silly gentlefolk, ever say it. I don't like it; yet the word's an innocent word."

" 'Tis the bowldacious way he speaks it," answered Culme, "with his nose cocked in the air, and his gert, stoopid eyes soaring over the heavens, as if he was expecting an angel with a golden crown for him. Always right, that man—in his own opinion. But if he only knowed what a lot he loses by being so damned cock-sure, he'd sing a little smaller sometimes, I do believe, and allow there was one or two above him in brains as well as manners."

"If 'tis 'denshiring' a bit of land, or selling a hoss, or breeding ponies, or mending a chair, or teaching a child, or drawing a glass of beer—'tis all the same," said Philip. "His way's the right way, and everybody else's way's the wrong way."

"Yes, 'tis," declared the water-keeper; "and when he comes to die, he'll draw 'em round the bed, if he's got wind enough left, and say, 'Now watch me, and do it like what I do, when 'tis your turn.' "

"Good for you, Peter—the very image of the man!" laughed Philip. "And more—all he's got be the best, while the rest of the world have to put up with second best. His drink and his wife and his brats, and his house and his old sporting pictures, and his dog and his cat and his false teeth—all can't be matched in the kingdom.''

"And what is he?" summed up Culme bitterly. "No more use to anybody than the hump on my shoulder. He's hateful on week-days, but o' Sunday he'd make the devil spit. Piety dribbles out of him, like gravy out of a cut joint, till you want to cuss and swear. And his beastly little children sniff just the same as him, and roll their eyes the very image of his way."

"A common habit with Methodies," said Miss Hext. "As for Gregory, I know the man—vain inside and vain out—though 'tis ignorance makes him what he is—not wickedness. But what's the result? He never gets a bit of good advice from one year's end to another. None will be at the trouble to give it him, because they know he thinks nobody born can teach him in anything."

Culme picked up his tea and candles and went away, but Mrs. Dury waited. Then a thought struck Ouldsbroom. It occurred to him that the water-keeper's days were but grey and his life cheerless. Therefore he followed Peter.

"Culme!" he shouted. "Will 'e come to my wedding feast at Stannon? There'll be a good rally o' neighbours."

"Ess fay, and glad to!"

"That's all right then. And bring your old mother. 'Twill liven her up."

"Thank you kindly, I'm sure."

"Bring your concertina likewise!"

"That I will!"

And the crooked Culme went on his way rejoicing.

"A fine chap," said Mrs. Dury when the men were gone.

"So he is," admitted Barbara. "But I wish he was as sensible as he is large-hearted. This is a terrible, barefaced thing he's done."

The other nodded.

"Pity he couldn't look elsewhere and leave them two alone. However, he's my sort."

"So he is mine. That's why I'm sorry for him. The girl that would take him as that girl did, for his farm and his riches, isn't going to be a good wife. We're all bred to trouble as the sparks fly upward, Betty, but he's brewed a double dose for himself, after the manner of all fools."

"He was strong enough to get Unity Crymes away from t'other; so he ought to be strong enough to break her in," argued the sick nurse.

"Not he. He's no woman-breaker."

"They ban't married yet, come to think of it. Perhaps she'll bolt with t'other at the last minute, like Jenny Webber did. And now I'll see some black, Miss Hext, if you please."

CHAPTER VIII

POSTBRIDGE is more ancient than the road of Roman straightness that strikes through it. Round about are numerous mediæval monuments. 'Clapper' bridges and miners' smelting houses, ruined dwellings and symbols of the Christian faith all stand within a walk of the hamlet, while, more ancient yet, though of yesterday contrasted with the stone man's relics, shall be seen a fragment of the Great Central Trackway or Fosseway, which extended from Caithness to Mounts Bay before the Roman landed. Fragments of this ancient, cobbled road still lie northerly of Postbridge, and traverse Dart at a shallow beneath Hartland Farm. Next, plunging into the prehistoric past, your antiquary enters behind the veil of time to trace Neolithic man through Dartmoor. Menhirs and parallelitha, hypæthral circles and hidden graves, the ruins of lodges and the shattered walls of many an aboriginal hamlet still stand upon these naked hills. Much is obvious, much remains to be understood of the vanished people. We have no Ariadne's clue to the granite labyrinth, though time may yet wake a dawn of knowledge upon the mystery and lift light above it. To-day this land of tumuli conceals some secrets still, and its monuments, behind their deep investment of the ages, challenge theory and defy proof.

Sunk in an eternal and frozen winter of antiquity the old stones stand. Some are obscure and need skilled eyes to mark their order for the work of men; others serve to arrest the attention of a child.

Twin, shattered circles, known locally as "The Grey Wethers," are of this latter sort, and excite an instant wonder in any intelligent mind. They stand upon the

60

eastern slope of Siddaford Tor, and, seen from afar, outlined against the sky upon the earth's shoulder, resemble
sheep so closely that no eye guesses the granite truth of
them.   Unlike the usual monuments of this character,
that spring rugged and splintered from the heath, these
stunted pillars have been worked.   Though no mark of
tool remains, and time has gnawed their contours into
roughness, the fact of fabrication can be proved

Now, upon the autumnal heath at gloaming, some
stood like square tombstones in a water-logged burying-
place of eld, and some were fallen   Stern, mysterious
and significant they spread; and by the gathering darkness round them, by the waste spaces all seamed and
scarred with storm, by the few that stood tirelessly
through the centuries and the many that had dropped;
by the cryptic writing of ebony and silver scrawled on
their faces, and by the emblem of eternity they dimly
shadowed on the hill, they might be known.   But the
hieroglyph of the lichen is not so obscure; the story it
tells of nature's beginning is not so undecipherable as
that of the Grey Wethers themselves, and the thing they
stood for to men's hearts in the far-off morning of the
Age of Bronze.

Henry Birdwood sat on a stone in the midst of this
local sanctity and waited for Unity Crymes to come to him.

The first great experience of his life had swept over his
spirit and left it changed.   Much was gone from it, and
the things that had aforetime flourished there were torn
out by the roots.   Their place knew them no more.   They
had prospered and made a fair show, as half-hardy vegetation under glass.   But the frost of reality slew them and
probed with steel fingers the soil that had sustained them.
What sort of crop would succeed none could guess,
neither did any man know if root as well as branch of
Birdwood's revealed characteristics had also perished
Whether the old attitude to life would put forth again
from his stricken heart, or whether a new sort of seed was
sown when Unity jilted him—that was hidden in time.
But Birdwood himself perceived and encouraged the
coming crop.

In the primeval forests that roll about the foothills of the Himalaya, it happens not seldom that tempest or man strips the indigenous pelt of the hills and leaves all naked. A verdure whose duration extends beyond human memory is swept from the face of the mountains; and then, out of the naked earth, spring, not the progeny of the vanished order, but seedlings of some autochthonous flora that have been sown here in still earlier time. For centuries they have rested dormant; yet now their long sleep ends; they germinate; they root, and rise to cover the hills with a vegetation unfamiliar to the age, but no stranger to the unchanging earth from which it ascends.

A like mystery had happened in the case of Henry Birdwood. Storms, as it seemed, had slain the direct and first-hand inheritance of his father's blood in his veins. That growth of Protestant instinct and simple religious principle was to all appearance dead. The soil that nourished it had been stripped bare by tornado; and it remained to find whether germs of deep-sown antecedent heredities would spring to light under the altered conditions, or whether what had apparently perished at this onset, yet held life and would presently rise again from its ruins.

One thing was certain the real man, for good or ill, must now appear.

Henry Birdwood looked down at his home far below, beside the brink of Teign, while rosy light faded off the hills and touched the river in the valley

Footsteps approached him, but it was not Unity. Ned Sleep appeared on his way home ,

"Have you seen Unity Crymes?" asked Birdwood, and the other drew up. scratched his head, and considered first the question and then the answer.

Henry, knowing his deliberation, did not attempt to hurry him.

"No," replied Sleep at length, "I can't in honesty say I've seen her. But a woman I did see, and she was in a very excited frame of mind, as well she might be In a word, 'twas Mrs. Dury, the sick nurse. She was travelling to Stannon so fast as her legs could take her."

"Why for?"

"The very question I asked while she stood a moment to blow. Mrs. Crymes be brought to bed. And Mrs. Dury is a wonder for looking on into the future, I'm sure; for, even at that great moment, her mind ran on and she said, 'However will they manage about the wedding? 'Tis the day after to-morrow!' 'A home question,' I said to her, 'and I'm glad I ban't the man to answer it.'"

"That's their affair. Perhaps 'twill be put off."

"So it might, so it might. 'Twould be a kindness in you to advise them to do that. They may not think of it; yet 'tis a very good idea," declared Mr. Sleep.

Not the least irony lurked in the remark. He was quite excited, and had been mildly wondering all the way home what was likely to happen; but the possibility of postponement had not occurred to him.

Sleep crept forward over the darkening hill, and Birdwood waited for an hour, but much impatience marked the vigil, and he walked up and down without ceasing. The stars were beginning to shine, and he was about to return to Teign Head when Unity Crymes appeared.

"I was just off; then Sleep brought news that things had happened to delay you. So I waited till now."

"My sister-in-law have just had a child—only a girl—worse luck for her."

"Will it make any difference?"

"No, seemingly. It's all happened so well as can be, and she says she could get up to-morrow if the doctor would let her."

"The marriage goes on?"

"Yes. How terrible patient you've been. To think you can forgive me like this! Yet 'tis a worse punishment than to scorn me. I feel a selfish wretch about it."

" 'Tis no odds. You'll get over that. Who knows what may happen? You may live to find even a farm isn't everything."

"Yes, I may."

"I love you too well to wish you anything but happiness all the same. You've took everything from me—

everything; and still I'm only sorry I haven't got more to give. You've stripped me of my religion and my hope and my trust; you've scattered me; you've done for me. But you can't choke me off loving you. And you can't choke me off knowing that you love me, for all your cruelty.''

''You'll find love far better worth than mine.''

''I've got yours—that's what I want to remind you. He can't take that It was all coming so steady if you could only have waited. Why, last week Twigg put two shillings more on to my money. I'm getting known.''

''You're a long sight too good for me Of course you're getting known ''

''And getting known to myself, too. This is the first knock-down blow I've ever had. You can't lose without larning. I've lost you, but I've larned a lot ''

She did not answer.

''Yes,'' he continued ''I've larned what was worth a pang or two Perhaps, as time goes on, I'll teach you a bit Your man be wiser here and there than I thought. 'Tis a fool's trick to ask Providence to help you Providence haven't got time. After I talked with Ouldsbroom and tried to move his heart, and found that I might so soon have tried to move this stone we're sitting on, I went home; and the queer feeling in my mind all the way was—not hate of Ouldsbroom—I couldn't hate him for loving you—but wonder at the terrific power of him 'Twas like talking against a hurricane. The hurricane hadn't no ill-will towards me; but if I got in the way—well, then I had to feel it, not because I was Henry Birdwood, but only because I'd got in the way He showed me that ''

''He likes you very well, and means to let you know it ''

''I'm sure he does. He likes everybody. But listen what I done 'You're strong, Philip Ouldsbroom,' I said to myself, 'maybe you're stronger than me; but I've got them on my side afore whose strength your strength be weakness.' Yes, I said that, and who did I mean? I meant Unity Crymes and my Maker. And first I come down, as you know, and prayed to you."

"Don't, for God's sake, go over it all again."

"I'm not going to. I only want for you to understand how 'tis. First I came and prayed to you, and you wouldn't hear. So that was my first hope dead And then I prayed to God, and reminded Him as I'd done His work very faithful and steady, and put the case afore Him out of a broken heart—for broken I was then But He didn't hear neither. And after a tidy week of torment, I began to see what the world really means and how the fight goes to the strongest, and how victory be won on our feet, not on our knees. D'you understand all that? If you don't, you will. Philip's right to go his way; he's a lesson to such as me. Ride rough-shod and don't think to interest God Almighty in your affairs, because you won't—not Him nor anybody else. He only remembers one thing about us, and that is when we've got to die. Then He rules us out of the book. And all this stuff about eternity is bosh too. For if He cared for us anywhere He'd care for us *here;* and if He was a just God He'd let us start fair and not handicap half the world to hell from the beginning. I've larned all this wisdom from the ways of your husband to be. A great teacher, him! And what's the outcome? I'm going to be strong too; I'm going to get my way too. You'll see —you'll see, Unity. And maybe I'll teach him a little some day, in exchange for all I've larned."

"This is awful news to me," she said. "I'd got to look on my soul as lost—but yours? Don't you go all wrong because I have."

"Never bleat that stuff no more! Be strong. This praying is tomfoolery—I've proved it. I know what I'm going to do. But the thing is to do it—not talk about it. Look at Ouldsbroom. Who is there don't like him and think highly of him? He's smote me into the dust. Who thinks the worse of him for doing it? Who comes to help me up? Nobody. I thought that mine was just a pattern case for God to handle, but 'twasn't 'Tis just a pattern case to show what a man's worth in

5

himself. And, afore another year's gone, I shall find out—and you will.''

''I know very well what you're worth. But don't let it drive you away from chapel, Henry.''

''Drop all that. 'Tis worse than cant from you Be strong, I tell you. Did you get the strength to throw me over at chapel? Was it God Almighty gave you to Philip? No, Ouldsbroom took you. Be strong—like your future husband is—and like I mean to be.''

''I'll never forget all you've been to me.''

''You never will. A lot's going to happen to surprise you yet—if I'm strong enough. If I'm not—then Sleep will find me some day hanging by the neck to the roof-tree in the barn down there; and he'll stand and look and wonder for an hour or two whether 'twould be the proper thing to cut me down. And he'll think it out and decide that he'd better not take too much upon himself and meddle in other people's business; and then he'll saddle the pony and ride off to Postbridge—or maybe over to Hartland—with the gay news.''

''You'll drive me mad.''

''I'll drive you—but not mad. Let the future look after the future. I'm a new man. The strongest physic's the nastiest. So all's said I'll go a bit of the way back with you. Philip wouldn't mind that. I wanted to see you first I'm going to see him next—and tell him all I've told you.''

''I don't understand. I only know I'm terrible miserable.''

''That's your weakness The strong are never miserable. You've done very well and been very wise. Each for himself. I've got something for you in my pocket— a wedding present 'tis. That shows what a lot I've been larning. A funny world—I never thought to give you any wedding present but myself. But now——''

He took a parcel from his pocket and gave it to her.

'' 'Tis just a little housewife's case with rows of needles and a thimble and such like. I thought it might be useful.''

''What a man you are! You talk about trying to be

large-minded and forgiving. I didn't know 'twas in men
to forgive what I've done.''

"There's nought woman can do that man can't forgive, if they love enough You'll use they needles?''

"And think of the giver ''

"Why not? And if Philip offers to be friendly with
me, you won't forbid it?''

"If you can be friendly—who are we not to rejoice at
it? You talk of learning from him—'tis for him to learn
from you.''

"No—no; I'm not worthy to black his boots—not yet.
He's older—such a lot older, you see. I'll never be able
to thrust my shoulder through life like him.''

Thus were Birdwood's perceptions quickening daily
and hourly. He felt them growing while he spoke to
Unity. He thought more than he said, and he remembered that the fox can go where the hound cannot.

Now he walked beside Unity to the hill above Stannon
Farm, and left her there.

"I shan't see you afore the wedding, but I'm coming
to that 'Twill be a plucky thing to do—about the first
plucky thing I've ever done.''

"You'll be welcome,'' she said.

"You want me to come?''

"Yes, I do.''

"That's my reason, remember. I wouldn't come if
you'd rather I didn't ''

" 'Twill sting me to the bottom of my soul to see
you there; and yet I wouldn't miss that sting,'' she said.

"Yes, I know what you mean 'Tis the worn-out edge
of your conscience cutting ragged and hurting I've
heard my old preaching father say that. Get rid of conscience so quick as you can, Unity Be like Ouldsbroom
and like me. We've got no conscience You can't run
with the hare and the hunt. You can't do what you've
done and keep a conscience on a chain. Choke it and be
free. Get happiness out of life. Good-bye.''

He shook her hand warmly and held it a moment.
Then he departed and left her to marvel at this amazing
change in the man. He was grown in a space of weeks

from boyhood to maturity He seemed to stand on the
ruins of himself. She admired him as she had never admired him. She told herself that had he spoken thus
when she met him at the sheepfold after Philip's proposal, she could never have left him.

CHAPTER IX

PHILIP OULDSBROOM entered into the state of marriage with many and varied resolutions. He continued, however, to be himself, and within six months the resolutions were forgotten. His wife, more stable, began the new life quite conscious of its large significance and found her nature well able to cope with the addition. She created another atmosphere at Hartland. The rooms were papered; the ceilings were whitewashed; broken walls were mended; broken gates were removed and new gates hung in place of them. The garden showed her handiwork; the very thatch on the roof signalled that Unity's reign was begun, and flashed gold out of the silver where it was mended. Old cracked crocks and cloam were swept away; old worm-eaten furniture was hacked up for firewood or given to those who coveted it. She set about her task steadily and with method. She made no violent alterations, but instituted a gradual and all-embracing change. The task was easy, for she could do no wrong in her husband's eyes. Each suggestion he hailed with delight and declared that none but she could have thought upon. His own ideas were usually of a greater size, involving no small expenditure; and the execution of these she negatived or postponed with skill and tact.

A man of Philip's pattern was clay in Unity's hand, despite her youth; and his transparent kindness and childlike errors of temper and judgment were readily perceived and weighed by his wife before they had been married six weeks. She liked him well, and even glimpsed the beauty of such a large spirit; but she never respected him and never feared him. She made him work harder; but seldom refused the pleasures that he planned for her, and rejoiced him mightily by sharing the things that he held good. She went to revels and other gatherings with him, she made no demur when he asked friends to supper or, on Sundays, to dinner She was always willing and always cheerful and hopeful. She hid exactly what she pleased from him, for suspicion was foreign to his nature They had not much in common at heart; but she affected to share his sympathies more closely than was in truth the case; and he believed her absolutely, and never ceased to marvel at the amazing parity of emotion that existed between them If he was angry, she simulated anger; if he was amused, she shared his amusement. She looked to his clothes, and made him dress in a manner worthy of his position. She worked with delicate touches to waken a wider self-respect in him She sought to raise him from his easy attitude of equality with all men. Here, however, she failed; but she did not blame him She blamed herself and cast about how to approach the problem in a light more favourable.

They both loved children, and wanted them. But any over-mastering desire is a weakness and throws the obsessed individual open to attack. A passion, in whatsoever direction, argues appetite so strong that judgment may fail before the strain and a fault in the armour appear.

Unity Ouldsbroom, having no doubt of the answer, asked her husband after they were married whether she might continue to attend the services of the Little Baptists. He laughed and said, "Just so often as ever you like; but I lay you'll soon get sick of 'em after you know my way better."

He was right: the larger attitude of Ouldsbroom and his contempt of her sect influenced her, while another defection did more, and decided her. Henry Birdwood returned not to his old worship, and none of his friends could prevail upon him to do so He had taken his disappointment in a manner that puzzled the people; and some held him a very wise man, and some called him a coward. But the experience changed his life, added years to his knowledge and self-reliance, and shook up the basal ingredients of his nature, so that they began to appear.

His father, the itinerant preacher, hearing that he had flung over the faith, came to see him, prayed long, and strove to prevail with him; but he was firm, and the old man went broken-hearted about his business. Ouldsbroom, who affected Henry's company after his marriage, and was not denied it, congratulated the shepherd on his pluck and aired his own nebulous opinions at great length, while Birdwood listened and flattered the elder man. And Unity, compounding, woman fashion, with convention and opinion, though she left the Little Baptists, became a member of the church congregation. She declared that since she had there been married, her sentiment determined her to worship there henceforth.

On a day in spring, Ouldsbroom met the shepherd upon his way to Postbridge, and they walked together between Hartland and the village. Sometimes Unity and her husband drank tea at Teign Head on Sundays, when the weather was fair and the Moor passable; but more often Birdwood accepted their hospitality.

" 'Tis nice going now up over," said Henry; "why for don't you and your misses come along next Sunday and have a dish of tea with me? I shall be lonesome, for Sleep is away. He've heard of a job to Tavistock and nought will do but he must see if he can better himself. He've been conning over it for a fortnight and will find the place filled, as usual, for he's always a week behind the fair."

"He don't get enough," declared Philip, "no more don't you, for that matter. Twigg's like all them Dissenters—hungry as a hawk for money. I should have looked around afore now to try and get you a better job; but I should be awful sorry to lose you from these parts."

"Thank you, I'm sure; and I should be awful sorry to go. I can't see myself away from Teign Head. I like the freedom and I like being in the saddle half my time. If the Moor-man—Twigg, I mean—would but raise it to twenty-five shillings, I could set up to stop here for ever."

"I'll see what I can do. But 'tis difficult now, because you've throwed over his meeting-house."

"That don't count really, though of course he's said so. He knows exactly how far he'd have to look for another shepherd like me. What does he care for a man's soul so long as his body be doing his work well and cheap? If I was to strike for more, I believe he'd pay it; but I shan't this year though I may a bit later."

"That's right," declared Ouldsbroom. "I like to see you with a good conceit of yourself. I taught you that, Henry."

"That and a lot else."

"Leave it till the end of this year, and then, if you and me together can't squeeze a bit more out of him, I'll cast about. Why, I might get rids of my chap and let you have his place; but ban't your job ezacally."

"Like you to think of such a fine thing. But that wouldn't do. I'll bide where I be for a bit yet. Who knows? Perhaps I'll go back to the Little Baptists again. Nearly all the chaps here with sheep be chapel members."

"Don't you do that. Keep free of 'em; hear Barbara Hext tell about em. She's so wise as a man in everything else; but where they be concerned she's all woman, and can sting like a hornet."

"Perhaps she've got good cause. I'd like to know her history. 'Twould teach us a lot about women in general if we did."

"You get a wife, Henry, that's the way to larn about 'em! Second-hand larning be nothing to having a female always on your hands—or in your arms. Pick the right one, and your days will be such that heaven couldn't beat 'em. I know—I know. Why, my dear man, we don't begin to live till we're married; we don't know we're born till we're married. And that's true, whether it turns out well or ill. We mess along—poor, half-finished things that we are—and we have a go at the girls off and on, and amuse ourselves with the naughty ones, and try and look as if butter wouldn't melt in our mouths when we'm along with the good ones; but 'tis all moonshine, and the naughty ones be just as much hidden from us as the good—may be more. We don't know nought *about* 'em inside their skins. But you marry, and then you'll begin to get a dim sort of an idea what a good woman is —if you marry a good one. And no doubt t'other sort let you see a bit of the naked truth too."

"No doubt, no doubt," assented Birdwood.

"Yes, 'tis so. I never had much use for women myself; but looking back I laugh sometimes to think I went blundering along, like a runaway hoop, all alone, and thought I was cutting a good figure in the world There's only one thing wanting, however——" He broke off and sighed.

Birdwood did not ask for information upon the point, because he knew to what the other referred. After a silence he spoke.

"Here's my way. And I'll count to see you Sunday if the weather holds fair."

"Better lock up your place and come to us. Come for the day. Ride over early."

"Your wife will want to go to church."

"I shan't."

"I'll come over then "

They parted, and Ouldsbroom, grown thoughtful at the shadow in his heart, went forward to the post office. He was soon cheerful again, and joined half a dozen children on the brink of the river.

"What's the fun, Sally?" he asked of a girl who stood holding a baby in her arms.

"Us be here to see my brother drown four chets," said the child stolidly.

"No, no," he said, and raised his voice. "Come here, you childer—all of you. I'll show 'e something better than drowning kittens up at Miss Hext's shop. Quick, the pack of 'e!"

He strode off, knowing well that they would all follow. Even the executioner did not delay. He flung the blind, useless life into the river and hastened after Ouldsbroom.

Fourpence was spent and the children departed; then Barbara asked Philip his business.

"Of course if there's a boy or girl in sight you must

drag it in here and waste your coppers,'' she said, ''but what have you come for?''

"Wish to God there was a boy or girl in sight at Hartland," he answered abruptly. Then he filled his pipe

"I haven't come for nothing in particular, but for a bit of a tell with you. You're the only creature with any sense in Postbridge."

"Thank you, I'm sure. 'Tis lucky there's more in my shop than sense, or I shouldn't have many customers."

"I've just been going along with Henry Birdwood. You was out there, for all your wit You thought I'd never win the man; but we're as thick as thieves now."

"Thieves always fall out sooner or late, however."

"We shan't I want to better him presently. The puzzle is how to do it."

"Find him a wife."

"Ah! just what I was saying, but easy to talk. 'Tis a ticklish task that. Yet good advice, too A bachelor lives like a toad under a harrow 'Tis a dog's life. But men have got to choose their own wives."

"Well, he did, didn't he? 'Twould be only fair if you could find what you took away from him."

"So it would. Though he's not much set that way Rather sour, in fact, against females in general, though very good friends with Unity, so far as I can see Always civil anyhow."

"We can't many of us see far. And 'tis the best wisdom of the rare, long-sighted people to keep their sight to themselves."

"Another child coming at Stannon," broke off Philip. "The luck some women have!"

"And never know it."

"A curious thing," he continued: "me and Unity do think so much alike that we often guess t'other's thought."

"A man's a fool to go guessing at woman's thoughts. He might so well pry into her cupboards."

"You don't know what 'tis to be one with a man through and through."

"No, I don't—nor any other woman."

"Unity does. We're hungering for a boy. That's what we both want more than anything on earth."

"I hope 'twill happen, I'm sure. Life must run easy if you can spend time worrying about that."

"Perhaps you never wanted to be a mother yourself? But a lot of women have a great hunger for it, and none more than my wife. 'Tis a bias of her mind. I'll catch her sometimes just thinking and doing nought. You'd never believe that she could be doing nothing unless she was asleep—would you? But off and on—even in the middle of her bustling days—she'll stand still and stare afore her as if she was struck. She'll let a pot boil over in them minutes; or a cat climb on the table. It comes over her like that."

"I should never have thought it."

"You don't like her," he said, and his under lip stuck out and his jaw hardened. "You never have liked her since she took me instead of Birdwood."

"I like a lot in her, Philip. She's a lesson to this lazy place in a hundred ways. But I don't like her so well as I like you."

"She's worth a thousand of me. She's made me. I look back at myself and feel ashamed of such a good-for-nought as once I was. And gives way to me, too, mind you! 'Tisn't all one-sided. She'll make holiday with me gay as a lark, and put her cares out of her mind, and sit on the green-side for an hour at a time by the river while I'm catching a few trout, or anything like that. If I tell her to come out, as I did three days ago, and listen to a pheasant calling, she'll come and take as much joy in it as I could wish. She's a wonder, and more wonderful every day of her life."

"I'm glad to hear these things. I hope your wife and me will know each other better."

"Come up," he exclaimed. "Come up Sunday and eat your dinner along with us."

"No, I won't do that. Later on, perhaps."

"There's only one small thing that ever makes her chide me," continued Ouldsbroom. "And that's my language. She can't abide a crooked word, for some reason—well used to 'em as she is.''

"More can I," declared Barbara "You do swear a great deal too much.''

"I know—I know,'' admitted the farmer; "but there is such a devil of a lot to swear at!''

"You've just said all's as well with you as can be.''

"With me—yes; but I ban't everybody. I mean round about. There's Duchy, to begin with. Who's going to help swearing at that? Then there's all these new things starting on the Moor, and the cannons that carry their beastly cannon-balls three miles, they say; and there's they Little Baptists and their little ways; and there's the hard trouble of getting labour. Why, every young man worth his salt be going off the land, so far as I can see. In fact, the times be enough to make any man swear; and they ought to make him swear. But I will have my way through it all.''

"The times was always bad and they always will be,'' she said.

He sprang to another subject with the customary weakness of relation peculiar to his mind.

"I offered for to be gossip to Quinton Crymes, his coming child. And he was content that I should be, but Gertrude wouldn't have it. Why for? Because she says I'm a man without God in my life. She wouldn't trust her child to me to teach it things Silly, moon-faced creature! But I talked to her. 'If I haven't enough sense to lend a hand to a green, young, newborn child, 'tis pity,' I said; 'and whether or no, I'd larn him to put a braver face on his own life and to start it with a better conceit of himself than ever you slimy Little Baptists will. You'll teach him to call himself a worm, and a slave to sin, and a wicked, useless creature not fit to be saved—not worth saving. But I'd teach him to be like me—a man that ban't wicked and ban't a worm, and be quite strong enough and sensible enough to save him-self!' That's what I told Gertrude Crymes, and she stared like a stuck pig and said she hoped the Lord would forgive me.''

"All good sense," declared Barbara. "If you were as clever as your words, I'd have no fear for you."

"I am; and a darned sight cleverer. However, I ban't clever enough to get a boy seemingly. Still I feel very hopeful about it."

"So you should. There's the telegraph!"

A bell tinkled, and Miss Hext went to her work while Ouldsbroom looked round him, found a little plum-cake, shouted to Barbara that he had taken it for his wife, and then left the shop.

CHAPTER X

THE colour strophe and antistrophe of the greater and lesser gorse is nowhere more easily observed than upon the slopes about Stannon farm. When the cuckoo cries. the greater furzes glow, and the linnet makes her nest in the fragrant acres of them; anon, after the blaze of the spring has died out, the smaller plant awakens, lights the rolling hills, and creeps to the very feet of its sleeping brother, now sunk into uniform masses of jade green. The lesser gorse twines into the rosy purple of the heather, and spreads the pomp of August on the heights and valleys It shines with golden warmth; the cloud-shadows scarcely lower its splendour of rich tone, through it twines the pink network of the dodder, and beside it twinkle the euphrasy and tormentilla and sweet wild thyme.

Over this autumn splendour on Merripit Hill came the man, Ned Sleep, upon his pony at an early hour. A heavy dew was on all things, and each grey cone of spider's web and blade of blue moor-grass glittered with moisture. But though the time was yet short of six o'clock, Sleep's passing had been observed from Stannon. A friend marked him and shouted to arrest attention.

Ned saw himself beckoned, pulled up his pony, deliberated, and then turned to the vale beneath. The distant man advanced, threaded Stannon stream, and presently stood beside him

"Morning Sleep! I seed you going along the hill and thought you'd be so good as to carry a message for me to 'Warren House.'"

"I will do so," answered Sleep. "I'm going to More-

ton to-day, and you might very likely wonder why for I
travel this road; but I've got to call at Mr. Twigg's upon
my way."

"So much the better. I meant to see him myself, but
I'm terrible busy getting in fern afore the weather
breaks."

"The fern's plenty this year. Us be going to save a
nice bit I cut down back-along. And what might you
want me to say to Mr. Twigg?"

Quinton Crymes explained his desires.

" 'Tis like this: my wife be going to have another baby
afore long, and she ban't doing very clever just now, and
doctor won't let her go to chapel or anywhere. My little
girl have got the measles also. And Gertrude's down-
daunted and crying out for a bit of prayer and pious
discourse. You know her sort. You and me be religious
men, and so's Twigg. And pastor's away sick, and, as
you know, Gregory Twigg be praying for the people till
he comes back. So there 'tis. I call upon Twigg, as
standing in pastor's place, to come and have a tell with
my wife and give her a bit of religion. That is, if the
man ban't too busy to do it."

"Let me go over what you say in my mind," said
Sleep; and for the space of two minutes he considered
all that he had heard.

"Mr. Twigg to come up over to talk along with your
wife and cheer her up, because she can't get to chapel
just at present?"

"That's it, Ned."

"Why for don't you pray? I've heard you fetch a
very tidy prayer more'n once of a Sunday."

"A woman don't want to hear her husband pray—she
knoweth a bit too much about him."

Sleep nodded.

"I daresay 'tis so. Their nature puts the stranger man
above the every-day one. Then it shall be done. I'll
give Mr. Twigg your message."

"How's Birdwood going on? Haven't seen him this
longful time."

" 'How's Birdwood,' " repeated the other reflectively.

"You ask me 'How's Birdwood going on?' Well, not
to speak in a hurry, I reckon he's coming back a little
nearer to grace. Yes, Crymes, I see a mark about him.
'Twouldn't amaze me if he was to be viewed again to
chapel afore we're all very much older."

" 'Twould be an answer to prayer "

"Not but what he's stiff-necked still, and I may be
wrong. 'Tis only an idea in my mind, and I beg you
won't let it go no further."

"No, no—I shan't do that."

"As for me," volunteered Sleep, "in confidence, I may
tell you I'm still on the lookout for a new billet. But it
don't offer "

"Well, good-morning, Ned I must get to work."

"So must I; so must I "

The men parted, and anon Sleep delivered his message
at the 'Warren House' Inn

As a result of it Mr. Twigg, who felt himself responsible for the spiritual welfare of the Little Baptists during their pastor's absence, walked over to Stannon late
in the afternoon.

Quinton Crymes saw the stout body of him descending
the hillside, hastened indoors, and gave his wife the word
that Gregory Twigg approached.

She sighed, with evident relief

"Keep him at the door for two minutes," she said;
"and I'll just whip aside and turn my apern and ope the
parlour window. 'Tis a thought stuffy in there, as we
haven't used the room for a good while "

She aired the parlour, made herself tidy, and issued a
few orders to the girl that worked for her.

"Get the tea," she said; "hot up they cakes as I
made last Saturday, and then keep baby quiet."

When Twigg arrived, Gertrude thanked him warmly
for coming, and found that the versatile man had quite
assumed the habit of the pastor.

"Thank Him who sent me," said Mr. Twigg "I have
been blessed with more gifts than what you'll find in most
men, Mrs. Crymes; but there's another side to it, and
the more gifts, the more work."

"I'm sure 'tis terrible lucky for minister that he can go off and feel you're pretty near so clever at the souls as him," declared Mr. Crymes

"It is lucky, as you say. In fact, so far as the natural skill goes, I'm better than him. 'Tis his business, and a very good and helpful man is Medlicott, and we're fortunate to have him in our midst; but the real touch is mine You may have noticed it. Practice has made Medlicott what he is. I've got what no practice can give —the Fire of the Spirit. Put a living soul in front of me and I lose sight of everything else and feel myself as great as Paul. I'm always astonishing myself and my wife with my flow of speech and the way I bring out an argument."

"I'm sure you astonish us too," said Quinton Crymes; "and I shan't forget your kindness in coming over—at a busy season of the year as 'tis with you at the public-house I should be terrible vexed if I thought we'd put you out"

"Have no fear for that. The mind that's regulated like mine don't get put out. I wake up of a morning and say: '1 thank Thee, O God, that I find myself ready and willing for everything that may come along.' Nothing's too big for me, because, though terrible big problems turn up and I often feel I'm Duchy's right hand, and know, when the bailiff appears, that he's coming for me to set right his great difficulties—yet my brain is large enough for all No man catches me in error I sometimes wonder whether the Prince of Wales have ever heard tell of me; for in a way, I've a hand in getting him his money, and no fair man can say I don't put many and many a pound in his noble pocket along of all I do to help Duchy."

"Without a doubt he's heard of you—or ought to have And now I'll be getting back to my work and leave you with the missis," replied Mr. Crymes "I shall take it very kind if you'll drink a dish of tea with us afore you go."

Then he edged away out of the room, and Gregory and the woman were left together.

6

" 'Tis a great misfortune to be cut off from chapel,"
said Mr. Twigg, "and with a man like Crymes you're
bound to feel it. When my wife has to hide herself from
the public eye, 'tis nought, because she've got me at her
side; and I'm like one of my own beer barrels: you can
turn the tap and get a drop of piety, or sense, or a bit of
fun, or just what your nature craves at any moment.
But 'tisn't given to every woman to marry the like of
me, and nobody knows that better than my wife. You
want uplifting to the Throne of Grace, and I dare say
Crymes haven't got the knack of comfort like me. I don't
blame him, of course. And now I've got an hour afore I
must be gone, and I'll pray for half of it and answer any
questions; and then I'll have a cup of weak tea."

" 'Tis most kind of you. A regular chapel member
like me gets to feel the want something cruel." declared
Gertrude.

"And so you should. Now you sit in that easy chair
The Lord don't want them in your state to kneel; and
I'll stand here and lift my voice to the Almighty."

He looked at his watch; then folded his hands over
his chest, flung up his eyes and half closed them, so that
the whites alone appeared After a few moments of
silent preparation, he began.

His voice had now entirely changed into a slow drawl;
but his opinions, his attitude to his Maker and to himself, continued as before.

"O Almighty Father, Maker of all things visible and
invisible, look, I beseech Thee, upon this visible woman
and also upon the invisible child that she is about to
fetch forth into the world. I pray Thee let it be numbered among the few who are chosen and not among the
many who must be rejected; let it be a sheep and not a
goat, O Lord, and hear the prayer of the just man, which
availeth much——"

Mr. Twigg proceeded in this strain for twenty minutes, then he varied his attitude by kneeling down. The
listener, with clasped hands, open mouth, and straining
attention, followed his efforts and obviously won immense
peace of mind and exaltation of spirit from them.

Towards the finish Mr Twigg tired and looked at his watch again; then he made a final effort.

"O Saviour of mankind and womankind, who art more ready to listen than we to pray, I ask Thee this afternoon especially to have mercy on Thy servant, Gertrude Crymes, to strengthen her and fortify her that she may be a valiant soldier in the army of the Lord, and that she may bring forth in due season, according to Thy holy will and ordinance, a child worthy to become a Christian child and to belong to Thy chosen Little Baptists, who are a light to lighten the darkness and the glory of Thy people Amen."

Mr. Twigg bent himself over the parlour sofa and completed the service in silence; Gertrude shed a few comfortable tears.

"There; and now if you've got the kettle boiling, a cup of hot but weak tea will be grateful," said the little man, rising. "I hope you find yourself better, Sister Crymes?"

"I'm a different woman," said she " 'Tis a gert gift, and you'm hiding your light in your public-house under a bushel. To think such a prayer as that all prayed for one poor, worthless woman."

"Not worthless," corrected Mr. Twigg "You are far from worthless. And, in any case, even the worst woman in your condition can't be worthless. You never know how great a servant of Christ be on the way. 'Tis nervous times now for you mothers, I grant; because if I read the Book right, and I can't say I know anybody who reads it righter, it looks very like as if Antichrist was upon us And a mother the Horror must have; and a father too, for that matter—if 'tis the Devil himself But you've no call to fret there He'll come out of the Upper Ten, if I know anything. God's a watchful God, and He won't let a Little Baptist have any hand in the monster."

With this comforting reflection Mr. Twigg joined the household at tea in the kitchen, he ate and drank heartily, and then, being reminded of a former subject, insisted on lifting another petition.

"Don't you go, none of you," he said. "I've got one more thing to say, and say it I will. It don't concern none of you; but Sister Crymes mentioned the matter, and if 'tis within the power of prayer to hasten it, as who shall doubt? let us do so."

Crymes and his wife, the girl who worked for Mrs Crymes, and the old labourer, James Coaker, all knelt down, and Gregory, rested and much refreshed, prayed for Henry Birdwood, that his backsliding might cease and that he might be rescued from the undying worm and the fire which never shall be quenched, even as a brand from the burning, and the widow's piece of silver which was lost and is found again. He hinted to the Deity that it was no ordinary individual who now interceded with Him for the soul of the shepherd, and he concluded by leaving the matter with confidence in the hand of Henry's Creator. He then wished them all well and went his way in perfect tune with finite and infinite.

"A man to be envied, if he wasn't so good that 'twould be wrong to envy him," said Quinton Crymes "I'll have a cup of tea now he's gone, but I can't eat or drink easy in his company: he's so much above me."

"A very heartening prayer he prayed—a good half hour, and all too short," answered his wife "When you see the man he is, I'm sure 'tis a wonder to me you can keep to church, James. Do your parson pray like that?"

"No," answered Mr. Coaker. "To be honest, he don't. At least I've never heard him get at grips with the Almighty same as Twigg can. 'Tis as if Gregory was talking to the Duchy Bailiff—and having the best of the argument."

"That's the man!" declared Crymes. "You've hit him in a word, Jimmy! He'll argue black's white, if 'tis to save a soul. Your chap sticks to the prayer book and ban't much more alive than the marker put in between the leaves. When you know a thing by heart—there 'tis—the virtue fades out of it Twigg takes the Kingdom of Heaven by storm—that's what he does He won't hear 'No' for an answer, that man won't. In his business with God, just the same as in his business with men, he will have the upper hand—to say it in a pious spirit.''

''There ban't no surprises to your church,'' added Mrs. Crymes '' 'Tis all rule o' thumb. You can go to sleep anywhere and, when you waken, pick up the stitch again, like knitting.''

''But look at the high class of the prayers,'' argued Mr. Coaker. ''When does a common man, like Twigg, light upon such fine, rolling words as we've got in our prayer book? He might pray all his wind out of his body and not come within shouting distance of what we ax for the Queen and Royal Family.''

They debated the rival virtues of their systems of belief, but neither convinced the other.

CHAPTER XI

PHILIP OULDSBROOM, his wife, and Henry Birdwood were driving back to Postbridge from Princetown fair. The farmer had sold six ponies to advantage; he had enjoyed all the attractions of the revel and drunk a great deal of beer and spirits. He was now market-merry, and his wife held the reins.

Philip chattered incessantly, and shouted jokes to the riders who passed his cart or the pedestrians he overtook. The pony sale had put him into great good humour; he was building important new projects upon the result of it

"They Cornish men know a pony when they see one," he said to Henry. " 'The very best ponies in the fair'—that's what they called mine. There's tons of cash to be picked up that way, if a man uses his brains. I shall put a slice of money in it—Unity willing—eh, Unity?"

" 'Twas a bit of luck," she answered. "It mightn't happen again."

"No luck about it—not at all," argued her husband. "Think of all I've done for they ponies, and how I brought 'em on, and the trouble I took to choose the sire. 'Tis sense, not luck. Sense, not luck, I say. A great future may come out of 'em, handled properly—not only for me, but for all of us in these parts—for all of us—for all of us."

"You're the leading man at Postbridge," declared Birdwood, "and 'twould be a proper thing if you could throw a bit of light on the subject and help other farmers to do the same. Baskerville, of Shaugh Prior, and you be the only men that really understand the business."

"Don't you get telling him that, Henry," said Mrs. Ouldsbroom. "My husband spends too much time as

86

it is 'pon other people's errands. If he's leading man in Postbridge, he don't behave like it. A child can order him about.''

"A child, yes," admitted Philip. "I'll do anything for the dinky dears. But 'tis I order t'others about; they don't order me, I assure you Birdwood here knows what I am—I say he knows what I am. My 'no' be 'no,' and my 'yes' be 'yes.' Show me the man as will order me about—I'd like to see him; I'd like to see him!''

He became truculent, and his wife expressed regret.

"I didn't mean nothing more than that you are a lot too kind, Phil—too kind and too easy.''

"So you are, Ouldsbroom—that's no more than truth any way," declared the shepherd. "How much money did you give all they mountebanks and foreigners and beggars at the fair? A good shilling or two, I'll warrant.''

"There was a terrible fine Italian woman there," said Philip. "Black as a crow her eyes, and her hair too. She was dressed so gaudy as her little parrot, and for twopence the blessed bird drawed out a card and told me —told me my fortune—damn the little liar!''

He grew grim suddenly with thoughts darkened.

"Hullo! what was it then?''

Without replying the farmer drew a card from his pocket and handed it to Birdwood.

Unity's lips tightened, and she looked at the horse's head. She had seen the card.

" 'A good wife and seven children—plenty of money and plenty of friends!' " read out the younger man. "Well, what's the matter with that?''

"The matter is it ban't true ''

"All true but one item, after all You can't expect a poll-parrot to do better, eh, Unity?''

"I reckon we'd sooner have all the rest a lie and that one item right," she answered, still looking before her.

Birdwood felt the matter too delicate for a bachelor's tongue and said so. He knew the trouble of this home well enough.

Talk drifted into other channels, and they began to

descend the hill to Two Bridges. Arrived at the bottom,
Ouldsbroom insisted on stopping

"I must have another drink," he declared. But his
wife persuaded him not to alight. She whispered to him,
and he gave a short laugh and yielded.

"All right—get on," he said.

Presently he explained to Henry.

"If you want a woman to do your bidding, you must
be very ready to do hers—mind that. Me and Unity be
two halves of a flail—one nought without t'other—one
nought without t'other I say, and 'tis as easy for me to
pleasure her as 'tis for her to please me. But you don't
find it so in every home, Henry—not in every home.
More often than not the friendship's a make-believe
thing, done to fool the neighbours. Wedded life be built
on give-and-take, and that's a duty in some homes, for
the apple-cart would soon be off the wheels without it.
But when you get understanding men and women that
have the luck to be wedded, and each—well, like me and
my wife—a wish is enough. We can't have everything,
I suppose."

They reached home at dusk, and Birdwood mounted
his pony, which had brought him very early to Hartland,
and set off for Teign Head. Unity asked him to stop
to supper, but he refused.

Their relations were openly cordial and secretly close.
Many opportunities to see each other alone occurred, and
intimacy had long been established between them. Ouldsbroom was a man to whom jealousy was unknown. He
could not feel the emotion, and his view of it showed that
even imagination was unable to picture it for him.

The subject formed matter for debate at Miss Hext's
upon the occasion of a tragedy in a neighbouring hamlet.
A hedge-cutter's wife had left her husband and run away
with a carpenter to Canada. Mr. Culme, the water-
bailiff, took a grave view of the event, and Gregory
Twigg, who was also of the company, agreed with
him.

"In Canada, or if not Canada, 'tis in America," said
the Little Baptist, "a man is divorced for the asking

and a woman for little more. ·Nothing is done against it, though for my part, if I was an American I should stand up for the married state and never vote a man to Parliament who supported such a loose way of living."

"Bah!" answered Ouldsbroom. "What do you and the likes of you know about large-minded people? A big nation takes big views, and so do I; and one of my views be this, that if a pair be sick to death of the sight of each other, 'tis tyranny chaining 'em together any more. And I'll go further and say that if one of the parties be sick of the other, no right-spirited man or woman would want to go on with it."

"Easy to talk—a man happily married like you," said Mr. Twigg. "But I, though I suppose no man ever chose his wife with much better judgment and forethought than me, can look around and see the danger of loosening the marriage bond. Those that God hath joined together, let no man put asunder."

"That's all right," allowed Philip; "but you know how many come together without any help of God, and to keep 'em in double harness for life be doing the devil's work, if there is such a party. If my wife comed to me to-morrow and said 'Phil, I've found a chap I like better than you,' d'you think that I should fret my liver rotten about it? Not me. I'd say, 'Then go to him You can live your life but once, and there's none of the glory of being men and women in heaven, by all accounts. So go to him—and I'll see what I can do.' What sane man would keep a woman in his house who pined to be out of it? What self-respecting female would stop in a man's home after she knew he was sick of the sight of her?"

"You owe your neighbours something, I should hope," said Mr. Twigg. "A good example we've a right to expect from every respectable member of the community."

"Be I going to live a lie to keep my neighbours calm, do 'e think? Not I—nor any sensible man. She was right to go with the carpenter. She'd have been a weak-minded fool to stop; and the hedge-tacker—a worm, not a man, I call him—he shows she was right and wise to leave him; for ever since she went he's spent his time whining in the public-houses and letting anybody stand him drinks because of his terrible misfortune.''

''So would you whine if you'd been left desolate with an old blind mother-in-law and a barrow-load of little sticky children,'' said Mr. Culme. '' 'Tis very well for the likes of you, with no family, to say these godless things, my dear man, but what about the young left without a mother to look after 'em?''

Ouldsbroom did not answer immediately, but looked at the hunchback with a sort of sulky frown in his blue eyes.

All roads seemed to end in the same barren wilderness; all discussions appeared sooner or later to drift upon this misfortune

''One or other of you fools be always ramming that down my throat,'' he said   ''Ban't I often enough put in mind of it without hearing you babble it? Don't every little one I pass in the road remind me? 'Tis very indecent in you to say any such thing, Peter Culme, and I'll thank you not to do it no more, for I won't stand it.''

Miss Hext endeavoured to still the farmer's annoyance.

''Be sure no living man, nor yet woman, would seek to fret you there,'' she said   ''We all know what you are with the children—and none better than me, that sell toys and lollipops. Peter here never meant to anger you ''

''Certainly not Why should I?'' asked the waterkeeper.

''These things be inside the law, and there are men in the world who understand 'em as well as we understand our affairs,'' continued Barbara. ''I was a very great reader when I lived in London, and I took everything that came and knew a lot then, though I've forgotten most of it since   But there's qualities be handed from father to son, besides the likeness of face or shape of shoulders One man will hand on a weakness and another hand on a strength   So it comes out with you, Philip.''

''My father was strong as a bear, and so be I ''

''But he never got but one child, for all his strength.

He wasn't a fertile man; and he was only one of two, for I've heard you say so.''

"Weren't his fault about children," answered Philip. "He married late in life, and my mother was getting up in years too. She was over forty when I was born."

They argued upon Barbara's scanty knowledge until Ouldsbroom stopped them.

"I won't hear another damned word on the subject!" he cried. "And if any man wants to quarrel with me let him name it."

" 'Twill be time enough to pull a long face when you've been married ten year instead of two," summed up Miss Hext.

But from that hour the report was spread that Philip and Unity, for lack of family, were not all that they should be to each other. Indeed lying rumour magnified the matter into an actual rift.

With passage of time a shadow truth might have been allowed to the story. There was no actual dissension, but the failure of a common desire existed, and both felt it. Had one alone done so, the other might have helped to heal the want, but husband and wife alike wished for offspring with intense fervour. Life ran exceedingly smoothly, and nothing happened to distract them from this ceaseless hope. It was the master-wish of each mind, and while the woman's larger reason and control fought with her disappointment, the man's feebler nature failed effectually to do so. Had he been more rational, Unity would have respected him and sought to emulate his common sense before a circumstance beyond their own control; but since he permitted himself large, vain regrets, she smarted too—at first openly; then, when he spoke harshly to her and flung the blame upon her, she brooded in secret.

Once she spoke to Birdwood on the subject.

"He seems to think, poor dear chap, that all the disappointment and hardship of it be on his shoulders. He may grumble so much as he pleases; but I mayn't. He catched me in a weak moment fretting about it when I thought he was long ways off; and he dressed me down proper, I promise you ''

"It beats me," answered the man, "why a pair of sane creatures can mourn for that. Look round and see what the children are worth—thorns—thorns I should call 'em If you'd married me, you might have had so many as you wanted, and more; but 'twould have been no pleasure to me to have 'em. I can swear to that.''

She considered his words at the time and remembered them afterwards.

CHAPTER XII

MR. TWIGG's hostelry was isolated, but since it stood upon the main thoroughfare of Dartmoor, he enjoyed a fair share of custom

The 'Warren House' occupied high ground at the limit of the Eastern Quarter of the Forest, and formed a good centre for the manifold industries of Gregory. But he had few friends, and his bar-parlour was not frequented. Upon the roadside custom he principally depended, because local men went only for drink, and not for company, to the 'Warren House' They wearied of the host, whose sole interests were centred in himself, and who had little leisure or sympathy for the temporal affairs of lesser men He would preach for the pleasure of it at an instant's notice, but his vanity kept him within the band of his own religious associates; and even some of them stayed away from chapel when it was known that Brother Twigg would conduct service.

Behind his bar Gregory was always didactic and superior. He could not help giving advice and he could not help drawing a moral—generally from his own achievements and victories

Ouldsbroom liked him little, but as Moor-man of the district, Mr. Twigg had dealings with all the local farmers, and sometimes it happened that Philip could not conduct business through a messenger and was constrained to go in person

Towards Christmas duty took him to the 'Warren House,' and after his business was settled he spoke awhile to Gregory and, at his invitation, drank a glass or two of sloe gin.

"My own brewing that," explained Mr. Twigg. "You can't get such a liquor outside these doors. I've arrived at it after years of experiments. The fox-hunters never pass here but they draw up and cry out for it. I'm told I could get fifty pounds in London for the recipe, and no doubt I could."

"Very pretty drinking And what's this I hear about Henry Birdwood? Haven't seen him lately to ax him myself. But you might know. Is he going back to your prayer-shop again?"

"He's coming back to the footstool of the Throne of Grace again, if that's what you mean."

"I can't believe it—not after all I've taught him about being a free man and to keep clear of you psalm-smiters. How d'you know 'tis true, Twigg?"

"We, who stand a little closer to our Lord and Saviour than the rank and file of people, often get first news of such things," answered Mr. Twigg "Of course a god-less man, like you, wouldn't understand that, and I wouldn't try to explain it; but I know 'tis true, which is all that matters He's coming back into Christianity; but whether 'tis to church or to us, I can't quite tell you. To us, I should hope."

"To church if anywhere. And I'll bet you half a dozen bottles of beer on it that 'tis my wife have done this! She's so steady as a rock for church ever since she was married in it And if you must go anywhere, 'tis better there than to your show, where any fool can get up and make a row if he wants to."

"How little you know, Ouldsbroom! Many religious men would be very angry with you for taking the name of the chosen in vain."

"Bosh! But if you want Birdwood, I dare say there's a way. Money's money. Tell him that if he comes back to you, 'twill be good for half-a-crown a week more, and very like he'd come."

"Not at all—not at all. Where's your manners even to suggest such a thing? Can we buy souls with money? I hope Henry will give me a chance to have a few words, because women don't understand, and never will. They mix up stained-glass windows and the organs going, and boys singing, and the rich cloth on the table, and all the rest of it with religion, and think because these things excite 'em that the Lord is near. But if you ask me——''

He was interrupted by Henry Birdwood himself. The shepherd had walked over, and now called for beer before he opened his business.

"You was the man in our mouths, neighbour," said Mr. Twigg, drawing half a pint. "There's a little bird have told me that you may be seen among Christian men again afore very long, and I'm terrible glad to think 'tis true. I heard the story a good bit ago, and have been hoping for six weeks that any Sunday might see you in your old place.''

"Never, Mr. Twigg," said Henry firmly. "I've no grudge against the chapel, but—well, if I go back, 'twill be to the church.''

"And why, if I may ask?" inquired the publican. "I'm sure your poor father would feel 'twas a cruel, left-handed answer to his prayers, if you did that. What's the reason?''

"I've bet Gregory six bottles of beer that the reason is my wife," declared Philip.

Birdwood laughed.

"Well, if he took the bet, you've won," he answered "She's death on my going back, and I'd do anything in reason for her.''

Philip crowed, and Mr. Twigg shook his head

"You've a lot to answer for, Ouldsbroom. This is all your bad work. First you take Sister Unity away, and now, through her, this man.''

"I took myself away," said Birdwood "Everybody knows that ''

"You think you did, but farmer here was at the root of it None can deny me when I say so 'Tis a shocking thing, because Ouldsbroom is nought himself and worse than nought. It might be forgiven if he was a deep believer. But look at him—he don't believe in nothing but the strength of his own evil nature.''

The farmer spoke.

"I told him you'd come back like a lamb if he put a bit on your wages, Henry; but when I said that, Twigg was off. He'd rather part from you than another half-crown a week; wouldn't you, Gregory?"

"I wish I could learn you manners, neighbour," answered the other "To say things like this before a man and his master is most improper, but you'll never understand—never. Your education was neglected, shocking, Philip."

"Yes—thank the Lord, if you're a sample of schooling. And now give me a thimbleful more of thicky sloe gin and I'll be going"

" 'Tis funny you should be talking about my wages," said Birdwood "You needn't haste, Ouldsbroom; I've got no secrets from you; but that's the very matter I'm here about. I've had an offer for after Christmas 'Twill take me to Chagford, and I should be cruel sorry to go; but there's a bit more to it, and I'm thinking seriously upon the subject I'm not like Sleep—always going to make a change and never doing it. The people came to me—not me to them And they're very good people, too, though I can't mention no names, being forbid to do so for the present."

Mr Twigg was much annoyed. Indeed, his indignation flushed him to his bald forehead

"This is most outrageous, and I refuse to hear of it," he said "You ought to know me better, Henry, and yourself too. Whatever is coming to the young men?"

"Sense," declared Philip "The world's waking up. Henry's worth what he'll fetch; and if he can fetch half-a-crown more than you'll pay—good-bye to you. That's demand and supply, that is"

"It's nothing of the kind. it's a piece of very unchristian ingratitude," answered Mr. Twigg. "However, me and Henry will talk about that 'Tis no business of yours, I believe."

"You Little Baptists!" retorted Ouldsbroom. "You'm like shell-snails sailing along with your heads in the air until somebody asks for a bit of cash. Then down come your horns, and you shrivel up and shrink into your houses, as if the devil and all his ducks was after you."

He left the bar, laughing loudly at his own joke.

He had not gone far, however, before Henry Birdwood also emerged and ran down the hill after him.

Ouldsbroom, on hearing himself called, turned and waited for the other.

"Hullo!" he said. "You wasn't long coming to the bargain."

"No. Greg saw I meant business from the first. He knows very well that I ought to have more. He wanted to make it a condition I went back to chapel, but I wouldn't. I've done with them."

"That's brave hearing! And presently, you screw him up a bit higher yet."

"I'm not anxious to work for him, and if 'twasn't for you, I'd so soon be down to Chagford as not."

Philip's heart warmed instantly.

"I won't have you go," he said. "You're the right sort, and I think a lot of you, and I'll be some real use to you some day—see if I won't. Me and my wife are very fond of you, and 'tis a lonely house at Hartland along of no family, so we can't afford to lose a friend."

"There's her people at Stannon."

"Yes; but I've no use for 'em. They wouldn't even let me stand gossip to the new babby. A proper, li'l, fat, chubby boy they've got, and always wants for to come to me, young though he is. They know somehow—the toads—that I'm that set upon 'em."

Birdwood said nothing, and Philip followed his own thoughts for a while. He preferred to speak than think, however, and presently broke into further words. There were links missing in his train of ideas, but Birdwood found no difficulty in appreciating them. Indeed, he knew all that was passing in the other's mind at this season, for Ouldsbroom's wife hid few secrets from him.

"Of course as a man I can stand it with a man's strength. I've my work and my plans—though work and plans be unfinished things if there's nought to work and plan for. But I've got Unity too, and I dare say, even

7

if we did have the rare fortune to get childer after all, they'd never be to me what she is. When I balance the thought of a son against her, 'tis queer how my mind jumps for a moment, but I always come back to her and put her first.''

"If even the thought of a child makes you hesitate, perhaps, when you do get one, you'll find it's more than anything in the world—even her.''

"No, I can't think that   The mother of any child of mine would be pretty nearly as much—quite as much, I do think—as the child. What I was saying is that as a man, and a pretty tough sort of man, I can face the disappointment; but I'm very sorry for her. She's awful cut up about it sometimes—for her own sake as much as mine. My life's full; but no married woman's life be full without children.''

"A lot don't think so, however.''

"Then they ban't women—only forked radishes. Let that flat-footed, hard-lipped sort herd together, and go out like tallow candles and leave nought behind. Unity's very different from that Look at her—'mother' stamped all over her. She'd sell her soul for a brave boy.''

"I can't understand such a fancy. I don't like children, and never did.''

"So much the worse for you. But 'tis ignorance, not vice makes you say it. 'Twould be wickedness to mean such a thing. Wait till you are suited with a maiden.''

"No more maidens for me. A good old salted widow some day—but not till I'm turned of fifty. I mean to be free till then,'' declared Birdwood.

CHAPTER XIII

THE trees of Postbridge stand in parallel rows—straight and crooked, slim and stout They are beeches for the most part; and now their foliage flew to join the crisp and copper-coloured masses gathering in water-tables and the hollows of the fields. They seemed a part of the life and the business of the place. Together with the river, the famous 'cyclopean' bridge that spanned it, and other inanimate things, the trees made a topic for the people and a plaything for the children. Their budding, fruiting, and fall were a matter of conversation as regular as the weather; and with autumn the harvest of them was a joy to the young, who gathered the brown, triangular nuts from road and meadows. The mast spattered the highway in November and covered it with white spots where wheels had crushed the kernels. This scattered food chaffinches and other small birds devoured.

Night crept among the trees and rain drifted through their ranks as the folk emerged from church. The service was held after noon, but the evenings were grown so short that darkness spread over all things before the people left their place of worship. A stranger would have been concerned for her attire; but rain to the natives was a matter so familiar that women only put up their umbrellas for the sake of their bonnets.

Unity Ouldsbroom, however, found an umbrella held over her, and it was her first love, Henry Birdwood, who did this service.

He was laughing at the mild sensation his advent caused, for in the little congregation of thirty souls he had appeared as a conspicuous figure.

99

"Funny to see 'em gaping," he said. "I felt a feeling that I should have liked to say the truth out loud to 'em and let 'em all know that I wasn't there for praying, but a better reason—just to walk back as far as your gate along with you of a Sunday night!"

"I can't believe it of you. 'Tis the sort of silly thing as my husband might do—not you."

They talked of Unity as they went through the trees, with the rain in their faces, to Hartland.

"You know all about me," she said. "What for d'you want to go over the ground so oft?"

"Because I don't know all about you. You seem all right—to the eyes of other people. They all say you're a marvel, and have trained up that man like a mother, and brought him to be twice the man he was. They say that's been your life's work these two years and more, and that you're a happy woman because your work's a success. But I tell them about the man and his shoe 'Twas a very tidy shoe and looked all that it should be in the eyes of his neighbours; but the person that wore it knowed where it pinched—and only him."

"I'm tired of that."

"Are you going to ax me to stop to supper to-night?"

"No. My husband's got a friend here. He wanted you to come, but Mr. Knowles isn't your sort, so I don't ask you."

"Philip hit a man down yesterday. I hear, for saying something about no children."

"Can't the people see that, whether or no, he's a child himself?"

"That's true. One child you've got anyway, and he's a handful too, I'll swear, for all you seem to manage him so easy."

"A child sure enough in many things."

"I wish I'd known more about him two years agone, when he went over me like a regiment of cavalry and left me dumb and dazed and weak as water. Knowing all I know now, and feeling all I feel, I can't hardly believe that 'twas this man flung me out of his way. 'A man' I call him, but he's a boy all through Sport—fish

—birds—childish things—always. All toys and to-morrows. Everything be going to happen to-morrow. To-day's never of no account with him. We may drink, or sport, or waste any amount of time to-day; but to-morrow we be going to do man's work. I could be sorry for the fool, if I didn't——"

"Stop that now. I won't have it, Henry. What's the sense to waste words so? Surely, between you and me, we've got beyond that?"

"You're one of the rare sort that can live without looking back," he answered. "I haven't reached so far"

"Learn from Philip, then, for all you despise him. To-morrow's better than yesterday anyway."

"It shall be; if you leave your to-morrows to me."

"As to that, you have enough of my time, I should think."

They were at Hartland gate, and they stood beyond the radius of a sheaf of light that fell across the yard from the parlour window.

Voices came from within, for the window was open.

"Ponies again I suppose?" whispered Henry to Mrs. Ouldsbroom.

"Yes, ponies. Phil be going to make everybody's fortune."

"A terrible kind chap; but the sort that mars more fortunes than he makes."

"With his own thrown in."

"Might have been so; not now. Hasn't he got two clever people on his side?"

"He's got me—who else?"

"And me too. Should you and me be such friends if it wasn't so?"

"What a word-shuffler you are! I hate it in you. Keep that sort of stuff for other people. 'Tis no use to me."

"I get that way of looking at things through my father. Preachers have to make words do all they can do. You can prove anything with words. You can bend 'em to any pattern, if you master them. I make words say I'm the true friend of Philip Ouldsbroom. And for that matter, who can say I ban't?"

"You're a mocking devil, and I ought to hate you if I was a wise woman. My husband's a wholesome creature, if he is tasteless, but you—you're sauce and poison both."

"Sauce to your life, anyway; and you know it. 'Tis the least I can be since you're the breath of mine. Hark! There's your cowman coming. I'll be gone."

The sound of feet lumbering up the lane struck Birdwood's quick ear. He kissed her and vanished to the Moor.

CHAPTER XIV

Miss Hext found it difficult to make her customers understand that at a certain hour her shop closed   Shutters she had none; but when four green blinds were drawn, the fact was supposed to indicate that business had ceased for the day   The folk, however, ignored this hint; and since many of her customers lived at great distances and were only able to visit her after their work was finished, she often declared that in truth her general shop never shut its doors.   During the long summer evenings the futility of attempting to stop work was specially apparent, and the bell often jangled till nine o'clock.

It was not far short of this hour when Henry Birdwood called for some articles of grocery on a night in early July.   Barbara protested while she served him.

"You selfish men will work me into my grave," she said

"Not a bit of it," he answered.   "You know you're coining money.   You ought to start a shop assistant."

"Don't tell me that.   'Twill be so, no doubt—worse luck.   It must come.   But not an hour before I can help it.   My heart sinks when I think of having to teach a young creature what this shop means   I was talking to my dog last night. 'You don't get no younger, "Sarah," ' I said; for in truth she's getting older, and that very fast.   And she sat there, and I seemed to fancy an answer in her eyes—as much as to say, 'No more do you, Barbara Hext.'   But an assistant is a frosty thought   I'm not sure if I wouldn't rather give up and sell the shop "

"I dare say there's a good few would be very ready to take it off your hands."

"Not a doubt of it."

He was preparing to leave, but the hunchback, Peter Culme, came in, and Birdwood stopped a little longer.

Miss Hext grumbled and lighted another lamp, for Peter's order demanded search in a dark corner.

"Just gave Philip Ouldsbroom 'good-night,' " he said. "He's in a merry mood seemingly, and more than fresh, by the sound of his voice. Was up at 'Warren House' on his pony, telling very loud to half a dozen men—something about his fine wife, I think 'twas—but I didn't stop. He just shouted out 'Good luck!' after me, in the cheerful sort o' way men do when they've had good luck themselves and feel large-hearted."

"Large-hearted always, he is," declared Miss Hext. "Never was such another."

" 'Tis funny to hear the fool sometimes, all the same," replied Birdwood. "We be very good friends now, as everybody knows; but for the life of me I can't help laughing to hear him bragging how he took his wife for her sense and wisdom."

"A left-handed sort of laugh from you, I should think," said Mr. Culme, "seeing how he served you."

"No; that's very near three year old. I'm not thinking of that. But to hear him tell how he took her for her sense, when all the world knows she took him for his farm——"

"She's the sort to keep at the helm of her own life and let none other steer her," asserted Barbara. "You can see that in her mouth. Rule she does; but he never feels it. He's the happier for it. She's a clever woman. I won't deny her that, though I don't like her, and never did."

Birdwood regarded the post-mistress curiously.

"Why not?" he asked.

"Why should I? She's not my sort. But her husband is. There's a finer nature hid in him than she can feel or guess at. But there 'tis: the match have worked very well, and long may it last so."

"As to that, she married him for his farm, you say, Henry," argued Mr. Culme. "Well, if you'm right, there'll come failure soon or late seeing to marry for goods be wrong."

"Don't you think it. Unity's a pinch too clever for failure. She never takes a step with her eyes shut, that woman. She ban't the sort that a man marries, come to think of it. You'd say of her she's the sort that marries a man."

"God help the man then," said Peter.

"Why, so He has," answered the shepherd. "Philip's got better luck than he deserves—fool's luck. We know the truth about most things a bit too late to be any use to us. If I'd larned the truth about Ouldsbroom when he took that woman away from me, I'd have got her back in time. I'm cleverer than him."

"He thinks that you are his best friend," said Barbara; "but 'tis time I warned him against you again—as I did before he was married."

"And I am his best friend, I dare say. I've given him the benefit of my sense more than once. I get older; he don't. He's where he was when he bested me; but I'm not. And don't you think to turn him from me, Miss Hext, because you won't do it. He knows very well that you don't like me."

Birdwood took his parcels and went out. He had not gone far when Philip himself appeared, coming down Merripit Hill.

Ouldsbroom was mellow and did not recognize Henry. But he shouted 'Good-night!' Birdwood, curious to learn the matter of this exaltation, stopped, and the farmer, at sound of his voice, recognised him.

"There now! Everything goeth right to-day! I was out over at your place with the news this morning, but you were to work, and Sleep couldn't tell where. Then I rode into Chagford and told a good few friends there; and then I went down to Moreton and told 'em there; and everybody's that pleased about it that what with drinking luck and one thing 'n 'nother, I've got a skinful—I've got a skinful, Henry."

"And what is the luck?"

"To think there's anybody don't know it, and you, of

all men! My wife—she's with child, my lad! 'Tis
beyond doubt, and I've been shouting the news to the
sheep in the lonely places! Couldn't keep it in—such
a fool am I!''

"That's great hearing and no mistake! Can you get
home, or shall I go beside your hoss?''

"I'm all right. Haven't done my round yet. Be
just going to tell Barbara; then I must get down to Two
Bridges—to Two Bridges you know. Masterman and his
wife at the 'Ring o' Bells' would never forgive me if they
heard the news from anybody else. And 'twill be over
the Moor like a flame of fire to-morrow!''

"I'm terrible glad, Philip, and I hope she's pleased.''

"'Pleased!' Good God! Pleased ban't the word—
I say pleased ban't the word. She've wanted a man child
ever since the day she was old enough to bear one. And
a man child 'twill be. 'Tis my will! I'll take no denial
of it. A blessed boy, I say; and he'll be born next February. Can't stop no more, Henry. Come over and
hear all I be going to do for the child. 'Tis all marked
out. Good-night, good-night!''

He trotted off and arrived presently at the post office.
Mr. Culme had gone; the lights were out, and Barbara
had retired to her kitchen. But the horseman soon
summoned her. He dismounted, made fast his steed to
the ring in an upping-stock close at hand, then entered as
Miss Hext appeared.

"Not a word,'' he said. "Don't you grumble to me,
Barbara, because I won't have it—I won't have it, I tell
you. I don't want nothing out of the shop. I only
want you. Be you alone?''

"I should think so; 'tis past ten o'clock.''

"You've got to hear me. I could talk for an hour,
but 'tis all said in a word. Fetch out something to drink
—your medicine bottle—you know; there's a dear!''

"No, I shan't. You've had enough. I'm ashamed
of you, Phil.''

"Who wouldn't drink? Not a stroke of work will I
do for a week to mark it—not a stroke. There's a lot
to be thought upon, but trust me. When I look at a

child now, I can scarce forbear to onlight from my horse and hug it And I wouldn't have let the day pass without telling you, Barbara; no, I wouldn't have let the day pass without telling you—not if a man was to have heaped up my hat with golden sovereigns, I wouldn't have done so.''

"Sit down, or you'll fall down, you silly man. What is it about then? I suppose you—that be always doing people a good turn—have had a good turn done to you? And then you get so surprised at it that you must needs take too much liquor.''

"I ban't drunk, or if I be—I say, if I be, 'tis with joy of it 'Drunk with joy' is a very clever word. Yes, a good turn has been done to me—a very good turn indeed.''

"Well, read Job and steady your mind. Who can tell what's good and what's bad? The thing that looks good often——''

"Don't you say that—I won't hear it! I won't hear it, I tell you My wife be gwaine to have a babby There 'tis!''

"That woman gets everything she wants sooner or later.''

"And so do I—so do I. There's nothing like making up your mind as you *will* have a thing. I would marry her, and I did. And all along I said I would have a son, and I shall. I'm the sort of man that makes things bend to my will, Barbara. I won't take 'no' for an answer—like some weak creatures ''

"She's very pleased about it, of course? Well she may be. A wonderful woman.''

"That she is. She'd open the eyes of the blind, she would. I say, I say she'd open the eyes of the blind, Barbara. I ban't easily astonished, but she astonishes me—yes, still she does. Never interferes with me, mind you. 'Man be master' that's her saying, and a good one. I tell you it's a good one But a cleansing terror in the house—oh, my stars!—a whirlwind of cleanliness!''

"You'll have to take care of her now, Philip ''

"And don't I always? If anybody said I didn't, I'd
—I'd—— But I will be obeyed from this day forward
by her I won't have her working herself dog-tired six
days a week no more I 'll put my foot down there She
shall be idle, though she hates idleness worse than the
devil I've seen her, of a busy morning, kick the cat
away from the hearthstone where he sat sleeping. 'Get
up, you caddling, loafing good-for-nought!' she'll say to
him 'Go about your business and catch the mice and
earn your keep!' That's Unity Ouldsbroom in a word "

"A rare towser for work."

"So she is, and yet that understanding with it, Barbara—that understanding, I tell you. She knows we
males have a bit of the boy in us always, though women
soon lose the girl in them I must fish and shoot and play
with the childer—other people's childer afore—my own
now—my own now She knows all that; she never says
'no' to such things, like some vinegary old maids might.
She understands everything, I tell you She's never
fretted nor troubled; and she never shall be while I'm
here But of course now she must do what she's told,
for the sake of the unborn."

"I'm very glad of this, Philip 'Tis the best thing that
could have happened, and I hope you'll take it in a wise
spirit, I'm sure."

"Wise! Why, if a man at my age—three-and-forty—
coming into fatherhood, can't be wise, 'tis a disgrace!
There'll be plenty of sense waiting for the child on both
sides, if I know anything. I've planned it out a 'ready
And he shall go to a proper school presently, if I've got
to starve to send him And I'm going to mark this good
thing somehow. You'll be able to help me there I want
a bit of rejoicing—d'ye see?"

"You run on so! Plenty of time for all that presently.
Well, I'm right glad, and I hope 'twill steady you down
and knock sense into your silly head. And mind you
keep the child away from the Dissenters when it does
arrive "

"No fear of that! My throat's a lime-kiln along of so
much speech. And now I'm off to Two Bridges. Master-

man won't grudge me a drink—I say Masterman won't grudge me a drink, though you do seemingly!''

She spoke to him for a further five minutes and persuaded him to abandon his idea and return home.

"To please me," she said. "And to mark the day—don't touch no more to-night, Phil. Get home to Unity and tell her that I'm very glad about this, I'm sure; and then, if you can see straight enough to do it, read a bit of Job—chapter twenty-eight. 'Twill steady you down."

"You'm right," he said "Come to think of it, after this news, I wonder how the devil I could keep away from her all day. I'll go back this instant moment—this instant moment I'll go "

"And lead your horse; don't you get on him."

He laughed.

"No call to be frightened for me. I'm sober as the river, and my hoss can carry beer, I promise you I say he can carry beer, Miss Hext. Not that 'tis very oft I ax him to do it. No man's ever seen me drunk twice in a year."

She watched him mount and go off. There was no night at this season, and a nimbus of pale, colourless radiance fringed the horizon where the sun stole behind the northern hills.

"Oh for the power to give that fond creature a pinch of sense!" thought Barbara

Suddenly the man shouted back to her

"I say, Barbara! I'll wager my boy will often and often come to you for sweeties, so soon as his li'l legs can steer him down over the hill!''

She heard him laughing until his voice died upon the distance.

CHAPTER XV

PHILIP OULDSBROOM was striding up and down his kitchen, like a lion in a cage at feeding time. In the window sat an elderly man, who smoked a pipe and looked uneasily out at falling snow.

"I hope this isn't going to get worse, farmer," he said, "for if it does, how shall I drive back to Princetown?"

But the other did not answer. His interests were elsewhere. He kept looking up at the ceiling. His under jaw was thrust forward a trifle and his shoulders were lifted. His hands were in his breeches pockets, and from one of them came the ceaseless jingle of a bunch of keys, where he fidgeted with it.

"The loaf-luck was right—right to a hair," he said "Perhaps you don't know what that means, doctor, but——"

A woman came to the door.

"Now, if you please, sir."

The grey man put down his pipe and followed her. Ouldsbroom set his teeth and tramped backwards and forwards faster than before. The strain on his mind called for air. He felt choking, and went to the farm door and drew in great gulps of the snow-laden north wind.

A boy was walking a horse and trap up and down in the yard, and the sight of him offered Philip occupation. He returned to the house, went through the dairy, reached the larder, cut a huge lump off a currant cake and took it out.

"Come in here under this shippon," he said "I'll fetch a cloth for the hoss. He ain't hot."

110

These things occupied but a few minutes, and he returned to the house again

His ordeal was not a long one. In half an hour a maiden, who ran about at the nurse's beck and call, rushed down speedily and told him that everything was well.

"A boy—say 'tis a boy or I'll brain you!" he cried, catching her by the shoulder.

"A very fine boy—'very fine boy' was the doctor's words, Mr. Ouldsbroom."

"Didn't I know it? Bring him down, then! How much longer be I to wait afore I see my son?"

"A longful time yet And Dr. Dickinson says that missis is as right as ninepence; and if you'll get away out of the house for an hour, 'tis the best thing that you can do—excuse me for naming it."

"Of course 'tis all right! Didn't I see it in the loaf this morning? I'll run round the village and send off a postcard or two and be back afore long. And make Doctor bide till I get here again. Tell him the snow ban't offering serious just yet."

He took his hat and rushed off.

On the Moor he saw two men in the distance, quite out of earshot.

"A boy! A damn fine boy!" he bawled out to them.

He hastened across to Stannon first, and burst in upon Gertrude Crymes and her brood of three.

"A boy!" he said. "A proper boy—the daps of me, no doubt, though I haven't seed him yet Come here, Maggie, and you, Jacky! Let 'em come, Gertrude, and hand me the little one. A proper cousin for 'e all, my darlings!"

"How's Unity?" asked the mother.

"Why, couldn't be better. As well I knowed it would be with her. There's a penny all round for luck! And Quinton must fetch you all over when the weather gets soft. Tell him all's well with his sister. I be going to send off a halfpenny card to Birdwood now—and a few others round about. There's a score and more of people will be terrible glad to know 'tis all right."

"Mr. Sleep heard from Henry yesterday. His father be failing slowly. He reckons he'll close the preacher's eyes afore a month's out."

"That's all one, since it's got to be. Well, you come over so soon as you can, Gertrude, that's a good woman. And give it tongue, will 'e? A very fine boy—to be named after me, of course."

" 'Twill make a confusion if you do that "

But Ouldsbroom stayed not to argue. He went off, shouted the news to Mr. Coaker, who was at work in an outhouse, and then hastened down to Postbridge.

The snow had ceased for the time, but it blew very coldly, and the wind was busy with a bank of grey that extended on the northern horizon.

Philip next met Ned Sleep returning home on his pony, and told him; but long before Ned grasped the great fact his informant had swept forward

Miss Hext was not in the post office when he entered, but he picked up a pen and shouted loudly to her.

"Barbara! Barbara! where are you got to?"

" 'Tis all right then?" she asked, appearing from her room behind the shop. "I see by your face 'tis all right."

"Of course it is. How should it be otherwise with such a woman as Unity? Everything right, and I be going to send off a card here and there to them who'll be glad."

He dropped the pen and shook her hand till she cried out and held her fingers.

" 'Twas all right from the minute she woke, and I rode off myself and come back with Dr Dickinson. He said he'd follow after; but that didn't do for me; so I fetched him along and galloped beside him. And at breakfast, if I didn't break the loaf in so true a horse-shoe as ever bread fell in! You laugh with all your town wisdom, Barbara; but I'll swear there's a lot in it! And I knowed from that moment 'twould all be right and never had another anxious thought. Did 'e ever hear them verses made by a true Dartymoor man back-along?"

"No, I didn't I blush for you—you who are above all this nonsense of churches and chapels both."

"There's things that be above either of 'em. There's the evil eye, Barbara—you won't deny that?"

"I'd so soon believe in witches."

"But the rhyme ban't a thing to flout—specially if it comes true Luck is luck, and you can't say you don't believe in that, because the world's full of it—good or bad. And if one sort of luck, why not another? Loaf-luck be a real thing, for all you scoff. List to this."

He repeated a rhyme

> "If the loaf bought on the morn
> When the little child is born
> Happens to be clove in two
> In the shape of a horse-shoe,
> 'Tis a sign that he or she
> All through life will lucky be."

Miss Hext laughed.

"And you believe that? Well, send your postcards and get off back to Hartland."

Ouldsbroom dispatched half a dozen messages and made half a dozen needless purchases. Then suddenly the thought of his prolonged absence from home smote him like a blow.

"What on God's earth do I mean by it—caddling about all over the Moor, and me a father? 'Tis shameful! All the same, I dare say I'll see you again come nightfall, Barbara."

He made haste to depart, but Miss Hext called him back.

"Here's my present for baby," she said, and gave him a little decorated box of fragrant soap.

He brimmed over with thanks.

"You good, large-hearted creature! My God, there's nobody like you—nobody. To think of that now! Unity will be terrible obliged—ay, and so will the boy. Mark me, he'll be a great friend of yours in a year or two Good-bye, good-bye!"

In half an hour Philip Ouldsbroom held the newborn

atom in his arms, and devoured its tiny head with his gaze

"He've got his mother's eyes, I see—ban't blue like mine," he said.

"A brown boy he'll be—all his mother's," answered the midwife.

Then she jumped, for the man's voice exploded like thunder upon her ear.

"Hell! Don't you be talking that stuff to me!" he shouted. "Mine, mine, mine!"

He went to see his wife.

CHAPTER XVI

THE child-hunger in Unity Ouldsbroom was sated when she held her infant to her breast She grew calm swiftly, and this new life henceforth dominated every other interest that her own life possessed. It was an instantaneous rather than a gradual change. Her husband best withstood the impact of it; others seemed likely to be swept aside, as of an interest, not ancillary alone, but in future quite non-existent. Philip, however, still appeared to her as neither more nor less than himself He bulked not greater and not smaller seen in the light of her motherhood. But her relations and friends—Quinton and Gertrude Crymes and their children, Henry Birdwood, and certain women of Postbridge who had been in some sort her intimates, were now largely diminished in her eyes. As yet they did not know it, but were destined soon to do so.

She went upon the high Moor with her child three months after it was born and walked slowly by the valley of Dart to an appointed meeting-place.

Her husband was from home, about the business of some stock at Totnes, and he would not return until the following day. Where the river bends back to the west under Broad Down she found a little familiar holt upon the hillside. Here a few great boulders fell together and made a penthouse against rain and wind. From the mouth of it the valley subtended and great declivities rolled round about. The place was familiar to Unity, though she had not visited it for many months. That she was expected might be seen, for some one had spread the little chamber with fresh litter of fern

She looked into a cleft in the stone and drew forth a

letter, as she had drawn forth many another	It was brief:—

"Expect me at one o'clock.—H. B."

She sat and looked out upon the spring world, fed her child and waited Around her were the first shy buds of May, and above her a stormy sky broken and cleft with sun gleams The more usual phenomenon of shadows upon light was reversed, and splashes of brilliant light roamed instead through ambient darkness. In gleaming patches, like great golden birds, the splendour passed. It flashed in the river valley, climbed the hills, winged onward to their crests and ridges, and so vanished again. But darkness was the note of the day; the wind brushed the song of the river fitfully upon the ear; the cleeves were calling to the rain.

Birdwood arrived punctually, and greeted her not without some emotion They had not met since the death of his father and the birth of her son.

"Well, well," he said, "we've both been through a bit since winter. I thought to have seen you long ago, but my poor old man took two months a-dying It steadied me a bit. 'Tis a teaching thing to see your father die I promised him that I'd go back to Chapel, Unity; but here am I, prattling about my concerns as if—— And you—how are you? How is it with you?"

"So right as ever I was—happy too You stare; but I am."

" 'Tis quite fair you should be. Childer ban't much to most men—no more than the paring of my nail to me; but to women they be nine months out of her life every time, and the heart's blood thrown in."

"All that and more A perfect child—perfect—lovely —sweet as honey—knows me a'ready and laughs at me."

She made to bare the baby's face for him. He showed no interest, however, and she desisted, but tightened her arms about it instead.

"And have it made you think much, Unity? Have it opened your eyes here and there?"

"What d'you mean?" she asked "Of course I've thought. That was sure to be."

"Have it showed you where I conquered him that said he conquered me? Have it showed you that I was strongest after all—in mind and body too? In body too, Unity?"

"I suppose so."

"You know so. I'm so strong that I don't even care to show him how strong I am. So long as you see, clear as crystal, that I've won every way and he's lost every way, that's all I care about"

"If you're strong, be strong always, and let me see how strong you can be."

"You cunning creature! But I see through you—even through one so deep as you Yes, strong enough and silent enough I'll be—except with you. I must have a laugh with you sometimes. 'Tis funny to see a man think he's got the kernel when he's only got the shell. A monkey would know better than that—eh? Poor chap! Well, I've got all I want of you—he can have the rest"

She was uneasy.

"I don't like you to be so terrible bitter. He's been a good friend to you."

"Yes, and I'm quite as good a friend to him as ever he was to me. I feel just as friendly to him as he did to me when he sloked you away and married you under my calf's eyes. Just exactly as friendly as that. The friendliness of the strong to the weak. Don't think I'm not friendly to the man I wish him nought but good. We're a regular David and Jonathan him and me."

His lips sneered and hers tightened. She looked on into the future and saw that her own strength, and only her own, would save the ultimate situation She glanced up under her eyes at Birdwood, but not with love. He might be stronger than Philip: she had helped him to be stronger for her own purposes But he was not stronger than Philip's wife. She knew that neither man possessed her tremendous force of character, subtle swiftness to win personal good out of any complication.

"Let me look at him. What's his name?"

"Philip Martin. Martin was my father's name."

She turned down the flannel from the baby's face. He stretched out a little arm, yawned, and showed his gums.

Birdwood looked at the infant and a strange expression—part triumph and part grief—brooded upon his countenance.

"Ouldsbroom be terrible pleased, I suppose?"

"You needn't ask that."

"So be it then. The Lord give him joy of my son!"

BOOK II

CHAPTER I

LITTLE Martin's life dawned upon the wild region of
Hartland—Hartland, in its immense amphitheatre of
hills and valleys; Hartland, with its coney-cropped turf
and crown of granite; with its feet amid the brakes of
fern and furze, and the cloud-feathers flying free on the
blue above. Dart wound beneath, now shrunk to a broken
ribbon of light in summer, now shouting the song of the
freshets And round about the homestead, when the
weather was fair, linen twinkled, fast held by thorn-
trees against theft of the wind To-day the sky would be
full of light, that burnt into a nimbus of splendour when
the sun sank behind Broad Down; to-morrow might
break sad-coloured, with low fog-banks rolling onward,
like armies under tattered pennons of silver, where a
watery gleam pierced through them. Now the west wind
roamed and roared; now the north wind brought up
winter on wings heavy with snow; now again the vernal
time returned; the Moor offered welcome of humble
flowers in marsh and heath, and the grey cuckoo chimed
his two sweet notes from dawn till even.

Martin presently created pet haunts in Hartland Tor
and shared them with the ferns and pennyworts, the
stonecrops, and dull rosettes of foxglove leaves that lifted
spires and bells when summer came. A great shelf of
rock faced south upon the tor, and beneath it, as years
passed by, he played for hours together. None shared
so many of these hours as Philip; but other children often
came, and the boy's cousins from Stannon were fre-

quently at Hartland. There were five of them by this
time, and Maggie, Jacky, Samuel, and Minnie might often
be seen in company of Martin at Hartland, or in the old
sheep-fold not far distant. They played their children's
games, made believe, took full unconscious joy of life,
and planned their great to-morrows full of mighty inten-
tions—all forgotten when to-morrow came For night—
to the adult mind but a curtain, often thin enough,
through which coming day stares forth with all its
promise or its threat—brings real oblivion and a great
forgetfulness to the little child. His connecting links are
feeble; he begins a new life every morning; and the dom-
inant present, with its instant claim and immediate desires, hopes, hungers, will often obliterate all the purposes that filled the small soul till sleep drowned them
and swept the mind blank for new impressions.

Martin was a slight-built, healthy, and hearty boy; and
as he reached the age of ten years his character began to
develop. Already he promised to resemble his father in
countenance, and his nature was staid. He had a
serious, speculative mind and took the lead among his
playmates. His eyes were dark grey, like his mother's,
his hair was black and straight. His intellect promised
to be very clear. He was an obstinate child, but Unity
did not find his nature difficult. Her great problem centred rather in Philip and his attitude to the young life.
Ouldsbroom fought to win Martin, and could not see why
all his striving should be so largely in vain. He exhausted his scanty ingenuity, and sometimes raged dis-
heartened at obvious failure, but then, with a great
awakening hope, redoubled his efforts before apparent
success. He built upon the future more and more, and
was swift to notice any closer understanding between
himself and the boy. A marvel arose out of the relation,
for even Philip learned a little patience, and though he
broke out not seldom, was swiftly contrite again. He
offered a spectacle of bitter import to those two who understood it; and as they watched year after year, their
estimate of its significance differed. For this cause, as
well as for other reasons, their friendship waned.

Philip kept open eyes and alert senses to catch every glimmer of himself in Martin. Physically they had nothing in common, for the farmer was all Saxon and the child all Celt; but driven from that expectation and hope, Ouldsbroom fell back upon deeper things, and, with such meagre power of observation as he possessed, looked out for his tricks of thought or speech, anticipated the appearance of his own tastes, his attitude to life, his general innate characteristics and method of self-expression.

A revealed shadow of these things put him in good temper for the day, and at first, thanks to the imitative instinct of infancy, Martin satisfied Philip; but every year saw the boy come closer to his own nature, and every year Ouldsbroom was constrained to admit to his fierce heart that the mother was prepotent in her child. And then again some spark or sign wakened his hope once more, and he blamed himself for impatience and unkindness.

Unkind indeed his nature never could be. From the first he poured out all the riches of an unreasoning love and won the affection of Martin absolutely. No young thing could have withstood such worship and devotion. The boy cried for his fancied father when he was sick or unhappy; he confided his brief woes to him; he crept to him when he had done wrong and knew it. But he did very little wrong. Rectitude and obedience to authority were natural in him, and his obstinacy generally appeared among matters of pleasure rather than duty. He was not often punished. His father had struck him once or twice—for no fault excepting that he was himself; and, after these lapses, Philip would beg the child to forgive him, and redouble his kindness. Martin's mother, on the contrary, corrected him with jealous care. She salved her conscience and excused herself for bringing him into the world by determining that he should amply justify his existence. In this ambition she felt her hope grow, for there was a strong bent to religious observance in Martin that appeared even in his games. She knew about these things, but hid them from her husband, and trusted that he might not discover them for himself.

Into her own heart Unity did not allow herself much time to look. She toiled without ceasing, and she devoted her leisure to her husband and only child. Her common sense assured her that by such devotion she might atone for the past. Her conscience denied it, and the growing facts of Martin's character denied it. She had not guessed that the boy's own nature and the accident of his paternity might breed a lifelong tragedy; she had never anticipated that her deed would cry out under her eyes for ever.

She was a pattern wife to the man, and that proved no light task as the years rolled on; because Philip, at fifty-three, continued for the most part unchanged. He thought himself as wise as his generation; he uttered definite opinions on all subjects of religion, husbandry, politics, and life; but such as were of any worth he had mostly received at second hand from another. His own views were entirely unpractical and made against prosperity, since he continued to judge mankind from the standpoint of his own trusting and generous soul, and built his estimates of all conduct on appearances rather than the facts underlying them.

The man's wife had difficult work sometimes to support his credit and character. But she prospered in the task and strove also, with no small skill, to gain to herself the business administration of Hartland. In some directions she succeeded, and then took good care that Philip won the credit. When praised, she always asserted that his mind controlled, while she was only the willing instrument. Her influence had grown enormous over him, and yet he did not feel it. Only when she was from home could he realise, by his discomfort, incertitude, and sudden desire for stimulant to bolster depression, how vital she had become to his well-being.

All Unity's ambitions centred in Martin. She looked far ahead and held no trouble wasted on Philip that could help to fortify her son's ultimate inheritance.

It puzzled the farmer to see how the boy resembled his mother in many particulars, and how his mother understood him. He was envious but not jealous. As Martin drifted farther and farther from him, nearer and nearer to his wife, Philip never felt one pang of jealousy. He assured himself that it was natural; he was quick to leap at a chance of bringing joy to the child; only in secret or out of Unity's sight did he give vent to his disappointment. Fault there was none within reach of remedy; and that made the situation absurd. The boy grew up good, cheerful, well behaved, and to advance this very fact as his grievance even Philip perceived was futile. Nevertheless, he did so sometimes, in the sole ears that could understand.

The inevitable had overtaken Barbara Hext and her dog 'Sarah.' The spaniel was dead; while to Barbara there came an assistant in the shape of Mrs. Dury's eldest daughter. The change was now some years old, and Kate Dury, with reason, considered herself a most successful shopwoman; but Miss Hext could never be got to admit as much. She seldom enjoyed herself so well as when Kate begged for a whole holiday and left the establishment in sole charge of the mistress as of yore. Concerning the postal department, Barbara, though growing a little shaky, continued to conduct that single-handed; and, indeed, the work was light enough.

Hither on a morning in winter came Philip, and with him he brought Martin. It was the child's tenth birthday, and he arrived to spend a shilling. The boy was very silent on the way to Postbridge, and Philip's prattle won little response. This annoyed him, yet nothing could have been more natural. The shilling had come as a great and splendid surprise, it was a large sum of money, and how to spend it to the best advantage demanded most careful thought. Martin, therefore, did not desire to talk, but to reflect.

At the River, Ouldsbroom bade the child go and play for a little.

"I want to have a tell along o' Miss Hext," he said. "I'll shout to you when you can come in."

The boy went off, but did not play. He climbed on to the old pack-horse bridge, and sat there with his legs dangling over the water and his mind upon the shilling.

Presently he took it out of his pocket and examined it, as though study of the coin might help decision.

Philip meanwhile spoke to Barbara. She had grown grey of late, but was comely still

"Bid Katey clear out," he said abruptly. "I want a tell with you"

"Kate can't clear out," answered the postmistress. "Come in my parlour, if you must see me. Where's Martin? 'Tis his birthday."

"He's outside. I told him to go and play, but of course he won't. Childer don't know the meaning of play nowadays His birthday and all, yet he's solemn as a judge. I've planned a surprise for him this afternoon—to take him out on a pony and have tea with the Mastermans at the 'Ring o' Bells.' But it looks as though the treats I plan for him give me more pleasure than the boy."

"Don't say that, or think it. He feels more than he shows," said Barbara.

"And then," continued the man, "my pleasure's turned to gall to see that he's got none. The things I've tried—racked my brain to remember all that was good to me when I was a nipper Damned if I can understand it."

"He's a wonderful thoughtful child, and old for his years—remember that The fault's not in him, Philip, 'tis in you"

"In me! And you say so, Barbara—you, who understand—leastways, I thought you did What can I do more than I do? Where be I wrong?"

"You're wrong for biding young into middle age," she said "You ought to be angry with yourself, not him Nature's played the fool with you and kept a boy's mind in a man's body. Well I know, for I'm a bit like that myself, and should have been more so if life had fallen out different I do understand, and I think 'tis a fine thing in its way to keep young at all hazards But the people don't, and of course the boy don't. How should he? He's not a boyish fashion of boy, and that you must allow for."

"But if he ban't young now, what the deuce will he come to presently? If a child but turned of ten—there, 'tis nonsense! I won't believe it He chatters all right sometimes and can make a game so well as any young boy. 'Tis I that puzzle him—same as he puzzles me. If I cuss, he looks through me and then at his mother. I catched him and his cousins playing at prayers t'other day on Hartland. My child playing at prayers! All the same, Barbara, years have brought a good bit of sense to me, and if I hadn't got it, my life wouldn't have run so smooth as it have. Therefore I'm very patient with him He's all the world to me—my only one; though I do wish to God I'd got a few more on a different pattern "

"The child's like his mother—the very tone of her voice sometimes."

"And couldn't be like a better woman. I'd set store on him for that alone. But I catch myself hankering—however, I needn't waste your time 'Twasn't that I come to say. 'Twas a message from Unity."

They discussed a matter concerning the price of food, then Philip beckoned Martin from the river.

"Now, my ten-year-old!" he cried out, "bring along your shilling to Miss Hext and her brave shop So set to work and let's see what you be going to buy!"

Martin smiled shyly, thanked Miss Hext for her congratulations, and began to look about him. The actual display bewildered his previous thoughts and plans. He suddenly began to think, and frowned; then he turned to the postmistress.

"I be wishful to—to spend threepence for something for mother," he said

"Ah, you copy-book boy!" cried Philip almost bitterly; and Martin glanced up at him with startled eyes

"Quite right and proper, Martin!" declared Miss Hext "Come along over here, and I'll see what we can find A nice bit of ribbon—how would that do?"

"I should think 'twould do very well, Miss Hext," he answered.

"And what colour would you like it to be, my dear?"

He considered this question and when she had him out of Ouldsbroom's sight, behind a pile of goods, she whispered to him:

"Shall you get anything for father?"

"But father 'twas that give me the shilling," he answered.

"Never mind that. Buy him a pipe. I'll sell you a fine wood pipe for threepence."

He looked at his coin doubtfully and she said no more. They returned to Ouldsbroom.

"I've bought mother a bit of shiny red ribbon for Sundays, father," said Martin.

"Well done you! And she shall wear it and not hoard it, I promise you. And now let's see what *you* be going to buy."

Barbara, wishing to relieve the child's anxieties, herself made him a present of a toy boat. He thanked her gratefully and his father did the like.

"Now get on, laddie, we musn't keep Miss Hext all day."

"I'll have a threepenny wood pipe for father," said Martin, peeping at Miss Hext inquiringly.

She made haste to fetch a pipe, and Philip shouted out the liveliest gratitude and joy.

"Good chap!" he cried "That's real proper of you, sonny, and I thank you, and I'll always keep that pipe— so long as I live I will—and only smoke it on great days!"

He hugged the boy and kissed him, and rubbed his muzzle against Martin's brown cheek. Then he dragged his tobacco pouch out of his pocket and stuffed the pipe.

"You shall have first puff, Martin, and then I'll always remember that yours was the first lips ever touched my pipe. Suck in!"

Martin rather nervously obeyed, while his father held a match to the pipe. The smoke made the boy cough and water at the eyes, while Philip laughed uproariously.

"Now your sixpence," he said. "What be going to do with that?"

Martin reflected.

"I've got this here butivul boat," he answered, "and I doan't want nought else, father. I'll put my sixpence in my money-box, if you please."

Ouldsbroom shrugged his shoulders and regarded Miss Hext.

"There!" he exclaimed. "Did you ever hear such a thing from a boy of ten? Be it natural?"

" 'Tis good sense anyway."

" 'Tis damn nonsense," answered the man. "I won't have him getting fond of money at his time of life. A saver at ten, good Lord, he'll be a miser at twenty! Look here, Martin, Miss Hext have give you a fine boat, and 'twould be very improper after that if you wasn't to spend your sixpence in her shop this minute."

The child was somewhat scared.

"I didn't know 'twas wrong," he answered. "Then I'll have one of they little brass anchors for **my** boat, please, if the money's enough."

Barbara abstained from arguing, for she knew that it would annoy Philip. Her sympathies were torn between the pair.

"An anchor and a good brass cannon you shall have," she said.

"And very like a sixpence in your money-box as well—who knows?" promised the farmer.

Laden with his gifts, Martin set off home, talked cheerfully of the day's doings and watched the new pipe in his father's mouth.

"Never knowed a pipe to draw more suent,"* declared Ouldsbroom. " 'Twas a very clever thing for you to think of, and I shall set mighty store by it, I promise you, and so will mother by the ribbon."

Then Philip had an idea.

"I'll give 'e some of my gunpowder after us have had dinner; we'll go in the yard and take your cannon and fire it off. I lay the chicken will all scream and go racing about for dear life when they hear it go 'bang'!"

He laughed at the picture, and Martin smiled—in sympathy but not in earnest. The spectacle of alarmed poultry had no charm for him. He was wondering whether another sixpence would be found for his money-box, and whether, if his father forgot the promise, he might venture to remind him.

* *Suent*—Easily, sweetly.

CHAPTER II

THERE is no loneliness in nature, and of Dartmoor it can never be said that it is empty. But watch some road, stretching inexorable mile on mile across the heath, and mark a solitary figure creeping along it. Then large loneliness is swiftly felt, as a quality of the human addition, not the place.

Such a figure proceeded on a summer day by no road, but across the heavy ground above Broad Down. It crawled, a mere atom, to the crest of the hill, and there, panting, footsore and hungry, flung itself down and fixed inquiring eyes upon the valley beneath. The little object was a boy, and he had travelled fifteen miles across the heart of the Moor, to find himself utterly exhausted above Postbridge

Now his anxious eyes looked ahead and instantly brightened. The troubled expression of his red and freckled countenance changed to happiness, and he rejoiced.

"Golly—houses!" he said, and instantly rose again to begin the descent to Postbridge.

The accident of his discovery banished a shadow of growing fear and put heart into him. His mind acted upon his body, and his physical fatigue, for the time, grew less.

He was a stout, square-built lad of twelve, with a large mouth, sandy hair, and a freckled face, now very red and hot with his exertions. He wore only corduroy knickerbockers, worsted stockings, and a blue flannel shirt. He had kicked the sole off one of his boots and tied it on again as best he could. His stockings were torn; his mouth was stained with the whortleberries that he had eaten on his way.

He was desperately hungry and weary, but he stopped beside the river, drank some water, tightened up his red braces and assumed a very determined expression.

The houses proved to be farther off than he expected, and his heart sank a little; but suddenly, round the shoulder of a hill, a farm appeared within a quarter of a mile, and he said 'Golly!' again and held forward

He was giddy and weak now. He reached the door of Hartland Farm, knocked, and then, with a swimming head, sat down suddenly on a trestle that chanced to be in the porch. With an effort he pulled himself together and rose as Unity Ouldsbroom appeared to see who had come.

"Please, ma'am," he began, then she cut him short.

"Be off!" she said. "Take your bacon face out of this We've got nought for beggars here."

"I'm beat," answered the boy "Please—please just give me a mouthful. I've walked all across Dartymoor wi'out any breaksis, and I'm that cruel leery,* I shall tumble down if I don't get a square meal."

"Be you alone?"

"Ess, ma'am."

"You want a square meal—you can have one," she said, with the ghost of a smile on her face at the jest. Then she turned to the kitchen and brought the boy a dog-biscuit

He thanked her abundantly and began to eat. He had big yellow teeth, and they soon crunched up the food.

She watched him a few moments and marked his natural strength. He was sturdily put together, with big bones and a fine little barrel He promised to develop into a splendid man if the fates were kind. He had turned up the sleeves of his shirt to the shoulder for coolness, and Unity noticed that his arms were well covered and that they shone in the sunshine with a delicate down of bright hairs

* *Leery*—Hungry, empty.

"Eat it up and rest for two minutes, and then go along," she said.

"So I will then, and thank you kindly, missis," he answered.

Unity, satisfied that the child was honest, left him; then Philip appeared, returning to his dinner.

"Hullo!" cried he, "who the mischief be you?"

The boy stood up and touched his head with his finger.

"Marnin', sir! I made so bold as to ax for a bit o' food, and the lady was terrible kind and let me have this here."

"Bah! You might so soon eat your nails as that mess. Give it to me and wait a bit."

He took the remains of the dog-biscuit and flung it into the yard. Then he entered his kitchen, where a dinner of pasties awaited him. He picked up the largest in the dish and carried it out.

"Here," he said, "stuff that down your neck. Whose boy be you, then?"

"Golly!" said the child. "That's pretty eating, that is. Can you spare it, master?"

"Get on   Yes, I can spare it."

"I'll do a bit of work later when I'm rested. Doctor at the Union said I was the strongest boy as ever he saw. An' I be a terrible fierce chap too."

"A workhouse boy?"

"I've runned away to better myself. I've runned all across the Moor from Okehampton. God's my judge if it ban't true! I'd got a job keeping birds from corn; and I chucked it so soon as the sun was up and miched off. Too fierce I be for that sort of work. And I thought I was done for; but then suddenly, atop of thicky hill, I looked down and catched sight of houses."

He ate with his eyes on Philip.

"What's your name?"

"Pancras Lyd they called me—after the church saint and the river to Lydford, where I was found. I was lighted on there years and years agone by a policeman when I was a babby; but nobody never wanted me. And none never found out wheer I comed from. But I don't want for to be called 'Pancras' I want for to be called 'Tiger' along o' being so fierce.''

Philip laughed heartily.

"You'm a rum, red rascal! Fierce—eh? And runned away to better yourself, did 'e?''

"Ess, fay. I want to be at something braver than frighting birds.''

"Quite right. How old are you?''

"Fifteen.''

"You little liar!''

The boy glanced up at Philip.

"I feel that old, master; and I be so strong as any fifteen-year-old chap. Look at my gert arms. They say I'm twelve, but if I said I was twelve I'd never get a job.''

"Cunning fox! But there'll be hue and cry after 'e come presently.''

"I want for to get work afore they find me,'' explained the boy. "Because nobody will be better pleased than them at the workhouse if I be took off their hands. They don't want fierce boys.''

"I'll warrant. Only the tame go there.''

Martin came in at this moment and his father called to him.

"Get this here ferocious chap a cup of milk,'' he said.

The other obeyed, and the children met.

Martin was much excited and interested. They left the wanderer to finish his meal, but Unity's boy had no appetite for dinner. He longed to return to the stranger.

He ran out soon, and found Tiger sitting among some pigs in a shady corner of the yard, with his back against the wall. He was drowsy and his head nodded.

He touched his forehead to Martin.

"Would you be so kind as to let me rest here, master— just for a bit? Then I'll get up and set to work and pay for my dinner.''

"You needn't pay,'' answered Martin. "My father wouldn't wish that—unless you feel you must do it. What's your name?''

"Tiger. What's yourn?"

"Martin"

Tiger rolled over and yawned hugely.

"Blessed if I ban't gwine to sleep!" he said.

In truth he slumbered immediately, and Martin ran in with the news.

"That boy's called Tiger; and he's gone to sleep in the yard by the pigs," he announced

"Let un bide then," ordered Philip. "The young rip's run away from Okehampton—to better hisself! Let him sleep it out I want to see what he'll do when he wakes up. You can keep about and watch him, Martin. 'Fierce' he says he is. Dartymoor's knocked the fierceness out of him to-day. Ha-ha!"

Unity protested, but Philip had his will, her son watched over the wanderer's sleep and took care to drive away pigs when they threatened to interfere with it. At four in the afternoon Tiger awakened, much refreshed, and hungrier than ever The latter fact he did not mention, but told Martin that he was ready to work.

"You'm a scholar, I see," he remarked, for Martin had been reading a book while the other slept.

"I can read books, and the Bible too. This is a story-book I got for a prize at Sunday School."

"Fancy that now! Be there any shows* in the book?"

"No; but I've got one with pictures."

"A beast book?"

"No."

"I seed a beast book open in a shop window to Oke-hampton 'Twas flung ope at a savage tiger. And so I said I'd be 'Tiger' too, cause the beast had such a terrible fine way with him."

"You wasn't baptized 'Tiger,' was you?"

"No."

Martin's face brightened with an idea.

"If you ain't been baptized, us might have a service—me and Minnie and Maggie and Jacky and Sam—and christen you. We play at prayer-meetings up along, and I be the parson."

* *Shows*—Pictures.

" 'Twould make a very brave game, I dare say."

"Yes, 'twould. We'll do it!"

"But I must go to work now. Do 'e think that gert man what gived me the pasty would let me carry out enough work to earn a bit of bread and dripping, or some such thing, for my tea?"

"Yes, I'm 'most sure he would."

"Well, what's to do?"

"Father's digging up there in the croft. You'd better ax him."

Tiger rose, and found himself lame.

" 'Twas my baggering old boot," he explained. "The sole dropped off of un and I had to tie it on, and took the tail o' my shirt for it. But I'm that fierce, when a thing like that happens I take no count of it. I suppose you haven't got a pair of old boots to spare a chap?"

"You couldn't get in my boots," answered Martin. "They'd be too tight for 'e. Your feet be whackers."

"Have you got a big brother or sister then?"

"No."

"Us'll see what the master says."

"He's my father, and he's called Philip Ouldsbroom."

They started, then Tiger stopped suddenly and clapped his hand to his trouser pocket.

" 'Tis all right," he cried. "I thought I'd lost un."

"What?"

"My Jew's harp I found it last Christmas in a dust-heap, and I've larned to play it proper. I'll play to you come presently, when I ban't busy."

They reached Philip, who was digging and trenching "I've come for a bit of work, please, master."

The farmer winked at Martin to show that he intended a joke. Then he handed his big spade to Tiger.

"That's a brave chap. You go on with this job while I smoke a pipe, and I'll see what you be made of."

The labour was impossible to a boy of twelve, and the spade came up to the runaway's breast, but he started valiantly, and puffed and sweated and struggled.

"That won't do," said Philip. "That's playing at it

You must break the ground to eighteen inches. You'm only scraping the top.''

Tiger thereupon tightened his braces, spat on his hands, assumed the fiercest scowl he could summon, and tried to dig deeper.

"I'd stand to it so well as growed man, if 'twasn't for my foot," he said, "but a chap can't drive home this gert spade in this here boot.''

Philip, however, let him go on, though Martin twice whispered to him to give the boy something else to do.

Tiger fought to the end of the ridge, then stopped to rest.

"Don't you think I be tired, master, 'cause I ban't,'' he declared. "I can stand to work so well as any clever chap. Never was known to be tired, I assure 'e.''

"That's the sort I like. Go at it!'' answered Ouldsbroom.

The boy struggled on. He grew very red in the face and his breath began to come hard.

"How much might I have earned now, master?'' he inquired presently, and stopped to pant.

"You've about earned the pasty.''

"There's the milk,'' said Tiger; and he set to work again. Hope of winning tea grew faint.

But then the man stopped him.

"Good boy! I see you be made of fighting stuff. I'll give 'e a bit of work you can do easier to-morrow. Where be you off to now?''

" 'Tis this way,'' he answered. "I want for to roam off to foreign parts. But I'm looking out to better myself for the minute, and make a shilling or two. Perhaps you might know somebody as wants a handy boy?''

"They'll send round the country to find you.''

" 'Tis all one, 'cause I've changed my name. I know you won't tell on me. I was called Pancras Lyd to the workhouse; but now I be called 'Tiger,' and a reg'lar tiger I'm going for to be.''

"Play your Jew's harp, Tiger,'' said Martin.

The child brought his toy from his pocket, set it between his strong teeth and played an old tune.

Ouldsbroom roared with laughter.

"Be damned if you can't do it proper," he said. "Here, let me have a try!"

He tried, made strange noises and failed.

Now Martin laughed and wanted to try too. Tiger was seized with the enthusiasm of the teacher.

"I'll larn you to do it, master! If you let me bide wi' you for just a day or two I'll larn you all the tunes I know—four and a hymn."

"What hymn?" asked the other boy. He reflected that music would be a great addition to the prayer-meeting game.

A voice called from the farm.

"There's mother," said Martin. " 'Tis tea-time."

"I'll have another go at this here spade while you get your tea," suggested Tiger, but the farmer refused.

"Come you down with us and play my missis a tune," he said. "She's a gert musicker, and can sing very nice when she's minded to, though it ban't often."

"She sings lovely to church," declared Martin.

But Unity was not much impressed by the Jew's harp. She showed no great interest in Tiger, and the more Philip encouraged the child, the less did she. It was not until the boys had finished their meal and gone out together that she relented.

"He's a very tidy nipper," declared Philip; "Martin have took to him something tremendous. I be going to let him bide for a day or two, till his foot's mended. He makes me laugh—and strong as a pony he is. Us'll see what use he may be. There's that in him will do Martin good, I believe."

"You'll have him on your hands afore you can look round," she answered. "They'll be very glad to get rid of him at the workhouse, no doubt, though they'll want his rags back."

"As to that, a boy can always get a job if he's got work in him. We'll see what character they give him from Okehampton. A bad one, I reckon. You might write off a letter, Unity, and tell 'em he's safe for the minute and ax 'em about him. Then we'll see if he's a liar or not. He's told me one lie a'ready—said he was fifteen—sly dog! because he hoped I'd think better of his usefulness. You write; there's a dear woman, and I'll go down and post it.''

In a matter of this kind Unity was always lightning-quick to make capital and establish a balance, to be drawn upon when her turn came for asking favours.

"What a fellow you are!" she answered. "Lucky for us we're off the road, or your silly way would be to find room for every tramp that set the dog barking. I'll write and hear what they've got to answer—since you say it must be so.''

"That's right! Who but you would be so sensible? And if they don't give him a good character, back he goes.''

"They'll know that, and say the best they can.''

Her husband, well pleased, went out to join the boys.

They were busy packing fern into an old broken barrel on the hill outside the farmyard

"Us be making a little cubby-hole for me to sleep in to-night, master,'' explained Tiger. "Martin says you don't set no store on this here barrel, and I can make a very fine lair in it, if 'tis all the same to you ''

"You may sleep in the shippon,'' answered Philip; "and you'll have to work like the devil to-morrow, because I be going to get 'e a pair of boots down in the village.''

Tiger rejoiced in the boots, but regretted the barrel.

" 'Tis cruel kind, master, and I'll work the flesh off my bones come morning,'' he said; "but, if 'tis all one, I terrible wish to sleep in this here old cask. 'Twould seem a bit fiercer like than being under cover I never thought to put my head under no roof no more when I set out this marnin'.''

CHAPTER III

PHILIP OULDSBROOM called at the 'Warren House' on his way home from Moretonhampstead. Mr. Twigg was not in the bar; but Millicent Mary, now elevated to the counter, served him.

There was an old man named Woodley in the corner—bent, dirty, and toothless. He drank gin-and-water, and regarded some young labourers with pint pots before them. Philip, marking the envy in his face, took his drink and sat beside him.

"What's wrong, gaffer?" he asked.

"Time's wrong," answered the patriarch. "Look at they youngsters swilling. 'Tis as hard a thing as we ancient blids can suffer to be reminded of what we've lost."

"Every dog has his day. We've drunk our quarts and turned night into morning afore now, too."

But Philip could not comfort the aged spirit.

"I ban't grudging them; but I be quarrelling with my own cruel luck," explained Mr. Woodley. "Here be I, not eighty year old yet, and dursn't let down beer for fear of shortening my life. And when 'tis so with a man, the angel of the Lord couldn't make him cheerful."

"What's the matter with gin?" asked Ouldsbroom. "Have a drop along with me."

Gregory Twigg and Henry Birdwood came in together. Mr. Twigg wore well, Birdwood did not. The positions between them were reversed in one particular. Increasing weight tended to keep Gregory out of the saddle and much diminish his activity. He had just resigned the position of Moorman to the East Quarter and Birdwood was about to succeed him.

"I've been telling Henry that it wouldn't surprise me if some note was took by Duchy of my resigning," said Twigg. " 'Tis pretty generally allowed, I believe, that

137

I've been the bailiff's right hand for fifteen year, and on a great change like this taking place 'twould be a natural and human thing to give me a feed and a piece of plate to hand down to my family when I'm gathered home. What d'you say to that, souls?''

The young men grinned indifferently; the ancient in the corner, from his cynical standpoint of seventy-and-seven, bade Gregory hope for nothing of the sort.

"Out of sight, out of mind," he said "You ought to know by this time what Duchy does; and bailiff's only the whip in Duchy's hand, when all's said."

Ouldsbroom, however, took a different view. The hope of a revel or merry-making was always meat and drink to him. Many a time had he been instrumental in getting up of little testimonials, and so adding to the amenities of his environment with good fellowship. He still laughed at Twigg for a vain humbug, but bore him no ill-will.

"A proper idea, Greg!" he said. "But you can't very well start a subscription for yourself, so you keep your mouth shut, if you know how, and leave the job to your neighbours. Next time I see bailiff, I'll sound him. We'll kill two birds wi' one stone strambang! We'll have a blow-out and a bit of fun and buy you a new top hat, or your missis a tea-pot, with what's left over!"

Gregory was gratified, but wished the proposal might come from a loftier quarter.

"You mean well, Ouldsbroom," he said. "And for a man without religion few could mean better. But do nought, I beg of you. This thing should be in higher hands. By that I don't mean my Maker, but Duchy. Do nought, and see what happens. When I think of the ocean of brain-work I've done for the bailiff, I can't suppose that a solemn thing, like my dropping out of the East Quarter, will pass as if 'twas nought."

" 'Twill pass like a shadow on the heath—same as you will yourself—and we all shall," said Mr. Woodley in the corner.

"Don't you talk that rummage," answered Philip; "you forget the five pounds us got together for you when your wife died."

"There's Millicent Mary's wedding too," continued Gregory. "I suppose 'tis known now far and wide that I've consented to her taking the carrier. He came shaking before me last Saturday."

"He didn't shake!" said Millicent Mary from behind the bar. "You know he didn't shake, father He ban't that sort of man. What have he got to shake about?"

"Go in the other room," answered Mr. Twigg, "and don't speak in that tone of voice, because well you know I never will have it."

The girl departed, and her parent continued:

"He came to offer himself; and though I can't say the Coombers of Dousland be all to my liking, there's nought against him He's added coke and coal to his other chores, and there's a modest manner and religion to him So it will happen "

"Be you going to bide out at Teign Head, or shall you come into Postbridge now?" asked a man of Birdwood

"I shall stop there There's no house in Postbridge for the minute."

"Build one, Henry," suggested Philip. " 'Twould be better every way if you was nearer Princetown."

"I might—later Must see how I get on "

"Don't be too hopeful," urged Twigg "I believe everybody knows the way I can handle figures Why, last year says the bailiff to me, 'Dammy, Twigg,' he says —he using the word, not me—'dammy, Twigg, you can make 'em talk!' And that's the truth. But with all my large skill, I never got anything to be called big money out of the Quarter, so you musn't expect to, Henry "

"You'll marry on the strength of it, I reckon," suggested a youth to Birdwood; but the shepherd shook his head.

"Not me, Samuel No wife for me. Philip here have been at me like a woodpecker at a tree—hammering, hammering it into me to take a wife; but not even for him would I do it."

"Silly mumphead that you are!" cried the farmer "What a fool is a man that flings away the best half of life and goes alone—eh, Twigg?"

"You might think so, neighbour, but remember Paul. Marriage is a great lottery. If you've got understanding, I say nothing. Perhaps no man ever chose so well as I did, along of the brain-power I brought to the task. But, with nine out of ten ordinary men, it is a lottery, because the female nature is entirely different from ours. You may have marked that."

" 'Tis the mixture of sense and silliness in 'em," said Philip. "The surprises be the salt of 'em—the ups and downs. If 'tweren't for the downs, the ups wouldn't be half so tasty. Laugh—I die of laughing sometimes."

"Do you?" asked the innkeeper. "Now that surprises me. What do you find to laugh at in your lady, if I may ask?"

"She've got more sense than any woman in Postbridge, bar the postmistress; and none deny it," said the ancient Woodley.

"She have—far more—far more sense than me, if you like; but 'tis women's sense, not man's; and women's sense do look so damn funny now and again," explained Ouldsbroom. "Their thrift—bless 'em—the way they overwork a half-penny, and don't see that to spend sixpence, and have done with it, would pay a long sight better in the upshot. My dear woman bought the boy a pair of shop-worn shoes for cheapness last year, and then blackguarded Martin because they was too tight for him! Darling creatures! 'Tis things like that make you love 'em."

"What's this I hear tell of a boy you've picked up, Phil?" asked Birdwood.

"Why, 'tis so. The rascal marched into Hartland a month agone, and he's there yet. And a proper boy too. My wife's a bit uncertain about it, but she'll come round, for there's plenty for him to do and he's wonderful handy for such a nipper. And my lad have taken to him; and so have I."

"A workhouse boy, I was told," said Gregory.

"So he is. They don't want him back if I'll keep him. He was found, as an infant child, by a policeman in Lydford parish, and be called after the river and the church.

But that won't do for him. 'Tiger' he's to be, if you please!"

"You'll rue it," foretold Twigg. "I lay my life he's a gipsy brat and full of bad blood. Keep him, and so like as not he'll cut all your throats whilst you sleep, or set Hartland afire "

"Not a chance!" declared Ouldsbroom "He's a red, freckled toad—nothing of the gipsy in him. They be all brown people And I've no quarrel with them, for that matter. I'd be very well satisfied with a van myself 'Tis a large-minded, sporting way of life "

"I should have reckoned that your own boy could have done a bit of rough work round the house by now," said Mr Woodley. "I was earning my living picking stones off the land when I was seven, afore all this silly foolery of sending childer to school began "

"No," answered Philip. "His mother have her ideas for Martin Come he's a bit bigger, he'll go to a proper school He's a clever child a'ready and can read out loud very nice."

"If this foundling boy had been a bit bigger I'd have took him off your hands, if he's as smart as you think," said Henry Birdwood "Ned Sleep will have to be gone afore another summer He knows it himself. He's riddled with rheumatism, and his breathing parts be giving out seemingly."

" 'Twill be the workhouse for him, I'm much afraid," said Philip.

"He knows that too He takes it as all in the day's work. Nothing was ever seen to fluster that man. He's so well used to looking forward and weighing things, that 'twill be no shock to him. He've got all the workhouse rules and regulations at his fingers' ends, and he reckons that on the whole he'll be more comfortable in than out He's been trying to better himself for twenty years, and though there's less liberty, he says that so far as clothes and comfort go, the union will be easier than Teign Head."

"He's right there," declared Ouldsbroom. "You don't know the meaning of comfort, Henry. I've often heard my wife say so."

Birdwood laughed.

"Comfort—what do men want with comfort? If you want to be comfortable, you can die."

He departed upon this sentiment, and Twigg discussed him.

"A cheerless man, though a godly," he remarked. "When his father was going home, he gave that old lion of the Lord his promise as he'd come back to the Little Baptists And back he came But I doubt he gets much out of it There's a screw loose in his spirit, and I wish he'd let me tighten it—for 'tis well within my power so to do. I can read the soul like you chaps can read a book 'Tis second nature to me to see what's going forward in the heart of a man Couldn't tell you how I do it—just one of my gifts. And I know Henry's not what you may call hand-in-hand with Christ "

Ouldsbroom burst upon these reflections with noisy scorn, and the ancient supported him. They wrangled over Birdwood's soul with some warmth, while the shepherd mounted his pony and struck off to the Moor.

He did not, however, return home directly. His business took him to Stannon Farm, and in half an hour he arrived there to speak with Quinton Crymes The men talked together for a while; then Henry went indoors to drink a glass of cider

"My sister be within," said Quinton. "She's walked over from Hartland at my wish, to see Gertrude. There's another coming. You know how 'tis with my poor wife She gets cruel low at these times, and believes that each one is going to be the death of her, and leave me a widowman and the childer without a mother's care. But I tell her that, after five successes, there's no fear of failure."

"Certainly not. She's all right, though how you can see this swarm getting thick as bees round you and fear nought, I don't understand "

" 'Tis nothing," answered Crymes. "They come gradual and take their places. I ban't in the least troubled for 'em I don't turn a hair for one of 'em No good being a God-fearer, like me, if you'm going to fret your gizzard about your offspring They'm the Lord's work, not mine. I do my appointed part by 'em and look for Him to do His. Why, I might so well fret about having six as Ouldsbroom do about having only one But I know my place better.''

Unity was just leaving as Birdwood appeared.

They had not met for a considerable time, and spoke with friendship but no particular cordiality.

"If you'll bide a minute I'll go with you," said the shepherd "Haven't seed you for a month of Sundays."

"Be quick then," she answered Then she turned to her brother.

"I've cheered her up," she declared. " 'Tis the same old story: she be going to die, of course, this time. 'Tis your second boy do fret her most, I believe. Samuel's a little cross-pot of a child and he's spoiled. You ought to whip that boy, else he'll whip you come he grows up. But Jane's a beauty. I wish that babby was mine. A dinky, chubby cheel, and I can't pass her without kissing her."

"More can't I," declared the father. "Jane's my favourite of the lot. She crows like a bantam of a morning—a sweet babe, I assure 'e!"

Birdwood drank his cider, assured Gertrude that he had never seen her looking better, and then walked away, with his pony on one side of him and Mrs. Ouldsbroom upon the other.

For some time they said nothing; then he asked a question.

"I suppose you don't see it different? But I needn't ask."

She showed impatience.

"No, I don't—I'm a sane woman, whatever else I may be."

"Devil doubt that. I was only thinking of your husband and the future of you all."

"So was I. You always forget the boy and his future."

"Perhaps it might work out better for his eternal future if 'twas known."

"You beat me," she said "Sure never was two men

in one skin afore! Sometimes I think you like my husband now better than you like me "

" 'Twouldn't be strange if I did, would it? Cast your mind back a bit, Unity—for a change I know you haven't got much use for the past as a rule. 'Tisn't in your nature, and maybe you've more reason than most to keep your eyes off it; but still, there 'tis, and you must remember that men don't live on air where women are concerned. You used me to please yourself and then, when I——"

"For God's sake drop all that! What would you have had?"

"I'd have had you," he said. "I'd have had you a little bit nearer—for a little bit longer. You dropped me rather short and sharp ten year back. You thought I didn't see it But I saw it very clear."

"Haven't I heard that often enough?"

"Perhaps you have."

"And didn't I make my side clear too? What does it all matter now anyway?"

"Nothing now—of course Only a man's temper changes and his anger wears out. Perhaps I do like Philip better than you 'Twouldn't be odd We've all changed, you see—all but him You like your son better than anything on God's earth You don't deny that?"

"I've never tried to hide it."

"But I'm no more to you than the stone that helps you over the stream "

" 'A man's temper changes'—'twas your word a minute ago," she answered. "And a woman's may do the like We did wrong—awful wrong—the pair of us. But the wrong can't be undone without doing worse wrong now. Surely you see that?"

"I see how you always argue for self. And I see how you always did You threw me over for him, because of his money; and then, when no children came, you threw him over for me, because of your own desires But I myself was never nothing much to you, for all your soft glances and whispers. When you'd got what you wanted —what then?—you turned pious and taught my child Bible stories, and told me that we'd done wickedness in the land and must spend the rest of our lives making up for it. 'Twas convenient to turn good then, when you'd got all you wanted out of being bad Don't you see what a damned hypocrite you've been?''

"What's the sense of this now? I'm weary of going over it again and again if you are not. If 'tis true I'm a hypocrite—what then? Don't I smart without you rubbing salt into the wound?''

" 'Twas your fault that I harp on it to-day," he answered. " 'Tis the things you said a bit ago brought it all up. God knows I think of it as seldom as I can. I've sworn to you never to tell him, though I'm tempted terrible to break my oath sometimes, when I see the man fighting so hard to win over my frosty child. Phil's worth the pair of us. And you said just now to your brother how you wished you'd got a little one like his babby. And that made me look back too, and set me thinking. Now I'll go.''

"And don't you quarrel with me, Henry," she said more gently. "Granted I'm a hypocrite and worse, remember I pay. Remember that life ban't a bed of roses for me neither. To marry the wrong man and hide it for ten years takes some doing—yes, and brings the grey into a woman's hair, I can tell you. Don't grudge me the boy; and don't grudge him what will be his And don't think I care nothing about you. Can a woman forget the father of her child?''

They parted then without another word from him.

A sound he did make in answer to her last question—a sort of inarticulate grunt, half amusement and half scorn. Then he rode abruptly away, and left Unity with a hearty contempt in her mind for his fond recollections. The past to her was past indeed; but she had imagination sufficient to perceive the different standpoint of the man. From a vanished year she had gleaned what was more to her than her own life; he had won nothing but revenge long foundered in bitterness—a revenge that had turned upon him, fouled his existence, grown up into a pestilent jungle round about him, and hopelessly hidden the pathway that once he thought to tread. Revenge is only food for the strong: it had poisoned Birdwood.

10

CHAPTER IV

THE boy Tiger by some accidents of character found no enemy at Hartland. Philip frankly liked him from the first, and Unity, glad to please her husband, was friendly to the child and began to seek for him a permanent home and regular work. But meanwhile Tiger, as he was now universally called, had won a stronger ally than the master himself. Martin rejoiced exceedingly in the sudden advent of this playfellow. To have another young thing under the same roof with him; to be able to practise those arts of teaching and improvement that belonged to his nature—this addition to life was very pleasant to Unity's child. She perceived it, and when she did get the promise of a good home for the unfriended boy, it was too late. Martin wept bitterly at the thought of separation; Philip also raised many objections. Tiger had already become useful. He possessed a good nature and a strong arm. It struck Philip that his amiability, physical pluck, and genial spirit would well serve the shyer and colder disposition of Martin. This he did not say to his wife, knowing that a comparison of such a sort might annoy her into antagonism; but he stood strenuously for the establishment of Tiger at Hartland, and the boy himself, assuming the utmost ferocity his freckled face could pretend to, declared that he *would* stay, and that, if sent off, he should come back again.

Martin's cousins also welcomed him, though Tiger at this stage of his existence affected a large contempt for girls. The children often met through summer days and played their games at Hartland Tor under Martin's ledge, or in the ruined sheepfold, or among the Stone Men's ruins on the hillsides of Stannon.

146

A little hut circle here was regarded by Maggie and Jacky, Minnie and Samuel Crymes as Martin's special property. It stood to them as a place of serious rites and solemn celebrations. Here Martin played at church, read from his prayer-book and made the other children sing. The boy would even preach sometimes, until Sammy Crymes laughed or cried. as the case might be, and broke down the illusion.

On a half-holiday Martin and Tiger went off to meet the former's cousins and perform a most important ceremony. One or two other children from the national school at Postbridge also promised to be present at 'Martin's church,' and the child himself felt greatly elated

Some washing fluttered on the thorn-bushes above the farm, and Unity's boy helped himself from it to one of his own night-shirts.

" 'Twill look properer," he said.

" 'Twill be solemn and holy like if you've got white on, though there ban't enough arms for you to hide your face in," declared Tiger.

They were going to the old barrow to baptize Tiger. It was a spot of sepulture from which the mortuary mound had long since vanished. An outer ring of stones still stood, and in the midst a ruined kistvaen lay. Martin decreed that the largest stone of the ruin was an altar, while the others furnished seats for the congregation and himself.

Evidences of an ancient track or stream-way ran immediately behind the old barrow, and thence Minnie Crymes, the second girl of Quinton's family, now brought water in an old meat-tin. She was a little, pretty child, with something delicate and dainty about her. Her small head seemed as a flower upon its stalk. Her face, like a bud newly opened upon the miracle of life, displayed ever a look of surprise. Minnie was indeed always wondering. Her mother declared that with 'I wonder' she began every utterance. Maggie belonged to a different order. She was a plump, hearty girl, and loved eating. Of the boys Samuel had a bad reputation as one prone to be difficult; while Jack, the elder, resembled

Maggie in face and soul. The children were a blend of their parents, save Minnie, who had harked back to some unremembered ancestor for her nature, or was, as her father proudly called her, 'a rare sport'

The fifth child of the Crymes family was also present, in Maggie's arms, and half a dozen other children had tramped over from Postbridge, being bribed to attend the ceremony by promises of cake at Stannon afterwards. Martin had long been Minnie's hero. Everything that he did was the right and proper thing to do, and she was always wondering what he would do next.

While the two boys from Hartland walked along, the younger arranged the ceremony.

" 'Twill be 'Baptism of such as are of riper years,' " he said, "because you can talk and have got your wits. But I wish you'd light upon another name. Everybody did ought to have two names at least."

"One's enough for me."

"Then Minnie be your woman gossip, and Jack will stand for a godfather, and if Billy Meadows do come up, as he promised, he can stand for t'other."

They arrived presently, and Martin looked blank.

"Billy ban't here," he said, "and none of t'other boys are old enough"

"I don't want no godfathers," declared Tiger.

Then he pointed to the hill

"There's Mr Sleep creeping along. Shall us ask him?"

Martin, however, refused

"We won't have no growed people. 'Twould spoil all. I'll be t'other godfather myself. 'Tis quite allowable; because when Mrs. Crymes had her last child christened, parson stood—didn't he, Maggie?"

"Yes, he did, Martin."

Martin donned his night-shirt and directed the congregation. None had brought prayer-books save himself

The rite proceeded laboriously with some interruptions. Once a flock of feeding geese came hissing near the barrow and made some small children cry; once Sammy Crymes flung a stone at a rabbit that suddenly popped up on the outskirts of the ceremony. Martin shortened the service a good deal and began at the address to the 'Well-beloved.' He then put the question

"*'Dost thou renounce the devil and all his works, the vain pomp and glory of the world, with all covetous instincts of the same and the carnal desires of the flesh, so that thou wilt not follow, nor be led by them?'*"

"Sure and sure and double sure!" answered Tiger heartily

Martin was mildly annoyed.

"Hush!" he said. "I made you rehearse it all the way here You know that's wrong."

"Sorry," answered Tiger. "I forgot. Let's see—I know—'*I renounce them all.*'"

Anon Martin whispered to Minnie, as he had seen clergymen whisper at baptisms, and heard from her the name.

"'Tiger, *I baptize thee in the Name of the Father, and of the Son and of the Holy Ghost. Amen.*'"

The boy dipped his hand in the meat-tin and drew the symbol of his faith on Tiger's brow All was ordered with the utmost gravity and seriousness, and the earnestness of Martin acted visibly upon the other children and kept them attentive. Even Tiger himself was impressed, and declared afterwards that he felt something quite out of the common had happened to him.

"'Tis cruel solemn," he told Martin afterwards, "and I hope to goodness as it won't take the fierceness out of me."

Presently all the children knelt and said the Lord's Prayer. Even the least joined in this, and the adjacent geese contributed a triumphant and simultaneous cackling, as though they too were conscious of the thing that had been done

Martin read the final admonition, and then, at Tiger's wish, the ceremony concluded with a hymn. The words were familiar, and Minnie, Maggie, and Jacky sang them, while Tiger played the tune on his Jew's harp Martin, however, preserving his priestly part to the end, knelt down and shut his eyes. From first to last his actions, attitude, and manner showed closest attention to his model: the village clergyman. He won immense, quiet pleasure from the ceremony. It was not a parody, but rather the best imitation possible with this material.

"A proper bit of fun, that!" said Tiger when all was over. "Lord! How you can be that solemn-like, Martin! I lay you was itching to take up a collection, wasn't you?"

"Now let's have a game of follow-my-leader—shall us?" suggested Sammy Crymes. "You promised us you'd play, Maggie, if I was good and sat it out."

The children scattered, drifted to the valley, and presently all arrived at Stannon, where milk and cake awaited them.

CHAPTER V

On a winter day Peter Culme called at the shop beside the river and met Gregory Twigg there. The innkeeper was talking to Miss Hext, and their conversation related to the master of Hartland.

" 'Tis with all men as it is with him," said Barbara, "but much more with him than most men. You be all more childish than us women. You never quite throw it out of you, like we do. It hangs about you to old age in your love for sporting and revels. We pretend to care for these things a bit—to pleasure you—but we don't really. We'd sooner be home. We are more serious-minded than men."

"Ah! I'd like to see the woman that's more serious-minded than me," said Mr Twigg.

"Look at the 'Warren House' and you will," answered Barbara. "As to Philip Ouldsbroom," she continued, "there's a man who be younger than his own son. He comes in this shop to buy him some childish thing and then plays with it himself, because the child won't. And next minute he curses and stamps his foot on the toy. I've seen him do it."

" 'Tis all along of his vain opinions," declared Twigg. " 'Opinions,' I call them; but you can't say his mind is rooted in anything. A feather in a gale of wind is that man; and if it hadn't been for his wife, he'd have been blown to perdition long since. It must come to that. 'Tis only a question of the Lord's patience."

"Still preaching!" said Peter Culme "Nature will out with you as with all, I suppose; but don't you know

151

your company better than to tell this here in Miss Hext's shop?"

"Sow enough seed and some will grow," answered the publican calmly "I don't despair of anybody, for I've known my gift of words win people terrible fixed in their errors. As for Ouldsbroom——"

He stopped, for Philip entered, and Tiger with him The farmer was excited and brought news

"Have 'e heard this gashly come-along-of-it to Shaugh Prior?" he asked. "Old Baskerville's only son, the bell-ringer, have strung himself up in the belfry!"

"All flesh is grass," said Mr. Twigg.

"So's sugar and bread; but you don't roll your eyes over them," answered Miss Hext "'Tis for that girl that flung him over—Mrs. Lintern's daughter, poor young man!"

"His opinions were parlous," declared Twigg. "'Twas well known that he held doubtful ideas and cared more for ringing tenor bell than the glory of Him he rang it for. Mark Baskerville was an atheist, and be lost for it, I'm afraid, under chapter and verse of the Book. Bible's clear enough, though 'tis the Church of England fashion nowadays to pretend plain English ban't plain English. If you want naked Bible, you must come to us "

"He was a very good young fellow and never hurt a fly in his life," said Ouldsbroom "Everybody liked him; but you, out of your narrow, frost-bitten heart, can damn him off-hand."

"Not me, neighbour. Damnation be God's business, not man's. 'Tis the case of a young fellow strong in works but weak in faith "

"It takes all sorts of tidy folk to make your hell, no doubt," said the farmer scornfully.

"Many men, many manners, and mostly evil," replied Gregory: "but there's only one sort in heaven, rest sure, Philip Ouldsbroom."

"And that's your sort I suppose, sir?" asked the debonair Tiger respectfully

Mr. Twigg regarded him with commiseration

"I'm happy to believe so, my poor boy," he answered

"You run out," said Philip. "Us don't want you here listening to this twaddle You can get down to the river and play till I call 'e."

Tiger departed, and Mr. Twigg went out after him.

"How about the testimonial?" asked Culme.

"There again," answered Ouldsbroom, growing calm. "Ban't my fault, for I've done all I can and still will do; but the people ban't tumbling over one another to start it, and that's a fact; and as for bailiff, he don't intend to do a thing. I put it to him, and he said he'd so soon start a testimonial for his turkey-cock as for Twigg."

"That's what he gets by all his nonsense And I'm right glad the thing be going to fall through, for it may open his eyes to his puffed-up silliness," declared Peter.

"More like to our ingratitude—so he'll call it. However, I'll see here and there. There's no great harm in the man, apart from his pious drivel, and a good feed and a bit of music one night at the 'Ring o' Bells' would cheer life up a bit these dull days. I dare say old Medlicott, their pastor at the chapel, would lend a hand."

"He'll be wanting a send-off himself soon," foretold Miss Hext. "He's nearly done He was in here yesterday—a nice, old, kindly man, and not so full of nonsense as most of his sort. But he's nearly fought his fight We had a very sensible bit of talk about Job. He knows it by heart a'most, so we met on common ground."

"I read it more than I did," said Philip. "There's things come home to you gradual as you get older Each year shows me a bit more sense in what Job says to they lantern-jawed, owl-eyed fellows that was the worst of his plagues, in my opinion. Martin pipes it out. 'Tis funny to hear such terrible things in his little cocksparrow voice. I laughed aloud last Sunday night while he twittered out they tremendous terrors in chapter ten."

"Do he get to understand you closer?" she asked

He shook his head, looked at Culme, and signified a desire for silence. Peter, however, withdrew a moment later and then the farmer answered:

"No, no, Barbara. You know the answer to that.

He'll never understand me   His heart's too wise, I reckon—or else too small.''

"Don't think it   'Twill grow with the rest of him God makes and man shapes.   There's a lot you can do.''

"And don't I try?   Ban't I always at him?   Good powers, Barbara!   If he'd only take a bird's nest sometimes, or break down a wall, or come in your shop and steal a sugar-plum when you wasn't looking—anything—anything to earn a whipping and make me feel closer to him.   His eyes—so steady and quiet—his little, good, childish thoughts—damnation—starvation, I tell you! I comed across the very thing in your book a bit agone, and laid it up in memory.   You'll mind the words, of course.   'Can the rush grow up without mire?   Can the flag grow without water?'   And can a man's heart go on loving his child without a bit of love back?   'Twill wear out—'twill cool off.   And yet how can I say such things?   He's different from me   Perhaps he feels too and hides it for shyness—eh, Barbara?   It may be there —'twill show presently.   I've a right to think that?''

"Every right   Keep your eye on his mother, and remember the boy was made out of her   That's what fathers so oft forget.   She don't wear her heart on her sleeve; yet show me the man with a wiser wife than you've got   The child's hers so well as yours—hers more than yours even, as often falls out   But you don't quarrel with her for being different from you, so you shouldn't quarrel with him ''

"He'll come nearer belike as he sees more of life and gets more knowledge?''

"Why shouldn't he?   I've known men—the best sort too—grow younger as they grow older.''

"That's just what I could wish for him.   You'm always hopeful, my dear.   And so be I, for that matter. And never found it fail me yet.   But there's a sort of cold gets round my mind when——''

A little girl rushed into the shop and set the bell jangling.

"Please, please, mister, Tiger's falled in the river——''

"Ah!" said Philip, "Martin never falled in the river —and never will."

He hastened out to find the drenched and dwarfed Tiger just crawling like an otter out of four feet of water.

"Crool sorry," said the boy. "I was showing Billy Meadows and Tom Dury that I could jump across from thicky stone to thicky stone. They dared me, and I went for it and missed."

Billy Meadows and Tom Dury were dancing on the bank and rejoicing at Tiger's downfall.

"Nip along home and get they clothes off. We'll go in the shop another time."

"Wait!" cried Tiger. "I can't be no wetter than what I be. Let me have another d—d—dash for it, master!"

He took off his coat and waistcoat, licked his hands, assumed his fiercest frown, and jumped again. This time he just managed to hold on to the further rock with hands and toes. Then he shouted triumphantly at the other boys.

"There! And now let's see if any of you have got p—p—p—pluck for it!"

Then he took his coat and set off at a run beside Ouldsbroom.

"That'll show 'em!" he said, "and if they t—t—try they'll fall in and be drownded, because they ain't got my fierceness. When I dropped, the water fetched me off my le—le—legs, but I wouldn't go under. I fought against it. I hope to God my Je—Je—Je—Jew's harp won't get rusty."

His teeth began to chatter, and Philip took off his own coat and wrapped it round the boy.

"You'll catch it come you get home," he said.

"Missis be terrible kind most times when you'm not there," answered Tiger. "That's because I work so hard."

"She knows work when she sees it."

"I wish you was my father and her was my m—m—mother," said Tiger earnestly.

"Do you?"

Tiger considered, and trotted forward. Suddenly a great idea struck him.

"I suppose now you never happened to have a li'l boy back along and forgot un, mister? Because if you had, and the boy was lost, I might be him!"

" 'Tis a very fine idea; but I'm afraid no such thing ever happened to me."

"Well, be it as 'twill," summed up Tiger, "I lay my father weren't half such a proper good sort as what you be."

"How d'you know that much?"

"Why, 'cause he'd never have gone and left me by the river to starve, for all he knowed. But, all the same, mind you, I wouldn't have starved—I ban't that sort—too fierce for that. I'd have lived on b—b—blackberries and such like, and made friends wi' the foxes."

"Perhaps you'll come across your father yet, one of these days."

"If I do, I shan't be none too civil to the man," said Tiger. "And if he thinks to t—t—take me away from you and make me work for him, I won't go. I'll never leave you no more—never so long as I live—no more than your dog wouldn't."

"I wonder, now, how true that's like to be?" asked the man.

CHAPTER VI

FROM no obvious quality in natural things may kindred qualities with certainty be inferred. The East wind freezes a man's bosom, yet around him flings a garment of atmosphere to augment earth's loveliness; the West wind salutes him with warmth, yet strips the world stark and suffers no sorcery of air made visible to cover her. Eurus may bear a scythe, but he robes the land in vesture of mingled magic and mystery, while gentler, franker Zephyr reveals the mother-naked truth about each far horizon, each ambit, and each article of many-membered earth.

On a day in August the Moor had receded, grown dim, and taken upon itself the enchantments of the East wind. Detail departed from distance, and the waste swept ridge on ridge and hollow upon hill, in semblance of grey and silver clouds, that rolled upon the sky, so that they might not surely be separated from it. The wind, with most delicate vapour, most tender tones of pearl and azure, wrapped heath and granite in a milky lustre, robbed the sternest rock-mass of its contours, and leavened the waste with the medium of its own opalescent colour. The lesser furzes took it, and the heath; the boulder was bluer for it, and the fading splendour of the fern more dim where the brake spread upon the hills. Colours swam together at the touch of this Orient breeze, and a melting, diffused quality of mingled tints was manifested through all things.

The heat was tempered. A fret of sunny foam drifted along above the cloud-banks, and into the air beneath Hartland Tor ascended long feathers of earth-born smoke from fires in a field. They rose in fulvous columns, then bent together westerly, thinned, lost their own sulky

157

hue and took the colour of the day upon their vanishing volume

About the fires were assembled the life of Ouldsbroom's farm. All hands advanced the work of peat-burning, for Philip was 'denshiring' a croft

To 'denshire' or to 'Devonshire' land (for the folkword belongs to the county, as the operation does) is a simple process of agriculture still practised before ploughing on spongy and barren soil   The turf is pared from the surface of the ground, gathered in heaps, and reduced to ashes.   The transformed matter, rich with chemical change of fire, is then spread once more, and the earth, thus invigorated, will bear roots or even corn, before it is laid under grass again.

Martin and Tiger worked as busily here as the men, and with tools called 'tormentors' broke up the turf or dragged it to the smouldering piles

Towards evening Unity brought up a great cloam jug of hot tea, and Tiger ran for mugs and the basket of bread-and-butter that waited for him.   He had taken his place now in the life of Hartland, and Philip held him useful in many ways, while Mrs Ouldsbroom conceded that the boy earned his salt, and was satisfied for her son's sake that he should remain

After tea had been taken in a corner of the field to windward of the smoking earth, Philip dismissed the children and told them that their day's work was done. They scampered off to the river, crossed it, and climbed the opposite hill upon the way to a favourite haunt. Tiger had found the natural chamber where, eleven years earlier, Unity and Henry Birdwood were wont to meet   He had decided that a den worthy of him might here be made, and with Martin's help had dragged rocks hither, built up the entrance, and suffered to remain a passage only wide enough for himself and his companion

"Us'll go to the holt and play games," said Tiger. "I left two gert pieces of that figgy pudden there ten days agone   'Tis time 'twas ate up, I reckon."

They considered the game to be played, and the elder made a startling proposition.

"I'll pretend as I'm bosky-eyed,* like your father was Saturday night, and you can talk to me, same as missis talked to him."

But Martin declined the suggestion.

" 'Twould be a very good game if 'twasn't father and mother, but being them, us better not do it We wasn't supposed to hear nothing about that row, and if you hadn't come in the washhouse. where I was listening behind the door, you never would have knowed. 'Tis a terrible bad thing to be drunk "

"I'm sure he seldom goes like it, and he's that awful funny when his voice gets up in his head and he squints——"

"Shut up!" said Martin hotly. "I won't have you laugh about it. Drink be nought to laugh at, but a disgrace to the nation. You heard my mother say so, and that was her word—'a disgrace to the nation and a wicked sight for children ' And nothing could my father say, because, bad though he was, he knowed 'twas true "

"Every growed man takes a drop too much off and on. 'Tis the manhood in 'em," argued Tiger.

" 'Tis the devil in 'em," answered Martin; "and don't you never stand up for wickedness afore me, Tiger, because I'll quarrel with you if you do."

"I won't have no woman reigning over me when I'm a man," answered the other doggedly

"If you dare to mean my mother!" answered Martin in a rage. Then, suddenly, he broke off, hopped on one leg and uttered a cry. From his lifted foot a glittering ribbon of black and silver fell and slid fast along the way to the nearest heather He had set his foot on an adder and been bitten by it.

Tiger, not knowing what had happened, pursued the snake, struck it with his stick and broke its back.

"I've killed the gashly thing, and that's twopence from your father. Twopence he gives for every snake us can show him."

"But—but—oh, Tiger, it's stung me!" cried Martin.

* *Bosky-eyed*—Drunk.

He had sat by the way and turned down his stocking
The mark of the viper's fang already showed livid above
his ankle.

"Aw jimmery!" cried Tiger. "Come on, start going
—us must run for dear life! But don't you get feared.
'Twill be all right if 'tis taken in time."

Martin had turned very white, and stared in front of
him without making any effort to move.

"Come, come!" cried the elder "For the Lord's
sake doan't 'e sit glazing there! Us must get back to
your father this instant moment "

The wounded boy rose and hastened. Tiger took his
hand and hurried him along.

"We must trust in God," said Martin.

"Not yet—not yet," answered the other. "There's a
lot of things to do afore we come to that. They'll make
a terrible pucker about it. But trust your father to save
'e!"

Martin faltered.

"It do smart cruel," he said. "I be going fainty
like."

"Don't think of it; don't think of it. Here, I'll put
my arm round you. Now us'll get on brave. When us
crosses the river, I'll shout, and your father will hear me
and come running."

They hastened on, but Martin needed the elder's arm,
for he was growing very sick. Anon Tiger bawled aloud,
and a man heard him and told Ouldsbroom.

"They childer be shouting for you in the valley, mister," he said. "They'm frightened. Maybe there's
something amiss."

Philip was in his shirt-sleeves at a fire. He dropped a
fork and started running where the man pointed Then
he saw Tiger supporting the other, and hastened to them
as fast as he could.

They told him what had happened, whereupon he
acted promptly but vainly. He tore down Martin's
stocking and revealed a limb swollen and of darkish
colour. Then he set his lips to the bite and sucked and
sucked. Martin had a handkerchief, and his father tied

it tightly as a ligature above the wound. It was, however, far too late for such remedial measures.

"Run on," he said to Tiger "Run home and tell
missis. I'll bring the boy; then you get on the hoss and
go like a flame of fire for doctor. Ride bare-ridged, and
ride like hell. This will show what you be good for!"

Tiger departed at his best speed, and long before Philip
had carried Martin to his mother, the elder boy was riding as hard as he could go to Princetown.

The question was what amount of venom the sufferer
had received, the event alone would prove it. Philip's
efforts were too late in any case, for the poison had
travelled through the boy's system long before he sought
to suck it out.

Unity acted otherwise, stripped the child, put him
between the blankets of her own bed, and gave him some
warm brandy and water. She kept a cheerful face, assured him that he would soon be better, relieved his
anxiety and hid her own. Presently she fomented the
wound with hot water to lessen the pain and reduce the
swelling.

The tension for both adults was terrific. They hung on
Martin's fluttering eyelids and gauged his colour with
straining eyes. Now he grew paler, and their hope fainted,
now he flushed a little, and they marked the change and
looked at each other and nodded Philip wanted to
drown the boy with spirits, Unity would not let him do so.

They whispered of familiar cases, and took heart in the
recollection that none they knew had proved fatal But
the youth of Martin made them fear. Unity was the more
hopeful and far the more self-contained The man
roamed everywhere, like a mad thing, and forced himself
away and killed time for minutes together; then he
rushed back again in dreadful fear that it might be to
hear worse news. He absented himself within sight of the
entrance, and each minute that Unity did not come made
him more hopeful; but suddenly his heart cried to him
to return, and he hurried indoors She meantime kept
by the bed with her hand in Martin's He was very
silent and drowsy, but he told her the pain was less, and

11

she fancied that after an hour had passed the swelling sank a little. The child continued very collected and presently inspired her with hope.

"I thought I was going to die," he said; "but now I don't think I am. Where's father?"

"He's close. I'll tell him what you said, Martin. 'Twill do him good."

"I'm afraid he's terrible put out."

"He's all right. Don't you be talking."

She left the child for a moment and went to the door; whereupon Philip, who was tramping round and round in a narrow circuit, felt a great pang shake him to the roots of his being, and rushed to her

"Not worse—not worse, for God's sake don't say it!"

"No—no—better, I do believe. He says he ban't going to die. I do think he's going on well."

Philip came in again to see the boy.

"That's a brave, dear chap," he said, trying to grin. "Of course you'll be all right. 'Tis nothing but a sting. Us'll all forget it to-morrow. And we'll go down to Barbara's and get the best toys in the shop—by God we will!"

"Where's Tiger?" asked Martin.

"He's off to fetch Dr. Dickinson. They'll be here in a minute, I reckon. I'll just go off and see if they'm coming."

He stooped and kissed Martin and hugged him; then he went out.

Ignorant of facts, Unity and Philip pinned hope on swift arrival of the doctor. They did not know in such a case that chance, and not belated medical skill, must determine the boy's life. Danger of death was long past before the medical man arrived at Hartland.

Martin, however, was still sick, and since the day had now sunk to night, the old physician yielded to Philip's entreaty, and stopped until next morning at the farm. Brandy, hot soup, hot bricks to his feet, continued fomentations, and some good sleep, found the patient stronger in the morning; and then the medical man went to Ouldsbroom, where he stood dishevelled at his door in the first

grey of the dawn, and declared Martin beyond any cause
for fear.

"Say it again; say it again!" cried Philip "Safe—
safe, doctor!"

"Safe as a church! I'll send a tonic—in fact, I'll
bring it this evening "

The father was distrustful.

"You'm a little bit feared, else you wouldn't come
again."

"Not at all. But come I shall, to-night, on my way
back from Moreton. I'm due there to-day, and will get
the physic made up there He's a fine, strong lad, with a
good constitution and good pluck Don't you have
another care for him. He's very nearly well again."

Philip shook the doctor's hand thrice; then he stalked
away alone to the top of Hartland Tor, and flung himself down there with a full heart

The regular life of the farm began beneath him He
saw the cows saunter in a row off the Moor, and wait at
the farmyard gate for the milker. He heard the dogs,
marked Tiger at his work, and noted a fan of blue smoke
deepen above the chimney.

Then his soul went out to the man who had done all,
as he supposed; and he hurried down the hill and called
to Tiger.

"I want to make a fine gift to him—poultry and cream
and the best we've got—to doctor 'Tis only a fortnight
afore their time. You catch a couple of they geese and
kill 'em, Tiger, and tell William to get on his apron and
pluck 'em."

Tiger had not been invited to describe the adventures
of yesterday, but now he did so, and his master com-
mended him.

"Nobody alive could have done it quicker, and I'll
never forget it to your credit; I promise you that You
rode very clever indeed, and I'm terrible pleased, and so's
missis "

When Dr. Dickinson prepared to start an hour later,
he found the back of his trap laden with the best that
Ouldsbroom could gather from dairy and farm.

"My dear fellow, what's all this? I'm not going to market," laughed the old man.

"Not a word, master, 'tis nothing at all. I wish the geese was packed with golden eggs, for you've earned 'em. And you'll be back to have a look at him before night?"

"I will; and if I must take this gift, I'll take it then, on my way home. It's ridiculous nonsense, Ouldsbroom."

Somewhat abashed to exhibit his present, Philip obeyed, and withdrew much produce from the back of the trap.

Dr. Dickinson protested anew at the sight, for it represented the value of a five-pound note

"Ridiculous man! And all for nothing! It wasn't I saved him. Fifty doctors couldn't have saved him after such a long delay. 'Twas your wife you've got to thank, if anybody, under Providence."

He drove off, the hour then being half-past six Philip found himself hungry and cried out for food.

The meal proved a little unquiet, because Unity had seen what was taken out of the doctor's carriage.

"If you'd knowed all he told me, you'd have understood that the danger was passed long and long afore he came" she said. "There was no cause for all that. He'll send in his bill just the same."

But her husband laughed.

"Let it go, and think of the boy. I'd got to make an offering of some sort to somebody when I heard Martin was all right. 'Twas bursting out of me to do it. 'Tis all to the good anyway; and what's a few birds and eggs and a bit of butter against Martin? And don't think I'm forgetting you. 'Tis all thanks to your wonderful cleverness, Unity, that he's alive this minute, no doubt; and if I don't do something to mark it for you, call me daft And Tiger too. He done his best "

She knew it idle to argue with him at this moment. The long-drawn strain was relaxed, and each felt the rebound according to their natures He, after a few deep and silent moments, fled to drown himself in praise of others, and in giving right and left, she looked into her own soul and was chiefly concerned with wonder at the wealth of the love that was harboured there. She had surprised herself during these hours. She was not aware that such deep places in her heart existed, or that, existing, they were full of Martin. She yearned still to be holding him in her arms, to feel her great breast bending—the pillow under his head. She could not be out of his presence through that day. Each mouthful that he took was food to her; each drop that he drank was drink to her; and when he laughed again, it seemed that the goal of her struggle was reached. Then, indeed—the first time for many a long year—she wept and hid herself from him.

During a week Martin slept with his mother, and Philip made a bed on the floor. Then Dr. Dickinson pronounced the boy well again. A boil, however, gathered on the snake-bite and had to be poulticed. Martin went lame for a while, but each day lessened the trouble, and he was soon able to frequent his favourite haunts. He showed the effects of the poison in want of energy and general malaise; but that also lifted before three weeks were past, and nothing remained save memory of his great experience and consequent fame. For some days he was a hero among his cousins and his friends.

CHAPTER VII

PHILIP's business took him from home for a week after Martin's illness, but it was understood that he should receive a frequent letter to tell of the boy's progress He had been away three days, and on the morning of the fourth, Martin, at Unity's suggestion, was writing to Ouldsbroom himself. The first letter that he had ever written caused the child great interest He had made two false starts and spoilt a third sheet with a blot, but all went well with the next attempt, and there came a visitor just in time to admire it before it was put into an envelope and sealed up.

Henry Birdwood called He was not aware that Philip had left home, and arrived with news of certain ponies that were to be sold.

"Two of 'em I know he'll gladly buy—and give money for," said the shepherd. "Martin here can put it in his letter, and tell him that Mr. Coomber at Dousland is open to a price for that mare and foal he fancies."

Unity beckoned Birdwood behind her child's back. She signalled and shook her head.

" 'Twill be time to name it to father when he comes home," she said "Now you can run along out, Martin, and play in the byre, for 'tis pouring wet I'll send the letter with mine."

The child went out, and she turned to Henry.

"Don't say nothing more about they ponies. I'm sick and tired o' ponies. They'm eating up too much of our money and bringing too little back. 'Tis all very well in a small way; but 'tis like chicken and bees and other things: if you go into 'em in a large way you lose by it."

"He's got plenty to spare."

"Has he? First I've heard of it then. You show me the man who's got plenty to spare and I'll show you a fool. Anyway, 'tisn't so with us Every penny's out to interest that I could get from him, and ready money's tight. And with a man like my man, the tighter the better. Things ain't quite so prosperous of late on the Moor, as you know. And I won't have no more ponies anyway. He's away now about some stock down in the in-country, Plympton way, and he's promised me faithful not to go a penny too far. You'd marvel if you heard his hopefulness still, and him up home fifty years old "

"I suppose he was properly terrified over the child?"

"He was. I never want to go through nothing like that again."

"Strange—so was I. Couldn't sleep for thinking of him. And you too, of course?"

"Yes," she said. "But the mark it's left on me be inside, not out. He goes off to boarding-school next spring To the grammar-school at Bovey. 'Twill be a pinch, but we're of a mind."

"What'll he do, I wonder?"

" 'Tis too soon to guess; but he's fond enough of farming, and my husband's will is that he follows on at Hartland Yet I've a fancy—hid close enough—that come he learns far above our learning, and sees the higher sort of life, and gets sense, he'll seek out something different and grow tired of our rough ways."

"You'd be glad if he did?"

"Perhaps so. Can't say that I want to end my days in this moil. How be you? Better?"

"I'm all right," he said "Tis only rheumatics. They'll lift again."

"You'm so thin as a herring. Why don't you eat more?"

He shrugged his shoulders.

"That boy's built on the same pattern, I fancy."

"No, no," she answered hurriedly. "He's stuggy—same as me. He's thin now along of his illness. He'll soon fatten again."

"Don't you believe it. He may be like you in his nature, and I hope 'twill prove so, but he's got my lean carcass and lank hair."

She showed annoyance.

"Don't be telling that stuff You might so soon say t'other child—that foundling—was like my husband."

"So he is—in a general way. You watch. Tiger will be more to Philip presently than Martin is, because he's built on Phil's own pattern. And I'm glad of it, for he'll be a comfort if he stops."

"How you do delight to prick me!" she cried

"As to that, 'tisn't so. But I wish to God you'd——"

The door opened suddenly and Tiger came in with a message from the farm

Unity was glad of the interruption, and remained no longer with Birdwood.

"Don't name the ponies, there's a good man," she said. "He will be back Monday, and then we shall count to see you And do, for goodness' sake, look to your clothes a bit more We're coming to the wet time now, and you'll go and be sick if you don't take better heed."

He went his way, but left her unquiet, and she slept ill that night

Birdwood was grown indifferent to his own existence, and the only real interests in his life centred about Hartland He felt a dreary discomfort in the presence of Ouldsbroom and knew that this long, living he was very hard upon his old enemy. Yet, to tell the truth now had meant issues so far-reaching that he shrank from it. His life was a hollow and cheerless one. He did not cleave to life In some moods he felt impelled to lay all bare before Ouldsbroom; then he considered Unity and the future of his child. He asked himself whether it was for his own peace or for Philip's that he felt prompted to speak; and he assured himself that mean personal motives alone urged him. All ways pointed to silence, and so he kept it But Unity began to fear whether he would persist in silence She knew that he had no personal stake in life, no personal ambition of future prosperity to make him a coward. He grew more dangerous.

In the dark that night she reflected on his indifferent health, and considered how much easier her life would be if Birdwood and his gloom were out of it. She felt him like an ever-present cloud, from which, struggle forward as she might, there was no emergence.

Ouldsbroom returned presently, and a carrier set him and his carpet bag down beside the river at Postbridge. He took farewell of the driver, invited the man to Hartland when time and chance allowed it, and then entered the post office before going home.

He had something to give Barbara, and something to show her. The gift was a bottle of old brandy from Plymouth.

"Physic," he said "You're not so young as you was, my old dear, and I know that a thimble of this stuff of a night will help you to sleep comfortable."

"Oh, Phil—was there ever one like you, you silly man? But thank you. I'll keep it against a rainy day."

" 'Tis good ancient drink, mind, else I wouldn't have fetched it. And read this here—a letter from my son that he wrote in ink. First ever he wrote, bless him! And where shall you find a child of his age could do better?"

Barbara put on her glasses and read the little letter.

"My dear father,—
"I hope you are well. I am quite well. Mother is quite well. Tiger found the snake that stung me where he killed it. He has taken off the skin and tried to stuff it with moss for a surprise for you. It looks rather humpy and smells horrid. But I hope you will say you like it, because he has taken a great deal of trubble with it.
"Hoping that this reaches you as it leaves me at present,
"I am your loving son,
*"*MARTIN OULDSBROOM *"*

"There! What d'you think of that?" asked Philip.

" 'Tis a nice little letter as you could wish," said Barbara. He folded it up and put it in his pocket-book.

"I shall keep that letter so long as I live," he declared. "And look here, Barbara; don't you remember what

I've said about the boy now and again. 'Twas all stuff and nonsense, spoken out of a fool's mouth. Good God! shall I be jealous of my own flesh and blood? Because he's a clever child and be going to have a big brain, shall I fret and fume like a zany and wish he was more—more like my own silly self? No, no. I'm sorry. I lay he'll welcome me home now like the warm sun—I lay he will. I've bought him a book down to Plymouth with coloured pictures—lions and missionaries and niggers—a good thought, eh?"

"A very good thought indeed. I'm glad to know it, because it shows that you begin to feel he's not just the same as every-day children."

"That's it. Now I haven't got no more use for such a book than a fox in a bush—and never had; but I know 'twill be better than a box of soldiers or the like to him."

" 'Twas very clever of you indeed."

"Not that I can take all the credit. Me and my wife have done a lot of talking on the subject of the boy since his illness, you may be sure, and she let a bit of light into me. She understands him better than I do—what don't she understand, for that matter? A serious mind happens in some children. Not often, thank God, but you'll see it off and on; and chance has just thrown such a mind into my boy, though you'd never have looked to see it in any child of mine. But there 'tis; and of course, as a man of my age, I'm serious-minded too, and must take things as they are, not fret because they ban't as I'd have 'em."

"Never heard such sense," said the postmistress. "Where have you been to pick up such wisdom?"

"Alone," he answered. "All alone with my thoughts. First night away I got along with a lot of fellows to Plympton Fair and took a drop too much. But after that I minded my business and kept apart and sober as a judge. And of a night I thought it all out and saw where I was mistaken. As luck would have it, there was a Bible in the bedroom where I lodged. And I had a good dip into your book. And I will say for Job that you never come empty-handed from the man. There's always something to catch upon. 'Who can bring a clean thing out of an unclean? Not one.' There's truth! And, knowing that, haven't I the right and the reason to be proud of getting Martin? Such as him couldn't have sprung from nothing bad. And so I can rate myself higher for being the father of him—eh, Barbara?''

"Surely; and I hope he'll be a fine fellow and the comfort of your age yet.''

"I look for it from him. I'm always the more trustful when I go away from home for a day or two. 'Tis worth it for the thoughts and for the feeling of the welcome that grows the warmer for tarrying.''

"You're a lucky man, and doubly lucky to know yourself lucky. That's your wisdom, and though once I never did think you'd grow up, I do believe you're beginning to do it. You'll be a man before your son yet!''

He laughed, and a spaniel came out from behind the counter and crept on his belly with wagging tail.

"Not a patch on your old 'Sarah,' '' said the farmer; "but a good enough dog.''

" 'Sarah's' been dead seven year to-morrow. I mind the date very well. How the years be racing, Philip! I shan't hold on much longer. I'm getting terrible shaky.''

"Don't you say that. I won't have it. I won't have you go, Barbara. Don't you dare to think of such a thing!''

"The time's coming. And when I drop, 'tis you will have to see me into earth presently. I don't want no parsons and no prayer-books.''

"I won't have it,'' he repeated. "And I won't have you talk about it. Stuff and nonsense! Me and you are the sort that go over fourscore.''

There was a silence, and then Ouldsbroom began to talk of his wife again. He praised her, and concluded with these words:

"And I learn more from Unity than what she says to me. 'Tis her life that's the lesson. But we can't have everything, and at fifty we begin to know it, if not before. She's like the boy in some ways: they ban't quite able to understand me, you know, though of course I understand them.''

" 'Tis the boy in you beats 'em, no doubt,'' said Miss Hext. ''The boy in man beats most women. Your son will never run after hares or fret till salmon fishing begins again. You musn't expect it. And now get along back to 'em. And thank you dearly for this thought of me.''

She looked into his face and marked the slight changes. He was wrinkled about the eyes more than of old, and his cheeks were a little heavier and looser. He wore whiskers that met on his throat, but clean-shaved his lips and chin. His hair was crisp and curly as ever, but shot with grey, his blue eyes were bright and the home of laughter still.

She bade him 'good-bye,' and watched him fling his carpet bag on to the crook of his stick and go up the valley. " 'Twill all blow down the wind when the fret and cark begin again,'' she said to herself. " 'Tis so easy to get away from everybody and be wise—all alone. The hard thing is to be wise with life and them you love jostling your elbow.''

Two small figures, long on the lookout for the farmer, marked him far off, and now came hastening down the hill from Hartland. Tiger outstripped Martin by many yards, yet some secret fineness in the boy stopped him before he reached Philip. He drew up while yet a long way from Ouldsbroom, and let the other go first.

CHAPTER VIII

THE children were making holiday, and the strength of Hartland and Stannon, with reinforcements from the village, had gone aloft to the high Moor. The business of the day was gathering whortleberries; the pleasure of the day consisted in a picnic—all alone, without company of, or interference from, any grown-up people

Maggie, Minnie, and Martin controlled the party, and the boys carried the food, while to Maggie's lot fell a rather heavier burden in shape of her small sister, Jane. A dozen children in all set out, and certain homes were left strangely silent and peaceful.

Now the party was eating and drinking high on the wind-swept side of Siddaford Tor. Much bread-and-cheese. cake, and three big bottles of milk made the meal; then Maggie cried out at the poor store of berries as yet collected, and called upon all to set to work with more energy.

They scattered presently, and the boys roamed far and near, while the girls, with greater method, picked together, and Minnie gathered more than all, though she did not stray fifty yards from her little sister, who lay asleep in the remains of the picnic. Martin worked industriously, but Tiger did not. His master had hinted to him to keep near Martin and look out for snakes, so he regarded himself as on a sort of special duty and prowled about near the younger boy. They talked together sometimes and noticed the familiar things about them; they called the girls to see the pad-marks of a fox in a mire; they collected odd treasures to be taken home Martin got a quartz crystal and a piece of white bog heather.

173

He put the flower in his cap for his mother. The boy Jacky secured hairy caterpillars and prisoned them in a match-box. The boys played and the girls worked.

Then came the first cloud, and Samuel, a child of unsocial spirit, accused Martin of trespassing upon a patch of fruit that he had marked for himself. Martin denied it; they fought, and Samuel fell under a fierce buffet. Then, after the manner of his kind, he retreated in tears to a neighbouring knoll. From here he hurled bad words and stones. One stone hit another child, and she shrieked. Then Tiger leapt forward, chased Samuel, caught him and pummelled him.

The incident was only closed when the time came for finishing the food. Samuel then rejoined the company and expressed regret at what he had done. After his share of cake and milk, however, he did evil once again, upset two baskets of whortleberries, and then finally fled to return no more. Tiger and Martin desired to give chase, but Maggie stopped them.

"Let him go," she said. "He's cranky to-day. I knowed he'd be wicked when we started, because mother made him carry a basket."

The day waned, and, under a sky of windy blue that lightened to a blaze above the Moor edge, the children presently set out to return home.

A strange sunset arrested the attention of the elders. From behind a long, squat cliff of cloud the sun shot strong rays upward and downward. They vanished in the upper blue, save where one broad mass of lofty vapour caught fire from them; and below, they burnt away the horizons of the earth in a flaming riot of splendour. The light fell upon many peaks and ridges and clusters of far-off tors, flung to the edges of the billowy land; while the solitary cloud from behind which all this glory escaped seemed scarcely to move, but stretched inert and sluggish from south to north. It had a snout and tail like a saurian, and crouched gigantic above the waste. Its back glowed with a rose-coloured crest.

The children, bathed in ruddy light, lifted their eyes to the sky as they tramped along. Their baskets were full of blue-black, lustrous colour, and their fingers and faces were smeared with purple stains. The duns and drabs of their clothes woke to radiance in the sunset. Life flashed and sparkled in their eyes: they moved, like fairy things, against the ragged, red gold of the heath and stones that made the way all bright.

Tiger it was who marked the shape of the giant cloud and called attention to it.

"If her ban't like a gert, monstrous dragon—eh?" he asked.

"So he is then—with head and tail and all," declared Maggie.

The sun began to sink from the hinder parts of the monster, and Martin spoke.

"There! And now the creature have laid a golden egg!" he said.

The surprise of the simile flung them all into a fit of laughter.

"Well done, you!" cried Tiger. "The cleverness!"

"Nobody but you would ever have thought of that, Martin," declared Minnie.

They rivalled each other in making likenesses for the cloud, and watched it until the sun passed behind the hills.

Then a man overtook them from the Moor, and Henry Birdwood, on his pony, hoped that they had done well with the berries. They showed him their laden baskets, and he applauded.

"Where might you be going, Mr. Birdwood?" asked Martin.

"To Princetown," he answered. "I've got a cough that keeps me awake o' nights, and won't stop. I'm tired of barking, so I'm going up to doctor for a bottle of physic."

"Mother would give you so good a thing as doctor, I'm sure," said Minnie. " 'Tis stuff she got a recipe for from my grandmother long ago, and she got it from a wise woman. 'Tis very nice, too, because there's honey and lemon in it."

"So 'tis then," added Martin, "for I had some last

winter, and I was terrible sorry when my cough went and I couldn't have no more"

"I lay 'tis very good," said the shepherd; "but my cough do come from down below somewhere in the tubes. I doubt if lemon and honey would reach it"

Minnie, however, felt hopeful that her mother's medicament might meet the case

"I'll bring you some when I can be spared to come up over," she promised

The man thanked her and spoke little. He was ill and weary of his days. His new work proved arduous, and, though he found himself likely to make money during the following year, the fact had no spice in it for him His needs were frugal, and for luxuries he cared nothing

Henry was about to bid the children 'good-night' and trot forward, when Tiger marked the approach of figures in the valley of Dart beneath them. Young eyes trained in these wide spaces are long-sighted, and the identity of the approaching people was not for a moment in doubt

"'Tis mother and father!" said Martin

It happened that Philip, the day's work done, found himself heartily tired of a silence and peace that had hung like a cloud on Hartland since the morning. So he went to his wife and asked her to come with him and meet the children as they returned homeward.

She consented, and now the parties fell together, and there was great clatter of tongues and showing of trophies. Ouldsbroom picked up Jane Crymes from Maggie's arms and bore the little thing along; beside him marched Tiger and Minnie, while the others came behind Presently the children from Stannon and Postbridge went their way and the company broke up. Then Philip proceeded to Hartland with Martin and Tiger, while Unity fell behind and walked beside Birdwood's pony.

The boys prattled of their day and the elder lad explained how sharp an eye he had kept for serpents.

"I was ready, I warn 'e, mister! But not one did I see. I doubt there's many left now."

"Fewer the better," declared Philip; and then, as

the way was still long, they asked him for some of his pixy stories. For these he was famed among the children, and they never wearied of the old familiar tales.

"Tell us about the good old woman and the tulips," suggested Martin; but the man felt not in humour for story-telling.

"I'll list to you now," he said, "and tell stories another time. The pixies be all gone from us nowadays, and won't never come back neither. That there ding-dong * at the church have frighted 'em away for good and all."

"Then they was very bad pixies," declared Martin, "and I'm very glad they've gone."

The farmer laughed.

"When you get a bit older, you'll see there's others beside pixies can't abide the bells," he said. "You must larn to be large-minded Martin."

"If your father don't go to church, that shows 'tis proper not to go," asserted Tiger stoutly.

A magpie got up in front of them and reminded the boy of something he had already thought upon.

"Can't say why 'tis, but they pies do always put me in mind of parson in his holy robes," he said.

"How so?" asked Philip, and Martin showed uneasiness.

"Why," continued Tiger, "'tis the way his reverence perketh and fluttereth in his black and white. And another thing: he holds his head like the bird on a bough, looking down crafty to see what's doing. 'Tis just so he counts the heads while his tongue be at the sermon verse."

"You oughtn't to say such things," answered Martin hotly; "and you wouldn't say 'em if mother could hear you, for she'd box your ears for it!"

They began to quarrel. Both were weary and both unconsciously suffered in the anticlimax of a good day, long looked forward to, but now over and gone. The farmer silenced their shrill arguments.

"No more holidays," he said. "If you can't abide friendly except on work-days, then we'll have nought

* *Ding-dong*—Bell.

else. Whatever be you thinking about, Martin, to say such cranky things?"

Then Ouldsbroom preached his simple gospel to them.

"You'll look precious silly, the pair of you, if I double your work and stop your play. But I'd be very sorry to do that, because work's only the half of life, and not the best half neither. I only work to make the play taste better; and so we all should. Play's nought without work, remember. But if the play be going to set you two by the ears, I'll have no more on it. You'm tired. Give me your berries."

He took both their baskets and, after a moment's silence, Martin made amends.

"Sorry I was vexed," he said. "I'm terrible leg-weary."

"And I'm sorry too, and 'twas more shame to me than you; because I ban't weary and never was knowed to be weary in my life," declared Tiger.

Behind them Mrs. Ouldsbroom walked, and listened to Birdwood. He told how Mr. Sleep had gone to the workhouse.

"Ned explained it all to me in his slow way. Time was never no more to him than to a toad under a stone. 'You see, Henry Birdwood,' he said, 'I'm not one who leaps before he looks. I'm pretty well known, I believe, to be cautious, and in a thing like this I wouldn't be rash. But there 'tis; I'm growing crookeder and crookeder with rheumatics, and 'tis just all I can do w'out cracking my bones to crawl up on my horse. So 'tis time to stop; and since I wasn't able to save, and haven't got no friends, I must come down on the parish. Such usefulness as lies in me be at their service.' And he's gone. And the new chap, Jonathan French, is hard as nails and would make two of me. I promised Ned to see him now and again when 'twas possible. I told him that very like I'd be after him afore long."

"More like you'll go into your grave," said Unity. "You'm coughing cruel and ought to come away from that God-forsaken hole you live in."

He, however, still harped on his old colleague.

"The only thing that troubled Sleep was a fear they'd make him go to church instead of chapel. He had a thought that all English workhouses was Church of England. But Gregory Twigg explained to him that it weren't so Greg promised him a Wesleyan service, though he was much afraid he'd miss the full flavour of us Little Baptists."

"Better he went to church and got larger ideas."

The man laughed without mirth.

"Don't you talk that stuff to me. Keep it for them who are in the dark. Church or chapel's all one to us, I reckon; and if you said your church tasted better than my chapel, I wouldn't believe it We shall live and die in a dirty lie, and that's all to be said about us."

She flushed deeply Until very recent years some cement of the past had held them together, though from the birth of the child her attitude had changed in all particulars of their past intimacy, but now the ghost of friendship was crumbled away She cared no more for him, and she knew that he despised her only less than he despised himself

Birdwood saw her colour come, but regretted not that she was angered. He brooded sometimes on the past, and had long ago reached the conclusion that it was she rather than her husband who had ruined his life

"A lesson to us, that man," he said—"him yonder, carrying my child's basket. I feel a beastly knave when he's by. D'you know 'twas him, and not Twigg, got me the billet I'm holding now? Twigg, in his grand way, took credit; but I was up at Princetown with the bailiff last week, taking over some papers, and I heard then that but for Philip, another chap than me would have had the job And never a word to me. I'll wager he's forgot that he did it. He'd want a far longer memory than he has got, to call home all the great, big, kindly things he does for us small, mean-hearted people. I never knowed his like."

"Better he thought more of what's due to his home," she said "I'd much wish to know where he'd be standing but for me 'Tis my thrift and pinching and wake-

ful night and grey hairs coming, that give him the
chance to be so mighty generous. But nobody ever
thanks me for aught. He'd be after Ned Sleep in a
year if I wasn't here. Yet everything must be just so,
and the boy's going to boarding-school in six months."

"You'll see to that."

"I shall do If there's one thing I'll screw and scrimp
for, and take no denial for, 'tis that He can spend on
whims and fancies; I'll spend on my boy's future. Out
of this he shall go, to get larger ideas and proper education, whatever happens."

"Philip thinks the same?"

"Yes, he's set on it now. Though 'twill fret him to
have Martin out of his sight."

"Not more than it frets him to have him in his sight."

"That's all changing, I hope. They be more and more
understanding and friendly since the snake bit Martin."

"And t'other boy?"

"He's very well. He's worth his keep, anyway, and
Martin be fond of him. My husband has taken to the
child something tremendous. He'd soon ruin him if I
wasn't here. Wanted to make him taste beer last night."

"Beer will be Ouldsbroom's downfall yet, if you're
not careful."

She did not answer, and then he surprised her.

"I'm beginning to think as I get old—for I'm getting
old terrible quick—I'm beginning to think, Unity, that
I'd be another man if I told your husband the truth
about that child and cut short his wild-goose chase."

You'll say that once too often to me," she answered,
showing her teeth through her lips.

"Use your wits and see it as I do," he replied. "If
the boy had chanced to be nearer to him 'twouldn't have
mattered so much. If he'd been like that nipper you
call 'Tiger'—a free-handed, hearty, common sort of
a lump of a boy—'twouldn't have mattered at all; but
see the trick fate's played us. The boy ban't even so
rough-and-ready as I am. He's cruel nice, and fond
of books and prayers and going to church. He's the
spit of what my father must have been when he was

young—good by nature 'Twould be easier for him to— but why harp about it? You know well enough how 'tis Haven't you traced him out to the very heart? And what I say is that the older he grows the farther he'll drift away from the man who thinks him his son There'll be such trouble bred of this that I'm doubtful if I can live and see it. I care a lot more about Philip than about the boy The boy's all right. He's got religion and your common sense He'll be a burning and a shining light, whatever happens. 'Twould puzzle him to go wrong more than it puzzles your husband sometimes to go right.''

''And what about me? Don't I count at all?''

''No,'' he answered, ''not in my mind. You've always looked damned sharp after yourself, and always will do I'm not troubling about you.''

She gasped with indignation.

''Go on,'' she said. ''Let me hear what else ''

''That's all—I only warn you You've thought of it too. I wonder what you'd do?''

He laughed sardonically, and his laugh turned into coughing.

'' 'Do?' '' she answered. ''Deny it: that's what I'd do Would he believe you afore me? He'd say you was mad—that's all And so you would be.''

''How if I pointed to the boy and axed where he got his eyes from, and his thin flank, and his——? What if I *made* him see? D'you know what he'd do? He'd strangle you to begin with.''

He looked down at her, and saw things that he had never seen before.

''And you'd like to strangle me, if you could— wouldn't you?'' he asked.

She kept her temper and smoothed her face.

''You've changed from what you were, Henry. What have I done to make you want to ruin me?''

'' 'Tis what you haven't done belike. You have everything your own way; and that makes a weak man like me a bit jealous now and again. 'Tis your iron-strong will. And yet——''

She began to feel the vital need for winning this man away from his own thoughts.

"I'll see more of you, and gladly," she said. "There's plenty of reason why I should, for that matter. You're ill—coughing from down deep by the sound. I'll come over on Thursday afternoon and fetch you some good stuff for your throat. See that your man be out and we'll have a long talk."

He concealed his amusement at her tactics, and welcomed them.

"I shall be very glad."

The boys and Philip had stopped, and were waiting for them at Hartland gate.

"Here's this poor man coughing his soul up," said Unity. "I've told him I'll get across Thursday with a pint of herby tea."

"So you shall, then," said Ouldsbroom. "And take something better too. If you wern't a fool, Henry, you'd have got a woman of your own to mess over you years ago. 'Tis madness thinking to live all your life without one."

Birdwood laughed.

"Wait till I see what it means to be Moor-man of the Quarter. And as for physic, I'm going up to Princetown now to ax doctor."

"And come in and take your supper with us on the way home."

"Does your missis second that?" asked the shepherd, and Unity assured him that he would be welcome.

He kept the appointment therefore; and when he returned with a bottle of medicine and some strong advice upon the need for care, he found Philip reading to his wife, while a cold supper waited on the table.

" 'Tis the twenty-eighth of Job," explained Ouldsbroom. "I always read it of an evening when I'm in a good temper, Henry. There's some brave things in it, and bits as you might say nobody could have set down without they knowed Dartymoor! 'Tis the ways of wisdom."

"I know," answered Birdwood "But what's all that

to you? 'The fear of the Lord is wisdom.' What fear
of the Lord was ever known in you?''

"But 'to depart from evil is understanding'—that's
the last word of the chapter,'' said Unity. "We know
it by heart very near; don't we, Philip?''

She looked without flinching into the younger man's
face as she spoke.

CHAPTER IX

PHILIP and his wife were walking home again after the wedding of Millicent Mary Twigg. The ceremony and subsequent feasting was marred for Ouldsbroom by the too unctuous propriety of the company and the Little Baptist sentiments of the toast-givers. He waited only to see the young pair drive off, then left the inn and played with Ethel and Alfred Twigg, Minnie and Jacky Crymes, and certain other children, including Martin, who had come to the 'Warren House' with their parents.

Unity joined him presently, and they started homeward through a crystal-clear gloaming, with frost already at work on the heights.

"Rabbit that man!" said Philip. "Can't even be jolly at a time like this. And that fiddle-faced fool who proposed the health of the bride. Talk about turning water into wine, like the Saviour did! 'Twas enough to turn wine into water to hear him drivelling about the solemn duties of the marriage state. Hadn't they heard enough of that stuff when they was being married?"

"Tom Hurley he's called—a very earnest young man, studying for the ministry, I believe."

"Is he? Well, if that's his idea of the right thing at a wedding, I should very much like to hear him at a funeral. I was itching to take him by the collar and ram him down into his seat, and so was the bridegroom."

"A pity Henry Birdwood couldn't be there."

"So 'twas then. I must get over to see him again at the end of the week. Doctor stopped five minutes at Hartland on the way back yesterday, and said he reckoned he was a thought worse."

Unity pursued her own reflections. Then Philip returned to the wedding and told the boy, who walked beside them, to run on ahead.

"Did you mark how Martin listened to their caterwauling?"

"He's always serious-minded."

"Worse luck. But what's going to come to a child that can't laugh at thirteen? Was there ever such a good boy afore, I wonder? Not many, I hope."

"He's got his faults," said Unity.

"You say that! I haven't seen them. But I should be very glad to hear about 'em."

"No, you wouldn't," she answered. "Because they ban't your own. They're mine. I see into him. If he was—well, what you are here and there—you'd say they weren't faults but virtues. But my faults ban't virtues in your eyes."

He whistled.

"I'm hearing things!" he said. "And what be your faults, Unity? 'Tis because the boy's your boy that I've taken it all so quiet, I assure you. When I've wanted him to be a bit more open-hearted and like t'other child, Tiger—faulty and full of surprises, so that you love the toad while you cuff his li'l, hard, round head—I've said to myself, 'Don't forget he's the son of his mother.' *Your* faults, my brave dear; and what be they? 'Tis strange as I've missed 'em."

"I've got plenty, Phil. And 'tis just because they look so small in your eyes that I've been able to hide 'em, perhaps."

"Get along with you!" he said.

"The boy's too fond of money, for one thing," she declared suddenly. "And that's me in him, not you anyway."

Philip was much intersted.

"Now I wonder if that be true? If 'tis, I'm sorry, for I'd sooner he was fond of pretty near anything else. Perhaps time will cure it when he gets old enough to be fond of better things—beer, or girls, or what not."

"Time don't cure that fondness."

"I doubt you'm wrong "

"I'm right, but I don't blame him. I'm fond of money too."

"Who isn't in reason? So be I. No harm in the child saving if the man spends."

"That's just what don't happen. If the child saves, the man stints. If the child's mean, the man's a miser."

"How you do run on! Be you a miser?"

She laughed at that.

"Small chance for your wife to be one. Maybe—if I'd married Birdwood——"

"Why, of course," he interrupted her. "You'd have had to save for him and been a poor woman all your life. But with me 'tis different."

"I've had to save for you harder than ever I should have had to for him," answered Unity. "I've had to stand between you and your capital like a wall these years and years. All your money would be on four legs, scampering away to other people long ago, but for me "

He was thinking about Martin, and full of a plot. He told Unity nothing, and kept his own counsel until the next day.

Then Martin rushed to his mother, white and frightened, with tragic news

"My money-box have been stolen!" he cried. "Tiger have just given me a penny for that old knife I found on the Moor, and I went to put it in my box and it ban't there!"

His mother helped him to make search, but she could find no sign of the money-box. The boy had a little room of his own under the thatch of Hartland, and in a corner, at the bottom of a larger box where he kept his treasures, the money-box was wont to stand. Martin carried the key on a leather watch-chain in his waistcoat pocket. He was positive that he had not moved the box from its accustomed place, and when its disappearance seemed certain, he began to cry. He accused the maiden who worked at Hartland, he then accused Tiger.

At dinner his father came home and heard the black news.

"How much was in it?" he asked.

"One pound, eighteen shillings and two pence," sobbed Martin.

"And—and——" burst out Tiger from his place at the table between two labourers, "I give warning, master. I'll go at the end of my month. I won't stop here no more—God's my judge! He says that I've took his money, and I'll beg my bread on the high-road rather than suffer it I've never touched a crumb, nor yet a straw, what didn't belong to me by rights; and after all you've done for me—to hear as Martin thinks I could do such a thing against him! And I catched him hunting in the little cupboard out of the back kitchen where I live—thinking to find his money hid there; and I wish I may die this instant moment if——"

"Shut your mouth!" said Philip, "and get on with your meat. I'll go bail for you, and for everybody else. There's none under this roof would take a pin as didn't belong to them I know that, and Martin knows it—or ought to. We must hunt elsewhere. 'Tis well known folk do queer things in their sleep. So like as not Martin have hid it himself somewhere."

The theory brought little consolation, however, and for twenty-four hours some anxiety and tribulation marked the life at Hartland. The household was distracted and suspicious. Each soul thought that all the others suspected him, and Ouldsbroom's reiterated assurances by no means allayed the discomfiture.

Martin, unknown to himself, was watched very closely by the farmer, and for once his fancied father saw unjust suspicion, unreasoning passion, as well as natural boyish bad temper, long protracted. That Martin should have suspected Tiger was a grief to Ouldsbroom. Martin's attitude before this disaster cast him down, while Tiger's rage, wild oaths, and large threats of terrific retribution, cheered him up again.

When night came the boys went to bed enemies, and Philip crept to Martin's door to watch him, if possible, through the keyhole. He could see little, but he heard a prayer. Martin made another careful examination of every corner of his chamber; he then sighed deeply several times. Slowly he undressed, and then knelt down by his bed and prayed out loud. His mind was now at peace, and no evidence of his past temper appeared in a mild petition to Heaven. He begged that God would touch the heart of the robber and so make him return Martin his savings. He added a faithful promise that, if they were returned, he would put two shillings into the church plate on the following Sunday.

He ended up with the words:

"And this I promise for Jesus Christ's sake, Amen."

Then he got into bed, tossed awhile, and sighed himself to sleep.

"You was right," said the farmer to Unity soon afterwards. "He's fond of money. I took it. 'Tis locked up in my desk. You ought to have heard him praying, poor chap. He's promised the Almighty two bob if his li'l box turns up!"

Next day, Philip, having slipped another shilling into the money-box, returned it when Martin was out at school. He then waited with eagerness to learn the boy's attitude to the great recovery.

He came down from his room breathless, flushed, rejoicing.

"It's got back!" he cried. "And there's another shilling in it. First thing I done was to unlock it and count over my money, and 'tis one pound, nineteen and twopence now!"

Childlike, he puzzled not at all to know how his little fortune went and came again. In fact, many children would have been more interested in that particular than Martin. Tiger, for one, ceased not to cudgel his brains as to what craft had been employed and why the robber had added to the hoard rather than subtracted from it, but upon this point Martin was able to explain.

"I prayed it might happen so," he said. "I asked for the money back, but, of course, I never thought to ask for a bit over. That's the Lord's idea, and now I'll only lose one shilling by it instead of the two I should have. I promised two shillings, and if I'd promised but one shilling I should have lost nought ''

He asked Tiger to forgive him, and, indeed, begged pardon all round for his ill-temper and suspicious The actual mystery did not trouble him; and he was only concerned to have his money back. Indeed, that night he prayed his God to pardon the sinner who had done this thing, and on the following Sunday, without being reminded, he put a florin into the offertory plate. He did it rather reluctantly, and was very silent for a long time afterwards

Henceforth Philip sought to enlarge the boy's mind and increase his instincts towards generosity. Perhaps the only result of this practical joke was a shadow of cooling regard between the boys. That, however, even Ouldsbroom perceived was inevitable. Their differences of outlook and intellect were not such as promised to strike a lasting spark of friendship from the contact Yet the farmer felt angry with Tiger for liking Martin less. To his wife sometimes he uttered the familiar, futile wish that the children could be melted together and cast anew with a different proportion of characteristics.

CHAPTER X

On a day in December Unity heard the rattle of hoofs upon the stones of the farmyard and saw young Jonathan French, Birdwood's new assistant at Teign Head, gallop off at a great pace to Postbridge. She was upstairs, and witnessed his departure from her bedroom window. A moment later her maid hastened to her with the man's news.

Henry Birdwood, who had been ill for some weeks, supposed himself better, disobeyed orders, and went about his business in bad weather. He was now stricken down and at the point of death. The doctor had stopped with him and sent French with messages to Postbridge. Birdwood desired, before all else, to see Philip Ouldsbroom, and French brought that message. The girl had directed him to Postbridge, whither Philip was gone. The messenger from Teign Head then purposed fetching Mrs. Dury, the sick nurse. He would carry her luggage on his horse, and she might walk or ride a pony. The inaccessible position of Teign Head increased the difficulties, but the gravity of Birdwood's case was doubly his own fault, for Dr. Dickinson had advised him, some weeks earlier, to leave his home and go into hospital. That he had refused to do, and then, when making a good recovery, he went afield too soon, and now seemed destined to pay for his folly with his life.

Unity Ouldsbroom found herself face to face with danger, and devoted her whole gift of energy to the task of conquering it. Why Birdwood wanted her husband, she guessed. The shepherd's troubled spirit thrust him this way and that, and at last, in fear of his end, he de-

190

sired to tell the truth to Philip before he should depart.
Her mind delayed not a moment. Indeed, there was no
time for delay. Had she seen the messenger, she might
have deflected his course and kept him away from Philip;
but now her husband would know what had happened
and set out for Teign Head. She must get there first,
and instantly she started. Her impulse was to go off
on foot; her reason delayed her at the beginning, to
make swifter speed in the long run. She was stout now,
and not a speedy walker. Therefore she went to the
stable, saddled Ouldsbroom's riding-horse, and, as soon
as she was a hundred yards from the farm, she mounted
and rode like a man. Two points were thus gained: she
would get to Teign Head quicker, and Philip would come
slower; because there was nothing left at Hartland for
him to ride but a cart-horse.

Much depended on the doctor, and Unity guessed that
he would be glad to hand the patient over to friends.

The horse trotted over the coarse integument of the
faded heath, all grazed close, all grey and harsh and sodden on the edge of winter. Only the asphodel's russet
death and blue rosettes of the moor grass, that had escaped the teeth of sheep and kine, still lingered, and
wove fading patterns upon the patchwork of the wilderness. Sere was the way and silent, save for a sourly
whimpering wind that roamed the wet miles of the Moor,
shook the woman's hair about her ears, and seemed to
wail fitfully, like a sick child.

From the soaking heights of Siddaford, above the Grey
Wethers, there spread northerly a mottled desert patched
with darkness of heather on a ground of livid and dead
grass. This wan covering brightened in the bogs, where
sedges perished in red death and spread dark, ruddy
stains, as though blood had flowed out there. The land
rolled desolate, water-logged, spiritless even to Cosdon's
rounded shoulders heaving to the north. Under Unity's
eyes in the cradle of Teign, where it now extended beneath her, stood the home of Birdwood—the loneliest in-
habited dwelling upon Dartmoor, but not beyond the
beat of death. A little reclaimed land stretched round

about, and the house showed no larger than a great, moss-grown stone flung here long since and now welded into the hillside. The lintels of the doorway were washed with white and flashed far off under a rusty red roof.

Overhead arched the cold, grey sky, fretted aloft with horizontal bars of dark vapour; while beneath them round wool-pack clouds lumbered up from the south-west, laden and leaking with the next downpour. The place of the sun was hidden, and the day was dark though noon had not yet come.

Unity now dismounted, and walked her horse down to the valley. She was soon at Teign Head cot, and the old doctor hastened out to meet her.

"Where's your husband?" he asked. "The man's crying out for him."

"He'll be here presently. He was away when the news came, and they've sent to fetch him. I came so quick as I could. How is the poor chap?"

"He's dying. I think he's conscious, but that's all. Nothing can save him. In fact, it was all over before I got here to-day. He's killed himself, as I told him he would long ago. I must get to Chagford now, and I'll come back this way, if I can, to-night; but none can help him."

"I'll stop till the nurse comes. Maybe he'll tell me what he wanted to tell my man."

"How he's existed so long in this den I hardly know. For years he has been weak and ailing."

Dr. Dickinson went in and cast a look at his patient; he directed Unity how to relieve him, and then got on his horse and rode away down the valley. It began to rain again.

Birdwood's bed had been brought into the kitchen and stood near the fire. The room was smoky and very hot. He sat propped up, with his shoulders lifted, struggling for air.

"Ope the window, for God's sake," he said when they were alone.

"Mustn't do that," she answered. "Lie so still as you know how."

He implored for the window, and she opened it.

"Where's Philip?" he asked.

"Coming. He'll be here soon."

Her eyes were on the distant hillside.

Birdwood was comatose, but conscious.

"I'm going to tell him," he whispered. "It's got to be I wanted to tell him once—for hate, to show him I was the strong one—not him. Now—now 'tis only for justice—I won't go on stinging the man from the grave. I——"

"Can't you think for the child?"

"Don't I? He'll be a shining light some day Born good, he was. Born good out of our wickedness. That's how things happen. Philip——"

He fell over on one side and she helped him and put her arm round him

"You—you don't count," he continued "You've hated me for years. You'd like to smother me now with my pillow—wouldn't you? Why don't you do it? I'd thank you, for that matter—dying by inches like this is hell."

"Don't talk."

"I'll wait for Philip. As for you—let your God get you out of this mess."

He grinned into her hard face. She itched to silence him, and he knew what was in her mind.

"Do it!" he said.

He became unconscious a moment later, and she thought that he was dying. She looked at the brandy, but put none to his mouth. He appeared to recognise her again presently But he began to sink

On the hill Unity saw a man She propped Birdwood up and went out. She ran to reach Philip as quickly as possible, and when she did so, they stood a quarter of a mile from Teign Head.

For a moment she gasped with her hand to her heart. Then she spoke

"I've got a message. He's thirsty and implores for a drink of champagne. 'Twill be his last drink on earth if there's time. I told him that I'd sighted you on the

13

hill and he said 'Ax him for God's sake to run over to "Warren House" and get me a bottle of champagne. 'Twill help me to die easier.' ''

"Is he dying?"

"So doctor says. He'll go to-night, or maybe last till to-morrow."

"What did he want me for?"

"Only to say 'good-bye.' You be more to him than any living man. He thinks the world of you But now he's cruel set on the wine. Will you get it? I'm doing everything the doctor directed till Mrs. Dury comes ''

Philip hesitated

"I'd like to see the poor chap again first."

"As you please, but he's terrible impatient for it. You'll be doing him a better service by getting the drink. His whole thought and longing be on it. 'Tis the last . thing you'll ever be able to do for him. When I said I saw you on the hill, he prayed as I'd run out swift and ax you. He thinks 'twill help him to go easier, and dying men be always right."

Philip looked round about him

"Let me see how the land lies. Yes—if I keep right over White Ridge and Assycombe. Tell him I've gone for it then, and will make the very best pace I can."

She feared that her husband would mention the horse, but he did not. He had not been home, and was unaware that she had ridden.

Ouldsbroom set off and she walked a little way beside him. Rain swept them heavily. He urged her to return, and presently she left him and did so

Her mind was full of uncertainty, and her hope centred in the belief that by the time Philip came back Birdwood must have passed out of sense, if not life. She wondered whether it might be possible to advance that end. She told herself the man was as good as dead, and that the welfare of the living must not be endangered by a moribund creature.

The patient had fallen forward when she returned to him and appeared to be quite unconscious Then a fear struck her mind that he might be simulating this state,

and would wake into life again when her husband returned He must be away for the better part of two
hours; the nurse would doubtless arrive sooner.

She did not lift or touch Birdwood, but went out into
the passage to reflect. She argued with herself that he
was virtually dead; she tried to make herself believe that
he was actually so.

She returned to him presently, and put her hand to his
heart. Poultices had slipped down off his back and chest
His eyes were open but unseeing. She could not feel a
pulse, and went out and left him in the same position.
Then she suddenly remembered that if young French or
Mrs. Dury came over the hill they would see her in the
yard; therefore she retreated and went into the parlour.
Mist was driving down upon the Moor, and herein appeared another cause for hope. Her husband might lose
his way back. Time, that she desired to crawl, raced
with her. An hour passed and she returned to Birdwood
He was still humped up with his head on his knees
Again she felt him and found his hands and feet were
cold. She laid him back, knelt beside him, and thanked
God from her heart that he was dead.

No doubt remained longer, and her attitude changed.
An immense load rolled from off her mind. She shut the
window and set about making some fresh poultices.
These she applied to the corpse. She could have sung.
Death never faced a more light-hearted woman. She
forgave Birdwood all that he had cost her of late. She
regarded him now with a stern complacency and traced
the lineaments of her own child in his. He was beginning each moment to look younger; and she believed that
presently, if his face was shorn, death would be found to
have taken ten years from it and ruled out many of the
deep lines and crosslines scored upon his forehead and
cheeks during that period Henry Birdwood had
stamped his image on their child's body. He had often
said so, and she knew it very well. She had watched
Martin growing more like his father, had marked the
thin, long limbs, colour of skin, and poise of head on
neck. She had speculated drearily on the future, and

marvelled at the blindness of the people who could not
note a thing so apparent to the eyes in her head and the
eyes in her soul. Only the greater gravity of the dead
man's personal threats had made this impersonal dread
less paramount And now all fear departed from her,
and took years with it, even as death was taking years
from the dead. She reflected on the slender accident
that might have turned that day from the best in her
life to the worst. Had Philip been at home; had the
messenger delivered Birdwood's cry to him, he, and not
she, must first have arrived at Teign Head Her husband, in that case would have been in time to hear the
confession.

"My sin is forgiven," she said to herself, and believed
an interposition of Providence.

She prayed that Birdwood's image might vanish from
people's minds as quickly as his body from their sight.
There was a photograph of him extant. Her husband
had a copy and one or two others possibly existed. One
hung close by in the parlour. This she now secured and
flung into the fire

Another hour passed, and then from the outer gloom
came shouts. She ran to the door, made answer, and
directed the fog-foundered Jonathan French and Mrs
Dury to Teign Head They had missed the way beyond
Siddaford and were wandering half a mile above the
cottage

The man rode and carried Mrs. Dury's bundle, she
tramped beside him, wet to the skin and much exhausted

"Look to yourself, Betty," said Mrs. Ouldsbroom, as
she received them, and settled her face into solemnity,
"It's all over, poor fellow. I got here hours agone, but
he was just flickering out then The doctor said he was
so good as dead before he left I've kept poultices to
him, but he's gone this longful time "

The nurse regarded Birdwood closely and satisfied
herself that he was dead.

"Take all they things away and ope the window," she
said "I'll change my clothes and then I'll lay him out,

poor blid. Where's the brandy? French and me had better have a drop hot. We're finger-cold.''

Within another half-hour Philip Ouldsbroom arrived breathless and soaking. His clothes steamed upon him with the haste that he had made. Unity met him at the porch.

"Thank God you'm come I thought you was lost!'' she cried.

"The biggest bottle in the pub,'' he said "and Gregory's going to get over to have a tell, if the fog lifts He didn't know things was so bad.''

"Hush—he's gone, my dear. His last thought was for you 'Remember me kindly—remember me kindly to Phil,' was the very last word I could catch Then he got dwaling and rambling. And then he died in my arms ''

"Dead—dead!''

"An hour and more.''

The man relaxed all over and exhibited grief. The great bottle he had dragged across the Moor fell out of his hand and broke. Its contents hissed into the mire.

"He knowed what you'd gone for. He said 'twas like you to go You'd best come in quick and get—or better still, take the hoss and ride home so hard as you can and change your clothes.''

"I must see him,'' he said, and pushed past her to look at Birdwood.

Betty Dury was washing the body, but threw a sheet over it at his approach.

"Do 'e think you could shave his poor cheeks, Mr. Ouldsbroom?'' she asked. " 'Twould make him look more vitty and like himself ''

Philip took Birdwood's hand and squeezed it.

"Good-bye, old chap; good-bye!'' he said.

BOOK III

CHAPTER I

HENRY BIRDWOOD was buried at Widecombe with his mother, and certain friends attended the funeral. Some walked with the dead and some rode on horseback. Gregory Twigg and Philip Ouldsbroom returned together with young French. They asked the latter whether he objected to stop at Teign Head alone, and he told them that he did.

The question of a new Moor-man for the East Quarter of the Forest was not yet determined.

At the 'Warren House' Philip alighted to drink, but Unity, who was in the market cart and had driven with Martin to the funeral, did not stay.

Gregory uttered some reflections upon the event of the morning for the benefit of Peter Culme and others who were in the bar. Then arose argument between Peter and the innkeeper, on one side, and Ouldsbroom and the ancient man, Nat Woodley, upon the other.

"He was back in the fold afore the end, and that's a tower of strength," said Gregory. "It was my work—of course the Lord aiding. I can see poor Henry coming up to me when I go over—I can see his hand stretched out and feel his angel hand-shake and hear him say, ' 'Tis all thanks to you, Twigg—all thanks to you.' "

"There'll be bands playing and banners flying when you go aloft, Greg," said Philip. "A regular revel, I reckon, and everybody given a whole holiday. How the mischief they can rub along without you up there be the puzzle to me."

198

Mr. Twigg reproved the farmer and turned to Woodley.

"I never heard tell the man was dead till an hour ago," said Nat. "I comed in this here bar for my afternoon drop and your missis told me. What took him?"

"What'll take us all, neighbour," answered Gregory "I saw him the next day, for 'tis among my chastening rules of life never to miss the sight of a corpse. If us living creatures saw more dead people 'twould be very good for us. I think there was victory on Henry's face I hope so. If anybody hadn't learnt to read the little touches that mean death, they might have said 'twas sleep."

"Death and sleep be cousins," said Peter, "at least that was the fansical way pastor put it in his sermon."

"Trash!" answered Ouldsbroom. "Don't you believe that, Culme."

" 'Tis true," declared Gregory. " 'Tis true beyond question. Sleep restores our natural powers of mind and body—don't it? It gives us a new life every morning; then why shouldn't death do the same and give us a new life altogether?"

"Doan't knaw why it shouldn't," said the aged Woodley "But I'm damned certain it won't. Sleep be rest, and there's nought in common betwixt that and death— pretend as you may. Who should know if I doan't? Why, death, as it gets nearer to us, kills sleep. What's my sleep now but a sort of dog's sleep, broken every time I turn my neck by a pang where death be hammering home his wedges? Death be death, and all the talk in all the Bibles won't get you out of his net when your turn comes."

"True for you, Nat," declared Ouldsbroom; "and 'tis a very manly thing in you at your age to face it so fearless."

"Death's no hardship to the dead—that's why I face it," replied the ancient. "We've got to go, and, if you live long enough, you're glad to go. And we, who know the meaning of life, would never call back any we cared about. 'Twould be cruelty to do it, and they wouldn't come for certain—even if they could."

But Philip denied this.

"You're out there," he answered. "I'd come for one —gladly and thankfully come. If I didn't drop till I was a hundred, still I'd crawl rejoicing back, if 'twas only to shake a man's hand, or hear a woman's voice, or list to a bird singing I'd come just to look at the sky and the clouds travelling on it. I'd come to have one drink along with an old pal. If 'twas only for five minutes I'd throw off death and come."

"You entirely forget what I hope you'd be leaving, Ouldsbroom," said Mr. Twigg.

"'Leaving'! Leaving a cheerful family of worms— poor company, Greg—you may take your oath of that. Bah! Give me another drop of beer to drown the thought of it."

"'Tis your narrow way not to look beyond the pit," said Mr. Twigg, "and Barbara Hext be largely to blame. We, who have understanding, can only pin our doubtful hope for you on the mercy of the Lord We don't deny your works; but works without faith be as much use to mankind as a bladder without wind in it to the drowning. The bladder must be blowed out with air, Philip, if 'tis to be of any consequence, and the human creature must be blowed out with faith, or else he'll sink to the worm which dieth not; and that's a very different creature from the poor churchyard sort."

"First time as ever I knowed 'twas faith as had made your barrel so round, Greg," answered Philip. "If 'twasn't for what we've just done, I could burst my sides laughing at that; for look at Medlicott, your minister. Faith haven't fattened him over much You can see through the man He'm little better than a dry built wall, that the wind and rain play hide-and-seek in."

"His work's over," answered Peter Culme. "He's going away to live the fag end of life in a lew corner. And there's another who be failing fast, and that's Miss Hext herself. A landmark gone she'll be—a very wise, kind woman—whatever she believes or don't. She judges none, and few can say as much."

"None but the Dissenters," declared Gregory. "We've

all our weakness, and that's hers. 'Tis a very sad and startling thing in her, and I can't understand it. To think she has lived all these years in the very shadow of us Little Baptists, you might say, and yet can't see the light. However——''

"Damn Time!" burst out Philip "The cruel wretch won't let nothing and nobody alone. Time's the only devil, say what you will, Greg."

"You've little to grumble at," declared Culme. "He'm gentle enough with you, whoever else he may be busy with He's taking your hair a bit; but that's nought."

"We ought to get old, and 'tis very indecent in you not to do it, Ouldsbroom," declared the innkeeper. "Why for you bide so young, and so foolish here and there, I never can understand or forgive in you. There'll come a day of reckoning. You may feel certain-sure of that. 'Tis better far for time to jog steadily and bring its weight of years and weight of knowledge with 'em, than hang fire like it do with you, for, mark me, 'twill come with a rush when it do come, and you'll go down afore it, like a green tree afore an autumn gale And what is there to stay you up when the storm falls? Now, I have always, as it were, spoken face to face with the Lord, like Moses on the Mount, and come away shining; and I can tell you——''

But Ouldsbroom felt no desire to listen further.

"Shine on," he said; "but you've shined enough for one day, in my opinion I be going down the hill to Post-bridge to tell a neighbour or two about the funeral now."

He went to see Barbara presently and, moved by the things that Culme had said, scrutinised her face narrowly.

"Left that fool Twigg chin-deep in drivel. Couldn't stand no more of it A funeral brings out the very marrow of the man I long to lift my fist and beat him down at such times."

"We're all humbugs, Phil, and other people's humbug always looks nasty to us But none are free of it. 'Tis certain in us, as that we've all got ten toes Every living creature has some dirty little holes sealed up and white-

washed over in their cellars   We pretend we have not;
but we know we have.''

"Don't you begin to preach too.   Remember as I
have had Twigg on my hands ever since we left Henry's
grave. 'Tis a very nice spot they've chose, and I be
going to put up a stone to the man presently. I knowed
more about him than anybody, and understood him better. His last word was 'good-bye' to me, and I shall
miss him a lot.''

"Did the missis go to the funeral?''

"She did, and so did Martin. I'll swear he got a spark
of pleasure out of it   But you know him. He'd be a
parson himself, I believe, if he could. But I told him a
bit ago that I'd sooner see him in his coffin than in a
white choker, and he looked at me—in that measuring,
doubtful way of his; but he said nought.''

"He's growing a fine fellow.''

"So he is, and getting clever at the farm too. I shall
have to talk presently, but I'm putting it off, for he'll
be away to school after Christmas, and that will enlarge
his mind a bit.''

"Certainly it will do so.''

" 'Tis that he wants. He's just, but awful narrow.
He judges right; but why the hell judge at all? that's
what I'm always axing him. 'Judge not at all,' says
Christ, doan't He? Then why do these prize Christians
want for to be always doing it, and casting a stone at
tramps and freethinkers and socialists and everybody
else, as don't walk head to head with 'em? I want my
son to be large-minded Justice is a good hoss, but
Mercy's a better one, Barbara, and the older I get, I
find myself that terrible merciful that I'll forgive anybody anything—if they'll only let me alone and mind
their own business.''

She laughed.

" 'Twill be a great strain for Unity parting with the
boy.''

"And for me. I shall miss him cruel, for all he——
You see, Barbara, somehow—what's the word? Well,
they do take sides against me. Yes, they do. I'm not

angry—I'm calm as a frog Haven't I just come from a funeral, and have I got more than two half pints inside of me? No, I haven't. But, in a way, they take sides. Not meaning to hurt, yet 'tis two for one and—and——''

He grew red—at pictures cast upon his mind by memory

"Think nothing of it. 'Tis the strength of your wife. But you'll ever find her safe on the side of wisdom.''

"That's as may be. A man must be master in his own house, Barbara. There'll be Cain let loose at Hartland if any creature thinks to come between me and the master's place. What right—what right, I say, has the woman——?''

He broke off, conscious that he was about to utter an unbecoming thing. He laughed

"There—there! We'm such old friends that I seem like to trade on it and wash dirty linen afore you. God forgive me for thinking to do such a thing. 'Tis only my stupid pride They meant nought. Ban't I the life and soul of 'em both? What would they be without me, or me without them?''

"That's right, Phil. Now 'tis you talking ''

But when Ouldsbroom went home he left Barbara with some fertile food for thought. She was not an inquisitive woman; yet she knew the character of Unity Ouldsbroom exceedingly well, and now she asked herself with interest what had happened. That Philip's wife had somewhere failed of her usual perfect tact and skill appeared That she had hurt and even angered Ouldsbroom was clear. He revealed the fact less in words than by the lifted voice and angry flush that accompanied them Miss Hext was concerned for him, and trusted that the incident had been isolated and provoked by some untoward chance not likely to recur.

She guessed that Martin's forthcoming departure to a boarding-school might diminish further opportunities for friction.

CHAPTER II

MARTIN'S departure was delayed until the spring Then came the great event. His box was packed, his farewells were made, and he drove off with Philip to a school at Bovey Tracey.

It was typical of the boy and man that Martin remained collected and calm, while Ouldsbroom became more agitated as the goal of the journey approached them Only when he left his mother did the lad's lip falter. He would not show Tiger his face when his playfellow, having carried the box to the trap, stood at hand to say 'good-bye.' Then Philip, marking the tears, signalled Tiger away Unity stood at Hartland door as long as the vehicle was visible When she saw that it was about to disappear, she waved her apron, noted the answering flutter of her son's handkerchief, and went to her work.

She hoped great things of this change, and had stinted for it through the past ten years. Her ambitions for the boy were high, but as yet he had manifested no special taste Secretly she pictured him a clergyman, since by that door his social position might most easily be lifted; but Philip raged so violently against the thought, that it never escaped her lips a second time. Martin's future was exceedingly safe with Martin. From that certainty she drew consolation, and her own rare powers of patience did the rest He was gone to be educated, to learn the first lessons of a larger life than Hartland could show him, and to mix with a higher class than his own She did not fear for him He was a kindly boy, and she had brought him up to obedience and consideration for elder people. His niggard instincts she did not deplore in the light of her husband's character They were a

shield to him, and she hoped for future fruit from them
A time must come when the lad's nature would enter
into closer union or combat with Philip's   That time,
indeed, was near, for the man continued little more than
a boy in many large particulars, while the boy had ever
been precocious, thoughtful, and not overmuch wedded
to childish things   He went away eager to learn and
eager to please   Unity therefore returned to her work
now with no tears in her eyes and a measure of peace at
her heart.

On Merripit Hill a group of children was assembled
to take leave of Martin   He did not lack for friends, and
among them were two of his cousins from Stannon:
Minnie and Jacky Crymes   The girl was shooting up
into some beauty. Her eyes still wondered at all they
saw; still asked their question of the world and its ways
as life dawned upon her understanding   Her affection
for Martin was very real, and he liked her well—better
than he showed   She seemed beautiful to him, and her
part of humble pupil and listener at all times, pleased
the boy. Few children would heed him when he was
serious, but she cared most for him at such hours, and
never wearied of his second-hand knowledge and youthful dogmatism   He and she often lost themselves in
speculations concerning the larger world and the things
that flashed to them sometimes from old newspapers.
Their mothers marked the friendship, and Gertrude
Crymes was pleased at it, but Unity hid her mind

Now Jacky flourished his cap, while the rest shouted
and Minnie waved a wet handkerchief. Philip, who had
pulled up a moment for the leave-taking, marked her
sorrow, and his heart went out to the little girl. He
thought of her afterwards, exalted her sentiments to
Martin, and loved her. And then, as they trotted along,
the man uttered his words of wisdom and, after his kind,
counselled much beyond his own power ever to put in
practice. Sometimes Martin secretly dissented; but he
listened quietly, made many promises, and often said,
'Thank you, father, I'll remember.'

"Be sporting always," said Philip   "There's no call

for me to tell you about being good, because you've got all that from mother. But there's just a few things a woman—not even the best—can teach a boy, and they be summed up in that word, 'sporting.' You'll have to play all manner of games that you ban't used to, and in the heat of 'em, if you be keen to win, as you should be, there come moments when there's a temptation sometimes to do things that ban't right or fair Always play fair, and think fair; and if you win, don't crow about it, and if you lose, don't fret. You'm a fine chap, with long legs and a great power of running, so I lay they'll be glad to have you in their games And nought will please me better than to hear they've chose you presently. The book larning will take care of itself with such a one for reading as you be, but mind and go in for the sport too.''

"So I will then, father.''

"And don't be near, mind. I wanted to give you a bit more in your pocket, but still, as mother says, you wouldn't know what to do with it Give where 'tis proper to give and share the hampers I be going to send you. And don't you think I shan't see you till the holidays, because I shall And I wouldn't wonder if a tempted mother over in a month or so for a sight of you She won't want much tempting, I lay!''

"It would be very nice to look forward to it. But mother won't do that ''

"Take my word she shall. A bit strange you must feel at first, but you'll soon settle down and make friends; and choose the chaps as be good out of doors as well as at their books. And write and tell me all about everything And mind you stick up for yourself from the first, Martin. I'd fought many a pitched battle afore I was your age; I took and gave and was none the worse Not as I want you to go fighting, I'm sure But the boy as quarrels with you will be the sort as wants knocking about, and if you reckon you can do it, or even if you fear you can't, go for him just the same ''

"I shan't quarrel with nobody if they don't quarrel with me.''

"Quite right, and if they do, don't you cave in, but

show 'em how a Dartymoor chap can hold his own. Then they'll soon larn to respect you. Mother will write how we go on, and I reckon Tiger will try his fist at it, though his penmanship ban't very grand.''

"I'll write to Tiger about things that would interest him.''

"Do so—'twill be good for him to know. I'm glad you thought of that.''

They parted presently, and the boy went out placidly to join two other new arrivals in the playground His father drove away, stopped in Bovey, made some purchases, drank with sundry friends, and then returned home. His wife heard every incident of the day, but declined Philip's proposal that she should call with him to see her son in a week or two

"No, no; that won't do,'' she declared. '' 'Twill only throw him off his books and make him restless I told him that I shouldn't see him till the holidays, and 'tis better far you shouldn't neither. I lay schoolmaster don't want you messing about at Bovey.''

"Quite right, quite right,'' declared Philip instantly. "Right as a nail; but, you see, there'll be hampers now and again, and my business will take me to Bovey sometimes, no doubt, and—what with one thing and another, I shan't be able to help catching a glimpse of the nipper off and on Couldn't help it if I would ''

She smiled and Tiger grinned.

Later on, as the term advanced, Mrs. Ouldsbroom, meeting with Gregory Twigg's wife, uttered one of her rare laughs and stated the case.

"My boy? Very happy, I do believe, and very good for sartin. 'Tis funny what a lot of business Phil finds to Bovey nowadays—a place as he never had no dealings with afore last Easter!''

"The boy draws him as the childer will the parent's heart,'' said Mrs. Twigg She was a watery edition of the innkeeper. She thought as he thought, believed as he believed, judged as he judged, and, in a fashion, even spoke as he spoke, and uttered tangled shreds and patches from his deep stores of piety and platitude.

"Yes, the boy draws him; but 'twould be better if he stopped farther off—far better."

"No doubt. The young must fight their own battles Us can only buckle on the shield of Truth for 'em and set them the example of steadfastness Martin be very like my Alfred in his disposition—a soaring child. He'll walk into the bar among grown men and they'll listen to him without a murmur. 'Tis a case of being actually born a Little Baptist. As Mister Twigg says, 'tis better than being born with a silver spoon in your mouth, like your boy 'Tis the silver spoon of the Spirit that our Alfred have got—to put it like my husband does."

There came a day when Tiger and his master went down to the great peat cuttings under Archerton Tor, to carve out winter fuel The weather of early July was hot and fine; the peat already spread—piled cake against cake—like tiny tents of some great fairy encampment on the heath.

A haunt of beauty was this place, whence came their winter warmth for the upland men Its lines and clefts brought ripe colour upon the waste; its dusky walls here shone, cut freshly from the peat sponge, here rose, weathered to rich harmonies of yellow and grey From agate to ebony the peat beds ranged in their colour. Within their chocolate-hued hearts, and on each shimmering pool, sedgy marsh, and shaking mire, bloomed half a hundred different flowers, the sphagna beds were brighter still and full of lemon and orange, emerald and purple. They massed and spread and made rich setting of the flower jewels of the bog, they hid the fount of the spring, yet declared its presence from far off.

Upon the peat beds cotton grass danced silvery, and the buckbean's fairy flowers ascended above their trefoil green The red rattle sparkled in its lacework of foliage; the heather sprang like a flower cornice along the black slab walls of the cuttings; and by rill and pool were lifted shy, small spires of the sun-dew and the frail atom of the butterwort's blossom—as though it had been a

little amethyst fly that hovered above each grey rosette.
Round about the land sloped upward from this bottom,
and to the north Archerton's flat crown of stones capped
a gentle hill

Tiger piled the unctuous slabs of dripping soil while
Ouldsbroom, who enjoyed peat-cutting, carved at the
ridge, and with rhythmic sweep of the knife made each
downward stroke, then used the peat-iron and flung cake
after cake upon the heather

He rested presently, and the boy brought him a little
runlet of cider.

"Only a fortnight," said Philip. "Only thirteen days,
to be exact, and he'll come home along. I be cudgelling
my brains a'ready to think of good sport for him."

"He'll want nought but that beautiful hoss," prophesied Tiger. "The only thing about Dartymoor as he
cares about be riding, and even then he'd never ride
along hunting or anything of that. He told me once,
when I slew a want,* that he hated killing things, and
he'd read in a book us hadn't got the right to do it.
'What about thicky long-cripple as bit you?' I axed him.
'Twas my fault,' said he. 'If I hadn't stepped on it I'd
have got no hurt.' But for riding you can't beat him "

" 'Tis the very truth," declared Philip, "built for the
saddle far better than me Have 'e marked how long
he runs from fork to knee? 'Tis so he gets his beautiful
natural seat. Wonnerful hands too. Might have gone
for a jockey if he'd been a little un."

Thought of Martin as a jockey made the jovial Tiger
laugh aloud

"Lord! the cruel funny things you say, master," he
cried in ecstasy

"Of course 'twasn't in his nature," explained Philip
"I ban't the sort that expects miracles, and I wouldn't
no more ax you to cram your head with book-learning
than Martin to do things what you do very clever I'm
only saying the cleverness was there."

"There's nothing he wasn't clever enough to do,"
declared Tiger.

* *Want*—A mole

14

Distance lent its kindly veil to the hearts of boy and man. They united in praising Martin, and when Tiger called up some feat of skill or trick of speech, Philip applauded him and capped the recollection with another.

Anon Martin arrived home in triumph: happy and healthy and full of learning. He brought with him a black eye and a prize for good conduct. The latter Philip regarded as inevitable; the former pleased him more, until he learned that it had only come from misfielding a cricket ball.

But there was rejoicing that night in the house, and ere he went to bed the farmer made Martin read aloud from his favourite chapter in Job.

"On great days, such as this be, I do like to hear the twenty-eighth," said Ouldsbroom. " 'Twas Barbara set me on to it scores of years ago, and there's fine things in it for every time. But nought finer than this. So wet your whistle, Martin, and let's have it."

The boy was very willing, and when he had done, all praised him and declared that his reading had now attained perfection.

CHAPTER III

FOR years had Philip continued to trust that, under the patent qualities of his mother, there might in Martin lurk latent some attributes of his own. With time this hope was called to die, and Ouldsbroom suffered in the process. He received and accepted it reluctantly; strove to evade it; at times denied it. But, while a man of little wisdom, his perceptions were not dull. He faced the truth and was constrained to allow that Martin varied from him as widely as boy could vary from man. Until the present this fact had not lessened his devotion. In his darker hours he fretted at it, in his happy moments— and they were still not few—he declared that it was well, and that a sane father should be proud of getting a cleverer son than himself But he was tenacious at certain points, and the hearty delight that he declared when Martin elected to be a farmer grew a little clouded in circumstances that followed.

Philip's sole vanity might have been said to lie in a conviction that his knowledge of Dartmoor agriculture was complete and final. He trod in the steps of his father and his father's father. Innovation was offensive to him, and he resented advice upon his business While, therefore, not jealous of others; while he was content that Martin should make new friends, enlarge his acquaintance, and win wider measure of attention, a thing that did not please him was the boy's attitude to his new and vital interest. Martin said that he wished to be a farmer, and Philip rejoiced, since such a wish brought the boy closer to him; but Unity did not rejoice, neither did she mourn, for she believed the wish a whim; she felt assured that education would lift her son's ambition to higher things

For the present, in holiday time, Martin addressed himself to the routine work of Hartland, and then it was that what had promised so great a delight to the master proved, in the event, a source of tribulation.

Because, now the growing child began to show more than his mother's qualities, and as the mingled oils of ancestry that burned in his lamp of life added each its own quality to his nature, there came the light of new things. Martin's character began to develop—clean-cut and decisive. He was religious-minded, he was thrifty, and he was thorough. He lacked imagination and the sunnier qualities—a want which, thus early declared, promised austerity when manhood dawned. He revealed not only a sense of justice, but also a strong inclination to judge. He thought a great deal and wondered a great deal about his father. His mother's attitude especially puzzled him. From the present standpoint of his experience, he could not understand why Unity condoned incidents and passed utterances that he knew won displeasure from her. His eyes grew round sometimes when his mother nodded, showed no concern, and said, 'Have it as you please, master,' to some assertion or intention expressed by her husband. Martin puzzled to understand why she hid her true opinion and even pretended agreement, when right well he knew that she thought his father wrong. Personally he had not yet dared to contradict Ouldsbroom; but each day found him better armed and at wider variance from the elder's opinions. His old, childish devotion to Philip was also fading away in the light of larger ideas and increasing knowledge. It was not in his nature to win much further joy of such a man.

The matter culminated when Martin, now home for the summer holidays, began to read a book lent to him by one of his schoolmasters. He interested his teachers, and they were willing to help him. The work concerned the chemistry of soil, and indicated modern methods of learning first the constituents of a given earth and then adding thereto the special properties required by different crops. Philip knew little of such a subject and cared less. He was wont to say that his stable supplied everything that the hungriest ground could cry for He pointed to his own produce, and was content to contrast it with that of his poorer neighbours Agriculture did not interest him, and his particular pursuit was breeding of beasts.

Now Martin began to air the new knowledge, and when Philip, thunderstruck, asked him what nonsense he was talking about, he blushed and burnt to the heart with a sense of injustice. He had planned his little items of information very carefully. He had taken the guide as infallible, for it belonged to his nature to trust books; and he brought out the modern opinions when walking upon the land in late August with Ouldsbroom.

It happened that what he said ran counter to Philip's most rooted convictions. The elder had just uttered some moth-eaten wisdom current in his grandfather's time, and upon it, seeing that the moment was apposite, Martin piped in with his chemistry.

" 'Tis in my book,'' he said with a wounded voice upon the farmer's rough challenge.

"Is it? Then you'd better burn your book; and if t'others tell the like trash, then burn the lot, and be damned to 'em and the fools that wrote 'em. Don't you never spout your books to me till I ax you to, my fine chap. Larning be all right, but it don't always square with facts—remember that If the know-nought fool who printed that stuff was to step up along from his chemist's shop to Dartymoor and listen to me for an hour, no doubt he'd tear up his twaddle and be sorry ever he wrote it.''

"But, father——''

"Don't 'but' me 'Tis lies, and there are three acres of ground under your nose to prove it. If you want to larn your job, come to your father, who'd forgot more than this book-writer ever knew, before you was born. And if you think to teach me my business, Martin, instead of coming to me to learn yours, then you'll do better to change your mind once for all and keep away from Hartland when you grow up ''

"I only thought 'twould be interesting to you to hear.''

"Don't think such foolishness no more then Teach

me all you can about the things I don't know, and larn
from me the things I do. And one thing is that nobody
on God's earth be going to get a better turnip out of that
field, or heavier oats out of t'other than what I can. If
you want to farm Hartland, come to your father, and
don't let's have no more silliness out of books. Good God
Almighty! to stick up that little thin atomy of a book
you pore over and put it afore what I know! I wish I'd
got the fool who wrote it here—to sweat for it and freeze
for it and drown for it a bit in the ups and downs of our
weather. Then we'd see what would become of his ideas
and all this blasted mess they tell about to fling upon
land nowadays. When they've poisoned a few things
and killed all the fish in the river, and so on, they'll begin
to believe the farmers understand best, I dare say. And,
be it as 'twill, I know a long sight better than to let any
of their trash inside my gate.''

"I'll say nothing more about it, father.''

"So much the better, Martin. And if you want to
please me, you'll burn the book and be done with it.''

" 'Tis a lent book. I must take it back.''

"And tell 'em what I say about it, and ax 'em, with my
compliments, to larn you a bit better.''

When he went home the boy put his book in his box and
presently told Unity of what had happened. She took
his side, yet bade him obey his father. It was one of the
occasions when her attitude puzzled his sense of justice;
but if she left him something to think about, the mother
herself remained with a still harder problem. Unity saw
the difficulties now rising ahead, and she perceived that
they must increase with Martin's advancement in knowledge and understanding. The line of least resistance
presented itself, and she felt that it would be well, once
for all, to wean Martin from farming as a future. Her
power over him was great and she did not anticipate
much difficulty. The danger of the task lay with Philip,
and she knew that if he guessed her purpose, or saw it in
operation, he would become deeply angered. Her patience
with him continued to sustain the home; but sometimes,
as at this juncture, she felt the severity of the strain.

Occasionally she found herself doubting whether patience was always wise, whether, as he grew more headstrong, some manifestation of her power, rather than her patience, might not prove more salutary and more sane.

Upon the other side there fell rare moments in the husband's mind, when he went under a cloud that shadowed his customary enthusiasm with respect to Unity. Once he confessed to Barbara that he had come from feeling the sharp edge of her tongue. He laughed it off the next day and accused himself of injustice and folly in ever thinking that his wife could be severe to him. He took all the blame, assured Miss Hext that he had richly deserved a scolding, and declared that the wonder was he received so few; but she understood. She marked how that his wife was rather less often on Ouldsbroom's lips, how his fits of admiration and shouts of applause at her cleverness and tact waned a little in their frequency. The thing had become a habit with him and the practice of praising Unity persisted; but the old emphasis, the sudden beam of countenance and rise of colour when he named her were rarer. None save the postmistress had noted the change, for it developed slowly through a period of years; but she marked it and grieved for it; she asked herself whether any sort of remedy existed, and knew that there was none.

Thought upon Philip's future often made this woman sad. She herself had aged of late, and sometimes felt sorry that she must pass before the crisis of Ouldsbroom's life broke upon him. But she comforted herself with reasonable trust in the possibilities of chance. Chance might lift the shadow yet for him, chance might thrust aside the threat of the storm and clear his horizon of a gloom that began to gather upon it in her ageing eyes.

The holidays, regarded as a period of joy and intimacy for Martin among his own, proved a partial failure. He was immensely delighted with the horse that Philip had got for him; but he spent so much time upon it that Ouldsbroom often failed to see him through a whole day. For fishing he cared not at all; and when September came and he spent long hours in carrying his father's game-bag over the bogs after snipe, he could only once be made to fire; and then he missed.

Coming home again he ventured to explain to Philip that, as Tiger had said of him, he did not like killing things; but an attitude more irrational in his father's eyes could ill have been imagined. Philip talked to the other boy about it, and gave it as his opinion that it was unnatural—a pathological condition in Martin calling for serious treatment.

He said:

"Sport be as proper to a lad as mousing to an owl. Martin must be sick not to like it. Who ever heard tell of a nipper near fifteen not wanting to catch trout or fire a gun?"

" 'Tis terrible coorious in him," confessed Tiger. "I never seed nothing so strange, but then he's different to us common boys. I lay there never was such a chap. 'Tis the great cleverness in him. He was always like that. I mind a year ago, when I found a gladdy's nest and strubbed it, he catched me blowing the eggs to put along with others for a necklace for Jonathan French's sister, and, if he could have done it, he'd have given me a proper hiding."

Philip was interested instantly. He looked at Tiger and compared the boy's large-boned, stout-built frame with the neater and taller and far lighter physique of Martin.

" 'Twould be very interesting to see you chaps have a set to in a friendly way," he declared. "You've got the powder, and you could take all and more than Martin could give, I reckon; but he's got the reach of you and he's twice as quick on his toes. I doubt if you could lick him, though he's younger."

This personal aspersion touched Tiger on a tender spot.

His old ambition to be fierce was now elevated somewhat. He desired at present only to be prodigiously strong, and he did all that he could to bring this condition about. He ate like a wolf and worked like a pony. He watched his biceps tenderly and investigated his ribs, loins, thighs and calves with profound affection. He measured himself once a month against the wall of the loft wherein he slept, and if his frank heart held one spark of envy for Unity's child, it arose from Martin's superior agility and superior height. That there could be a shadow of doubt as to his power to thrash Martin, did such an unthinkable necessity arise, Tiger would not dream. He was quite startled that, of all men, his hero and exemplar entertained a question upon it. He felt, however, that the subject was delicate, and some spark of feeling silenced him now, though he grew very red and opened his mouth to answer

Philip marked the emotion, but could not appreciate the silence.

"You think they fat arms of yours would soon polish him off. But we won't talk of it. I'd get two pair of gloves to-morrow, only he'd never don 'em. He ban't the fighting sort. Though plucky enough, mind you, Tiger. For all he's so terrible unnatural, he's got pluck. I've seen him show it with a bull afore to-day."

"So he has," acknowledged Tiger. "Besides, the missis would soon send me to the right-about if I get sparring along with Master Martin "

"None sends you to the right-about but me, my bold hero 'Tis to be 'Master Martin' now—eh?

"Ess, it is."

The farmer considered.

"Did he ax you to, or missis?"

"Him! No, he never would She said so yesterday. 'Tis to begin from when he comes home next time "

It was Philip's turn to keep silence though tempted to speech, and he left the boy abruptly.

Martin's solitary rambles, his rides, and his occasional visits to his cousins at Stannon, made up the chief pleasure of his holidays He went with his mother twice to Tavistock market and drove her proudly. Then came the time for going back to school, and he faced the ordeal without regret.

In Philip's heart there dawned a vague sense of relief when the boy was about to go, but it vanished instantly, and sadness took its place after he was gone. Fond hope

—his soul's heritage—awoke. He explained everything away.

"'Tis always the winter our lad likes best, I do believe," he said to his wife. "Us'll give him some proper fun come Christmas time, and if he once goes out for a gallop when hounds meet hereabouts, he's bound to get the hunting fever. Something tells me that he will do so, for 'tis a very common thing with they fox-hunters that they never care a brass farthing about any other sport. No doubt 'tis the king of sports for that matter"

CHAPTER IV

On a day when autumn was far spent and winter again at hand, Unity called at the shop of Barbara Hext and fell into conversation with the postmistress. They were not friends, but entertained a very genuine respect each for the other. His wife knew Philip's regard for Barbara and was aware that her husband heard nothing but sense from her. The elder woman had sometimes served Ouldsbroom well and helped him to wise conclusions when Unity's arguments proved powerless to do so. She felt in debt to Miss Hext, and never hesitated to acknowledge it. They discussed the farmer frankly, and he knew that they did and cared not.

Of late Barbara had marked a little acerbity on the other woman's tongue, and she had guessed correctly at the reason.

"No currants," said Philip's wife. "Such good things ban't for us just now Time enough for currants when Martin comes home."

Barbara nodded and ceased to weigh a weekly ration.

"Keeping your boy at this big school calls for thought."

"It does, and I'm always reminding my man that we must remember sixty pounds a year be a lot of money. But what cares he? He's never felt a pinch, and he snorts if I say a word. I'm feared of my life for our savings sometimes. He's too old to be so rash, Barbara."

"He'd sooner be rich in friends than money."

"A fool's wish; because the one only lasts as long as

219

t'other. You can't buy friends in this world, you can only hire 'em, and if pay day comes round and the money's gone, you'll soon find what nine in ten be worth."

"A bitter word," answered the other; "but I don't say it's less than the truth. Philip knows nought of human nature; he never did, and never will. He counts to find every man a proper man and every woman so clever as his wife. Yes, he asks women to be reasonable and fools to be wise. Yet; when you offer him reason and wisdom, 'tis any odds but he'll scorn 'em. But what a nature he hath, Unity! Who that's worth their salt but cares for him?"

" 'Tis a prettier nature for outsiders than her that's got to guide it. He's more difficult than he was, and I'll tell you for why. As he gets older he gets busier, and I ban't let into every secret now till it's too late."

"He does love to surprise folk with his little tricks and plans."

"Too well I know it. Such a thing be making me sore this minute," answered Mrs. Ouldsbroom. "But last week he thought to give me a mighty surprise, and he went and made a bargain in Tavistock market that Tiger wouldn't have made, let alone my son. He was fresh, of course, at the time, as I got to hear afterwards through Jonathan French. But there it was. He came home full of a great secret, and wouldn't let it out till morning. And then he surprised me all right, no doubt; but 'twasn't the sort of surprise he'd hoped; and when I explained, so quiet as I could, the things that he hadn't remembered, and the cruel nonsense of flinging away five pounds—for 'twas little better—then——"

"I know. I can see it all and hear every word he said. I admire your patience."

"There's other things beside money. I can speak to you, because you don't tell again, Barbara, and you know Philip better than anybody living after me. There's a thing now that's growing into mischief, if it ban't mischief a'ready, and that's Tiger. I've nothing against him; he makes no trouble in himself, but I can't but fear he's no longer the best companion for Martin in holiday time. What should you think?"

"He's got his work."

"Yes; and Martin will oft go and help him at it They be as different, of course, as chalk from cheese. And that's not all neither· my husband relies more and more on Tiger—so far as a man can rely on a boy. He thinks a lot of him."

"Why shouldn't he?"

"No reason, perhaps; but a mother's quick to smell danger for her own. Suppose that Philip so far forgot himself as to set Tiger before Martin? He's just the reckless creature to do it, in my opinion Something might gall and vex him and he might dash off and——"

Miss Hext interrupted. She was amazed to win confidence from one who gave no confidences; but she was quick to feel the mother's fear and glad to allay it.

"Don't dream of such a thing. Nobody—not even you, I see—can tell exactly what Philip feels for his boy. He has wearied my ear—yes, wearied my ear, Unity, with praise of Martin. He's taking a point of view about Martin that's very much indeed to his credit, in my opinion. Jealous I doubt he couldn't be; but there was a time when he growled a lot to think his son was so different from himself. For years he made a sort of silly grievance of it—you know he did as well as I do, but that's all altered. He's as proud as a peacock of Martin now. He'll tell me by the hour of all that he said and did last holidays, and what a wonderful thing he feels it to have got a son who is cleverer than he is himself. There's no danger there. He likes Tiger very well; but he loves Martin with his whole heart."

"Tiger can do more with him, however."

"That's natural too. Love can't always be counted upon to see sense; and the more we love people, the more our view of them is twisted out of clearness. He comes to Martin with all his senses strung up—he's cruel tender in that quarter; and if Martin says a word he weighs it and looks at it from a dozen points of view, and makes too much of it very like, or doesn't understand it, or

reads something mistaken into it. With Tiger he meets
the living likeness of the boy he must have been himself.''

"No, he don't," said Unity. "Tiger's got a lot more
wits already than my husband. And that's why I begin
to doubt about him. Suppose he grows crafty come a
few years? Suppose he was to creep up my husband's
sleeve and do harm to Martin? 'Tis idle to shake your
head Such things do happen.''

"I laugh at you," declared Miss Hext. " 'Tisn't often
anybody does that, Mrs. Ouldsbroom; but knowing what
your husband thinks of his boy, and what Tiger thinks
of him too, for that matter, I can't help laughing. Nothing on earth—and Tiger last of all—will cut your son
out with his father. 'Tis only Martin's self that can ever
do it, and for my part, seeing the goodness and nice,
quiet ways of the boy, I'm positive sure that 'twill never,
never be. He's growing up, and his brains are growing
up even quicker than his body. Such sense you seldom
see in such a young creature; and that sense will very
soon teach him to understand his father and see the greatness of his father, and let the real, solid part of Philip
weigh against the other things I do hope that is what
will happen; and then they would be more to each other
in the future than ever you could expect them to have
been in the past.''

"It sounds a hopeful saying," answered Unity, "and
I'll try to find it so. And, if you want to do me a kind
turn with my husband, you preach thrift to him in season and out—that and steadiness. I've opened my
mouth wider to you to-day than ever I did in my life
afore to mortal man or woman. But I know you'll not
put what I've been saying to evil purpose. 'Tisn't often
in such a small place as this you'd find two women with
the power of holding their tongues; but you and me both
know how to do it.''

Unity went away, and the elder's conscience pricked
her a little. She had been surprised into saying smooth
things that were not quite her honest conviction. She
reviewed her recent assertion, and shook her head at her-

self. That the sense of Martin would ever see the bright
side of his father, or appraise the worth of him as
weighed against the worthlessness, she knew was impossible. The growing sense of Martin must disapprove
more and more emphatically; there was not in him the
power—even had love inspired a wish—to understand
or appreciate the qualities that made such a man as
Philip precious.

CHAPTER V

UNDER the shoulder of Bellaford Tor there stands a little grove of ragged pines. Many have perished, yet still they rear, stark in death, among their living neighbours. Behind them, on an evening in December, sloped Bellaford's shoulder, all shining with light; and below, Dart wound with many a curve about the foothills of the tor. Earth and sky melted together in one fuliginous darkness; but in the notch of the hills behind the wood a brilliant orange flame glared out like a cresset of fire, sent flashes down the glen, touched the twilight murk, and flamed upon the fir trees. The hour was mild and reeking with moisture. Torrential rains had fallen until after noon, and the sky threatened to brim over once more ere night should come.

Against the savage radiance between the hills there moved two black specks in the direction of Postbridge. A boy and girl sauntered together homeward, and Tiger shortened his stride to keep pace with the feet of Mary French. She lived with her brother Jonathan at Teign Head, for the youth had succeeded his dead master and was now a shepherd under the new Moor-man of the Eastern Quarter. Tiger was Mary's 'friend' in the technical acceptance of that word. It signified between them mutual amity and an understanding closer than any existing with others; but it meant no more. Neither stood committed, and each was at liberty to establish another friendship if he or she pleased to do so. Tiger, however, in whom the dawn of sex now glowed, hoped for greater things from Mary, and her flaxen hair, long legs, and very red mouth were good to him. As for her,

224

she was well content to be in his company, and she knew that with a rise of wages Tiger would formally invite her to become betrothed.

Mary had reached seventeen; but Tiger's birthday was hidden in obscurity and his exact age uncertain. He had always regarded himself as older than the workhouse people thought; and when he learned the date of Mary's birth, decided once and for all that he must be considered exactly a year older.

They talked of their little interests and hopes, and the lad was concerned with the return of his master's son; while Mary, too, felt concerned in this subject upon a side issue.

"Minnie Crymes be properly fond of him," she said. "I often wonder why, for she ban't his friend. She'm terrible serious-minded, and did ought to suit him down to the ground."

"For that matter she do I lay his hoss will take him to Stannon oftener than out fox-hunting, for all master's so set on it for him. I'm going back now, this instant moment, to help with some fuzz-bushes and hurdles we'm setting up in the big meadow. They be for us to jump Master Martin's hoss over, and teach un to be clever against he comes back. He's taking to it kindly too—the hoss, I mean."

"A lot kinder than your young chap will, I reckon."

"Very like. But the master be so resolved, that I do hope as he'll see his way to go after foxes. I wish to goodness I could. All the same, Mr. Ouldsbroom be such a grand hero hisself, and so fond of sport, that I will say he don't grudge me a bit of fun now and then. I be a very good shotsman, Mary, and next time I shoot a game bird I'll bring it up over to you."

"Thank you very much, Tiger."

"Just had a wonnerful feed to Squire Blackall's. I went down at daylight with a pony that he've bought from us for his little girl. And I stopped to the kitchen dinner, and I never want to eat better food or more at a go. A footman said that 'Tiger' was the right name for me, after he had seed me let down my meal And I

15

axed if they'd like to look at my arm muscles, but they
didn't—for shame, no doubt, being a skinny lot.''

"I lay they was nought beside you for strength.''

"Nought, though grown up. I told 'em they didn't
know what work be. 'You chaps,' I said, 'breaks out in
a presspiration if you've got to carry a box of coals in
the parlour. But I—I could drag a hundredweight sack
ten mile and never turn a hair,' I said to them. Of
course they wouldn't believe it—true though it is.''

"You couldn't expect indoor servants to be like you,''
said Mary. "I never yet seed an indoor man as hadn't
got a cold in his nose. Poor, pinnicking things, I
reckon.''

As they approached Hartland, Philip, at work in a
croft, marked the boy and shouted to him.

"Come here, you caddlin' rogue, and you be off, Polly.
I lay you've had enough of the rascal for one day.''

She laughed, and went on her road, while the boy
hastened to his master.

"After the girls a'ready, I see,'' said Ouldsbroom.

"Not me. I don't care nothing for 'em in general.
But she's different. We'm friends.''

"Glad of it. I ain't got no use for the frosty sort.''

"Us might go so far as to get tokened come I get a
rise,'' said Tiger, striking while the iron was hot.

"You'll have to wait a bit for that. Money's tight.
Did Squire like the pony?''

"He did then, and nothing would suit miss but they
put the saddle on that instant moment.''

"Lend a hand with these hurdles,'' said Philip. "And
to-morrow us will have the hoss out and you can take
him over 'em.''

The hurdles were set up, and next morning Tiger enjoyed some exercise on Martin's horse. All went well,
and the beast appeared to enjoy himself as much as the
boy. Philip was in high good humour and praised the
steed and its rider.

"Always knowed there was a bit of hunter in him, and
if he can jump 'em with a solid lump like you on his
back, he'll fly over with Martin.''

"So he will, no doubt," declared Tiger. "He rides a lot better than me, of course"

"He does—not that you ban't very clever, but he's built for the saddle and you aren't."

They practised the horse daily until Martin returned, and he—warned by his mother of the trouble that had been taken—essayed to show interest He felt no fear of the hurdles, and leapt them well, but the prospect of hunting gave him scant pleasure. To satisfy his father, he attended three meets, and Philip heard afterwards that the boy had ridden straight and kept well up as long as his steed could gallop. But when the beast became distressed, he had stopped He excused himself from another attempt, and his father used harsh language at finding a last hope dead

Martin was regretful, but the incident revealed a flash of something new in him. He showed unexpected firmness. He explained that the horse was his own, that it was not a hunter; that even under his light weight it could not live with an ordinary Dartmoor field

"Then you ought to make up in cleverness what he lacks in pace," argued Philip "You know the Moor inside out, and you ought to be so well up in short cuts and dodges, that you ought to take your hoss where t'others dare not go, and be in it all the time—specially with the harriers. I won't say nothing about fox-hounds if you'll stick to the harriers."

"I'd rather not, father. I'd much sooner just go out quiet and take my own way and think about things. 'Tis no pleasure to me to be in a crowd of hounds and people and all the rest of it."

"You might think of my pleasure, then, and remember I'm a bit wiser than you still and a bit longer sighted too A time will come, as you mean to turn farmer, when you'll be sorry you didn't know the country-side better. The way to do it is to be friendly with your own generation and make friends and get well thought upon Then, when you grow up and take your share in the work of the world, there you are: you've got friends waiting everywhere around."

"There's other ways of making friends, father, besides hunting," declared Martin; but the farmer lost his temper and called the boy a milksop and a psalm-singing young humbug.

The sabbatic temperament of Martin soon learned to value these outbursts at their own slight worth. They rose and passed like a summer storm, and the boy mourned them, yet did not suffer largely from them. He tried hard to please Philip, and in some directions succeeded.

Martin spent a good deal of his holiday time at the house of Quinton Crymes, and he liked his aunt, Gertrude Crymes, right well. Her piety was genuine. He discovered that religion was more to her than to his mother. And Minnie proved very serious too.

He took walks with Minnie and imparted much of his growing knowledge to her. She loved him now, and dearly loved him, while he felt pleasure in her company and a lively satisfaction at her trust and faith in all that he said or did.

He talked to her of Tiger.

"I'm very fond of him," said Martin; "but I wish he'd let me tell him a bit about serious matters, Minnie. He's took father for his model in all things, but there's another side to it—good as father is, and so kind-hearted. He doesn't say his prayers no more—Tiger, I mean; and when he used to, he only prayed to be made fierce; and when he gave up that silliness, he only prayed to have the biggest muscles on Dartymoor. He told me so, and when I said 'twas wrong, he said that a chap naturally prayed for what he wanted most."

"He's awful good and kind."

"In a way—yes; but you want more than that. You can't live your life without help, Minnie."

"No, Martin."

"Tiger hasn't had any troubles yet. He has nobody to care for."

"Yes, he has. He's friend to Mary French."

"That! That's nothing. I mean he hasn't got a father or mother or any brothers or sisters."

"That's not the same as troubles, Martin."

"Not with you. But father is a trouble sometimes, because I know he does wrong things, and it isn't my place to interfere."

"I suppose we all do wrong things sometimes, Martin. But my mother and father never seem to do any."

"More does my mother. If father would only listen to her more. She's very wise, Minnie."

"So mother always says, Martin."

"Tiger, you see, hasn't got more than bare reading and writing, and doesn't want more. I offered to give him some lessons of an evening in figures, because I'm pretty good at figures for my age, but he said that he hadn't got no use for them at present. What interests him about school are the fights and games, and so on."

"You're so different, Martin."

"Games are very interesting, but I don't care for any but cricket."

There had come a new pastor to the chapel of the Little Baptists, and Martin asked Minnie what her mother thought of him.

"Mother's not very pleased with him," she answered. "She says he's too young to have got to know what sorrow and trouble mean. And a pastor as don't know that, mother says, ban't going to be useful yet awhile."

Martin considered.

"Has he got a fine run of words?" he asked.

"I don't know," she replied. "You'd better ask mother. He's shorter in his prayers than what Mr. Medlicott was."

"What does Mr. Twigg think about him?"

"I couldn't tell you, Martin."

"I should like to hear him for myself," declared the boy; "but I always go to church along with mother, and I don't know whether she'd like for me to go to chapel."

"Perhaps she'd come. I've heard father and mother say that she always used to go afore she was married."

"I know; but she's a thought against the Little Baptists, if anything, now. Father's so hard on 'em that he's set mother against 'em a bit, I fancy."

"She might come and hear the new gentleman, now-ever"

"I never thought to ask her to do it But there wouldn't be no harm done in asking her"

Martin was impressed with the idea, and kept silence for some time while he reflected upon it. The children went home to tea presently. His holiday was nearly at an end, and he had come to say good-bye to aunt and uncle. Now he asked Mrs Crymes concerning Gregory Twigg's opinion of the new pastor.

"Mr. Twigg haven't given me the benefit of his judgment yet," she answered, "only I happen to know what he said to his wife He's a little uneasy on doctrine, he's going to speak to Mr. Bewes himself and throw some light Mr. Bewes is only thirty-four."

But this seemed a great age to Martin.

"I should like to hear him," he said.

"There's nothing against his words He's very earnest and his face shines. Beautiful words, and a voice that makes you jump, after so many years of Mr. Medlicott's weak pipe But there's no warmth to the man He ban't a very patient person by the sound of him But no doubt 'twill all come."

The boy parted from them presently and returned home again Minnie went as far as the gate with him, and there were tears in her eyes when he said 'Good-bye.' He saw them, but they did not move him except to words.

" 'Tis very, very kind of you, Minnie, to be sorry I'm going, but you must remember how good it is for me. I wish your father was rich enough to send you to school But, as he can't, you must let me hand on such things as you'd like to learn."

"You've taught me all I know already, Martin"

"That's nothing yet. But I'll try and teach you a lot more come next spring."

"Do you get any holiday at Easter, Martin?"

"Yes, I do."

"And shall I write you a little letter next month on your birthday, Martin?"

"Yes, Minnie, and I promise to answer it. But don't send no present or anything like that. If you think to give me one——"

"Of course, Martin!"

"And very kind it is. But keep it till I come home. No use wasting money to send it by post. I shall think just as much of it when I come home."

"So I will then, if you'd rather I did."

"Yes, I would. It's a great thing to be saving. I wish my father wasn't so free-handed I often see it worry mother. But there's one thing. He gives me a lot, and I tell mother on the quiet that it's all safe in my money-box, so that makes her feel happier, because she knows I don't waste it."

When Minnie had gone, Martin thought about her, and told himself that she was good and kind and fond of him. He felt that he was fond of her too; and, upon returning home, talked about her to his mother before Philip.

Ouldsbroom agreed, and praised Minnie heartily.

"She's a dinky maid, and if 'twasn't for all the psalm-singing at Stannon, she'd be a cheerful one," he said. "Uncle Quinton's all right, Martin; but don't you give too much heed to your Aunt Gertrude. She's a bit given to——"

His wife interrupted him.

"Now we've agreed to drop that, father. And as to Minnie, none likes her better than I do. And Martin is right to like her, and like her brothers and sisters also, for that matter. They be all nice, sweet childer—save Samuel. And when he goes off next year to the training ship at Devonport, he'll soon be so good as the rest."

"He's the best of the boys now," declared Philip. "There's a pinch of the devil in him, as there ought to be in every nipper."

That night, when they were gone to bed, her husband began again to talk to Unity on the subject of Minnie Crymes.

"I'm a great stickler for boys to marry early," he said, "though I didn't do it myself—luckily for me. But if

Martin has a liking for that quiet girl, I don't think we
ought to stand in the way of it."

"They're children. You do run on so."

"Children now; but she'll be wife-old afore you can
look round, and Martin would be of age to marry in three
years."

"Don't put no such folly into his head."

"You needn't fear that. He's got no use for my sense
—or my folly either. I only mean that 'twould be a
settling thing for him, come presently, to be properly
tokened to her. 'Twould keep him happy, surely, and be
the light of his life if he loved her."

"The light of his life will never be a woman. To be
straight, Phil, I don't reckon such an arrangement would
be very clever—even if Martin thought of it. Let him
look around and see life and learn his lessons. He's not
the girl-loving sort, and a good thing he isn't. He'll see
plenty of girls higher and cleverer than Minnie Crymes
presently. 'Twould be a silly business to get tied up
to her before his eyes be opened."

"You want for him to find somebody as would take
him away from Hartland and into another business than
farming?"

"I don't want to find anybody or think of anybody,"
she answered. " 'Tis little less than ridiculous to dream
of such a thing for a child. Why, he don't know the
meaning of love yet. How should he at sixteen?"

"I'll grant that," answered the man. "But I've a
notion that come he did, it might be the saving of him
and get him to take larger views all round and be a little
kinder to everybody."

"He's kind enough. But 'tis one of them rare natures
that can't understand the temptations of people, because
'tis so seldom tempted itself. You know his master said,
when he wrote last Christmas, that he was an extraor-
dinary good boy."

"I know; and he wrote it as if he was a bit disappointed in him."

"Nonsense, Phil!"

"Well, I do wish with all my heart he'd fall in love

with Minnie presently. Such a thing might make him larger-minded. And it might tempt him to spend a little out of his precious money-box. He was asking me yesternight if he'd got enough to put out at interest. Lord! To hear him!''

''That was Barbara's fault. He has ten pound in the Post Office Savings Bank, and she's told him he could get better interest elsewhere. And that's troubling him.''

''I wish to God something bigger would come along to trouble him. And maybe when it does——''

''Don't be fretful. He's going on all right. You'll be proud of him yet, Phil.''

He snorted, and expired a great impatient breath.

''Well, here's another holiday ended anyway,'' he said.

And when Martin had been at school again a week, his father was already planning the first hamper and deciding upon what day he might go to Bovey. Neither did he forget Minnie Crymes, but went more than once to Stannon on purpose to see her. He felt as though he had discovered her. His mind already wove romances round her. He pictured her his daughter-in-law. He found out that Martin was her hero, and he listened to her telling stories of the boy's wisdom and greatness. To learn so much of Martin from a new point of view was pleasing to Philip. He shouted Minnie's praises in and out of season to many ears. He gave her presents. These somewhat embarrassed her, because the farmer whispered with them that she was not to mention the gifts to anybody.

''Things may happen,'' he said, ''and I'd be very well pleased if they did, Minnie. And I want for you to know that, whatever does hap, I'm your friend and on your side—and on Martin's side.''

He prattled on and hinted of possibilities; but he was talking over the girl's head, and only puzzled her. She looked into his great beaming blue eyes, felt his hand grip upon hers, and wondered what he meant. But she saw that he was happy and hopeful, and that he liked her the better for liking Martin. Therefore she felt vaguely happy too. When Martin's birthday came,

Philip heard of the arrangement concerning Minnie's present.

"You send it," he said; "and don't you never let him dictate to you in matters of money. He's a thought too fond of money—to say it lovingly, and you mustn't help him to hoard: you must help him to spend—if you want to please me "

Minnie understood, but she was old enough to feel that the master-wish of her life centred in Martin's pleasure, not his father's. She kept the present until Martin returned, because he had told her to do so.

CHAPTER VI

A YEAR had passed, and Gregory Twigg, grown elderly now, but otherwise unchanged, gazed from the door of his home into a wet and stormy gloaming toward the end of December. Before the 'Warren House' there stretched wide spaces of former activity, where once tin miners had worked; and more than this dreary, broken region of rotting mounds, dry watercourses, and deserted machinery could not be seen, for the air was full of a shouting storm-wind and of driving clouds that shut out all things save the water-logged foreground.

Mr. Twigg looked forth without depression He was a man whose heart carried him high above such minor tribulations as winter and harsh weather.

" 'And the fountains of the deep were opened,' " he said to himself. Then he was about to return to his empty bar when a sound of wheels and a galloping horse arrested him.

Along the road from Moreton they came, and Mr. Twigg delayed a moment to see if the traveller might stop.

A market cart appeared, with a man and boy in it. The vehicle proceeded swiftly, and in two minutes Philip Ouldsbroom, with Martin beside him, drew up and greeted Mr. Twigg.

"Never better pleased to see you and your shop, Greg. We'm storm-foundered and wet as fish; but I ban't going no farther without a drop of hot Scotch, and Martin must have some too."

The boy, who had not expected Philip to stop, spoke, under his breath, for fear of hurting Mr. Twigg.

"Wouldn't it be better to keep going right home, father? We're very wet."

"Stuff! Get down and take the hoss round the lew side of thicky shippon. Then come in the bar. But throw the tarpaulin over him Us won't be five minutes"

Martin obeyed, and presently joined Mr. Twigg and Ouldsbroom. The latter already stood by a big peat fire. His clothes were steaming, and upon the mantel-piece a tumbler of hot drink also steamed.

"The same for the boy, Greg. You needn't roll your eyes He's a teetotaler most times—ban't you, Martin? But the whole Ancient Order of Rechabites would want a drink if they was catched out in such weather as this."

"Regarded as medicine, or as the means to keep a chill out of the frame, I've never heard anything against whisky." declared Mr Twigg; "and I'm the last man to speak against it. Such as me respect liquor, same as we respect all good things; and just as I wouldn't have a bad servant on my staff, so I wouldn't have bad liquor in my cellar."

He helped Martin, and the boy sipped and coughed

"Put some more water, please, Mr. Twigg," he said.

Gregory, who esteemed Martin very highly, was about to obey, but Philip stopped him.

"Not at all. Let him taste it and 'twill brace him and make a man of him. Down with it! And don't pull faces, else Greg here will be cross."

"Far from it," declared Mr. Twigg. " 'Tis the last drink for boys, speaking at large, and I'm the last man to give it to boys—that or beer either—in a general way."

"Give me another, anyhow."

Martin fought with his liquor, and waited, cold and uneasy, while his father drank. He liked Mr. Twigg, and was always glad to see him and listen to him Now, when Philip was not looking, he poured the greater part of his glass into the sawdust, and when Ouldsbroom urged him to take more, he refused.

The innkeeper supported him, and the men argued, while the boy went out to look to the horse

Philip lighted his pipe and set his feet to the fire.

" 'Tis worth while waiting a bit," he said. "I reckon the weather will break presently. And what d'you think of my nipper, Greg? He'll be pretty near so clever as you yourself at the gait he's going."

"You are blessed in a very proper boy," said Mr Twigg. "I've watched him grow in wisdom and favour with God and man, neighbour. He's the sort to leave the world better than he found it—as I shall have done myself when my Maker calls. My wife was saying to me that, little though I see him, he's got my mark on him already. He's serious-minded and a seeker after the things that cannot perish."

"Don't you talk about 'your mark.' Keep your mark for your sheep and ponies. 'Tis his brains I set store by. Sharp as a needle and full of great ideas. Damned if I ban't most frightened sometimes when he comes home for the holidays! To walk him round be kicklish work. A lot of silliness too; but that's not his fault. You can't go to school and not larn a bit of worthless stuff along with the rest. I tell him that they can't teach him how to farm Dartymoor down to the in-country. For why? They don't know. But 'twill come right."

He drank, and talked, and drank again.

"Between ourselves, there's a fault, however. He's terrible religious, but he's near. For my part I wish he was neither; because you religious men be not a rap more certain in your dealings than the likes of me—not when it comes to business; but nearness is a vice, and if you can tell me how to stamp that out of him, I'll thank you."

"We must be just before we are generous," declared Mr. Twigg. "Still, the saying is often an excuse for a man to be mean. I grant you that. He who giveth to the poor lendeth to the Lord. I'll speak to Martin and tell him that the saving spirit can be pushed too far."

"He's all for putting money out at interest, and such like."

"Don't prevent it; don't prevent it. But show him where the best interest can be got. However, you haven't learnt that yourself, so you'd better leave the teaching to me. I shouldn't take another, Ouldsbroom—really I should not. You've got to get home."

"Damn it; don't I know that? I say, don't I know

that? 'Tis because I've got to get home I want another —and another on top, very like.''

Martin returned.

"The dark is coming down," he said.

"Let it," answered Philip. "We know our way, I believe Twigg here wants to talk to you, Martin. He's marked what I have marked in you; and 'tis a beastly fault—I say 'tis a beastly fault, and you're got to stir yourself and do better ''

The boy flushed deeply under his brown skin and looked from one man to the other.

"Don't be troubled," said Mr. Twigg. " 'Tis a fondness for money, my poor boy—not a fault exactly, if kept in the bounds of reason and religion; but it often grows to be a canker in the human heart, till we lose sight of what money is given us for and give worship to it for itself. You mustn't get fond of filthy lucre, Martin Oh no, you must remember that we are stewards, and that a tithe is not ours at all. You mustn't rob the watching, loving Lord, Martin You——''

"Stop!" cried Philip. "If you be going to talk that twaddle, Greg, I'll be gone Give me another of the same and then I'm off. You put it all wrong. I say you put it all wrong—wrong. I can preach better than that—so can his mother.''

Mr. Twigg was hurt and startled.

"If you really think so——''

"Gimme my drink; and you can pay, Martin. Out wi' your cash! I know you've always got a store. Be you one to deny your father a drink? I'd break your neck—I say I'd break your neck if I thought so. I'd break any man's neck—I'd——''

The distressed boy brought forth a little leathern purse, and his father made him count the contents

"Dammy, he's rolling in money—rolling in it! Five and twopence.''

"Two shillings are mother's.''

"And mine. Be us to have separate purses—us three? Mine's yours and yours be mine, and all's mother's And now us had better get on the road—I say us had best to get on the road, else they'll think we'm drowned ''

Mr. Twigg helped Ouldsbroom into his trap with some difficulty, and he was glad that the farmer made no objection when the boy took the reins.

Philip began to sing a bawdy song, and Martin felt dull anger throbbing in him as he drove swiftly forward. Great indignation burnt in his young heart. To him this display was gratuitously wicked. He resented his father's drunkenness, he resented his song; above all, he resented his indictment. That his father could complain of him to Mr. Twigg left Martin bruised and almost bitter. There was none whose good opinion he valued more than Gregory's.

A tramp approached them as they descended the hill into Postbridge. He was ragged, lame, and dripping. The man stopped as the cart passed him, and touched his hat; but Martin paid no heed. Then Ouldsbroom bade him draw up.

"Hullo, my brave hero, you'm a thought wet seemingly," he said.

The man began a sorrowful tale, and Philip cut him short.

"I know—I know—a hell of a world if you draw a blank. Give the chap that half-crown out of your purse, Martin''

"Father!''

"Yes, 'father.' Give him that half-crown, and be quick about it. Who be the like of us to keep him standing in the mire when he wants to get on his way to food and shelter? I say who be the like of us? Be quick, or I'll fling you out of the cart!''

Martin obeyed; the wanderer uttered a flood of thanks, and the boy drove on. Out of his eyes dropped fiery tears. He felt sick and frightened. He did not speak again, but his father did.

"That'll larn you to be large-minded. You don't know your luck yet. You don't know all the good fortune you're born to. And that poor, harmless dirt there —just so good as you or me once, I dare say. Just so good as you or me. Maybe a damned sight better. And that bit of money will be the turning-point for him so like as not. 'Tis time your mind was stretched a bit, Martin, and I be going to stretch it—to stretch it, I say.''

That night the boy slept little. He had spoken to his mother when Philip went to bed, and she had counselled patience, and foretold that, with another day, he would find the master sane and contrite. But she smarted much in secret, and looked without joy upon the future when Martin must return home to leave it no more.

Meanwhile the boy debated many things, and, before he slept, determined that he would speak quietly to his father when morning came, and try if he might influence him. He would approach under the ægis of his mother's name. He would speak as one who loved her only less than Philip himself loved her. For while Martin could not understand the man's failings, he had sense to mark that Philip's affection for Unity was the leading, reigning principle of his life. To her, when sober and self-contained, he was always loyal; against her none had ever heard him say an unkindly word. He might grumble to Barbara, or protest to his wife herself at some passing failure or difference of opinion, but Unity continued his abiding beacon. And Martin knew it. He planned his little remonstrance, therefore, and fell asleep rehearsing the form that it should take.

He met Ouldsbroom in an evil hour next morning, for the man was suffering from his intemperance of the previous day. He endured physical discomfort, and shame had made him sulky.

"May I speak to you, father?" asked Martin as they met in the farmyard; and the other answered:

"Yes; if you've got a drop more sense in you since yesterday.''

"I—I—you see, father, it's cruel to be so hard on me. I know how 'tis about money, and how you've got to stint to send me to school, and I—— Of course 'tis your money, and all I've saved be yours too. It came from you——''

"Ban't I always saving myself—or trying to do it? But there's a sort of saving that loses all. You're so beastly mean, and I won't have it. I ban't going to give you back a penny of your money—not a penny. And you can grumble as much as you please."

" 'Tisn't that. I'm not fond of the money for itself, father. Only mother is always saying to me to look ahead. My way pleases her, and I save for her sake, and I wish that you too—for her sake, father——"

Then Philip raged as no man had seen him rage before.

" 'For her sake'—'for her sake'! God damn you, you whelp! D'you think I want you to teach me my duty to your mother?"

He lifted his fist and struck Martin a heavy blow on the head. The boy fell stunned, and while he lay on the ground, with his hands lifted to his forehead, Ouldsbroom cried out again. His words tripped each other, and he roared.

"Let that larn you sense and decency. 'For her sake'! You unnatural dog! When you can love like I can, when you can worship your mother like what I do—when you've got a heart in your cur's body that's the shadow of your father's heart—then come and tell me how to treat your mother, and not afore! You dare to preach to me again, and I'll do more than hit you down—I'll break your blasted neck. To your own father—to dare! And to name my duty to her! I could weep, I tell you— ess fay, I could shed bloody tears to think a child of mine—— Get up and crawl out of my sight, and ax your blessed God to teach you your duty to your father—as have done his duty to you, faithful and loving and true, since the day you was born. Get going, and don't you see me no more to-day."

The boy rose and slunk off, the man, panting and raging, strode to his stable, brought out his horse, and went away bare-backed into the Moor.

He did not return till dusk, and by that time the evil of yesterday's drink had departed from him, and he mourned to think what he had done. As the hours passed a great grief settled upon him and in the silent places aloft his act looked awful to his eyes. He perceived that the words Martin let fall with such deadly force were

16

meant otherwise than he had understood them. He
judged that his boy did not know the meaning of the
thing he had uttered.

Philip returned at nightfall, contrite and ready to
make amends. There was a bruise on Martin's forehead,
and the lad was tearful and very nervous in his father's
presence. But none spoke of the incident, and Unity
did not allude to it even after her son had gone to bed.
She waited for Philip to do so. The matter was on his
lips in a moment.

He told her everything, declared that he had wickedly
misunderstood Martin, blamed the drink of the previous
day, swore that the fault was all his and none of Martin's
making. She answered that the boy had cared nothing
for the blow.

" 'Twas that he had not made his meaning clear what
hurt him most, not your fist," she explained. "He's
terrible fond of me and—well, least said soonest
mended, I reckon. The sooner he's back at school the
better."

She sighed, and Philip saw that she had been much
perturbed. He talked, but she said little; then he went
upstairs to see Martin. The boy was speaking aloud, and
did not hear his footfall. At the door of the little room
Philip stood a moment and listened. As a gift handed
down to him—perhaps a donation of heredity from his
preaching grandfather—Martin had an instinct to offer
oral prayers and, when moved, he often did so. To-night
he called upon his God to make him better and wiser—to
forgive him for wakening his father into such anger, and
to pardon his father for being angry. Philip heard and
was crushed to the earth.

He went in to Martin, and lifted him from his knees,
put his arm round him, gripped his hands, and begged
humbly for forgiveness. He promised amendment; he
showered censure upon himself, he explained to Martin
all that he was doing and planning to make life better
and happier for Unity. He made Martin forgive him and
promise to understand him better. He vowed that now
indeed he knew what Martin was, and that no shadow

could ever come between them again. The boy, tearful and hopeful, slept presently; but it was long before his mother or her husband did so.

Philip's excitement would not abate. He talked on for hours after he and his wife were in bed. He exhibited an absolute trust in what to-morrow must bring forth. That day had seen wonderful things, he declared. It was a day to be marked with a white stone, albeit no morning had ever dawned darklier.

"Us be nearer together than ever before since the snake bit him," declared Philip. " 'Tis as if a shadow was lifted from between us. Never, never again will there be so much as a frown separate me and him. I see what a wonder he is, and I see that he can't but do right and reason with the love of you he's gotten. You be his guiding star, same as you be mine, Unity; and with such a light upon us, how can us be anything but close, close father and son? 'Tis impossible, I tell you. I know him inside out now, and he knows me too—so well as a child can know a man and the depths of a man. Henceforth there'll be such a friendship grow up as will surprise you. By God, there will! Give and take, mind. We shall please each other, Unity—we shall plan how to do it. 'Tis all clear as light between us. We've talked it all out; we've forgived each other; we'm heart to heart a'ready, you may say—in a fashion we never was till now."

She listened.

CHAPTER VII

Time passed, and each holiday of Martin's dawned in hope and set in gloom. As for the boy, his observation quickened much and he progressed steadily in understanding.

He spoke to Tiger two days before he returned to school after his summer vacation

"You're older than me, and you've the knack to do things that I can't do," he said. "I've come to see of late what a deal father thinks of you, Tiger, and quite right too, for you please him properly and you think like him."

"He've made me," declared Tiger; "I owe him and missis everything, and I'd do anything in my power for 'em."

"I know. You feel very properly to him, and you ought to. If you went to church and felt thankful for all the good that's happened to you, Tiger, you'd feel properer still. As it is, you thank father for all, instead of looking beyond father, where you ought to look. But the thing is that you have got a power over my father."

"Never, Master Martin!"

"Yes, you have. I'm very fond of my poor father, and I'm very wishful to help him. You know what I mean But I can't get at him like you can. Don't pretend 'tisn't so In a word, I want you to do everything you know to keep him—to keep him steady, Tiger. I don't say 'tis in your power, or anybody's, to do much good. If my mother can't put it right, 'tis very sure you can't

and I can't; but he does turn to you a lot. And he'll
take from you what he wouldn't from anybody living,
for I've marked it. 'Tis your rough-and-ready way, I
suppose. I've often wished you were a bit more serious-
minded, Tiger, for you might have worked wonders with
my father if you had been."

"Not me," declared the other. "He'd wince away
very quick; he'd soon have no use for me if I was that
sort. And I ban't that sort, and don't want for to be.
He's good enough for me and good enough for anybody
What's cussing and swearing against the things he
thinks of? What's his words against his deeds? I'd
sooner be large-minded like him than pious-minded like
other people."

"Whether or no, he drinks too much, and each time I
come home I see him drink more; and 'tis turning my
mother's hair grey. He forgets his age. 'Tis very bad
for him, and an evil example to the men and you."

Tiger was silent for a moment. Then he spoke.

"I know you're right enough there," he said. "And
I do try, so far as I dare, and I will again."

"That's what I ask, and I tell you that you could do
a bit towards it. You're said to be eighteen years old
now, and you're strong and sensible. I beg you, Tiger,
for my mother's sake, and because we've been friends
ever since we were children, to do what you can. I've
got another year at school, and then I shall come home
for good, and do all I know to help mother with father,
and pay them well for all they've done for me. But a
year's a long time."

"I'll bear in mind what you say," answered the elder.

And he kept his word. But there developed from
this attention a difficulty that neither of the boys had
guessed at, and Ouldsbroom's wife was the first to perceive it. A glimmering dawn of jealousy against Tiger
had faded for a time, and now it revived and waned no
more. After the promise to Martin, the older lad pursued a part agreeable enough to himself and sought his
master more than formerly. He had always entertained
a profound admiration for Philip, and as Tiger entered

into manhood this regard increased with his own waxing understanding. He was built on a mental pattern to see little more than the goodness of his master. He liked the genial and reckless nature of him; he desired to be such another, and imitated Philip as much as possible. And Ouldsbroom gradually grew to find Tiger a very vital feature in his life. The lad had more common sense than the man; he was able to retain Martin's goodwill; he had often succeeded in bringing Philip back into friendship with Martin after a quarrel. He had steered him out of strife in other directions. All this Unity perceived and welcomed; but she also awoke to the fact that Tiger was no longer a boy; and she suspected that his control threatened to become supreme with her husband. That the influence worked for good and peace she could not deny, its force alone she began to fear. More than once, in a passion, Philip had openly wished that Tiger and not Martin was his son. After such explosions he did indeed lament and redouble his affection for Unity's child; but she knew well enough that nature bent Ouldsbroom more and more towards Tiger, and she asked herself what might come of this as the man grew weaker and the youth more strong.

There was none save Barbara Hext to whom she cared to speak upon this subject, and even there she hesitated, because she guessed that the postmistress would laugh at her Philip's farm was not entailed. He might do what he pleased with it. She felt no difficulty in picturing him making a new will and handing everything to Tiger. So mad a step he might regret and possibly revoke when effected; but the likelihood of it made her uneasy; she felt that Tiger's influence for good upon her husband was too dearly purchased by the increasing trust and amity that Ouldsbroom displayed towards him.

Unity spoke to none; but at last there came the needed inspiration, and she decided to appeal to Tiger directly. Well she knew him, and well she knew that he was loyal and honest. He had never dreamed of the thoughts in her mind; he had never asked or hoped for anything better than presently to work for Martin and rise to be his right hand. But Unity knew how ambition ripens with age; she guessed at the conversations held between man and boy; she felt positive that the time had come for Tiger to leave Hartland while yet his mind was clean and unsullied by vain hopes and hungerings. She judged him by herself, and remembered what, at his age, had served most to influence her thoughts and actions. The difficulty of getting him away would be considerable; but she did not shirk it. She understood him and guessed that an appeal to his nature would cut the knot. He must go of his own free will. He must desire to go and insist upon going, no matter how hardly Philip might try to keep him. She decided to be exceeding frank with Tiger. He was the heart of frankness himself and might best be influenced in that spirit.

Unity matured her scheme and weighed her words before uttering them. Then there happened an incident that postponed her intention; for trouble and a threat of great loss fell upon Philip, and she felt that this was no moment to bring further care upon him. She was shaken in another particular also. Martin had told her of his speech with Tiger and of the boon that he had begged. She watched, therefore, and was constrained to admit that Tiger had come between Philip and the bottle on more than one occasion. He had a power that now Unity herself began to lack. Her old authority over Philip was diminished, but she could not tell how or by what means it had decreased. And the lost credit promised to belong to Tiger presently. She was jealous at this; she even found it in her heart secretly to rejoice when Tiger failed, as he often failed. Her pride resented it that Tiger should possess a power of control lacking in her son; yet, while she felt angered in thought, reason told her plainly enough that the thing was inevitable if not desirable.

She was about to speak to Tiger when Barbara Hext fell ill and postponed her action.

The postmistress had for some time been failing, and now she suffered a stroke and came into the shadow of death. She could speak freely, and her mind was not obscured. She desired to see Philip on the morning after her attack, and he hastened to her. They were left alone together, and he sat beside her bed

"The end, Phil," she declared. "I'm well past three-score and ten, remember. Seventy-five this year, and not sorry to go."

"Don't you talk of it. 'Tis just a warning that you musn't work so hard—no more than that."

"I'm not sorry to go, I tell you. And I want for you to see me under ground. I thought to be taken across the road long ago, and I've chosen my place. There must be no nonsense talked over me, Philip. I must be buried as I have lived—free. If there's anything after, then I shall have my share in it. If I'm wrong in what I believe, I shall be glad. But as it is with me, I go to a dreamless sleep and can't believe in any awakening. I want you to read a bit of Job beside the grave—nothing else at all."

"Yes, I will, then. But 'tis bad for you to run on so. Time enough. I don't believe you be at your latter end, Barbara. You don't look like it. Your voice rings so clear as a bell."

She shook her head.

"It can't be long, even if I get over this. 'Tis a stroke, Philip. We tough old people that Death can't sweep away at a breath, he tackles different. He gets the thin end of the wedge in, like a woodman. Then 'tis all up with us, and he only waits his own good time to drive it home and bring us down. I'm sorry to leave you, Phil. I'm very, very fond of you, and I know what you are better than any living creature."

"You can't go—you shan't go! I couldn't get on without you, Barbara. Your sense be a big part of life to me. None ever had such understanding—none."

They talked, and she told him that she had left twenty pounds to Martin and twenty pounds to Tiger. That she had willed a hundred pounds to Philip himself, she did not mention.

"My little estate goes to my nephew at Plymouth," she said. "I like him, for he's a freethinker and an

honest man and a good one. He has five children and a
sick wife. 'Twill be light on their darkness. He's a
watchmaker, and well thought upon and badly off.''

Philip rose presently to go; but not before he had
promised to come and read with her on the following day.

"Kiss me, Phil," she said. "And to-morrow—and
to-morrow us'll go bit by bit through Job, and fasten
on such few words as I could wish spoken to them that
may stand by my grave.''

He promised to obey; he then departed from her much
cast down. For the first time he pictured life without
Barbara and found it very empty. He had lived so near
her and seen so much of her that he had not perceived
her approaching end. He forgot her age, for age sat
lightly upon himself. He felt surprise now to learn that
she was nearly seventy-five. He himself approached
close to sixty, but nothing spoke of it to him. He was
strong and hale as ever. Only his hair had grown thinner
and whiter. On his good days, the genial life of him
still bubbled over, and generosity and sympathy continued to be the notes of his character.

He returned home sorrowful, and walked thrice again
to the valley that he might learn how Barbara fared.
The last report was good, and he went back to Hartland
more cheerful. That night he read aloud from Job, and
when his throat grew husky, he made Tiger continue to
do so.

"I'm to speak from it over her grave,'' he explained
to Unity after they had retired. "She's not going to
have no parson say anything. She's going to be buried
as she's lived—free. But I hope to God the time is far
ways off yet. She's got all her wits, and that's saying
a lot. She's gived our Martin twenty pound—bless her
kind heart, and she's gived Tiger twenty too.''

His wife guessed that this might be an opportunity
to approach Tiger, and even considered whether she
should now discuss the possibility of his departure with
Philip himself. But he spoke on while she debated, and
soon she learned that the shadowed death of his friend
had sorely troubled him. She had never seen Philip so

despairing, so stricken; and before this grief she perceived, for the first time, all that Barbara Hext had been to him.

She determined to delay any step in the matter of Tiger until after the threatened misfortune.

CHAPTER VIII

PHILIP read Job to the sick woman, and she bade him mark this verse and that. The exercise gave her considerable satisfaction and occupied some hours on several mornings. Then, little by little, the evil symptoms were modified and a new lease of life was granted to Miss Hext.

Its duration promised to be precarious, but for the time she enjoyed comfort and some return of strength. Her activity was much curtailed henceforth, yet as soon as possible she came again to the shop, sat in the midst, and directed the two girls who now worked for her. A young man from Plymouth was in temporary control of the post-office.

Philip rejoiced extravagantly before this recovery, and his exultation extended to many others. None but was glad to know that a leading figure in the hamlet, and one well liked by most of her neighbours, might still for an uncertain length of days be spared.

There met by chance a gathering in the shop near Christmas, and the people were happy to see that good store of the season's luxuries adorned Barbara's counters and decorated her windows as of old.

Peter Culme, the hunchback, was there, and Mr. Twigg of the 'Warren House' had called. Mary French, from Teign Head, came for Christmas shopping, and there entered also Philip Ouldsbroom, and Tiger with a basket in each hand. Miss Hext sat in a comfortable chair behind the counter and directed her two assistants. She trembled often to leap up and serve herself; but the time for that was over. At best she needed now two sticks to guide her going.

251

The egregious Gregory was in a large and retrospective mood. He condescended to include Miss Hext in the flight as he ranged back upon his brilliant past.

"Neighbour Culme here and a few others must listen and learn from such as us," he began. "I may say that I have walked in a sphere not to have been expected from my beginnings. They were as humble, or nearly so, as Tiger's here. But there was that in me that soared from the womb. I was never even a common suckling child. The Light came to me at a very tender age. And understanding men soon saw my nature and were proud to lend a hand. You and me, Miss Hext, have mixed in a better class of society, and much has been naturally revealed to us that is hid from Postbridge. Religion is a great bond and also a great uplifter. I had it so abundantly that it couldn't be hid, and my betters—so to call them—soon found out my nature. Hands were stretched out to me on every side. 'Twas the case of the humble being called to the place at the upper end of the feast. It often happened, and I can say without boasting, that 'twas an everyday thing for me to eat at the tables of the rich."

"Their kitchen tables—yes," said Tiger. "So have I."

Philip laughed, and Gregory was much annoyed.

"Is that your manners?" he asked sharply. "But there—you are what you are. If a man's godless, 'tis ten to one but he's also without any veneration. But don't you speak again, please, when I'm in company. I ask your master to forbid it. Respect I have from my own generation, and so much the more should I command it from the next. If you took upon you a decent name, and went to chapel, or, failing that, the Establishment, you might hope to cut a properer figure in the world than ever you will cut, you indecent boy."

"A boy no more," declared Philip. "He's a man—eighteen-year-old, and big and strong at that. He's my bringing up, ban't you, Tiger? and I'm proud of him."

"Then teach him modesty to his superiors," answered the innkeeper. "The young ought to be on their knees before the face of such as me or Miss Hext here. Fun I allow in its proper place, but not familiarity. The new generation is too familiar, and it's all summed up in that We, as have the solemn awfulness of age upon us, ought to be treated according. But grey hair's a laughing-stock now, and a bald head's a joke.''

"Things must be as they must," said Barbara. "We can glimpse what's coming, but we shall be taken away from it. I don't say 'the evil to come,' but the changes to come. Good changes, for certain."

" 'Twill be evil," declared Mr. Twigg "We're drifting to Antichrist faster and faster. We've got to go through it, and just the blessed few will weather the storm and keep their lamps burning to help light the battered world again after 'tis over. But he's got to come first and work his terrible will, and we can't hope for any lasting improvement till he's been and gone. That's how I read Scripture, and I've not heard that anybody reads it truer.''

"Us shall be away afore he comes," said Peter. " 'Tis something, no doubt, to have escaped him; but such as have childer and grandchildren ought to be careful to warn 'em.''

"Tell these old men they be damned fools, Barbara.'' said Philip.

She laughed.

" 'Tis what they are nourished on," she said. "If you eat child's meat, you'll be childish. You chaps—you that take a big size in boots and a terrible small one in hats—are prone to think your view's the only view. You cling to the old ship, and fancy you can set the world right from her sinking deck. But the world's looking the other way. It can't be saved by you. 'Tis you that will have to be saved by it, if you live long enough. The old things are worn out—full of holes—beyond any more patching. They've tinkered and mended till there's nought of Christian Gospel teaching left. What you've got now is only the shadow of it. You may wade chin-deep in words, Gregory; but where's the man or woman can build their deeds on the Bible now? 'Tis impossible, because the world's always moving, and it's moved on beyond."

"Pray God 'tis moving in a circle, then, and will come back again," said Culme.

"There's the Spirit to quicken, if the Letter is dead, Miss Hext," suggested the young man who controlled the post-office. He was very earnest and of a religious mind.

"You and the likes of you miss the Spirit," she answered " 'Tis because the Spirit is missed that the thing has died "

"We show different," declared Gregory. "We Little Baptists shine with the Spirit; and if all men don't see our good works and glorify our Father which is in Heaven, then that's because they are blind, not because we are wrong."

"And what do the world want now, Miss Hext?" asked Tiger.

"It wants to be more brave," she answered. "It wants to face change and not stick its head into the past, like an ostrich thrusting its beak in the sand There's a number of things outlived, and 'tis no good that we pretend they are alive any more, because they're not. We must give heed to them that tell us so; not to them who pretend different. We're too weak and too soft. We run in herds, and think in herds, and crowd together to keep each other's courage up. I'd say to a young man, 'Branch out, get away from all this dead stuff; break loose, and look before you—not behind ' 'Tis like Lot's wife—them as be always staring back be turned into stone."

" 'Twould be a terrible world if that happed," said Mr. Twigg. "If the young shouldn't look back to the tried wisdom of the old, where should they look?"

"To the untried wisdom of the new," she answered "The old goodness is played out, I tell you It's served its turn, and now we want a new goodness "

The post-office clerk asked where higher goodness could be found than in the Bible.

"To seek for it is seeking better bread than can be made of wheat," he said.

"And why not seek?" she asked. "Is wheat the last word about corn? Everything's moving; and you good, Bible-believing people—I don't trust you—I don't believe in you. You pretend—you fool yourselves"

That a woman could say such things made Mr. Culme suspect possession

"She've got an evil spirit crept in," he whispered to Philip.

"Have she, Peter? Then I wish to God 'twould creep into a few more of us," answered the farmer. Thereupon he laughed, and told Miss Hext what the hunchback feared for her

"Evil or good, 'tis the spirit of the hour," she answered "'Twill cure a lot of sickly thinking when you start to serve man instead of God. Maybe our whole duty to the one is our whole duty to the other, if we could see it"

Martin Ouldsbroom entered at this moment, and most of the people in the shop left it. The boy had returned for his holidays three days before. Now he shook hands with Barbara and declared how very glad he was that she had recovered

"Thank you, Martin," she answered "What a man you grow—not much more schooling for you till you go into life's school now!"

They talked, and Martin bought a Christmas present for his mother. The action inspired Ouldsbroom; he bade Tiger and Martin depart that he might make various secret purchases

After they had gone, Philip found himself alone with Barbara. They left the shop, and he helped her into her little room behind it. Then he spoke to her.

"I want for my son to smoke, but be beggared if he'll larn," he said. "'Tis the hardest thing that's happened to me, for I've reached a point now when I know that whatever I hit upon as a happy thought will strike him just contrariwise. Cold—cold—and colder to me every time he comes home. Never wrong, that boy—never wrong! But his cold goodness have bred hot wickedness in me. I thought back-along that I'd larned the secret of him, and I could have shouted for joy. Things promised to go better; but they didn't. He's come back now that pushing and that full of ideas. Not an uncivil word, mind you. No chance for a bit of a flare up and friends again—I could endure that. But just silence when he ain't of my opinion—and that's most times."

"How does Tiger do with him?"

"They'm like starlings—always quarrelling, though they will keep together. He raps out at Tiger and Tiger raps out at him. 'Tis fire and water, and if I come along and take Tiger's part, as happens now and again, then Martin, instead of keeping up his end of the stick, shuts down and says no more."

" 'Tis out of respect for you."

"I don't know. Silence be a sort of disrespect, I think. Ban't I worth arguing with? Be my wide knowledge of life and experience nothing? Can't he larn from me? Be I a man behind the times? 'Tis the boy that's behind the times, with his stiff-starched larning."

She considered.

"I know the sort, Phil. You must take him as he is, and not fret. You and me are simpler—commoner. I'm not a stickler for the grand virtues. They've got no friends—only admirers. And oft enough even the admirers keep their tongues in their cheeks."

"Such virtue stinks," said the man hotly. "I hate it. 'Tis unnatural. He's a mountebank of virtue—a thief of virtue—stole it without paying for it—about so virtuous really as my grandfather's clock—ticks good time and nothing else. That's not virtue; 'tis machinery, and he ban't no more inclined towards anything but this parched-up, frozen, heart-breaking goodness than a wheel's inclined to do anything but turn round and round."

"His nature leads him mostly to right. He can't help it. He's a creature of good habits," she said.

"If you can't do wrong, you don't know what it is to do right," he answered. "I feel this—it's been seething in my brain for years and it's showed me wonderful things. 'Tisn't goodness, I tell you, to be like him—no

more goodness than an acorn's good to grow into an oak
Goodness have got to be fought for, not filched. He's
never paid the price. He's made good. He's born good.
And they talk of original sin! Where the hell have his
got to, I should like to know? All gone into love of
money—the only thing I couldn't forgive. And my son
—my blood in his veins—me, a sinful, loving, breathing,
feeling human man—have got this horrid lump of perfection. That's the damned sickening thing. How can
I tear it out of him? How can I make him like Tiger and
like me? 'Tisn't his mother neither. I'd forgive it all if
it was. She's a wonder, but she's a woman too—a woman
with hopes and fears and a heart, and a temper also, for
that matter. Should I have married a graven image?
She can do wrong so well as right. She knows how to
suffer and how to weep. We have words, and we own
up our sins and love again. We're one in pinching and
scraping to keep him learning anyway. But Martin——"

"Be patient with him. He's himself, and presently,
when life begins to pound him, he'll be softer and more
understanding. There's nothing like the fret and tear
of living. He's got a fine, lofty nature, and life will
give it an edge. I believe in him. If you can only keep
him from being pious—try to do that, Phil. It's death—
death and frost-bite and ruin."

"Don't I know it? But how?"

"I'm hopeful of the world, I tell you. Let him see
sorrow—better still, let him feel it. 'Tis the only thing
that ripens some natures. 'Tis the only thing that
ripened mine."

"I want for him to marry in a year or two. I'm hopeful that will be a good, useful eye-opener to him. He's
got blood in him somewhere, he must have—my son."

"Be sure 'tis so. A wife of the right pattern might
do much."

"Yes, she might. But he'll choose the pattern, not
me. I know the girl for that matter, and I've nought
to say but good of her, save that she thinks too well of
him and would spoil his shadow if it could be done. But
Unity and me ban't of a mind there."

17

"Be hopeful—very hopeful," she said. "After all, such a son is better than a bad lot—a rip that would do nothing but wrong and end by breaking his mother's heart, perhaps. He's human and he's very young."

Philip nodded.

"I feed on hope, you might say. And I look back now and again. See here."

He produced a pocket-book and took an old letter from it.

" 'Twas what he wrote after the snake stung him. I swore I'd never part from it, and I never shall. Somehow I feel the little chap that wrote that letter must be my son all right."

They talked awhile longer, and she cheered him, so that he made great purchases and went home in good spirits.

Christmas was the prime event of the year to Philip, and he planned mighty things on this occasion. His wife, as usual, had much ado to modify his schemes before the time of their fulfilment came.

CHAPTER IX

THE interest of life shifts so slowly that those still in the heat and turmoil thereof perceive not when they begin to drift from the central position. But surely, steadily, as the adult become old and the young take up the burden, the focus centres on new faces; those who were children enter the midst of it as men; while they who formerly figured there pass into the blur beyond and are protagonists of the play no more. They guess it not themselves, and suppose that still the throb and pulse of life beats at its highest where they sit by the fire, or in the sun; but others know differently. The most filial, the most dutiful, understanding that the prime concern lies beyond their fathers. It is their children who call loudest to those that bear the heat of the day.

Philip Ouldsbroom was the last man to grow old with any distinction, or accept the inevitable in a philosophic spirit. He resented the slightest hint or suggestion that his physical strength was upon the wane; yet he did his best to further its declension by carelessness and intemperance; he quarrelled with his wife when she essayed to limit his energies or hint at the gathering weight of his years and the dignity and increasing repose proper to them. Unity and her husband provided matter for discussion between Quinton and Gertrude Crymes.

"If I—a man ten years younger than him—can slack off and leave heavier work to Jack and the hind, how much more did ought he? I cited Coaker to him but yesterday. 'You mind Jimmy Coaker, who worked for me long years ago?' I said. 'Your end will be like his if you go on at this gait. Coaker didn't know when Time

259

had beat him. He'd have dropped here if I hadn't made him go, and as 'twas, he shortened his life by his own silliness. The things that be little to youth be big to old age. Yet foolish men will cling to youthful ways and fret when Time says, "No more of that!" Coaker would walk two miles on the high road, fine or wet, every day of his life to the end of it. No matter how coarse or how cold it might be, out o' doors he'd creep over they two weary miles. Then he'd pipe out in his age-foundered voice, "Nought's wrong—nought's wrong with an old man as can travel two mile under the hour like what I can." Go he would, and he went once too often when the wind was in the east and he had a bit of a tissic in the chest. It cut his carcass down like a dead leaf off a bough. They found him halfway home again by the roadside—asleep as they thought; but 'twas death.'"

"You told Philip that?"

"I did so, and he only laughed at me and said I was a lazy old man and the shame of such boys as him."

"If Unity can't get him to see sense, 'tis pretty sure you won't."

"I'd hoped that Martin would have a bit of power over him. The sooner the better."

"The very thing his mother said. And it will come, but not afore Phil's a bit weaker and the boy's a bit stronger," foretold Mrs. Crymes.

"There's one, however, as can hold him in a trifle, and that's Tiger."

"He can," admitted Gertrude, "and even Minnie marked it. And so did Martin too. There's no nonsense about Martin. He knows what use Tiger is. He's got a touch with Philip that none else have."

"Because he's so much on the same pattern," declared Quinton Crymes. "In my judgment, and in my sister's, 'tis a great question if Tiger is any use really. He'll get Phil past a public sometimes, or make him keep his money in his pocket when he wants to bring it out; but in the weightier matters I hold with Unity that he's no great good. There's a danger, too, that Unity sees better than we can. Phil turns more and more to Tiger. That can't be denied. And Unity feels pretty strong about it. In fact, she's told me, private like, that she'll breathe easier when the young man's gone. And you know what that means. The next bit of news we shall hear, very like, is that Tiger's said 'good-bye' to Hartland.''

''Philip would never suffer it. There'd be a terrible upstore if such a thing was so much as hinted at,'' said his wife.

''Trust Unity. She has her way still in all the big matters, along of giving him his way in all the little But 'tis harder and harder to manage him, and she don't deny it She's pretty well praying for Martin's schooling to be ended. He's a tower of strength to her, of course.''

''She told me not long since that Martin can make his mark now. 'Tis his education, she says It won't be denied. There's nought like learning to make a fool cower afore you. Not that he'll ever make his father cower; but Unity hopes, with time, that he'll force a little sense into him.''

''And he'll have to make my sister see clearer too, here and there,'' added Quinton. ''You know what I mean. If anything is certain on this earth, 'tis certain that Martin will care about our Minnie presently.''

''He do now. 'Tis wonderful how much he shows it— seeing how little he does show at any time.''

''Of course he does, and why not? Even Phil sees it, and you know how he's took up with Minnie in consequence. The presents he gives her! Phil's longing for it to happen, and would like to see 'em wedded out of hand so soon as the boy comes back from school; but Unity——''

''She wants something more in exchange for all that schooling than our Minnie,'' explained Gertrude calmly. ''She's an ambitious woman—as all be with an only son. She'll prevent it, and don't you think otherwise.''

''I don't say that Martin's stronger than her already. But it rests with him. If he wants Minnie, he'll have her.''

''Well,'' answered his wife, ''I'm the last to wish a

quarrel with your sister. I may be a bit frightened of
the woman's intellect, or I may not, and I own in her
young days I didn't like her, but she's strong and
straight, and we've got no call to be anything but her
friends. She's a wonder to have steered that man so
long."

"And does still," he said. "They are very good companions for all his vagaries. Their quarrels come to
nought, and, when he's not drunk, he's still handsome in
his praises Well, he may be, seeing he's all to blame."

"Her patience is amazing. Will it last for ever?"

" 'Twill last till he's in his grave," answered the man

Minnie came home at this moment She had received
a few lines from Martin which were enclosed in a letter
to his mother.

"I've got the letter Martin promised," she said. "He's
gone in the first class as he expected There's four new
boys to school this term, and one he likes and t'others
he don't."

Quinton laughed.

"You'll have to mend your speech come Martin gets
back," he said "You ban't talking so finicking and
nice since he went away."

She blushed.

"I try to remember," she said

She had grown into a tall and handsome girl. Her
eyes were large, dark, and a little sleepy Her breasts
were small; her hands and feet were small; there was
already the fragrance of budding woman about her, and
many young men were haunted by the thought of her.
As yet passion had not touched her and her deep love
for Martin was unfinished

She was depressed at his absence; she felt secretly
very glad that, when another winter came, he would
return home to leave it no more.

"Martin sent his love to you, mother. But he's a
good bit worried. He's been called upon for two shillings One of the masters is going away at the end of
the term, and they be collecting for him to present him
with a silver inkstand when he goes, and Martin says

that he's been paid for the work he's done and is going to a bigger school and better money, so there's no call, in his opinion, to do any such thing. And he's standing out against giving up the money, and the other boys aren't very kind about it.''

"They wouldn't be," said Quinton "I dare say they don't know the value of money so well as Martin does He always understood the worth of it in a way very surprising for a young chap ''

"What ought he to do, mother?" asked Minnie.

"He'll put it to his conscience," she answered. "Never a boy had such a good, working conscience as Martin. He takes his puzzles before the Throne and gets 'em answered ''

"He won't part," prophesied the master of Stannon. "You mark me, his conscience will tell him the two shillings be better in his pocket. They'll poke fun at him and call him 'miser' and such like, but he's not the sort to mind that.''

"Did he ax your advice, Minnie?" inquired Gertrude.

"No, he never does. He's decided what he's going to do. 'Tis at the end of his letter. He's going to give threepence, after making it a subject in his prayers.''

" 'Tisn't for us to judge him; but if ever a poor boy promised to be a rich man, Martin's that boy," summed up his uncle

"He gives money to charities, however," declared Minnie. "He wouldn't tell me how much, because he says your right hand oughtn't to know what your left hand doeth ''

"Do his playmates like him, I wonder?" mused Quinton.

"Oh, yes they do—very much," replied Minnie "Martin says they do, and he never would say it if they didn't. He says they often bring quarrels to him, because they know how terrible fair he is They oft make him judge among them.''

Sammy Crymes entered He was at home for a holiday from his training-ship

Now Sammy hated Martin more than he hated any-thing else in the world.

"I wish I had the judging of him," he said. "I'd judge for him to be took in our duck pond and held down under the dirt till he was drownded "

"You ought to blush to say such a thing," cried Minnie indignantly. "He's done nothing to you but try to im-prove you."

"Beast—beast!" answered Samuel. "I never knowed a proper chap yet that didn't want to fling stones at him."

"You wait till you've been to sea, my son, and larned the ways of a boatswain's mate," said Quinton. "Then you'll take another view of things."

Sammy was not convinced.

"If they'm like him at sea, I'll very soon escape and swim back ashore again," he answered. "But well I know they won't be. I'd sooner be lathered and cussed and kicked to pieces than stroked and preached to, any-way. Me and Tommy Bone and Will Westmacott have all sworn to God we'll catch Martin Ouldsbroom out in a crooked deed some day; and when we do, the air shall ring with it!"

"You never will—never," declared Minnie fiercely. "He's as high above all you wretched boys as the sun above the moon."

"You're as bad as him," answered her brother; "you was pretty decent once; now you'm under his thumb, and no good to anybody."

CHAPTER X

WHEN presently Philip Ouldsbroom announced he had raised Tiger's wages, in order that the young man might save more money, Unity was reminded of former anxiety. Her cares in this matter had slumbered of late, but now they woke again; she marked the close-woven texture of the friendship, and knew that never a day passed but Philip praised Tiger and sought his company. She remembered her former intention, therefore, and prepared to act upon it. But first she sounded her husband.

"I suppose, after Tiger marries we shall have to say 'good-bye' to him," she remarked on an occasion when she and Philip were driving into Tavistock.

"'Say good-bye to Tiger'!" he cried. "Me! Never —never. Tiger stands for me. I've made him. His sense, his mind, his way of looking at things—all be mine. I've made Tiger. I tell you—everything but his thews and sinews; and I'be mighty proud of him. When fools doubt me and cold-shoulder me, as I've been stung to mark here and there, then I say, 'Look at Tiger. There's a chap that be me over again; and who has a word against him?' To go! I'd like to see him go! He won't be wedded yet awhile—not till he's of age at earliest, for I forbid it sooner; but come he does, then we must see. I'd rather build him a cottage with these hands than let him go. For that matter, he wouldn't go if I was to try and make him. You must be daft even to think such a thing. And Martin too? What would Martin say?"

She calmed him down and set her thoughts to Tiger. He was now nineteen, and while, indeed, largely imbued with the spirit of his master, displayed as well a native

265

sense that he had not gleaned from Ouldsbroom He
worshipped Philip, if he worshipped anything, and would
have laid his life down for the man. It was no hyperbole
that made him actually declare as much when Unity
advised him to leave Hartland She chose a moment apt
for this direction, and waited to speak until her husband
was from home on business nigh Exeter. Then came a
day when she gave Tiger his favourite dishes at dinner
and treated him with unusual kindness. The meal ended,
she bade him light his pipe and come upon the Moor.

"You'll stare that I should waste my time or ax you
to waste yours. But 'tis not to do that that I want you,
though it may seem so. Your sense be very great for
your age, and I rely on it now I'm going to say what
I wouldn't say to any other young man no older than
you And 'tis a difficult and a hard thing to say. But
I ban't feared to say it to you, Tiger. Only mind this:
I don't speak it out of any unkindness. Far from that.
You know how many depend upon me, in a manner of
speaking And of course my son and his father come
first. Their good is your good—isn't it? Say it is."

"Be there any need to? I owe them everything Every
hope I've got in the world pretty near depends upon 'em
What they've been to me I shall never forget and never
be able to repay If me and Master Martin have a tussle
now and again, 'tis nought, and we're no worse friends
after. He's far away cleverer than me, and well I know
it And as for master, I'd give my life for him—God's
my judge."

"I know you speak in earnest, and that makes it easier
for me to go on There's things harder than giving your
life, Tiger—harder far. I know what I'm saying, for
I've had trials and sorrows deeper than fall to the lot of
many women. Life's no great thing—though you can't
offer more, because, to the young, life looks everything
Now listen to me. I want you to do something, and
'twill be the greatest thing you ever have done, or be
ever likely to. And first I'll tell you what 'tis, and then
I'll tell you why 'tis."

"For master, or Master Martin?"

"For both of 'em. For their future peace and future friendship; for justice and right and reason; for every proper cause you can think of."

"Then I'll do it, ma'am, whatever it is."

"Don't you be too sure. 'Tis a hard thing, mind, and I've had many an hour of trouble thinking upon it afore I could screw myself up to ask. Don't think I ask it with a light heart—far from that. None will feel it more than me if you grant it. And if you refuse—but you won't refuse. I know you won't refuse; and 'tis that that have made me hang fire so long before I asked. But I know, so well as I know any mortal thing, that it ought to happen for my son's sake."

"It shall happen," answered the other. "If you say 'tis right, then I'll do it."

"Master's just put up your money, he tells me. And very glad I was to know it. And I know more than that. I know a man who'll give you half-a-crown a week higher yet. We can't, because we've got to think of Martin's schooling for a bit longer; and I may tell you now, it have been a very great drain and struggle to find such a lot of money; but for him—our only one—we did it gladly. But it means close living, and I warn you 'twill be years and years afore you can hope for another rise."

"What's that to me? I'm more than satisfied. I never axed."

"It must be something to you. Look forward. You've got a wife in sight, and a rare good girl too. Life's different then, and ought to be different."

He considered a moment and an expression of dread crossed his face.

"D'you want——?" he began. Then he stopped.

"I'll be honest, Tiger." continued Mrs. Ouldsbroom. "I won't pretend I'm saying these things for your own sake only. I put your wisdom first; now I'll put your duty. Master's very fond of you—very fond of you, Tiger."

"I'd sooner know that than anything in the world, ma'am, and I'm terrible proud to know it."

"And so's Martin fond of you."

"I believe he is."

"Are you fond of him though?"

"Yes, I am—wish I may die if I ban't."

"The case is this. I've hesitated long to tell you; but now I must. Martin's father finds Martin difficult. 'Twas bound to be so, because they have different natures. And, because Martin's what he is, despite his hard efforts, he can't quite win to my husband. You've marked that?"

" 'Tis only now and again. Master very well knows the wonderful rare sort his son be."

"No, he doesn't—he can't; and I'll tell you for why. He looks from Martin to you, and in you he sees what he likes a thousand times better than his own son."

"Never!"

" 'Tis truth, and 'tis natural it should so fall out; and I don't blame you at all. Never have and never shall. But master's proud of you; he sees a quick pupil and a ready learner in you. He's made you what you are largely, and of course we'm always proud of the thing that we've made ourselves."

"And I'm proud to be like him, I'm sure. But Martin's higher and finer than me, of course. And the master knows it."

"Martin's different. I don't say he's higher and finer. You're a good, straight chap, Tiger, and you deserve to be happy, and you will be; but, as things are, you won't be happy here—just for this fatal cause that you are more to master than his own son."

"Never! Such a thing couldn't be in nature."

"Such a thing has come to be. And such a thing won't breed happiness presently. I'm not frightened of it—for why? Because I trust your growing wits to understand the master better than anybody but me myself; yes, better even than Martin can. You're like Philip in a lot of ways, and so you see and feel about him in a fashion that Martin can't. His mind is different, you see, and the things that he likes and the things that he shuns are different from those his father likes and shuns. And so it's come about that while my husband is proud of Martin and sees his gifts and virtues, yet he turns to you more and more for companionship and understanding. I trust you, as I said before. I know you're honourable and high-minded and would never influence my husband against Martin——''

"Good Lord, missis, how could I?"

"I know, I say; but you've got to ask yourself this question. Is it good for Martin for you to be here? If you are at his father's ear all the time, how can Martin get to it? If he gives heed to you always and hears his own ideas and opinions echoed from you, is it helping Martin to get any nearer to his father? I don't say that you are anything but on the right side, and I know, young though you are, you've got a bit of power with master and have used it to help him to be wiser on a Saturday night once or twice, and at other times also—I don't deny that. But I do say that if there's a shadow of fear you are coming between him and his son, or even drawing him a thought away from his son, then, Tiger, you must bethink yourself and look how your duty seems I'm only a woman, but I'm a mother and jealous for my boy. I'll say no more than that, because I've a great opinion of you and a great opinion of your sense and judgment."

He nodded and gloom fell upon him

"You want me to go?"

"God knows I do not," she answered. "I've felt like a mother to you these many years You're a good chap, and the place will be the darker for your going to all of us. I don't want you to go, any more than Martin wants you to go, or your master wants you to go. But I'm quick-sighted and far-sighted And I see that what's brewing will be a cruel bitter cup for more than one of us. I only want you to see it too I don't bid you go; I only bid you think. There's no hurry at all Turn it over in your mind Look all round it. Remember Mr Ouldsbroom's nature, and the fiery unreason of him, and the rage that sometimes flashes out of his powerlessness to understand Martin. Remember that in right and justice none should even cast a shadow between a father and his son Ask yourself your duty You'd

lay down your life for the master. You said it and I
know it. And I told you there was harder things that
men and women be sometimes called to do than to die.
Think of it—think of it with all your brains, Tiger. Say
not another word upon the subject, and come and tell
me what it all looks like in a month from now. And,
mind this, I'm your friend always, whatever you may
decide to do for my son's sake. It all comes back to
him. I won't deny that."

Tiger nodded slowly. He was already occupied with
the great problem.

" 'Twon't take a month," he said. "I'll turn it over
right away and decide so soon as I can. What you think
is always right—I know that. Who don't? I set great
store on all you've taught me, missis, because, of course,
you'm wise and up in years and know the ins and outs
of people."

She was a little moved.

"Go and think; go and think," she said. "You're a
good boy—and you've been a real help to me—more of a
help than you know; but there it is. I've spoken, and
I can't call back a word of it."

She left him then. She had not played a part. Her
words, while subtly chosen, reflected the truth. She
felt kindly to the young man, and would have been content to let him take a son's place at Hartland had no
son existed. But, for Martin's peace and prospects, she
believed that her husband and Tiger had better part,
and she had spoken accordingly.

She entertained no doubt of the issue. Tiger was as
good as gone. She knew him. He would not question
her. It remained to help him to go. The departure
must be difficult, and Tiger would need her help. Already
she began to consider the problem and how to appease
Philip when the trial came upon him.

She believed that she had won Tiger; she also guessed
that only after a cruel rupture would the young man
break away from her husband. The quarrel must take
place and must be painful. The brunt she trusted to
throw on Tiger if possible. It could not hurt him after

he had left Hartland; but there was nothing to be gained and much to be lost by involving herself in differences with Philip. Tiger must give warning; and he must let nothing shake him into changing his mind afterwards. That attitude would certainly estrange Philip, and thus the desired end must appear. If absolutely necessary, she was prepared herself to be embroiled, but only if absolutely necessary. One thing was vital: that Martin should not suffer. She saw clearly that he could not do so, since he cared well for Tiger and would stand on his father's side against his friend's departure.

Thus she argued, not without comfort to herself, nor guessed how the interests of another woman would bring her deftly woven web to ruin.

Tiger mourned this position very heartily. It bewildered him and even tortured him, for his young heart was large; his life was full and joyous; he had dreamed of no change, and his highest ambition in life was to have Mary French and a cottage at Postbridge; to rise until he should be head man at Hartland; to work for Philip, and for Martin after Philip in the future. To be torn away from the only world he knew—to be faced with this grim necessity—quelled Tiger's spirit as life had never quelled it until now.

He shook his head very wisely, very mournfully, to himself, and went back to his work after leaving Mrs. Ouldsbroom.

"I knowed it couldn't last," he thought. "Something told me that life was going too suent with me; and now— but 'tis a facer sure enough. Yet who could have put it afore me wiser than what she did?"

He turned his mind to Mary French, and there came a fleeting doubt whether he should ask her advice, or merely tell her of his decision.

"She'll be all for my stopping and try to drive me into it," he reflected. "Mightn't be ezacally fair to ask her—especially as my mind's made up."

He decided without telling his sweetheart. Three days later Mrs. Ouldsbroom met him returning from Postbridge alone.

"I've settled, ma'am," he said "You know best about it I'm hopeful that you'll let me come up over sometimes. I couldn't bear to think I wasn't to be welcome to Hartland Master's been more than a master to me—a father a'most—to say it respectfully, I'm sure I'll tell him come Monday and give him a month's warning."

"I knew you would," she said. "I know what you're made of. Remember all I've told you and be firm about it, Tiger. 'Twill be difficult to go; but you're right; and, come presently, you'll know you're right."

"I'll stick to it—say what he may."

"And I'll talk to Mr. Chave at Runnage. He's been wanting you this longful time, and he'll be thankful to get you at your own money, I believe."

He shook his head fiercely.

"Don't—don't," he cried. "For God's sake don't name money, missis. 'Tisn't for that—'tisn't for that."

CHAPTER XI

JONATHAN FRENCH'S sister was a girl of some character. The lonely life at Teign Head pleased her but little, and she looked forward with keen anticipation to her marriage and a home in civilisation.

To find her sweetheart cast down and abstracted was an event so amazing that Mary sought now to learn the reason. The lovers met upon a Sunday and walked over the Moor together. But Tiger's pipe remained in his pocket and an unfamiliar gloom clouded his brow.

The girl strove to cheer and charm him. She told him to put his arm round her; she bade him rub her soft cheek with his ruddy one. He did these things, and more; but he relapsed again and again into his own thoughts, and once, when she asked him a question, he did not even answer.

Such a state was intolerable, and Mary set about ending it.

"Pitch on this stone," she said "I ban't going a yard farther. I'd sooner walk along with a bear than you Sit down and fetch out your pipe and light it, and then tell me plain what have happened I know you well enough—better far than you know me, for that matter—and never, never afore have I seed you so down-daunted So out with it and hear if I can mend it."

"You can't," he answered. "If 'twas in the power of mortal woman to do so, of course you would, Molly But this—well, 'tis a terrible bad business and I won't pretend different. Mind you, it's got to be I see that clear enough. But I be cut up—cut to ribbons, you might say "

"You ought to have told me long ago, then, and not left me to find out "

" 'Tisn't a thing of long standing. I meant to tell you, of course; but I had to make up my own mind first "

"I doubt if you'd a right to make up your mind about anything without telling me," she declared. "Suppose I don't hold with what you think?"

He lighted his pipe and did not answer immediately.

"You've got to hold with it," he said presently.

Then he told her of his conversation with Mrs. Ouldsbroom and of his decision to leave Hartland.

"You be going to be Mrs. Tiger," he said, "and my secrets are yours, and my good's yours and my bad's yours, though I wish I could keep that to myself. And so I make a clean breast of it to you. But 'tis done, understand. To-morrow morning I tell master that I'm away in a month. That will be just afore Martin comes back for the summer holidays, you see."

" 'Tis a hugeous upheaval," she declared blankly.

"So 'tis, then, and I can't see my life going on away from Phil Ouldsbroom. But it's got to be. And I shall work at Runnage—for Farmer Chave, it seems."

"But you don't want to go?"

Tiger stared at her reproachfully that she could ask such a question.

She knew him well and understood that his mind was made up; and she loved him well and set about considering whether this blow might be averted. Mary herself cared not where he worked She liked Philip Ouldsbroom, for he had smiled upon her romance, told her what he thought of Tiger, and praised her as a sweetheart worthy of such a valiant spirit. Mrs. Ouldsbroom, however, had ignored her, and Martin she scarcely knew. But the meaning of his home to her lover was very clearly understood by Mary, and she entered straight into his heart now and sympathised with its soreness. She came and sat close to him and put her arm round his neck.

"Be there no way out?" she asked.

"Plenty," he answered; "but there's no way to bide in. I've told you all the woman said. She's terrible wise

and never wrong She was kind too—kinder than ever I
knowed her to be afore. I might have been her own son.
She said that she felt a'most as if I was."

" 'Tis for her own son she's done it. She's frightened
for him. She thinks more of him than of her husband
I'm sure I never should feel like that."

"If us had ten cubs, your old Tiger would always be
first ?"

"Yes, he would "

"I know it," he declared. "Never a couple loved
each other like what me and you do. 'Tis terrible out
o' the common—I can see that, and it may not happen
again in the world Why, you look round among the
married people, Molly, and you'll see at a glance they
don't feel half, nor yet a quarter, of what me and you
feel! None of 'em don't. But love you as I do, I ban't
company for you this afternoon I'm thinking of to-
morrow. I hate like hell to hurt that man. After you,
he's more to me than anybody in the world. And the
cruel thing is that I can't tell him why I be going."

She reflected, and his words woke the needed inspiration. But she kept it to herself. She even concealed it
falsely with a sigh.

"No," she said, "you can't. What shall you answer
when he asks you why you want to leave?"

"Tell me 'Tis here you can help I had it in my
mind to ax Mrs. Ouldsbroom that very question. Then
I thought you was the properest one to help me. I want
to go off without angering the man I should be wisht to
my dying day if he didn't forgive me. Set your wits to
work on that."

"I shall," she promised. " 'Tis right that you come
to me, and I should have been properly vexed with you,
Tiger, if you'd kept this a secret till 'twas done."

" 'Tis done—or so good as done. But if you can find
how I'm to put it to him clever enough not to hurt, then
I'll say you're the wittiest woman ever comed out of
Dartymoor."

"It'll take a bit of thinking on," she replied. "For
the minute you must do naught I can't be expected to

light on the proper thought all to once. You must give
me a week, Tiger—a week at the least. I will have a
week. And little enough time for such a job, I'm sure.''

He readily admitted this

''A week more or less don't signify now,'' he answered
''And a week you shall have. I'll tell the missis I shan't
speak till Monday after next; and I'll tell her for
why.''

''Don't name me. Not a word about me.''

''No, no I'll just say that in giving notice I want
to weigh my words very careful 'Tis natural I should;
and so long as I'm gone afore the holidays come round,
her turn's served.''

They dismissed the subject, and Tiger grew a little
more cheerful, now that Mary shared his burden; but
it was her turn to become silent

She excused herself for it by the magnitude of the
problem that he had set her.

''All the same,'' she said, ''you can keep up your hope,
for I feel 'tis a thing quite within my reach to tell you
the right word ''

He doubted it, left her presently at the door of Teign
Head cottage, and returned home.

Then Mary began to think in earnest, and she followed
a conclusion that had already flashed upon her mind
Left alone, without the distraction of Tiger's presence,
one resolute thought took possession of her, and she determined to act before the day was ended

She well knew the course of events in Hartland, and,
at evening time, when it was certain Mrs. Ouldsbroom
would have gone to church and Tiger be out of the way
upon the farm, Mary French paid her visit Fortune
favoured her, and she found the master at home. He
stood at his door smoking and talking to a mounted
friend who had ridden over from Princetown At sight
of the girl he was about to lift his voice and shout for
Tiger; but she stopped him.

'' 'Tis you I want to see, sir, and I'll be very much
obliged if you'll not let Tiger know I've called.''

Fearing a lovers' quarrel, Philip prepared to soothe

her. The visitor trotted off, and Ouldsbroom invited Mary to come in.

"You and Tiger haven't had a row? Don't you tell me that, for I won't believe it," he said. "Too sensible for any such nonsense, I should hope."

" 'Tisn't very likely," she answered "He says there never was two tokened in this world as thought such a lot of each other as him and me do."

"I could tell him of another such a pair—not that he'd believe it, of course. He's a lucky young devil, Molly, as I've often told him."

Tiger was heard outside, and the girl put her finger to her lips. Philip thereupon went out, sent Mary's lover away on an errand to the other side of the farm-houses and returned to her.

"Now then—out with the trouble," he said; and she obeyed. Mary took fewer words than Tiger had taken, but they were well chosen, and swiftly she burst the thunderbolt of Tiger's intended flight upon his master's head.

"And whether 'tis wicked of me to tell you, or whether it isn't, I don't know," concluded Mary. "But loving Tiger like what I do, and knowing how awful he'd feel it to go, I had to tell you or die for it For I won't keep my tongue inside my lips and see that Tiger wronged. and you would have wronged him if he'd done this here thing and gone and given you no reason So I want for to tell you the reason, and that is because your missis be feared you'm too much addicted to Tiger And I hope you'll forgive me for speaking, and I beg to goodness as you won't tell Tiger I've been here I promised him I should hit on a plan when he axed me whatever he should say to you; but I didn't tell him what the plan was, and I'm very doubtful how he'd take it if he knowed I'd been so busy. Still I felt 'twas only fair to him——"

"Say no more and get home. If you go down the lane and up the stream he won't see you Leave the rest to me. By God! we'll have some thunder and lightning over this! You've done right—dead right. And you can set your mind at rest and be off."

He turned his back upon her and forgot her existence. A mighty storm beat up black over the blue sky of his mind, and its genial horizons vanished. He looked at his watch and perceived that Unity would not be home until an hour had passed. He strode about—for an age it seemed to him—then he looked at his watch again. Five minutes were passed, and he had thought that fifty were gone. Dusk began to darken the earth as he went out hatless towards Postbridge to meet his wife. He burnt with a sense of unutterable injury. His soul was poured out upon this matter. It dominated him as the first and only thing in the world. It bulked larger and larger as he thought upon it. From every aspect it appeared a shameful, wicked, cold-blooded plot against him. It meant so much. Not only had she planned to take Tiger away, but she had so ordered it that Tiger, by the act of departing, must make Philip his enemy; and that she should have thought such a step was necessary at all could only mean that she doubted her husband's love for Martin. He worked himself into a fever of rage before she appeared. Then, as Unity proceeded alone up the lane from Postbridge homeward, Philip stalked out from a gate by the way and immediately fell upon her.

"What the hell's this I hear about Tiger? I'd like to know what it means afore I speak, and if 'tis true and if 'tisn't. Let God judge me if—why don't you answer—why don't you answer me?"

"Has he spoken to you?"

"No, he hasn't; but somebody else, as seemed to know what she was talking about, have done so."

"What have you heard then?"

"I've heard this: that you—you—behind my back— I very near told the girl she was a liar. But jolly soon I saw she wasn't. You and only you it is. You've gone unbeknawnst to me and told him to go—the chap that I've liked better than anybody but my own son, since poor Henry dropped. Shameful, I call it—and a damned silly thing too; for don't you know me? Be I the sort to let my will down afore—there—speak—speak, can't you? Why be you so quiet? Tell your story, if you've got one. I'm patient—ban't I? I know you—'tis some stupid twist in you. I'm reasonable, and I know you. Get on, then, say what 'tis all about and what bee's in your bonnet now.''

They were standing midway between Hartland and the village. A man came running up from Postbridge, but neither heard him.

Unity answered

''You say you'll be reasonable, Phil, and that's all I ask. You shall know all about it. But first tell me who told you?''

''That girl Tiger's got. It seems he's going to give me notice, because you've axed him to do so on the quiet. That's the case in a nutshell, and I want to know whether 'tis true or false.''

''You must hear the——''

''Is it true or false?''

''It's true; and now list to the reason——''

''Damn the reason! There's no reason but some maggot in your fool's brain! I told you back-along, when you hinted he might go, that I'd never suffer it. He's mine—body and soul, and if he was to fall on his knees to me to leave, I'd not hear him. And knowing that—behind my back——''

She considered bitterly.

''How easy to be misunderstood,'' she said. ''How the carefullest plan may go crooked—once a man's hitched to a woman! But I know you'll listen to me now. Perhaps I was wrong; but you're not one to condemn your wife unheard, Phil. At least you'll let me tell my side.''

''Tell it then; but all the same you've got none.''

She was going to speak when they were overtaken, and the running man reached them.

''Be that Mr. Ouldsbroom?'' he asked.

''Yes, it is; and what do you want?''

''I want you, and 'tis good chance you'm on the way. Barbara Hext's going. She's been struck again—but an hour ago; and they'm with her, and Mrs. Dury says she can't last the——''

Philip heard no more. For the moment his own affairs vanished from his mind, and he set off instantly to Postbridge as fast as he could go.

The old woman was dying, as it seemed, but she retained consciousness and showed pleasure at sight of her friend. They had got her to bed and sent for the doctor. He came presently and directed treatment; though he held out little hope that she could survive until another dawn. Philip stayed with her, but the thing she desired to impart she could not. She indicated that she wished him to stop and he did so. He talked to her, and the hours passed. Presently he remembered his own affairs, and told her of what had happened. It was doubtful whether she could understand him, but the recital awoke his own indignation, and the nurse in the next room heard him lift his voice and shout so angrily that she hastened in to silence him.

He expressed shame, and spoke no more. At midnight Unity sent down Tiger to know how the sufferer fared. With him the young man brought Philip's supper and a pint of beer in a can; but Ouldsbroom refused to eat or drink and bade the other carry these things home again.

"I'll talk to you to-morrow," he said. "This isn't the time or place. And you can tell missis to write off a letter to Martin and post it to-morrow morning. He's got to be at the funeral; and so have you; and so will every decent person in the neighbourhood. And I be going to read Job over her, though God He knows how I shall bear myself. Now, you'd best be gone."

He returned to the passing woman and felt at work that force odylic—that power of gravitation men call death. It was drawing her back and drawing her under. Earth called out for this pinch of dust again, and Barbara yielded, as autumn yields to winter, twilight to darkness, matter to time. Life departed gently and tenderly from her, as though sad to go. Philip did not know that she was dead until the nurse told him.

He was reading aloud from Job, and had done so for an hour. Then Mrs. Dury bade him cease and depart.

He went out into the first elfin light of another day—
a trembling blink on the edge of dawn. For a long time
he roamed up and down in front of the little shop, then,
as the morning came on feathers of fire, a thought took
him to the churchyard. He went to the spot long since
selected by the dead woman. He stood there and looked
down at the dew-drenched grass of it and he felt suddenly that she was indeed gone from him. Anon he
crossed the burying-ground, left a green track in the cob-
web-coloured dew, and then went homeward.

His thoughts next turned to Tiger and fiercely fastened there.

"Only him now," he said. "Only him—after Unity
and Martin. And to try and take him from me! Let
'em take my right hand—they shall do that sooner!"

CHAPTER XII

On a drowsy summer day, when the beech groves of Postbridge made murmuring through their panoplies, and the cuckoo called with a broken note, Barbara was buried. The stern rite that she had directed came swiftly to its close, and Philip uttered over her a dozen verses from Job. Three score of the folk attended, and not a few wept when the small coffin sank out of sight.

Martin and his mother were there, and Tiger stood beside Mary French, who had come with her brother from Teign Head Farm. Peter Culme was also present, with Mrs. Dury and her family. From Stannon came Quinton and Gertrude Crymes, with Maggie and Minnie, Jacky and Jane. Under protest, Mr. Twigg brought his wife and unmarried daughter. He listened in lofty pity and forgiveness to the faltering thunder of Ouldsbroom's great voice as it stumbled over the prescribed portion.

Martin also gazed with secret regret upon Philip, and would have gladly heard and seen a more conventional ceremony. But the service ended swiftly. The people departed, and at last only Philip and the chief mourner remained to see the grave filled.

Miss Hext's heir was a man who kept a small jeweller's shop at Plymouth. The bulk of her little fortune went to him, but she had left numerous trifling bequests, and Ouldsbroom found himself the richer by one hundred pounds, while Martin and Tiger each received twenty.

Young Saul Hext, the eldest son of Barbara's dead brother, asked Philip some questions, and invited his opinion on the worth of the shop at Postbridge.

"My business is nothing of much account," he said, "and my children are ailing. D'you think that this little shop would pay for taking up and improving?"

"No doubt 'twould pay for taking up," answered Ouldsbroom, "but as for improving, 'twill want a better man than you to do that. This here priceless creature under us—she knew everything there was to know worth knowing, and especially about the business of keeping a shop of all sorts. To her dying day she was for ever thinking upon it and how to better its usefulness. Never was known the like, and if you think to take it over, you'll do well to abide by her plans in everything."

"I must go into her books."

"And wonderful books you'll find them. Nothing she couldn't do, I tell you; and you were a bit of a fool not to see more of her, for she was a rare bird. Like brother and sister—her and me. That understanding—such a brain—and such a heart. I've no power of speech, but if I had, I would have spoke a word or two to the people and told 'em what they've lost. Ever doing kindly things and ever thinking them. No power of unkindness in her—always for seeing the bright side of the darkest people—always for making excuses. Only one thing roused her hate, and that was humbug and falsehood. Afore them her eyes would flash and her tongue would scourge. She looked through and through human nature, I tell you. She was like me—patient with the fools. She taught me patience, and I must be patient now she's gone, but—oh, how I shall miss her, young man! Cruel —cruel I shall miss her. From her heart came every-thing, but she'd never let it out till the thought had filtered through her head. That was her rare wisdom. A very learned woman, mind you. Schoolmaster was dust afore her, and he knew it. ' 'Tis all true what she tells,' he said to me once. ' 'Tis all too true, farmer; but I dursn't listen to her, because my daily bread de-pends upon my teaching the children different.' These here schoolmasters and mistresses, you must know, have to walk in chains—so Barbara said. They've got to re-member the parents' eyes and the parson's eyes and the

squire's eyes all be upon 'em That's what Barbara was
down on. And I hope you're the same And now 'tis
done "

He referred to the filling of the grave

"You'll set a brave stone here presently, I suppose?"

"Yes, I certainly shall," said Mr. Hext "She was
the right sort, and I hope I'll show you I'm the same, if
I come to these parts "

"Better walk up the hill and have a drink along with
me then. I was her first friend here. Us'll go to the
'Warren House,' and I'll show you the sort of man your
aunt couldn't abide at any cost. He was at the funeral.
and he looked at me as if he was praying to his withered
God to forgive me. I dare say he was Gregory Twigg.
I mean—innkeeper and preacher and Little Baptist—a
very sleek, well-meaning man, but getting old now; lives
on his own fat, like a dormouse, and drips piety "

They walked up Merripit Hill and presently reached
the inn.

A brisk conversation stopped suddenly as Philip entered with the dead woman's nephew.

"Ah!" he said "D'you mark that—as if they was
all struck dumb? They was talking of Barbara Hext.
and Gregory was telling 'em she've gone to the bad place
Wasn't you, Greg? Out with it—you that always boast
to tell the naked truth "

"Shows how little you understand us, Ouldsbroom,"
answered Gregory, passing his hand over his bald head
"I was saying that the prayer of a righteous man availeth
much. I was explaining to Culme here, and these other
neighbours, that for my part—though many think 'tis
a parlous doctrine—I don't see why that text should run
out and finish at the grave Our pastor, Bewes, he says
that 'tis flat popish idolatry to think otherwise; but I
withstand him there."

"To pray for the dead be one step more foolish than
to pray for the living," said Saul Hext, and Gregory
shook his head. But Philip clapped the young man on
the back.

"You're the joker for me!" he cried. "It might have been your aunt said that."

They drank, and entered upon a barren discussion wherein none convinced another. The debate only brightened at the finish.

Mr. Hext proved a dry and humorous thinker.

"I'm a watchmaker," he said, "so, in a sort of way, I've the right to speak, and what I say is that if God made us in His own image outside, 'tis a thousand pities and a great oversight that He didn't make us in His own image inside too. God's the only machine I ever heard tell about that can't go wrong, and He ought to have built us on the same pattern, in my opinion. And why not?"

"I'll tell you for why," answered Philip. " 'Twas just His sporting kindness. He knoweth, and none so well as Him, how deadly dull a thing it is to be perfect. Look at Twigg here, if you doubt me. And so God gives us all the chance to get off the rails a bit, just to add a pinch of salt to life."

"And most people jump at the chance," said Peter Culme mournfully.

"Even God Almighty on His throne must have His holy work," declared Gregory, "and ban't His work regulating our wicked hearts, like this man's work is regulating clocks? Some of us be too slow in righteousness, and others of us be too fast in sin. And there it is—God's work be never done, so long as a human creature's left wandering in this vale."

"The better a man is, the duller he is," said Philip; "and a real, right down good man be the dullest sheep you'll meet with in any fold. I'd sooner go with the gipsies, or herd along with the grey boys to Princetown prison, than keep in step with your Little Baptists."

"Have you ever thought upon where you'll go when you die, Philip?" inquired Mr. Twigg.

"No, Greg; but I shall meet a good rally of friends there—wherever it is."

Hext and the farmer left the bar, and Ouldsbroom relapsed into melancholy.

"God forgive me—laughing and chattering with they fools," he said. "To think I could do it, and her but now sunk back into the earth."

"She'd sooner you laughed than pulled a long face," answered the other. "She hated even a child's tears. A very understanding woman, and left the world better than she found it, in my opinion."

"She did—she did—if ever woman did. And I'm mighty sorry I didn't know your parts sooner," answered the farmer. "For if I had done so, I'd have called upon you to say a few words afore the earth closed over her."

CHAPTER XIII

A RARE day of ineffable splendour crowned Dartmoor,
and to the seeing eye, even upon this desert, was displayed a vision wonderful—a dream of life mating with
matter, of the protoplasmic element flying, swimming,
growing, ripening, multiplying, and displaying its
eternal miracle upon the bosom of the sun-supported
earth. The colour was of a cloudless noon in August,
the forms were familiar hill and stone-capped tor, broad
marsh and glittering stream, roaming herds and flocks
scattered widely upon the undulating land. The earth
and the fulness of it rolled out glorious, ridge on ridge,
to the transparent blue of the horizon, and not an inch,
not a morsel, of these ascending planes and shining slopes
but made a home for life and theatre of war. Æons
have brought this scene to its present polity; unnumbered
years have gone to order its present precarious adjust-
ment. To the fleeting eye it appears changeless, yet
hourly it changes, and will change hourly so long as it
exists. No permanent peace is here; not even a temporary truce shall ever be proclaimed, fierce battle rages
at all points and for ever under this apparent concord.
Death's warp it is that threads each woof and completes
the web, for full half this far-flung glory is founded in
disintegration and decay; full half this grand harmony
is rioting and rooting in blood of perished things.

Martin Ouldsbroom and Tiger stood upon a great hill
and rested after climbing it. The latter saw no more
than a sunny day, felt only the heat, the former ex-
perienced a little of what such an hour might mean to a
young and thoughtful heart.

He looked about him, renewed friendship with the hills,

287

and smiled at the immense world unrolled beneath his
feet; while the other youth puffed and wiped a wet face
and neck.

" 'Tis on a day and in a place like this that one can
feel the weight of some words,'' said Martin. "Take
these: 'We bless Thee for our creation.' Don't they
mean a lot, lifted up here like this in the sun?''

"I wish I was such a dry man as you," answered Tiger.
"You haven't turned a hair seemingly This is Fur Tor,
and I be going to have a drink and a pipe afore I travel
a yard beyond it ''

"There's no need to go farther. 'Tis somewhere about
here that the plant grows My schoolmaster saw it in
a book. He's a great botanist, as I told you, and he
explained that in time past a sort of bilberry was used
to grow here—the only place on Dartmoor where it does
grow. 'Tis easily marked if seen, because its fruit is
red instead of black, and its leaves are like to a box plant.
I'm hopeful to find it for him and fetch back a good root
or two for his garden ''

"I'll help presently,'' promised Tiger, "but not afore
I've cooled down and drunk my tin of cider.''

Martin had begged for his friend's company, and Tiger
made holiday with his future master The question of
his departure was for the moment in abeyance. Philip
suffered much from the loss of Barbara Hext, and Unity,
judging that this was no time to bring further trouble
upon him, held her peace She had not spoken again
of that matter to the younger man, and did not design
to do so until Martin was back at school again

Now Martin hunted over the wild shoulders of Fur Tor
and stopped twice to survey the scene spread round
about him. Infant Tavy glittered to the west, and suddenly, turning his eyes therefrom back to the shattered
granite by his way, he found what he was seeking and
marked the Mount Ida whortleberry gemmed with scarlet
fruits.

He shouted to Tiger, who joined him.

Neither had seen the plant before They dug up some
clumps of the little shrub and tasted the berries

"I shall go over to Bovey with them," declared Martin. "The chief's away on his holiday, and I shall plant the things very carefully and well, and 'twill be a great and glad surprise to him when he comes back, to find them there."

They ate their lunch and spoke of personal interests. Their friendship was still close, despite their opposite natures. Tiger admired Martin's cleverness; the other valued him for his kind heart and good temper. He also believed that Tiger was of service to Philip. Yet shadows were growing on Martin's mind, and much that the elder youth said both hurt and angered him in secret. With his actions he could not cavil; but his opinions, gleaned from Philip Ouldsbroom, sometimes struck at what was very precious and vital to Martin. This happened now, and Tiger spoke of Miss Hext's funeral with approbation.

"A lot better than the usual way," he declared. "Jolly fine, I called it, and if I was going to be buried, I'd like nought better than to be treated the same."

"If you was to read the proper burial service you'd think differently," answered Martin. "There's a right and a wrong way of doing everything, and after hundreds of years and the thought of many wise and religious men, it isn't likely that common, everyday people can make a better thing than the prayer-book service. I'd be very glad if you'd read it."

"She wasn't church, nor yet chapel. She always stuck up for Job; and so does your father. He often asks me to read it out to him of an evening after supper, for he can't see by candle-light very well now."

"I don't say anything against Job; but I'm all for law and order; and we oughtn't to take a solemn matter like the burial of the dead into our own hands."

" 'Twas her wish, and she left you twenty pound anyway."

They talked and ate. Then Martin began a long catechism on the subject of his father.

"Though I've been home a fortnight, I've had no chance to ask about him," he explained. "But now I

19

can. I do hope you've got good news for me, Tiger.
He seems a bit short and abrupt to mother since I came
home; and he goes about alone more than usual,
too.''

'' 'Tis because of Miss Hext's death. He was terrible
fond of her and spent a lot of time with her.''

''But I can't see why he should be short to mother.''

'' 'Tis the sense of loss on his mind. He's short to
everybody, for that matter. 'Twill soon come right
when the sad thing be pushed farther back into his
memory.''

''If anything, it ought to be the other way. Only my
mother has such a wonderful steady temper. Nothing
ever makes her hot.''

''Like you. But how do you mean that it ought to be
t'other way?''

''I mean that my father has done a good bit more to
vex her than she has to vex him. Not intentionally,
Tiger I don't mean that—very far from it He always
means well to everybody. But he dashes at things so,
and doesn't look all round a bargain or a sale before he
closes.''

'' 'Tis his long experience. He's no need to take so
much time as other men. He's got it all in his head.''

''Yes—all the past; but he's slow at making room
for new ideas. Even I see that If the world was run
like it was when he was a young man, all would go well,
I dare say; but you're young, like me, and you must
know, Tiger, that we've got to change. Farming isn't
what it was at best; and if you won't take up with the
latest improvements and ideas, you get left behind ''

''He's not like that. He's a very inquiring man He
goes to all the shows and sees all the new things.''

''He sees them—yes But he's been rather unfor-
tunate of late. My mother was telling me about it. Of
course father didn't The new sheep weren't what he
thought.''

''A man lied to him at Okehampton cattle show.''

''But father ought to have known better.''

'' 'Twas late and far on in the day, and——''

Tiger stopped.

"And he was fresh. You may as well say it. Of course he must have been, or else he'd have seen they weren't Dartmoors crossed with South Hams."

"Yes, they were; but just happened to be a poor lot."

"There are other things. He seems not to take mother's advice like he did."

"I'm sure he does then. He's a reed without her. I never knowed another man so terrible fond of his wife. I'm like that too. I shall be just so fond of my Mary when I'm sixty year old as master is of missis. I'm no more than a copy of master. And I was proud when a man told me so. And as for your mother, why, when she travels, if 'tis only for a day to Moreton or Princetown, he's glum as a raven without her—misses her something cruel; and when she went for four days to her relations at Exeter, the man couldn't suffer it—not after the third day, so he went up after her and fetched her back home."

Martin continued his questions. He was civil, even filial, but he was remorseless. Tiger writhed under the inquisition. Some points he evaded, and once or twice he said the thing that was not. Even in his discomfort he had time to marvel that a son could stand in such stern judgment on his father.

Upon the subject of money Martin spared no investigation, but over the question of drink he was especially pitiless. At last, indeed, he did a thing that much astonished him and woke Tiger into sudden fury.

"God damn it!" shouted out the elder, "haven't you got no heart in your body? Can you tear your own father to pieces? Ban't it for you that he strives and stints? And if he makes a faulty bargain now and again, who don't? And, be it as 'twill, the money's for you, not him. What does he care for cash—save for the joy of spending it on somebody else? Such a man never was seen, and he's like the sun to the shadow among all these here frosty people, who go suspicious of their neighbours and with never a kind word for a fellow-creature. Why to God don't you see his vartues, and copy 'em, instead of always being down on his faults?

I tell you the very faults of such a man be vartues against the mean and crooked spirit of most of us Granted he drinks. Does he ever drink as much as he pays for others to drink? Does he ever think again of the good he does, or expect to get it back in his turn? Does he ever remember all the little deeds to make this child happier or this woman easier in her mind? No! Never. He don't take no more account of his quick, generous acts than the summer sun of the work it's doing. And if such things can be overlooked and forgot by all others as well as himself, then damn all the men and women— that's what I say. He's too good for 'em!"

"I know all that, Tiger."

"Then why don't you remember it? Why must you for ever be looking at the other side? That man's never hurt anybody but himself—not since I've had the under- standing to know him."

"But he does hurt himself. That's the point. And 'tis for us, who care about him, to stop him hurting him- self. I don't ask these things for pleasure, but for duty. I want to do my duty to my father, just as much as you do. You've kept him out of many a public-house and been useful to him. I only want to know all about his weak places, so as to help him to make the weak places stronger. He's been a good father to me—according to his lights—and why shouldn't I want to be a good son to him?"

"Can't you be a good son without judging him then? I hate and loathe to hear you sigh over it—as if you was a schoolmaster hearing tell of a naughty boy I know drink's bad for him, and I know it makes him quarrel- some and breeds enemies for him; but I say that when he's sober, no decent man can be his enemy. You mag- nify what's wrong in him.

"No, Tiger, I don't. I see it in its proper light, and I see the danger to us all. 'Tis the danger that you can't see. You don't look ahead like I do. And well may I sigh when you tell me he's not better. If he's not better —then he's worse. There's no standing still with father. He may be large-hearted—though you ought to be just before you are generous—but he's very narrow-minded; and since I've been educated I see that more and more."

"He's not—he's not, I tell you! And if he was, did he put you to school to larn you how to see his faults? Is that what your folk teach you? If he'd sent me to school, and the people had told me my father was this and that, I'd mighty soon have made trouble."

Martin perceived the hopelessness of explaining his standpoint.

"We won't fall out, Tiger. I know what you mean, and I wish you could see what I mean. But I'll try to show you when my schooling is done. I come home for good and all after next term. And I shall be sorry to leave, and yet glad—very glad to be back I love my father in my own way. I'm disappointed that you can't see my side. What more natural than that I want to be of use to him? What more natural than that I want him to learn some of the things he's paid for me to learn? But it's so difficult, and I look to you to make it less difficult. You oughtn't to side against me—especially where you know I'm right and father is wrong."

"I don't know you'm right," answered Tiger obstinately.

"Yes, you do. I mean to do what's right, and I want to find the way to show him I do. Take farming Half my time at school goes into that now, because it is going to be my business. I'm coming back full of work. I want to lift a lot off father's shoulders. But you know how hard it is. You know if I say such and such a thing is done differently now; or if I mention this or that new way of doing things down in the in country—what good is it? He always laughs at the 'in country' and says no sense can come out of it. But you know I'm right in many things."

"I do," admitted Tiger. "I'm not saying you are not; and I've argued with him too. He's a great deal gentler about knowledge than he was He well knows your cleverness, and he well knows that the world doesn't stand still. He's not narrow-minded really—far from it Anybody can get him to see sense, if they only go the

right way about it. I've preached you to him many a
time, and more than once things you've said and he's
refused for the moment, he's done after, when I've reminded him about them.''

This cheered Martin.

''I'm very glad to hear that,'' he said. ''Don't think
I'm jealous of your power over him, because I'm not.
I'm getting on very well with him too—so far—these
holidays I'm working more than I used to do, and
he much likes to see me at it. But 'tis very natural that
he should put you before me. I'm not hurt about that.
You've the knack to get at him far better than I can.
And I want you to teach me how to do the same.''

The genial Tiger instantly came to his knees at this
gentle speech.

''Forgive me for speaking coarse, and swearing,'' he
answered '' 'Twas very unmannerly in me, and I'm
awful sorry I did it 'Tis only because I see such a lot
of your father that I've got his ear a bit. But I'm nought
to him really, and you mustn't think so, or fear so. I
shan't be here much longer myself.''

''He would never let you go.''

''Don't say nothing about it, Martin. But, taking one
thing with another, it might be better. He's amazing
kind, and too prone to think that them he likes are far
better than they be, and them he don't like are far worse.
I'll speak more about that another time. But I've heard
some wisdom on the subject from your mother, and she
don't waste words or tell a chap what it isn't useful to
him to hear. We had speech about my going just before
Miss Hext died, and then, owing to her sudden end, the
matter dropped. But I haven't forgot what missis said.
My girl mentioned it to Mr. Ouldsbroom and there was
a bit of a flare-up in consequence. But, as I tell you,
I haven't forgot it and shall do what I ought presently.''

''This is the first I've heard of any such thing,'' answered Matrin ''And I'm sure I hope you will do nothing at all, Tiger. Just think what father——''

''Leave it,'' interrupted the other. ''Whatever you

may think of the governor, there's no two opinions about your mother. She's wisdom alive—and kindness alive too—I will say that. Shut up about it, Master Martin, please, and trust her to know better than you or me.''

Martin, wondering what this could mean, kept silence; and when they spoke again it was upon another topic.

At the earliest opportunity, however, Unity's son asked her for information. She showed no small interest that he had learned the thing in Tiger's mind; but she would not discuss the matter at that time.

''There was trouble,'' she said, ''and then came a greater in the shape of Barbara's death. That put it out of your father's head altogether, and 'tis far too soon to bring it back again. Leave it alone. Tiger knows all there is to know. He'll do the right thing presently.''

Martin showed concern and asked many questions, but his mother bade him leave the problem for the present.

''All's going well,'' she said, ''and father's getting back his spirits. That's the first thing. You and him be closer friends, seemingly. And nought's ill if that but lasts.''

CHAPTER XIV

MARTIN's conduct at this season satisfied Philip Ouldsbroom. The boy understood a little of the man's recent loss, and followed his mother in respecting it. He showed very active interest upon the farm, and revealed an intimacy with those crafts that the wear-and-tear of Hartland put into constant requirement. He displayed some skill as a carpenter, and prepared a surprise or two for the farmer which gave Philip immense pleasure.

Together they went on a serious pilgrimage round and about the property, and the perambulation was a success Very slowly the elder began to yield in certain particulars. The process was so gradual that neither man nor youth could be declared conscious of it; but another marked the dawning influence of Martin, and was glad. Will-power exercised without deliberate design must prove more pregnant than any intentional invasion of one mind by another; and Martin, as he came to man's estate, developed a nature calculated to influence those with whom he came in contact As yet he was a boy, and life had not strung his character to its ultimate strenuous, cheerless, and austere attainment. A little of the suavity, a little of the indecision, a little of the helplessness of youth still clung about him But his didactic instincts developed He went to his mother, indeed, to learn, and her judgment and certitude in all things he accepted with no question A bond of absolute sympathy obtained between them—a link beyond life's power to break; but none else stood in any such relation to him. He had worked very hard at school, and was keenly awake to the advantages of his education and the position it enabled him to occupy. He loved teaching.

and while he went to his mother to learn, the ruling passion appeared in his dealings with all others. Experience had taught him to restrain this impulse in the company of Ouldsbroom; but with nobody else would he submit to conceal his own attainments. Nobody else, indeed, desired him to do so. He was a welcome guest at Stannon, and Gertrude Crymes drew satisfaction from his youthful wisdom. To Minnie he was life. Sammy, the only spirit in that home who never could endure him, had now gone to sea, and an atmosphere of simple piety brooded unbroken at Stannon. This pleased Martin well, and other friends always welcomed him at 'Warren House.' Mr. Twigg was now grown very corpulent, and his health had become indifferent. He flourished unchanged in all other respects, and accepted his somewhat harassing private circumstances as put upon him for secret but beneficent purposes by the God he served. To Martin the publican appeared a very wise, religious, and improving person. He reaped satisfaction from their intercourse, and, in his turn, led Gregory to prophesy for him a future of wide usefulness on the side of the angels.

"It is borne in upon me," declared the elder, "that you have been sent into our midst to do a good work here, Martin. I have been the Lord's willing tool for fifty years—indeed, you might say for much longer than that. They catched me giving a halfpenny to a beggar not more'n a year after I was short-coated. Not that I would do so now, because too well I know that charity breeds a multitude of sins as well as covers 'em. But there was the Spirit already stretching out of me to help my fellow-man, and you can't blame an infant, only just able to walk, for not being up in the truth about promiscuous alms. But, as I was saying, my active usefulness must soon be a thing of the past. My great intellects will still be at the service of my Maker, so long as He is pleased to want 'em; but for His own ends He's built up the flesh on me in a way that much limits my powers of running on His errands as I was used to do. And I'm very much inclined to think that He may have His eye on you, Martin, to continue the good work."

The boy flushed with pleasure

"I want to do His work, and no other, Mr. Twigg."

"You're young yet, and it isn't given us all to have what I had. Elisha was never a patch on Elijah, in my opinion; but, nevertheless, he had the mantle. And a very good, earnest man too, though we may say that he never had himself quite so well in hand as the other prophet "

"The bears and the children," suggested Martin.

"Just so, they bears was a very harsh answer to a lot of naughty little creatures—just let out of school and full of spirits, no doubt. I've often put the case to myself, and I'm bound to say that if I was going through Postbridge and the childer mocked my bald head—and balder than me Elisha could not have been—why, to call forth bears? No, no. I should go among 'em and talk to 'em and reason with their unfledged minds and make 'em say they was sorry."

They debated this nice point, and decided, with the deepest deference, against Elisha.

"As I grow older," continued Gregory, "the light from the Throne of Grace, that has always beat so fierce upon me and showed me the narrow path, gets mellower, you must know. 'Tis often to be marked with the great minds that, as age creeps over 'em, they get just a thought more trustful of their fellow-men and a thought more hopeful that the mercy of the watching Lord can reach the publicans and sinners."

"For certain, Mr Twigg."

"Yes. Just you listen to me; don't you talk. Now, like Paul afore me, there comed a very great light upon my mind not a month ago. I was awake by night puzzling how to bring in they people at Dury Farm. To bring 'em into the Little Baptists, of course, I mean. They're newcomers, and they are hovering in two minds between us and the Establishment. And firstly my thoughts ran into a channel of great dislike against the Church Then flashed upon me the saying of the Lord: 'Other sheep I have which are not of this fold.' What could be clearer? He meant the Establishment! He's

there too, Martin! He's there too! In fact, the puzzle
is, not so much to say where He is, as where He isn't.''

"Mother and I are Church of England," said Martin.

"I know, I know—at present. But remember that she
was a Little Baptist once, and she may be again And
if I lived to get her and you back to us, I should feel very
much inclined to say to myself 'Well done, thou good and
faithful servant. Enter thou into the joy of thy Lord '
Especially if you go on as you are going at present. But
the point I'm talking about for the moment is my mel-
lowing opinions. Of course in some men there might be
a danger of going too far; but not in me. Commonsense
comes into it, and I've always carried my commonsense
into the House of God, and always shall do—very different from so many among us, who take it off and put
it aside with their hats till they come out again."

"You can't let in everybody to Grace?" doubted Martin.

"Certainly not. Too well I know those that must bide
for ever outside; and they call themselves Christians,
too, and fondly think they are so, and will go on thinking
it till the dread day of awakening. But 'tis a painful
subject, and I can honestly say I was thankful to find
how many of my poor neighbours have a right to hope."

"I'm often in a mind whether I wouldn't sooner be
with you than where I am," ventured Martin "There's
more freedom; and if the Lord puts it in a man's heart
to get up and say the healing word to his fellow-man, 'tis
hard he can't do it."

" 'Tis wrong he can't do it," declared Gregory; "and
the longer you bide at church, the more you'll feel it, if
it happens that it is with you as it was with me. Look
at the scores and scores of messages I had for other people! In my early middle age, never a day dawned but
it come to my pillow with a light to lighten the Gentiles
And was I to be dumb just because I wasn't a paid minister? Never! You'll come back to us, Martin—if ever
I knew anything, I know that Yes, and your mother
too She've taken our teaching into her life, and see
what it's made of her. In common gratitude she ought

to come back, as I've always told her, and always shall
do."

"I don't think she'd much mind if I was wishful to."

"Well, come—the sooner the better. And in the meantime your work is to your hand. I mean your father.
That's the first call of the Spirit on you; and if you
can save that stubborn soul, then we've a right to hope
for a great deal from you."

Martin nodded.

" 'Tis what I want to do more than anything else in
the world," he declared.

His last school holiday drew to a close, and only one
more term remained. The weeks passed swiftly by, and
Martin's ripening judgment was able to evade much of
the friction of the past. Then there happened a misfortune which clouded many subsequent days.

Philip had been overreached by a stranger at ewe market, and he went to his wife smarting with the tale. For
once her patience failed, and she protested and asked
him why he had not taken Tiger. Thereupon he turned
suddenly to a grievance tacitly buried since the death
of Barbara Hext, and asked her why she suggested trust
in Tiger, when she wished him away altogether. This
provoked her, she said some bitter things, and quickly
reduced him to silence. Wounded and indignant, he
went his way and came upon Martin working in the tool-
shed.

The lad handled a cold chisel and Ouldsbroom warned
him against it

"Have a care," he said. "I ground it but three days
agone. 'Tis as sharp as your mother's tongue."

Martin flinched, but said nothing. Then Philip, in a
troubled and cloudy mood, called him away from his
work and bade him walk again about the confines of the
farm

"You'll be off soon, and I'd have you look round, so
that you may know what's doing and to do," he said.

Martin put down his tools and followed the farmer.
He was hurt at the allusion to Unity, and said little
Ouldsbroom asked him many questions, but received very

short answers to them. Then Martin criticised unfavourably a piece of work This much angered the other, and he spoke in wrath.

"That's because Tiger done it! If another had, you wouldn't have thought of the thing again. 'Tis just your mean spirit to say that A dirty trick learned from your mother. I see through it, and if you knew how I see through everything, you'd not be pleased. Look at t'other side—if you know how to Look at what Tiger's taught you. You think you've got nothing from him; but I tell you that you've got everything that's worth having from him. And the more you get from him, the better for your nature and for your future."

"I didn't know this was his work, father."

"Liar! You knew it well enough. And I'll tell you this; and you can tell your mother if you please to: the pair of you won't get him out of this place—plot and scheme as you like. He's my man—bred up by me on my own pattern; and he's all I've got—all I've got; d'you understand that?"

He strode on, and Martin followed

"Please, father——" he began; but the other silenced him.

"Get back! Go to heel! I've done with you for the present. You've seen enough. All's wrong here in your eyes I'm old and behind the times I'm letting Hartland go to the dogs. I know nought. I'm such a damned fool that I can even pay to teach my son to despise his father; stint myself and live hard, so that my son shall grow clever enough to despise me! Yes, I'm a fool all right. But you—there, begone! I forgive you—I forgive you—d'you hear that? I forgive you 'Tis all my fault. Everything's my fault "

He moved rapidly onward and Martin stood still. This terrific storm out a clear sky staggered him and left him battered and helpless. He walked away upon the Moor by himself; and when he was far off and alone, he prayed about the matter Then he returned home comforted and ready to allay Philip's rage when the opportunity arose.

Unfortunately the day had worse things in store for Ouldsbroom. Upon this unhappy hour, by most malevolent chance, came Tiger with his warning. He had debated long, but felt that further delay was treason to Unity and her son. He could not appreciate her argument, yet had wit to see sense in it. The very storm into which Philip had fallen when the matter came to him was proof, so Tiger thought, that some ill to Martin must happen from his continued stay. Therefore he nerved himself to depart, and in this hour declared his purpose.

Philip came to him somewhat calmer, and told him of the thing that had happened; whereupon Tiger laughed.

"The job wasn't done," he said. "I've got a way of breaking the heart of a bit of work, then going all over it again. That ground was set aside for to-morrow morn. If you'd looked upon it after noon o' Thursday, you'd have seen a very different sight."

"And didn't I know it?"

"But here's a good time and chance to go back to what fell out when Miss Hext went. I must go, yes, I must go, master. There's more reasons than one that I should."

"Didn't I shut your mouth last time you said that?" Tiger laughed.

"Ay; and you threatened to do so again wi' your fist. But I know you'll not be rough. You'm the wisest man in these parts and have got the biggest heart; and I've heard you say that the greatest good to the greatest number be your rule of life. Well, so I must go—for the greatest good to the greatest number. 'Tis so, and if you'll consider, you'll know 'tis so. I can't say what I owe you. I can't even think upon it. 'Tis beyond words to measure or deeds to pay again. And I ban't going to return evil for good. I see my duty and I'm going."

"I've heard you patient—amazing patient," answered the elder. "And if you knew what was tormenting me at this moment, you'd wonder at my patience; but now you'll hear me. I'll not let you go. You've come to be

to me more than a hind—far more than a pair of hands
working for wages I've seen you grow from child to
man. I've put into you all the wisdom and all the friendship for folk in general that I've got myself I've made
you see life the right way—same as I see it. All that
I've done. And so it comes about that you're well
thought upon by everybody, as you deserve to be But
you shan't leave me—you can't, Tiger 'Twouldn't be
decent, boy; 'twouldn't be honourable The chap I've
taught to think as you think—the chap I've——you
can't turn your back on me—I say you can't do it.''

"No; God knows that," said the youth warmly. "Turn
my back on you! I'd sooner make a hole in the water.
Who be I to dare lift my eyes to your goodness? You're
as much above us all as—there, this be cruel. Don't I
know what you are? And shan't I always be proud to
black your boots to my dying day? And don't I know
right well there's not a man in Postbridge worthy to do
it? But that's all by the question. I must go I must
I won't live for myself in this matter. I'm outside your
life—much though you are to me And there's others
inside it. And 'tis for them I'm going; but for you first
—for you first, master. 'Tis a seemly thing. But not
far off—always ready and thankful to do your bidding
if you call to me ''

"My bidding is that you put this trash out of your
brain There's no sense in it—nought but the folly of a
woman who ought to know better. Ban't I the soul of
justice? Should I do wrong or lift you up into the place
that belongs to my own? 'Tis a gashly insult and a sin
against me to think I could do it; and I'll never be the
same to her again—never But that's not for your ear.
I order you to stop—I order you.''

"No, master, you mustn't do that.''

"Then I beg it—I sink the mastership—I'd scorn to
remind you of what's gone You know in your heart
where your duty lies, but I don't touch duty. I say as
a friend—man to man, I say 'Stop, please, Tiger. Please,
Tiger, stop along with me ' ''

"I can't; it wouldn't never do—never—not now.''

Still the other was patient and pleaded.

"A good few have turned against me of late—God knows why. 'Tis a terrible sober generation, and a merry chap like me, as sometimes takes a drop too much—— There's sour looks here and there. Perhaps I haven't got any real friend now—none but you—you and my own folk. But even they—at times, you know. Of course you know—what don't you know? And now she's gone —Barbara——"

There was a silence; then Tiger shook his head and picked up his spade

" 'Twill be better I should go—you'll say so presently."

"You can go after my kneeling to you—kneeling to you to stop?"

"I must. 'Tis awful hard for me too."

"Go then! Go—and may hell clap close on you, and every devil in it hunt you to your dying day so soon as you be past them gates! Go—pack your fardel and begone—and never—never see my face no more, you canker, you blight! Go—and get better money—go and get a kinder friend—go and win your reward—like Judas afore you. Sell yourself—and then hang yourself and sink out of the sight of honest men. And keep my name off your blasted lips for ever! Not one man left—not one—that's fired by common gratitude in all this world! 'Tis left to the dogs to feel it. And if they'd said to me that Tiger's like the rest, I'd have struck 'em to the earth with this hand "

"I tell you——"

"Don't you answer. Shut your mouth. You've said enough. I never want to hear your voice again. Ingratitude made alive—ingratitude on a man's legs walking the streets for childer to spit at! 'Benefits forgot' shall be your name—a thankless thing—a thankless thing—worse than hate—worse than murder—worse, worse to me than the darkest evil in the darkest heart of living man."

Ouldsbroom seemed to sweep the other away, with a great gesture of his arm flung out from the shoulder.

Tiger did not reply. He went on digging, and his master passed out of sight.

That evening, according to the custom of the house, Unity, her husband, and the two youths, sat together in the kitchen after supper The time was nine o'clock; the cloud hung heavy and storm-freighted; silence held them all. Then Philip broke it.

"Get the Bible," he said to Tiger. "You'm my servant still; and for your month you shall work and obey. I'll not mar you—don't fear that—a very good character you shall have from me. But orders be orders Read out the sixth of Job at my command."

Tiger obeyed, and all listened. Unity was working, but her husband told her to set down her needle

The poet's despairing grief throbbed upon their ears, and none spoke when Tiger had finished.

"Now read the tenth," said Philip. "Time was when I laughed at Barbara Hext for making me cleave to Job. I little thought that him and me would one day be birds of a feather. Read the tenth

Tiger obeyed

"'A land of darkness, as darkness itself; and of the shadow of death, without any order, and where the light is as darkness.'"

He finished, and turned his eyes to his master questioning.

"Now go—the pair of you," said Philip. "Get you to your beds and chew on it—and if it don't stab, it ought to. 'Where the light is as darkness'—remember that's in an old man's heart."

They went away silently, and Unity marshalled her wits to soothe him. But he was in no mood to hear her then.

"You'm of the other side," he said. "You'm the captain of the enemy. Us'll be all above board and fair. I don't blame you, Unity. You think you are right. Where you're consarned I'm terrible easy and always shall be. But you're wrong—wrong—and, be it as 'twill, you can't work with me and against me. Go straight. Crookedness is the only thing I can't forgive.

20

Myself be my only company henceforth; you can't
neighbour with me in this matter, for the trouble is your
breeding.''

She tried to stay him; but he wandered afield and did
not return home until after midnight. He came back
happier. Out of the turmoil of his spirit had risen a
great hope. It was agony to him to think of losing Tiger;
yet he saw now that only one being looked strong enough
to change Tiger's determination. And that one was
most involved by it. From Philip's mind vanished the
heart-tearing scenes of that day. He forgot alike what
he had suffered and what he had inflicted. His new
inspiration thrust all else into the oblivion of the past.

"I'll go to Martin—I'll ask Martin—I'll call upon
Martin to stand up for his father!''

He said this over and over to himself as he turned
sleepless by his sleeping wife; and he longed for another
day to come that his appeal might be advanced.

CHAPTER XV

Soon after light had dawned, Phiiip was up, and before six he tramped his farmyard and awaited the appearance of Martin. The boy rose early always, but the time seemed long to Ouldsbroom, and presently he went round the house and called up through Martin's open window.

"Come you down," he said "I want to speak with you."

Five minutes later they walked together on the Moor The morning was dark and still. The heath seemed as yet unawakened and mist hung over the high lands.

" 'Tis this. Tiger be set upon leaving us. I'm very much troubled along of it, and I dressed him down properly yesterday for daring to think of such a hateful thing. But sense came in the dark of night under the stars, as it often does to fiery men like me. There's a reason for what he's done, and the reason have brought me to you. Your careful mother—I don't blame her neither—she's jealous for you And ban't I? She's in fear of the future A very bitter blow to a man like me to be mistrusted in anything. But this—this is worse than gall, because you're the matter. Ban't you as much to me as to her? Haven't I done so much for you as her? I know she understands you best, because in understanding of the human heart her equal's not left in Postbridge now Barbara be gone. But ban't you my son too? Ban't I loyal and true to you as well as her? Answer that, Martin."

"Always, father."

"Very well then. And ban't I to be trusted to do what's honest and right by you? Is it within the mind

307

of any that know me, to think I'd pass you by for
another, or let another come between you and what's
lawfully yours?''

"I'm sure not "

"Thank you, Martin. I thank you for that. You're
my son, and dearer far to me than any living creature
after your mother. I'm a very reasonable, steadfast
man, Martin. Staunch to you—staunch to you; and if
I've my impatience and hard words—what is it? No
more than the wind in the trees. And now this here
Tiger I can't move him. But you—don't you let him
go, Martin. Don't you let him go away from me. I
care a lot about him. I've made him. I'm proud of
him, because he's a rare good un, and he understands
me and my ways. And I couldn't part with him. You'm
growing so strong and trustworthy now—such a man—
that perhaps you—— Will you be my side, Martin?
There 'tis in a word. And to be honest, it have cost me
something to ax it.''

"He shall stop if I can make him,'' said the boy
thoughtfully. "If you was to tell mother what you've
told me——''

"I'll tell her nothing! I'm proud—damned proud;
and if I wasn't, I'd wish to be. For her, who knows me
better than anybody in the world—for her to doubt me!
. . . There—leave that. You're my side. And when
ever was heard that a good son wasn't his father's side?
Don't I know best?''

"Tiger shall stop if I can make him,'' repeated the
boy. "He shan't go, father. 'Tis natural that you
should set store by him. There's a lot of usefulness in
him.''

"And good in him—a lot of good in him. 'Twas a
sort of silly goodness that made him want to go. I swear
that, Martin.''

"I believe it was. Still, he could get higher wages
somewhere else. He'd think of that naturally. I
wouldn't blame him either.''

"Wouldn't you? But I would. Curse wages! 'Tis
an unclean thought between me and him: and he knows

it, and if I believed 'twas wages was drawing him, I'd let him go and help him to go with my boot. Wages —wages—the minds of the people reek of wages and nought else; and that's why I hate a good few of 'em But Tiger—no, 'tisn't his good but yours that was going to take him away And so I've had the terrible witty thought to come to you.''

''I'm your side about it, father. I like Tiger very much. But if I try to make him stop, I must talk to him I'll be set over him when I come home for good at Christmas. I'll be master then, under you.''

''Of course you will And them that pleasure you will pleasure me. Have I made you what you are for smaller men to flout you? You'll be my right hand, and well I know it.''

''Then, look here, father, I'm your side, and all I do and all I say is for the good of Hartland, and for your good I'll be the best son I know how to be, and I want you to believe in me.''

''Why not? I shall believe in you—I do.''

''Then I'll talk to Tiger, and I'll make it a subject of prayer first.''

''I want you to talk now. I can't wait while you go praying. I must have this off my mind to-day—afore breakfast—this instant moment.''

''I'll see him then. I'll say straight what I think; and I'll remember what he is to you—I'll remember that, father.''

''Don't forget you've growed up together. Don't forget what a great man he thinks you are. He'd go to the moon for you Poor devil—don't he want to do even what's harder for him, and go away from Hartland? I saw it all in his face; even while I was white-hot and cussing him to hell, I saw it. Not a word he answered. He's good, Martin. He's a rare piece! Deal gentle with him. Remember—remember! 'Twas him that went for the doctor when the snake bit you; 'twas him that——''

''You needn't tell me these things, father. I never forget a kindness that's done to me. And I'll speak to mother too—if you'll let me.''

"I'll let you do what you please. I'm proud of your sense. Thank you, Martin, shake hands, Martin. You've took a weight off my shoulders—a weight heavier than I'd care to own to. I'm getting old, I suppose—not real old yet, thank God—but getting on And 'tis right, with white hairs, that a father should trust to his son's shoulder sometimes This is a very good day—to be marked with a white stone, as they say. Thank you, my son. I'm terrible beholden to you. Make him stay; and for God's sake get it done afore breakfast. Then I can eat again You'll find him milking "

" 'Tis breakfast time now "

"Damn breakfast! Get to him—quick! I'm on thorns till you've handled him Tell him how 'tis with me—though well he knows it. He'll be down on his own luck poor toad You won't need to ax twice, I reckon."

They parted, and Martin went where Tiger might be found, while Ouldsbroom looked at his watch and calculated, like a child, on the length of time that must elapse before the desired thing was done He sat on a stone and watched the minute hand crawl.

"Now they'm together," he thought; "now Martin's begun on him; now Tiger's answering I'll give 'em ten good minutes, if I can stick it so long, then I'll go down."

He rose, and strode this way and that. Then he heard, thin and far away below, his wife's voice at the farm-house door.

"Breaksis! Breaksis! Breaksis!" she cried

Meantime Martin spoke with Tiger where the latter sat on a milking-stool at work

The shallow vein of sentiment that belonged to Unity's son still persisted, and as yet life had not dried up the trickle of it He felt for his father in this matter, and if slight, his emotion was genuine. The inevitable battle of wills between Ouldsbroom and this boy had yet to come. For the present Martin was flattered by his fancied father's praise and by the great commission upon which he now found himself. His mother also came into his mind, and for the future he feared nothing. She and he, between them, were strong enough to control the master of Hartland. He felt sanguine even of Ouldsbroom in that hour. He trusted that Philip would rely more and more upon him. He remembered the voice of Mr. Twigg, and believed that it might yet be his proud privilege to save an erring parent's soul.

In an exalted frame of mind he came upon his errand; but the fervour waned and he quickly grew businesslike and practical.

"Good morning, Tiger. Go on milking. I can talk. I want you, please, to listen to a rather serious thing I've just been hearing my father about you. He's very much troubled as to what fell out between you and him yesterday."

"Can't be more than what I am," answered the other. "I'll swear I woke up twice in the night."

"You oughtn't to go from here, and you mustn't go."

"You say that!"

"Yes, Tiger. This is rather beyond me altogether and I'm a bit helpless over it. But I think I understand how it is. You see there's mother on one side and my father on the other, and I'm between Mother thinks that my father is too fond of you and might shut me out come presently; but I don't think so. He's a very wild sort of man, because he's got no religion; but I've never heard that he did anything not honourable. Have you?"

"He couldn't—no more than I could jump over Hartland Tor."

"So I've told him I'll ask you to stop I trust you, Tiger. I know what you are to him. I'm pretty quick at seeing. He comes to you for a lot of things that I can't give him; because if I know he's wrong, I won't say I think he's right And he comes to you for sporting; and old as he is, sporting is a lot to him, because his mind is rather simple. I'm not saying anything unkind. There's many like him. I suppose you'll be the same He comes to you, Tiger, for what I can't give him; and therefore you'd better stay."

"What about missis?"

"Mother will see it when I put it to her."

"I'll stay if she says 'Stay,' but not else. I'd rather face his rage than her."

"Then you'll stay," said Martin. "Mother and I always agree. I'm very glad. And now, hear me, Tiger. I don't want to set myself up over you, or anything like that. We've all got our faults—me as many as another; but Providence has a way of letting us see the truth about one another, though it hides the truth from us about ourselves. And we ought to tell one another and bear one another's burdens and point out one another's faults. And we oughtn't to take it in bad part."

"That's all right," answered the elder.

"When I come home for good at Christmas," continued Martin, "I'm going to speak to father straight. I shall be in my right to do it then; because I shall take up my duty in the world and do what I was called to do. And my father must tell me about the will he's made and have no secrets from me. I've done my duty at school, Tiger, and worked hard to profit by all my parents have done for me; and when I come home, 'tis my pride to think they'll see their trouble wasn't wasted. I'm going to take a lot of work off my father's shoulders; and I must hear about the money, and how it is to be left for mother, and where I stand and so on. That's right and justice—especially with a man like my father. He owes it to me and mother, because his way of life is uneven, and he may come to grief some day in his cups."

"You'll have to be terrible clever to win round him."

"I know where to look for the cleverness, Tiger. We'll leave that, because that's my business and not yours. Now about you; I put it to you whether you mightn't work a bit harder for your money. What d'you think?"

Tiger laughed.

"Who mightn't come to that?" he said. "But no doubt 'tis so. He'd spoil the devil—master would."

"I'll say this. Don't go off sporting with him so often. Now 'tis shooting, now 'tis fishing, now 'tis to draw a badger, now to see hounds meet. Let him go alone. He's old, and there's no harm in him slacking off. I want him to slack off when I come back—the more the better. He was never called upon to work very hard in his life, or want for money, and he'll never know what real hard work or poverty is, I suppose, now But you—eh, Tiger?"

"Yes, yes, I see I've struggled against him, but never was a man who less liked 'No' for an answer. I've got into an easy way, I'm afeared. But I'll tighten up against him if I can. I've felt troubled afore to-day, I promise you He lets t'others work, but—well—'tis always 'Knock off and come along of me, Tiger.' And then, again, there's my girl 'Tis always, 'You pack away over the hill to Mary—don't want you no more to-day.' And where a sweetheart's in the wind, a chap be weak. He do so dearly love to see everybody having a good time "

"Not everybody," corrected Martin "I've watched his way, of course, and I mark he's a terrible hand at making favourites. He never tells Will Rogers to knock off—more likely he'll use coarse words to him for being idle. He's not all of a piece, my father But you're different, and you know very well what a day's work ought to be "

Tiger did not immediately reply. A flutter of indignation lifted his breast, but he stilled it He wondered how long he would stop at Hartland after Philip passed therefrom; and he knew that the days would be few For the present, however, he was very thankful to remain.

"You've spoken and I've heard," he answered at length; "you'll not have to speak again 'Tis all sound sense and reason that you say And I thank you for showing me what I knew already for that matter. I've been wrong here and there But I'll right the wrong so far as I see how "

"Thank you very much indeed, Tiger. I know well what a good chap you are—and clever too There's only one more thing. I do wish you'd try to go with my father when he buys That's the dangerous time."

"It is," admitted the other, "and that's just when he never will have me. Always finds two men's work for me when he's off to market. Tender ground there. But I'll do what I may.''

It was then that Unity cried aloud and bade them to breakfast. Tiger had been milking while he talked, and now, with two pails, he returned beside Martin

"I'll go forward and tell them," said the younger; and when Tiger had washed his hands and come to table, he found Philip in great spirits and full of noisy rejoicings.

"You young dog!" he shouted. "And so Martin's cleverness brought you to reason—eh? Well I knew he'd soon get the length of your shoe, though I couldn't. But never you say such things to me again, or I'll wring your neck for you!"

He chattered, ate mightily, and planned a whole holiday for Tiger and himself.

"Us'll keep you company, Martin," he said. "Us'll go up over after the snipe and have a proper bit of fun. Fog's lifting very clever, and we'm like to have a grand day. And mother—dammy if mother shan't come too! You'll have the pony, mother. I'll take no denial—none at all. 'Tis years since you was that way, and a breath of air will do you a world of good. You look after the meat and I'll get the bottles, and you chaps can carry 'em, for I shall have my gun. And Barbara would forgive us—she'd be glad. Not a mourning band she allowed. She ordered me not to put one on afore she died."

He insisted upon his plan, and departed soon with Tiger to leave directions for the day's work after they should be gone. To the youth he turned then, and put out his hand. He did not speak, but shook and shook.

"Never you dare again!" said Philip at last, and neither dwelt more upon the subject.

Unity, albeit her own purpose had thus failed, cared little before the exposition of her son's dawning power. It came as a revelation to her and caused her great comfort. Martin's tact and strength of mind impressed her deeply. They pointed the way to future peace by a road she had never considered. That her son would develop resources great enough to cow and restrain her husband.

was a possibility beyond her hopes. Yet now the thing looked within reason and likelihood. True it was that Martin had only done what his father begged him to do —a course not difficult; but the significant circumstance was that Philip should have appealed to Martin, that he should have exalted Martin to this task; that he should not hesitate to admit that Martin had succeeded where himself had failed. She was gratified and even light-hearted when she thought upon these things.

Then Martin himself approached his mother concerning an ambition now grown great to him. Three days before he returned to school, he asked her to come for a walk and invited her to consider an idea.

"I was talking with Mr. Twigg on Monday. He's infirm now, and I think it cheers him up to see me, because I'm serious. So I visit him. And he was on at me about the Little Baptists; and, somehow, to me they do seem more real and alive in a sort of way than our people at the church. There's more fire in them and I—well, suppose I was to say I'd much like to join them and go back to the people you——? You was a Little Baptist yourself, mother. How would you like to go back to them? I only ask to hear how the thought strikes you I wouldn't do it if you didn't like it."

She did not immediately answer. Memory's veil lifted for her; more than twenty years rolled away while the boy spoke; she saw herself again, a maiden standing beside Henry Birdwood and singing out of his hymn-book. She remembered the shape and the colour of his thumb upon the page.

" 'Tis all much the same to me, I think—now," she answered presently. "I wouldn't say but 'tis a very natural thing that you should feel this come over you— yes, a very natural thing."

"You don't hold it wrong in me to hanker to change?"

"Nothing wrong surely. The Crymes folk was always that way of thinking. Leave it till you come home, Martin. Then, if you'm still set on it, I'll go back with you. 'Twould be old ground to me. Yes, I'd go back."

Her easiness lightened his mind.

"I've been a good bit troubled by it," he confessed, "and I'm sorry now that I didn't speak to you quicker. There's none so wise and large-minded as you, mother. D'you think 'tis in the bounds of hope that we'll ever get father to come?"

"I'd have said 'never' ten days agone," she answered; "but now, knowing what I know, and seeing as the old grow weak and the young get strong, I'll not say that anything—not even such a thing—is outside the bounds of hope."

CHAPTER XVI

YOUNGER boys were sometimes wont to come to Martin Ouldsbroom when in trouble; but none ever approached him with their joys. He moved through his school-life soberly and with credit. His ability was not remarkable, but he worked hard and stood high in the school when the time came for leaving it. He played games and played them well, yet not with all his heart. Success or failure at cricket and football left him indifferent. Enthusiasm he had, but it was spent on other things. His patriotism belonged to matters of religion and was hidden from the eyes of his fellows; his thrift he could not hide, and it made him enemies. His masters thought well of him, yet found him uninteresting, colourless, and a prig. He gave them no trouble, and they slighted him accordingly. He lacked humour and the power to cajole or charm. 'The Sabbath of his mind required no levities,' and he moved in a sort of twilight of reserve and self-contentment. The passions and sensations that came to other young men appeared to pass him by. He hid what nature made him feel; he asked for no light upon novel emotions; but he was always glad to throw light for others, and liked nothing better than to spend a half-holiday with the smaller boys and improve their knowledge. His instruction was quite sound, and if he did not know the answer to a question, he always confessed his ignorance. At the end of his school-days he often read prayers, and sometimes he took a junior class at his own wish. He was arid and lacked sympathy. He inculcated habits of self-control in the matter of food and pocket-money, and his advice left smaller boys cold

317

His career seemed pretty clearly defined in the eyes of his masters. They feared nothing for him; neither did they hope much. His agricultural life promised to be uneventful and prosperous. His probity and justice would be balanced against a lack of humanism and tolerance with the faulty human machine. They trusted that life would soften him and make a fine man of him, but his lack of imagination promised to come between him and any right understanding of mankind. They wondered what were his temptations, but could not guess One sanguine usher suspected that a woman might save the situation, but the idea was ridiculed. Martin's solitary revelation of himself was greed; and love of woman is not potent to cleanse that impurity

So he reached the close of his school-life, and chance willed that it should be shortened by a fortnight.

There came a telegram from Postbridge at the earliest possible moment on a Sunday three weeks before Christmas, and Martin was shocked to learn that his mother had fallen dangerously ill.

For once emotion did mark his action; he departed as swiftly as possible and omitted all amenities before setting out. The telegram found him coming from school chapel, and he rushed away before breakfast and drove home as fast as a horse could take him.

Philip was waiting for Martin half way down the cart-road from Hartland He carried his right hand in a sling, and two heavy strips of sticking plaster crossed his left check. He was haggard and stricken. His great shoulders had bowed of late; his voice was broken.

"List to me," he said, "and hear the worst from him who did it. Your mother's in no danger for the moment She may live, but she's very bad, and she may die For my part I know she'll live, because for her to die of this would be the awfullest thing that ever happened on earth. 'Tis too awful to happen—that's what I tell myself over and over "

"Was it an accident?"

" 'Twas an accident brought about by me. I ban't going to hide any of it, though no doubt she'll try to.

Yesterday I drove her into Tavistock market. By evening I got very drunk, along of meeting a man I thought was dead. Such was my joy about it, that I took enough for half a dozen, and then, when mother wanted to drive, I wouldn't let her. I very near got back, but just afore you come to Postbridge it happened. I ran into the wall going down the hill and killed my hoss. Us was thrown out, and I thought she was gone. I shouted, and a man or two came along. They carried her home, and she comed to presently. Then they sent for doctor, and he was here all night along with her. He can't say much yet, but he don't like it. As for me, I comed off very near scot free, as drunken men will. My elbow was put out and my leg torn and my face scratched. That was all. I needn't tell you what I feel about this here. I be going to take the pledge—God's my judge if I don't— the day she's out of danger."

They went in together. Mrs. Dury was waiting on the sufferer, and Martin could not see his mother immediately, for she slumbered. He asked for food, because he was hungry. Then, since his mother was still in peaceful sleep, he went out and spoke with Tiger.

"You needn't mind telling me everything," he said. "My father has made a clean breast of it."

"He meant to tell you everything himself. 'Tis a cruel bad job all round. None can throw a ray of light for him if you can't. I hope 'twas in your power to comfort him a thought?"

"I didn't try to," answered Martin. "You must remember how I felt myself. I've got my religion, and at times like this we know the meaning of it. But how can I comfort my father?"

"I hope and pray missis will live. Mr. Ouldsbroom be sure she will."

"That's his way always. And I hope—for his sake before even my own—that mother will live. I knew some terrible thing would happen sooner or later; but I little thought—— 'Tis the curse of wickedness, Tiger, that the punishment often falls on the innocent."

"He's punished enough. The very dogs see it. They

go wagging their tails to him to try and cheer him up as he passes by. If your mother is took off, you'll have to watch him close.''

"But he swears she is going to live.''

" 'Tis all bluster to hide himself. Only doctor knows, and he's not over hopeful. He told me.''

"I can't think of this place without mother. Such a life—such a life to be thrown away—at least not that— to be called away. Prayers must be offered up at church and chapel to-night, Tiger.''

"They prayed for her in church to-day, for that matter —so Rogers told me.''

"Not my father's work?''

"No; her own. She explained to Betty Dury last night that she was very wishful to live if it pleased God; and she axed Betty to have the prayers of the people called for. I went down this morning to parson with the message.''

The arrival of a medical man cut short their conference. Tiger took his horse and Martin entered the house with him.

Mrs. Ouldsbroom was seen, and her husband and son waited for the report. Guarded hope marked it, but they learned that time must elapse before any definite pronouncement for good or evil could be made.

Martin spent half an hour with his mother, and found her very calm, very weak, and free from pain. Herself she was not sanguine. Her mind continued clear, and she spoke not of the past, but the future. Unity indicated to her son the way his course must lie.

"Be patient with him,'' she said. "All I can say in that matter is 'Be patient.' You've larned the art of that from me, Martin, and when you'm sore driven and galled by the poor man, remember me and my word ''

She broke off and presently spoke again.

"And be in no haste to wed. Plenty of time for that. Go slow and get well into the saddle here. Let your father see that you know what you are talking about, show him gradual that the new is better than the old. Don't press him too far home, but case off when he begins to get restive. Remember that he's never quite grown up, so to say, and he never will now. You'm clever at humouring children. So you must be clever with him."

He said nothing, but listened to her.

"And let money be a servant, not a master, Martin. Don't you let it rule over you. You must rule over it. You'll marry presently. But I say again, be in no haste to do that. Choose one that feels as you do yourself and ban't too worldly nor yet too fond of herself. Choose one who's seen the rough edge a bit and don't come straight out of a warm nest. Choose a girl that knows work and the worth of it. Let her be one you feel can help you where you want help. Don't shut her out from helping. The happy wife's most always the helpful one."

An expression of pain crossed her face. Martin's brow furrowed and he reflected the suffering.

"Don't you talk if it hurts you, mother."

"Hold my hand," she said. "And be so gentle with people as you've always been with me, Martin. Don't be stiff-necked. Try to find out what's good in the neighbours, and if you can't, blame yourself, not them. There's good in all, and the true Christian is him that has the wit to find it, no matter what dross overlays it. Be gentle to your father. This is worse for him than us."

Unity's talk became incoherent, and she suddenly realised that she was wandering. Therefore she spoke no more.

"Go now," she said, "and tell Betty to come in."

"I'm seeking Mr. Twigg to ask for them to pray for you at the Little Baptists to-night."

She smiled on him and he went away.

Philip, Martin, and Tiger ate together presently, and the meal was taken in silence.

Martin indeed began to talk, but Ouldsbroom bade him desist.

" 'Tis no good pretending," he said. "You mean well; but there's only one subject in our minds, and 'tis treason to try and get away from it."

He was unshaved, and Martin noticed that his chin

had upon it silvery bristles His right arm was useless at present, and Tiger cut his meat small for him, so that he might eat with his fork. Philip drank nothing but water.

"I wish to God the old doctor had lived to carry through this job," he said suddenly. "This man be too young for such a life-and-death matter. I'd have felt a deal more hopeful in Dickinson's hands "

"Mr. Forde is very clever for certain," declared Martin "And, remember, he said just before he went, that he would have another opinion to-morrow He's written to Plymouth."

"The world's in the hands of the young now, seemingly. God knows it ban't for me to grumble neither—not after my work yesterday "

He rose abruptly and left them.

"Keep him in sight, Tiger," advised Martin. "I'm going to walk up and see Mr Twigg And to-night I'm going to help watch over mother."

Unity Ouldsbroom had leisure for thought before her case was determined, and she brooded with herself over many things The past homed upon her and she lived in it. Again and again she turned from them, but the vanished years fastened upon her spirit; the secret of her life came out of memory and huddled its wings close round about her It was insistent, imperious, almost visible and articulate It cried to be answered and proclaimed. It clamoured to be voiced by her and she had to begin to fight it. An instinct to speak and tell her husband the truth wakened in her and set her shuddering physically The nurse feared a rigor, and guessed that she was worse. Unity put this temptation from her, but it returned She began to doubt her strength, she dreaded sleep. A suspicion settled upon her that at the last she might speak, ere death hid up all for ever Regret the truth she did not. It was incarnate in the form of her son—the most precious experience that life had brought to her.

Birdwood rose from his grave and came to Unity then. She saw him as a motionless, watchful creature amid the other watchers She was indifferent, and neither welcomed nor repelled the shadow of him.

A second physician presently visited her and gave some hope, but two days later serious symptoms appeared and an operation became necessary. It was performed, and the patient sank under it. She continued conscious to the end; Martin never left her; Philip came and went Like a shadow he stalked the farmyard and the wild places round about. He saw darkness roll over the eastern hills and light fade above the west They called him at last, when the evening star glittered above Broad Down from out a dim green sky. Then sable-footed, gentle, swift came the December night that saw the end of Unity Ouldsbroom.

She could speak, and her mind was clear and collected. Her breath grew fainter, and sometimes she smiled Martin was close to her and talked to her He repeated texts from Scripture. He did not look at Philip, but kept his eyes on his mother

In her mind was still a strife, still an uncertainty. Her problem centred round Martin's future, and she wondered whether revelation would mar it, or make it a finer thing. She had never anticipated this great problem, and came upon it now too sick to see all that a decision involved That confession must for ever ruin her own repute did not trouble her. She cared nothing for that. Nor did she suffer Philip to influence her now. Once she thought of whispering the truth to Martin. But she guessed that he would not keep it a secret after she was gone. Then she remembered his instincts and believed that possibly he might hide it. To put such an ordeal upon him was not just or necessary; yet to know the secret might influence his whole life for good She battled with the problem, and no conclusion came. Twenty-four hours before her death she still doubted.

Time swept onward, and the last minutes of her life ran out. The hour was near six o'clock in the evening, and her son sat beside Unity and held her hand He pressed it, but she could not press back

Elsewhere Tiger walked and strove with his master and sought to abate his raving.

"What have I done for this to happen against me? Tell me that Let anybody tell me that. What devil of a God would turn a man's hand against her he loved best on the whole earth? If she's to die, I'll do such things—I'll lay all waste—I'll fire the farm—I'll strike back—— But there's no God—none—and this job proves it."

He raged about, and then they called him, and he came to his wife and grew silent in the shadow of death Unity passed away peacefully, with her husband's left arm round her and her hand in Martin's.

She died dumb

BOOK IV

CHAPTER I

THE petrific hands of frost were laid on Dartmoor in the winter that saw Unity Ouldsbroom die The waste was frozen to its heart, and days of low, weak sunshine and nights of starry cold followed monotonously upon each other By ill chance, little work called for Philip's hand to do, and he had the more leisure to feed on misery

The man suffered as he had not suffered until now. His nature was such that remorse ate him alive. He could not bear the sight of his fellows, and spent most of his time roaming the hibernal wilderness alone. He flouted the harsh cold, and would have been well content to perish. The thought of self-destruction, indeed, haunted him, and he came near it more than once. He lost all touch with life. There seemed a barrier lifted between him and reality He moved in a dream; he could not hear voices, his son and the folk of Hartland were called upon to thrust his knife and fork into his hands at meal-times and to tell him the hour was come for going to bed. A woman, one Martha White, his wife's right hand at Hartland for many years, had most power over him. He associated her with Unity. He skulked far from all human habitations and exhibited shame.

When he met tramps upon the roads—strange men— he fell into speech with them, poured scorn and loathing upon himself, told them that he was a murderer, and explained how the crime had been committed Then he would give them money and stride away and leave them staring. In time he sought these wanderers and won a strange satisfaction from revealing to them all that he had done and suffered Sometimes another mood swept over him; then he shook his fists at the sky and cursed the unconscious universe and the gods supposed to control it.

On a day when the world was white with frost, all roseal under the risen sun, Philip went out into the Moor. The very spirit of light glittered from the facets of the ice crystals and flashed for miles upon the rolling earth around him. Cast out of the east, a horizontal radiance lit the Moor and touched each candid hill with crimson. This splendour faded into pale gold as the sun climbed a cloudless sky But deep blue shadows brooded in the valleys, and Philip's own shade, cast forth before him, struck darkness along his shining way He went up over Broad Down, then turned towards the west and tramped heedless along, for the earth was hard as iron, and might be traversed with safety anywhere save upon the quaking hearts of moss-clad bogs that never froze.

Mapped with dry-built walls, ancient broken reaves, tracklines, dykes and boundaries of old-time miners, the white hills exhibited a network of man's industry stretched over their bosoms. Some of these demarcations spoke a doubtful history; some dated back no further than Norman mining grants; and some were of yesterday.

Near the upper waters of West Dart, upon the breast of a lonely hill, Ouldsbroom passed by a ruin, known as 'Brown's House.' Local tradition declared that the builder of this dwelling (sequestered here from the sight of any other roof-tree) was a jealous husband who, for the green-eyed passion, mewed up a lovely wife and suffered her existence to pass unseen in sadness away. Not guessing the significance of this heap of stones or its relation to his own future, Philip went on. He roamed without special object, for his mind was buried in a project Then, crossing Dart and holding forward by the hither hill, he came upon Crow Tor, and stopped there. The great mass stood sharply up, and at its feet was a frozen pool He climbed the tor, and found upon its head other jewels of ice, hard as the granite that held them

It has been noted that a perpendicular plane exhibits more of sublime force in its contours than any inclined one; and the survey of rock forms will furnish further proof that a beetling crag, a projecting shelf, a cornice, inspire still more active emotions of awe. Because in presence of an overhanging precipice the law of gravity is threatened; and though a spectator may not consider the fact, unconsciously he feels it. Hence, above the solemnity of the spectacle, deeper than the grandeur, awakes a sense of possible peril; and nature's threatening frown upon some cliff-face imparts an added instinct of jeopardy to the first homage at its wonder. We know that there is an endowment of these giants to fall untimely; that their occasional destiny is to slay man

Crow Tor, in its wild and lonely glen, served well to illustrate this fact. On a bog-foundered slope above the gorges of Dart in mid-Moor it stands, and seen afar from beneath Wistman's Wood, ascends as a prominent landmark among the hills In form, at this remote range, it suggests some mighty saurian or hump-backed snail, creeping aloft from its lair in the marshes; while observed at hand, the tor presents an irregular, huge mass of granite piled forty feet above the earth, cleft, torn, and weathered from base to crown. Upon one side the ledges overhang heavily and shut the sky from any who walk beneath them; the summit mounts northerly of this pent-house; and in the midst of the mass is a little plateau of vegetation, dwarfed almost to a carpet by its elevation and the ceaseless pressure of great winds. Like a green cushion on a great grey throne, here spread the close, springy textures of whortleberry and moss, grasses and heather The place is starred with golden potentilla in summer-time, and chance flowers, little to be expected, lift their nodding chimes in the late spring, for a colony of bluebells flourishes aloft upon this vantage ground above the world, and makes a scented company, unseen, unknown, where they nod and dance to the buffet of vernal winds

This spot, though uplifted in the midst of the tor, might easily be approached, and Philip Ouldsbroom climbed it now, sat down there, clasped his hands between his knees and stared before him. His Dionysian neck, ripe lips, and plump hands, were changed from their old, rich fulness His chops had thinned, and the white hair on them was also thinned; his nape had grown wrinkled under reticulations of countless fine lines, that ran into each other and branched and ramified every way over its red surface. His mouth was little altered, save that a vanished tooth or two had broken its firm lines by withdrawing the internal support, but his hands told of withering age; their fleshiness had shrunk; their moisture was lessened; the veins stood out corded on the atrophied muscles beneath, the skin grew drier and tighter.

He stared at the world; but he saw neither the plastic work of Nature, in the great hog-backed hills before his eyes, nor her glyphic art, where through the centuries, with chisels of frost and lightning, she had sculptured this granite colossus that now supported him.

He thought to destroy himself, for life seemed no longer tolerable. He argued fantastically with his soul, as he had often argued with wayside wanderers since his wife's death He was a murderer, and the State should pay him a murderer's fee 'Here be I that have earned hanging—why for don't they hang me?' Some had laughter at the question. some had shrunk from him in fear that they walked beside a madman. For a time his wits were on the razor-edge; then he grew sane, and to-day he was affirmed to act and make an end of living.

While he cast about for the means, Philip's name was on the lips of other men At the 'Warren House' Mr. Twigg sat behind his bar and talked to Peter Culme and Jonathan French from Teign Head As they spoke together, Martin Ouldsbroom rode to the door. alighted, made fast his horse and entered.

He was dressed in black, save for his cap, which bore

the colours of his school and made him look youthful
still. He was wearing it out.

"We're heartening Mr. Twigg here," explained Peter
"The rheumatism have got into him something shocking,
and I, that know it to the marrow in my bones, be telling
him of a very good physic what one of they fishermen
sent me back-along. And he's going to buy a bottle
And I'm wishful to say that we was terrible sorry to hear
of your trouble, Martin Ouldsbroom, though never a
woman was called away in a hurry that left the world
readier to leave it than your mother, I'm sure."

"She was ready enough, Peter."

"I'm afraid now your poor father——?"

"Yes; he's feeling it very cruel. He was bound to
feel it, seeing how it happened. He's got a kind heart
but no religion. There's nothing to be done for him,
because he refuses to listen. We must leave him to his
Maker."

"Job's his book," declared Twigg. "He feeds on it
and will say pages. 'Twas Barbara Hext led him to that.
I wish it had pleased the watching Lord to put the Gospel
into him instead. Job's well enough in its place and
time; but 'tis cold comfort for the bruised heart. I've
steadied a hopeful, puffed-up spirit with it before to-day;
but a man in your father's case wants the cheerful
whisper of angel voices, and his face lifted up to the
place where there shall be no sun and no moon."

"I can do nothing to make him any more at peace."

"He's in the Lord's hand; and 'twill take even the
Almighty power all its time to hold him now. Nothing
would surprise me. In fact, I've run over the things he
might do. If 'twould bring him to his knees, then your
mother wouldn't have given her life in vain, for greater
love hath no man than this: to lay down his life for his
friend; how much more a wife for her spouse! But
there's no sign that the Spirit is working in him yet."

"There isn't, Mr Twigg," answered Martin. "Or if
it is so, the work's going on out of sight."

"I was exalted in heart to see you at worship on Sunday, however, along with the people from Stannon," de-

clared Gregory. "And they new folk—the Coplestons from Dury farm—was also there, so 'twas a glad day for the chosen. Have you had a tell with Pastor Bewes yet? You'll find him a very eager and hopeful man. He might help you with your father."

"He's got his reverend eye on Mr. Copleston's daughter," asserted Jonathan French; "and that's why they Coplestons have turned Little Baptists. Farmer's very anxious to get his maiden off, as she's getting a bit too far past thirty for safety. And I dare say 'twill happen now."

They talked; Martin discussed the use of the Little Baptists, and learned from Gregory their tenets on certain matters of dogma and the sacraments. He was glad to join them, and he considered other organisations also that appealed to him. The Order of Rechabites especially attracted Martin. He thought that by joining it he might help his father toward more sobriety. Philip had taken no strong drink at home since his wife died, but he had once returned to Hartland intoxicated since her funeral.

Now the boy went back, and, having stabled his horse, came suddenly round the corner of a barn upon Philip. The farmer carried a rope. His hat was off; his bald brows shone, and he was clearly labouring under some fierce excitation. He hastened past, and Martin called to him.

"Can I do anything for you, father?"

Philip turned. It seemed that he heard the voice, but not the words.

"What d'you want prying after me?" he asked. He was perspiring freely, and a gentle steam rose from his head.

Martin repeated his question, and the other stared and laughed.

"Not you—no, you can't. Perhaps you might though —if you thought 'twas your duty. Duty—eh? 'Tis a word that always sounds like a rat-trap going off to my ear. No, I'll not ax you; but since they as ought to do it wont, then I'll do it out of hand."

"Do what, father?"

" 'Do what, father?' Why, hang a dog, father—hang a useless, worthless dog that's lived too long and done evil too long."

He shook the rope and went on. Once he looked back, but Martin made no movement and did not see the other turn to regard him. When he was gone the younger, not a little puzzled, stood still and wondered at this thing. His father had been drinking. His feet moved unsteadily and his face was red. It happened there was actually a troublesome dog on the farm. The creature had been badly broken in, and Tiger vowed that he ran sheep. There was talk of shooting him, and Philip's voice alone had saved the brute thus long. Yet now Martin supposed that his father must be bent on destroying this dog. He reflected for some minutes, and then, in a flash, the truth of Ouldsbroom's saying burst upon him. He staggered and gasped. For a moment his soul turned to ice and his feet to lead. He felt torpified and fettered in heart and limb before this horror. Then his conscience stabbed him for an instant's delay. He rushed round the corner of the byre beside which he stood; he ran forward, shouting with all his might; he hastened and cried out, looked into a barn and then proceeded to other shippons. But Philip was not visible, neither did anybody else answer his clamour.

A few moments later, however, he saw Tiger talking to his master a hundred yards away beside the Moorgate, on the north of the farm. Neither of them marked or heard him: but from the angle of a toolhouse he watched them now, and did not lose sight of them. For twenty minutes they stood and spoke together, and Tiger was earnest and minatory in his manner, while Ouldsbroom displayed wild gestures and a fierce demeanour. Then the elder seemed suddenly to crumple up and shrink and grow old. Tiger took his rope away from him, and they returned side by side to the farmyard. Toward the end of their argument, Philip had pointed with scorn where he and Martin met, and the watcher guessed that he himself was the matter between them. But later on, when he met Tiger alone and strove to learn what had passed, the elder was evasive, and answered merely that he had met Mr Ouldsbroom in a state of great excitement and fury, and that he had prevailed with him to return home and not go into the Moor at that time.

"He was out over this morning," explained Tiger, "and he came home terrible cold, and got drinking rather too deep on an empty stomach. I doubt he'll be all right presently. He's gone in the house to sleep it off."

But Tiger erred in both his statements. His master had often spoken of self-destruction before this occasion, and he had guessed, on seeing Philip hurrying off, exactly what the frantic and drunken man was about. He had taxed him, then stopped him, and then listened to Philip's account of his meeting with Martin.

Concerning the second assertion, Ouldsbroom had, indeed, withdrawn to his chamber, but not to sleep. As his mind grew clearer and the first strange sense of having returned to life by a short cut passed from him, he fell back upon his speech with his son; and the more he thought upon it, the more terrific it appeared. Swiftly it bulked into the most awful experience of his life. Its significance appalled him for some hours. He glared with great agony of spirit at the wall before his eyes, and rehearsed to himself the thing that he believed had happened to him.

"My son—my first and only son—and I tell him that I am going to hang myself, and he lets me go. Lets me go to do it. Doesn't seek—doesn't care—waits and wishes me dead. To let me go was murder. I'd have murdered him belike if he'd tried to stop me; but why for didn't he try? Didn't the blood in his veins shout to him to save his father? Nay—'twas dumb and cold. He stood and let me pass by. He wouldn't have cut the rope if he'd found me twisting on it. A man can endure no more than that. 'Tis the end, and I wish to God I hadn't met t'other, for I'd be out of it this minute if I hadn't."

He sat upon the side of his bed, sank his head upon his knees and wept the first tears of his senility.

CHAPTER II

OULDSBROOM could not conceal this new grievance, though
his was a sort of heart only to be wounded mortally from
inside. Hope healed most hurts, even while the scars
might remain As a child Martin tortured him; but the
torture was tuned by time into a thing bearable. Under
the last torment, however, he would not rest For some
days he fumed in silence, then an accident of passing
difference with Martin unsealed his lips and he burst out
upon his wrongs.

"You saw me going to my death, and lifted no hand to
save me! You knew the thing I meant to do in a dark
hour, and you let me do it; and doubtless you was cruel
sorry when you found that another had come between
And now you are my son no more—mark that! Never
again will I so much as call you son, or think of you as
son!"

Then the younger explained patiently, fully, thankfully.

"Did I ever tell you a lie, father?" he asked. "Right
well you know I never did And before you judge me,
hear the truth. I can't force you to believe it; but if a
solemn oath will make it truer to you, then I'll swear
before my God it's true. I'm thankful you spoke upon
this matter and let out the dreadful thing you've had in
your heart against me. I thought you meant what you
said—I thought you were going to kill a dog—that you
were going to hang that useless cur we've got here now.
And I stood, after you had gone, and wondered why you
meant to do it in such a clumsy way. Not till I'd done
some thinking did the real meaning of what you had said
come home to me Then for a moment I was frozen, body

and soul, with terror, and then I ran after you—I ran after you, and searched right and left, and shouted as loud as I knew how. A minute later I saw you with Tiger, and, well knowing that Tiger would do what he might, I hid and watched. And if you'd gone on and left him, I should have followed after you; but I saw you coming back, so I went away. That's the truth, and I've hungered to speak to you since about it, but I didn't dare. But now I'm very thankful you have spoke about it, for if I had known this awful thought was in your mind, it would have drove me mad."

He stopped, and the farmer looked at him in doubt.

"Didn't Tiger say nothing then?"

"No, I gave him the chance, but he never told me anything."

"Of course not! You'll hear no word of my mistakes from him. You swear and swear double that you've told me truth?"

"Yes, I will; and 'tis a cruel and awful thing to me, father, if you doubt it. You can't do that?"

"Then I'll believe you Martin—and thankful to—thankful to believe you. I can almost find it in me to be glad this have happened for the sake of finding I'm wrong. To let your own father put a rope—no, no, never could my Unity's son have done it. I forgot you was her son. I forget many things. But there 'tis, we'm reconciled. We've come together close—eh? You care about me, Martin? You don't wish me away, or anything like that?"

The youth assured Philip that he cared much for him and was concerned very deeply for his welfare.

" 'Twas almost the last thing mother said to me, to care for you and seek to please you," he declared.

A riotous amity sprang up in the elder. He shook Martin's hand thrice; he spoke hopefully of their future. then he shook hands again."

"Shoulder to shoulder we'll work," he said. "I'm ten year younger since I've heard you speak! I'm sorry to God I ever thought of doing any such thing 'Twas a base doubt I harboured against you, and 'tis one more grief to me, along with all my other griefs, that I could have sunk to do it. But I'll make it up to you I'll trust you with my money; I know what a wise chap you are.''

So he talked, and from that day there ensued a period of peace and cheerfulness at Hartland. Philip, to Martin's secret discomfort, often dragged him away for long rides over the Moor. For a while he exhibited a desire for Martin's company at unseasonable times; but the gratification of this whim soon killed it. Nothing could break down the radical disparity of their natures, ambitions, and opinions. Philip, therefore, summoned the lad less often, went upon his business or pleasure alone again, left Martin to control and direct. He rarely criticised now, and if he grumbled occasionally to Tiger, the latter was usually able to justify Martin and prove him in the right.

Indeed, the hands of the farm were well content. If they toiled harder, there was so much the more to show for it And Martin himself set the example, for he proved a very steady and keen worker. He took the opportunity of his father's prolonged absences and indifference to get a firm grip of affairs; and when Philip, by gradual stages, recovered in a measure from his loss and began to show renewed interest in life, he found much in Martin's hands that could not again be taken out of them.

He accepted the situation with tranquillity, and only differed at minor points These Martin readily conceded, and a sort of lifeless understanding subsisted between them. Philip rarely praised the innovations; he felt it enough that he should suffer them without protest; while Martin had long ceased to hope for Ouldsbroom's commendation on the farm, but, none the less, went his way with resolution. He was haunted by the fear that Philip might at any moment assert authority and overturn his cherished schemes and improvements; this, however, did not happen, and as time went on he gained confidence and felt his way to further changes

Upon some subjects they were at one; and these agreements lessened the strain on other occasions, when it threatened to reach a breaking point

After her death, Unity was elevated and extolled by Philip at all times. When a year had passed, and he could again endure to speak about her to the people, he did so without ceasing, and wearied his hearers in long-drawn praises of her wisdom and kindness, her patience and perspicacity. But one alone tired not of this subject; one alone rejoiced when the topic was Unity, and never found Philip tedious upon that theme. Martin dearly loved to talk about his mother and listen concerning her. Of the things that she had done at Hartland and the ordinances that she had laid down, he sought to alter none. Her name stood for all that was wisest and best in his knowledge, and he revered it. He had suffered when his mother died; and it might have been expected that his grief would have drawn him somewhat closer to his fancied father; but this it did not do. He could not forget how Unity came to her end; he lacked imagination to judge fully that by so much the more terrible must be her husband's agony and grief; he held Philip's suffering to be stained with remorse and of a colour less pure, a depth less profound, than his own.

Philip rode much at this season, and found himself the better for it. During the year that followed his wife's death, he was more temperate; then the habit of drinking gained upon him again, and brought evidences of a weakening will. He came home one day with a new horse, and Martin was summoned to see it.

"Five-and-forty pound he've cost," said Philip—"a stiff figure, but not dear. I've long had my eye on him. The very hoss for me—well up to my weight, and can carry a drop of beer too, if need be. And I wish you'd get yourself a new hoss, Martin. 'Tis time you had one. Christmas be at hand, and I've got a present for you as you may hear about now so well as later."

"I don't want a present, father."

"Nonsense and stuff! Of course, in a manner of speaking, all mine is yours, and I'm sure all yours be mine; but a present's a present. We've had a very tidy year, thanks a bit to you, and I'm going to give you a hundred pound for yourself.

Martin was moved at the size of the sum. He did not decline it, for he felt that it would be safer with him than in his father's hands. Moreover, he knew of an excellent purpose to which it might be put. There was a cottage of four rooms with half an acre of neglected garden at Postbridge, and he had long desired to buy it. The instinct of his mind hungered for possessions, and now, together with his own savings, this great gift made the purchase possible. The farmer asked him what he should do with the money, and was pleased when he replied.

"Can't begin too early. Go ahead, and you'll buy up all that's to be bought of the village afore you're my age. House property—eh? Well, why not? The people must have houses. I've been leading man here these good few years now; but you'll take my place soon, I warrant you!"

"I shall spend twenty pounds on repairs," explained Martin, "and then I shall put up the rent by thirty shillings a year."

"Well done you! A landlord afore you'm twenty-one! 'Tis your mother in you—not me. 'Tis her care and cleverness and rare trick of looking ahead and never putting all the eggs in one basket. She'd be terrible proud to hear tell of this."

"What credit belongs to it is yours as well as mine," answered the other. " 'Tis true that I've saved up and hoarded very close since I was a little chap; but without this splendid gift, father, I should have lost the chance."

Philip, however, refused any praise in the matter.

"Not so," he said. "Why, I didn't so much as know the house was going begging; and lucky for you I did not—else I might have swooped down and bought it myself. And as for more rent, you'll have to wait your time for that. They old people, Mercy Maine and her mother—sixty and eighty-three are their ages. You can't shift them while the gammer lives, and you can't ax 'em a higher rent. 'Twouldn't be proper."

22

"But their lease expires next Lady Day."

"Damn their lease! They must stop, I tell you. But leave it for the moment. We'm all cheerful and gay to-night. I know as you'd never do anything improper —else I'd——"

The subject was dropped; but in a week Martin had bought the house, and a secret throb of satisfaction warmed his heart and lighted his eye henceforth when he passed it. From that day he would often speak gently of 'my house' to Minnie Crymes and other sympathetic listeners.

Martin frequently visited Stannon, and between him and Gertrude Crymes obtained the closest friendship. He brought to her not a few problems, and she was able often to help him in the conduct of domestic affairs at home. These had long remained in the hands of his mother's old servant, Martha White, but now Martin, true to himself, looked into household matters, and found no little waste and loss. He mentioned the situation to his father and suggested a change, but Philip would not hear of it.

"If she was good enough for your mother, she's good enough for us," he declared. "A better, honester thing don't go on two legs, and I won't have her away. You mind your own business and let her mind hers. I've no patience with men-folk as poke and pry into women's work. You be the sort as would waste half an hour cheapening a bunch of carrots. Take life larger. Martha's very well, or my wife would never have stood her for fifteen years."

Martin brought this difficulty to Stannon, but Gertrude could not help him.

"Come a few years she'll be too old to go to market; then you'll have to get another," she explained.

Her eyes rested on Minnie as she spoke. There was a ready and an easy way out of the difficulty, but as yet the young man failed to perceive it. He and Minnie were close friends, and she loved him in secret. Others had courted her, but they were shadows to the substance of Martin in her eyes. She waited patiently, and hope

hid in the core of her heart, but she let no gleam of
it appear, and would never discuss the young man even
with her mother. Yet both her parents knew well how
it was with her, and sometimes they permitted themselves
impatient speech upon the subject when secluded

This happened on the night after Martin's complaint
concerning Martha, and Quinton Crymes, fired by inspiration, advised a definite deed.

" 'Tis clear we can't bring him to the scratch, but
there's one who might, there's one who's only less fond
of our Minnie than we are ourselves, and that's Martin's
father. A week ago—no more—he was grumbling to me
that his boy didn't bring a wife to Hartland 'Here's
Tiger fixed up, and to be wedded inside a year,' says
Phil, 'but my frosty chap goes on without a girl, as if
he'd got no blood in his veins nor heart in his body. And
well I know all the time he's—he's——' something. I
forgot what 'twas he said; but he meant that Martin
thought the world of Minnie in his chilly fashion. I
changed the subject, and I'm sorry now I did do. There
'tis, however, in a nutshell. Phil can speak, though we
can't; and he would be only too glad if it came about
He's wanted it to happen for years."

" 'Tis far too perilous a thing," answered his wife.
"To interfere in such a matter never could come to
good. Martin's slow but sure. If there was another girl
in the wind 'twould be different, but there is not Let
him take his time Would he sit beside her to chapel
every Sunday of his life, just like Henry Birdwood used
to sit beside his mother, if he hadn't got his ideas about
the future?"

But Quinton Crymes did not argue the subject. He
matured a plan, and the next time that he met with
Philip he spoke He overtook Ouldsbroom on the way
home from Moreton, and told his tale to willing ears

"Nothing better could have fallen out," said the master of Hartland "In fact, the wonder is I didn't hit on
this a bit sooner Not like me to be so dull For three
year I've wanted for Martin to have your girl, and I'll
rub it into him this very night. What be young chaps

made of nowadays? If I wasn't old enough to be her grandfather, I'd offer for her myself! A sweeter maid don't live, and well I know she likes him, for haven't I seen it in her eyes many and many a time when I spoke his name? The chap be one-and-twenty next February, and it shall be done "

"Go crafty, however. 'Tis the matter of old Martha White put me in mind of it. Martin says to my wife that Martha ban't no use and lets a penny slip in every shilling she handles. I don't know nothing about that, but of course if you had a young woman so clever as our Minnie to reign over Martha—why, 'twould all be very different, and you'd get modern ideas and such like "

"A very capital plan, Quinton, and if you hit on it single-handed, you're a cleverer man than ever I thought you," returned the other. "I'll keep quiet till Martin whines about Martha's ways again, then I'll dash at him and see how he takes it. His sort often want a bit of shoving forward where a girl's concerned, and I'm his father and the man to do it."

"Don't you saying nothing to my wife, however. She'd never forgive me. But this I'll tell you—in secret, mind. You're right about Minnie caring for him. She does—a lot. So do we all for that matter. He's very different from the rough-and-tumble sample of young fellows, and of course there's all the education he's got behind. But I'm a proud father also, Philip, and I'll stand up for it that, good as he is, my Minnie's the equal of him and worthy of him every way."

"Didn't I say so to your wife two year ago? If I can't read a young thing, who can? Don't the childer come to me across the road? Don't I understand 'em— boy and cheel alike? She's a bowerly maid, and I've sworn that she shall be my darter-in-law; and what I swear happens. Say no more. You'll hear further on it inside a fortnight, or my tongue have lost its cunning. Here's the 'Warren House.' Come in and have a nip along with me."

Philip was as good as his word, and when, some few days later, Martin again grumbled at their housekeeper's ignorance of the price of tea, Ouldsbroom startled him by thrusting in upon the tenderest theme.

"Now, look here, young shaver, if you want a female in this house to please you, why the devil don't you get one? I can't help. You know very well that I've been at you afore to-day to fetch home a wife; and you know very well that she'll be welcome as the flowers when you find her I say 'find her,' but surely to God she's found long ago. And don't let me hear no more about Martha, because the remedy be in your hands. Marry—that's what you've got to do, and the quicker the better for my peace, if not your own."

Tiger supported this attack heartily, and Martin, somewhat flustered, soon retreated before them and made an early start for bed. Tiger fired a final shot after him.

"And don't you waste no more time. You ain't the only chap in the world, and come you wait a bit longer, you'll find some more dashing blade swoop down and take her from under your nose!"

When he was alone Martin turned the matter over in his mind and reflected upon it into the small hours of the morning. He cared for Minnie deeply, and in a sense regarded her as his own property. He had done so for ten years. They had passed from childhood into adolescence together, and their love grew into reality so gradually that it seemed to him it had become a recognised state between them without any necessity for declaring it. Now, however, he perceived this was not so. If he desired to marry Minnie, he must court her and win her. He knew that he had won her without need for any labour. He desired to marry her, and that circumstance entered as a factor into his plans for the future; but he had not proposed to himself to do any such thing immediately. Tiger's last warning did not alarm him. He felt that Minnie would wait as long as he pleased; but was there any particular need to wait? Might not his father be right? He pictured Minnie at Hartland He had trained her in his own opinions, and she knew the value of money.

A slight emotion of pleasure awoke at the thought of

Minnie married to him. He determined to see more of
her for the next few months   Then, if all went well with .
the courting, he would formally ask her to wed

Upon this decision he rose from his couch, knelt down
and asked the blessing of Heaven on the thing that he
was now to do   He returned then to bed and occupied
the remainder of his waking senses by planning the arrangements of Hartland when Minnie should enter it
'Father would have to give up the big bedroom,' he reflected. He also wondered whether Quinton Crymes
would give his daughter any money. He knew the financial position of most local people and guessed that Minnie's father could do but little for her in the matter of
dowry.

CHAPTER III

ON the next occasion of a walk with Martin Ouldsbroom, Minnie Crymes found out that a change had come over him. She was a gentle girl. Life had offered no room for the fragrant little sprig of sentiment that belonged to her nature, but though it could not flourish, it did not fade. Flower of wonder and fruit of kindness were still put forth by it. She had a heart for sorrow and her sympathy was ever ready for the sad. Many women loved her and she did what little good she might, suffered unhappy people gladly and lessened their grief where she could. Upon her tender nature and spirit of pity before the grim truth of the world, Martin's strength and assurance were a precious influence. And now, as he spoke with her and she found that his strength and assurance for once were gone, as she heard his level tones falter; as she saw his straight young glance tremble and fall, she knew that at last the amazing thing, banished with blushes from her maiden heart to reappear in dreams, would soon be a dream no more.

The youth himself, having given rein to impulse, found all changed. Deliberately he set to work to love Minnie and in a week he did love as a man loves. Entrance once admitted to the virgin closes of his heart, passion grew with healthy vigour and, for a season, its fine luxuriance hid the permanent and indigenous products of that garden. Martin was in love, and he came nearer to Philip Ouldsbroom while the fever lasted than ever he had come before or was likely to come again. A decent humility marked him. Minnie had nothing to complain of. Until the deed was done, until she had promised to marry him

343

when he pleased, until she had felt his fresh, warm kisses, nothing could have been more beautiful and perfect to her than her lover's way. He surprised her. He revealed a tenderness, a quickness, a devotion that even her worship and affection had never guessed at. The sleight put upon him by his passion transformed him; he did things, said things, even thought things that belonged to his condition, not his character.

The result was joy for several different people; but they made the mistake of supposing that the change was radical.

There came the day when Martin asked Minnie to marry him. Fierce storms were breaking over the Moor, and they stood together in a shed at Stannon, waiting for a tempest to pass by. Martin had come to fetch Minnie, that she might drink tea with his father at Hartland.

"He says that he hasn't seen you for a week and can't go any longer without a sight of you. He's been in the house now for ten days with a cough and a bad chest. But he's nearly all right at last and means to be out again to-morrow."

"I'll come, of course, Martin. I must fetch my hat and jacket."

They waited for the weather, and suddenly Martin, turning back from the door, brushed his cheek against Minnie's. She had followed behind him and he did not know that she was so close.

The accidental contact served to loosen a tongue that had long trembled to speak, yet failed till now of utterance.

"Minnie, Minnie, I can't hold it in no more. Look at me, Minnie!"

He put his hands on her shoulders. She looked a moment, but her eyelashes quickly came down, and soon her head sank till he could only see the crown of it. He marked the thick hair; then he lowered his head to her shoulder and put his lips to her ear and whispered into it.

"I love you, I love you, Minnie. I'm not good enough, but there 'tis. Oh, Minnie dear, will you marry me? I wish I knew what to say. But all I know is I can't do without you I want you for my own. I've always cared a lot about you, ever since we were just little things and ran about together; but I never knew the sweetness of you and the loveliness till I grew up. And of late, Minnie, I seem as if my eyes had been opened, and I've been wondering how in the name of fortune I could go on year after year so near to you and never——"

He stopped and put his arms round her.

"Look up, you beautiful thing!" he said. "And tell me if I'm mad to hope for it, or if——"

She looked up then, quite speechless and pale. But her brown eyes held more than tears, and he knew, if he had needed to know, that it was well with him.

For once Martin was a joyous, irresponsible young man in love. He smothered her with kisses; he babbled; he hugged; he hurt her. They panted together in a wild embrace, and he thanked God—not piously—but riotously, triumphantly. It was a grand flash of frenzy that left them breathless, dizzy, faint with longing and with love. But it never came again—not even in the hour when first he possessed her.

Minnie walked beside her betrothed to Hartland. He had grown perfectly calm before they reached his home, but she could not so quickly recover. Her legs shook and she had to take his arm. To feel it made her still more unsteady. To touch him at this time brought a sort of delicious vertigo upon her. His return to sobriety strengthened her and helped self-control. His voice was measured again, his face was cool, the swollen vein on his temple had vanished before they turned into Hartland. He even seemed a little ashamed of himself, and asked her to excuse him for being so rough.

Then it was Philip's turn, and Minnie saw the old man turned into a happy child before this news. Her heart responded, and she listened to him while Martin smiled— a little self-conscious and uneasy.

Philip chattered.

"When this fine thing happened to me—which it did do at Stannon, and I blessed Stannon evermore because of it—I got on my hoss and rode like hell-fire to Tavistock

for the ring. No—no, I didn't neither I got the ring
first—afore your blessed mother said 'yes'! Ha, ha,
ha! That was the sort I was But there ban't many
would have the cheek to do that nowadays We ban't
less cocksure in youth now than we was then, but we
ban't so brave However, you shall have it to-morrow,
Minnie, if I've got to drive him off with a hosswhip to
get it!''

"No need for that, father," laughed Martin "Next
market-day, when I'm in Tavistock——"

"Next market-day! Get along with you! You command him to fetch it to-morrow, Minnie; don't you stand
none of his cold-blooded nonsense no more You order
him about and make him run the soles off his boots, my
pretty darling—that's what you've got to do now. Let
him larn all it means to win the beautifullest maiden
in Dartymoor ''

He promised mighty gifts and foretold all manner of
delights Presently he got up to leave them Then he
stopped at the door and turned, his eyes twinkling.

"Kiss her!" he commanded Martin. "Let me see you
kiss her—just once 'Twill be meat and drink to me—
you can't refuse your father that I command you! Go
on, Minnie!''

Such a fleeting caress as might be imagined at this
order passed between them. Minnie indeed minded not
the audience, for her future father-in-law had long won
her heart, but Martin was uncomfortable and even vexed.
Such an incident savoured of indecency, to his mind. He
complied quickly, then the farmer with a snort of contempt departed He had not wit to perceive the performance must be vain.

"Practise! Practise!" he cried. "You've got a lot to
larn yet. But Minnie will teach you, if I know her!''

The lovers talked for half an hour, and Martin returned to himself in discussion of Philip Ouldsbroom.
But he was gentle still and no cloud shadowed Minnie's
halcyon hour

"Poor father," he said "He does make me feel so
old, Minnie. I feel as if he was my son, instead of me

being his son, and I catch myself feeling pretty much as real fathers feel, I should think. But he'll never grow up to sense now. If only we could get him to chapel— just to give it a try, Minnie. How I've thought and thought and planned to do it. But I can't shake him. He hates the whole business and won't listen. 'Tis very puzzling, because you'd think, with all his good parts, the Lord would make Himself heard. He's too kind-hearted, you'd think, to turn the still small voice away from his heart. It must sound there often and often, as it does on every heart, but he won't listen to it.''

"I've loved him dearly this longful time. And my father does too. Father says that he's his own enemy.''

"More than that now. He's making other men his enemies too. He's uncertain, and you can't rely on his word like you used to. That's the fatal thing that drink does. It makes a truthful man a liar. When you come to Hartland, Minnie, you must see what you can do to help him.''

"Be very sure of that, Martin.''

"You never know the Lord's chosen tool, Minnie. Mr. Twigg foretold that I should be the one to get father to see the Light. But I don't think that ever I shall by the look of it. But perhaps you——. He's terribly fond of you, and always has been. He'll go pouring out money for you now, I'm afraid. But you must be firm and not let him do silly things.''

"He's wonderful to me. So simple and childlike.''

"But you must be firm and not childlike—firm from the first. You must begin as you are going on. You may save a soul by it, Minnie.''

"His soul is saved, if ever a soul was, Martin. His eyes are so blue. Oh, how blue they are! He'll come with his troubles to my father sometimes and call me to listen, and hold my hand while he tells; and I've looked into his eyes under his sad, old forehead often and often, and thought they was like little peeps of clear sky through a storm of clouds.''

Martin stared at her. He had his arms round her

while he was speaking; but for the moment he let go.
Surprise and admiration shared his voice.

"That's poetry! Well, I never, you clever girl! It
is, Minnie, for I know what poetry is, because I had to
learn bits of it at school."

" 'Tis true—poetry or no," she said

He put his arms round her again.

"You'll save my father if 'tis in mortal power to do it.
And I'll be very quick to help. There's a lot to think
upon now There must be changes all round When
we're married will be the time to make them. And
there's a great deal to be done first, too. Hartland must
be turned inside out for you, Minnie."

"No, no, Martin. I dearly love it as it is. I wouldn't
change a stick."

"That's for me to say. You shall come into a home
worthy of you. But we must go gradual and clever.
Father will do anything for you—so that's to the good "

"And I'll do anything for him—anything in the
world," declared Minnie.

They relapsed into love talk and the time flew.

Philip gave them two hours while he sat over a fire in
his bedroom, smoked, and built castles in the air. He
had ordered Martha White to leave them alone, and she
had gone off to the village with the news of the betrothal.
Then he returned to them All was dark, but he heard
the murmur of their voices At last he came to the door,
knocked very loud, heard a flutter and movement of
chairs, and laughed Then Minnie opened the door and
he found the kitchen chilly, for the fire had gone out

"A damned good sign, that," he said "You didn't
feel the lack—eh? Catched enough heat and to spare
from each other, you rascals!"

Then Minnie lighted the fire and presently Martin saw
her home He was radiantly happy and full of ideas.
He desired to speak to Quinton Crymes Upon the subject of the date of the marriage he did not speak, and he
neither pressed Minnie to name a day nor thought of
doing so.

When her father presently asked him his views on the

subject, he declared that much must be thought of before the wedding; but he hoped that Minnie would see her way to wed within the year.

His father asked him the same question when he returned home and received the same answer.

"Within the year, you frosty toad!" he shouted. "Good Lord, what's come to the human race? And you just one-and-twenty and can wait a year! Well, well— think better of that—think better of it, Martin. 'Tis a poor compliment to her, I assure you. Force her into it afore Lady Day. A year—Dammy! I want to be a gran'father in a year—don't I, Tiger?"

Tiger laughed and the lover withdrew.

But the reason for the delay appeared soon enough. Martin was methodical. He left nothing to chance in the great event of his life. He had long conversations with Minnie, and if he was loverlike he was businesslike as well. He taught her to keep accounts on his own system; he indicated branches of learning calculated to be useful; he enlarged her mind and declared his own theories of what married life should be. She seldom found herself at any difference from him, and such friction as existed at Hartland he concealed from her. She heard of it, however, from Philip; but she never mentioned trouble again to Martin after the first time. Then he distinctly told her that she must support his view in everything, at all costs, and that if his father was to be happy in the future at Hartland, a course of unyielding firmness would be necessary.

"You mustn't spoil him 'Tis bad for all created things to be spoiled," he told Minnie.

She promised, but always found herself weak in the presence of the old man, and Martin quickly discovered it. New problems rose from this circumstance, and he saw that with Minnie at Hartland, Philip might become increasingly difficult. He argued with Minnie and she promised amendment.

Philip, for his part, rejoiced over the approaching changes and himself made many suggestions and proposed a hundred alterations at Hartland But his ideas did not commend themselves to the better judgment of Minnie's future husband Martin often left Ouldsbroom chilled and disappointed. The farmer's surprises fell flat, and objections to them seldom failed on Martin's lips; while, conversely, the things that he proposed to do and invited Philip to sanction were usually of a character that annoyed or openly angered the elder man.

Philip talked with Tiger on a summer day when Martin made holiday and took Minnie to a revel.

" 'Twas all I could do to make him go He hates a bit of fun like a drop of drink. 'Good Lord,' I said, 'you don't know what a girl likes. I know better than you do. Be off with you and spend a bit of money on her and put her in the round-about and play kiss in the ring, and all the rest of it You won't be young much longer,' I told him 'For God's sake keep young while you may ' "

"He never was what you might call young," declared Tiger; but Philip denied this.

"Once he was—long afore your time Comed to me with his baby sins in them days and axed me to make his mother forgive him. Young then—that was afore he'd got into double figures We understood each other then. And, like the fool I was, I always longed for him to get older quicker. so as he should be more and more to me He said to me a bit agone—puzzled like—'How is it, father, the little things in life seem so big to you, and the big things seem so little?' There 'twas in a nutshell."

"And what did you say?" asked Tiger.

"Why, I asked him who was most like to know what was big and what was little I said, 'Can you, with your score of years, judge better than me, who have got more'n threescore behind me?' Still, there it stands. and my plans for him miscarry and my thoughts miss fire Of course, he'll live to see what matters and what don't; but that's no gert use to me, for I shall be under the daisies afore he finds out the truth of things."

"His wife will larn him."

"I'm very hopeful of it She knows a bit about the

joy of life, and the proper worth of money and the right uses for it. But he's that terrible strong, Tiger, that 'twould take a very wilful pattern of female to——"

He broke off.

"Here—here—this be treason I'm talking!" he cried. "We'll back Minnie—you and me—and we'll help her, and if three to one can't knock a bit of nonsense into my boy, 'tis pity. 'Tis they Little Baptists, in my judgment, Tiger. T'other religious people don't scowl on all that's best in life—not to the same tune any way, but that slim atomy of a Bewes—why, I do think 'tis a sin and a shame for the sun to shine in his opinion. His hatchet face and icicle nose always make me cry out for a pint whenever I run on 'em. A barrow pig knows more happiness than him—and has a larger heart."

"You're quite wrong there," declared Tiger. "His outside's the worst of the man. He's all right, and he's going to be married hisself, and that's a sure sign of grace, as I've oft heard you say."

CHAPTER IV

The work of getting his life and its environment fitted to marriage was done very carefully and very thoroughly by Martin Ouldsbroom; and the approaching responsibilities did not decrease his sobriety. No intelligent man of thirty ever made ready to leave the single state with more deliberation than this youth of twenty-one. The only difficulties centered in his home, and they were serious; because Philip thrust himself into the preparations with immense ardour. Often when Martin differed from him, the farmer went to Minnie; and when she clove to her lover and ventured to think his way was the better one, Philip would be hurt

"I won't be left out," he said once to Martin. "Anybody would think I was expected only to look on and see everything done without lifting a hand to help. But I'm not that sort. Haven't I been through it all? 'Tis but yesterday that I was setting this place straight against the day your dear mother came into it. I must be heard, I tell you. I've given up the big bedroom; I've given up—there, what haven't I given up? But I won't give up all, and you oughtn't to want for me to Martha White have got to stay She's used to me and I'm used to her; and Tiger have got to stay for the present. When he's married, then he must find a house, and not till then."

This sort of thing was spoken by the master of Hartland daily. Sometimes he put it in mild language and sometimes in coarse. For the most part Martin answered with policy and conceded what he felt to be right; but once it happened that, harassed by some private problems and weighted with thoughts and small cares of which Ouldsbroom knew nothing, he was surprised into rare petulance and made a sharp retort.

"Time doesn't stand still, surely!" he cried. "Don't your own hair tell you that, father?—and sense doesn't either? You beat me—you beat me. Can't you ever see how it is with life and what life means? We grow wiser as we grow older—up to a point. And then we go down hill again and, if we last long enough, end off where we started from and are twice children. But you —you're not old enough to be so foolish."

"And are you old enough to be so wise?" asked the elder. "Well, I suppose you think so; but I'd have you to know that you're little more than a child still, whatever I may be, and 'tis the childishness in you thinks that I'm childish, not the wisdom in you. You've sucked a lot of damned nonsense from books, and 'tis my hope that life will knock it out of you—life and trouble too. 'Tis trouble you want; and when you've seen half so much as I have, and larned the truth about man's days, then you'll look back and own up that I was right."

At times a season of amity obtained between Martin and the farmer, and as the date of the wedding drew near, many differences were permitted to pass unchallenged. Philip was proud of the match and took great personal credit for it. The situation enlarged and became more cheerful towards the end; but then, just as those concerned were thankful to believe all must take place happily, there fell two incidents that threatened disaster to the actual ceremony and promised for a time to cloud the future.

Martin was a fanatical teetotaler and had made Minnie one. He especially desired that his principles should be respected at their wedding feast, and when Quinton Crymes objected that such a frosty welcome would be felt by the guests in general and by the bridegroom's father in particular, Martin explained his position.

" 'Tis for him—for my poor father most of all that I do it. You know his weakness and how hard it is to fight

23

against it. If I could but take over his temptations for him, I gladly would. But we've got to conquer the devil ourselves Nobody can do it for us, Uncle Quinton. Even our Saviour can only help us to fight. And knowing what I know, and seeing what I have seen, I hate liquor like I hate sin; and if I can bring it about never to have one drop inside Hartland, that I shall do It's death and damnation both. So I want father to see that I'm firm from the first. He's giving me authority now, and I shall exercise it for his good, when and where I can 'Tis no kindness to him to put temptation in his way, and I won't do it willingly. You can explain to the others—they'll be very quick to understand.''

"Us must drink the health of the bride and groom,'' declared Quinton

"Then do it in water. I'm going to be above silly things like that, and so is Minnie. 'Tis the duty of every serious man to set a good example in the world, and if I know from bitter experience that drink is poison to body and soul—as well I do know—then it shall never be said that I helped the cause of it.''

"Your father won't come if he hears tell of this.''

"Do right and leave the working out in Higher Hands.''

But Quinton Crymes enjoyed liquor and had a great sense of self-respect He apprehended trouble, and he took steps to avert it. The threatened danger passed, for Quinton went privately to Hartland, and with a guilty heart avoided Martin and sought the master.

"Your young wonder was all for a wedding breakfast with water,'' he explained in the privacy of a byre "Don't you say nothing, Phil, or I shall have him down on me like a ton of bricks. but rest sure that I ban't going to do any such ondacent thing.''

Philip was in a mild mood and said little save in kindness

"You are right, Quinton. There's a proper and an improper way To give 'em water! No, no! 'twould be remembered against the party for years—never forgot. I tell you a marriage begun in water would end in ice, so like as not. Give 'em generous drinking, and them as don't want to drink can pass it. I ban't the sort to dictate to any man. And if the boy and girl won't touch it, we'll touch it for 'em and wish 'em well in the prettiest liquor we can run to. I'm glad this has come up, for I want the drinks and baccy to be my share. You remember when I took your sister away from Hartland—my dear wife that was—that I forked out for the drinks and baccy. And, by your leave, I'll do the like again—just for old sake's sake. 'Twill soften the sadness of it to my heart, Quinton. Because 'tis going to be a queer, creepy thing for me, however well it goes. I shall see myself there—five-and-twenty years, is it? Somewhere about that now. Young, gay blids were we! And Unity—what a woman! What a bosom she had for a maiden! By God, how cruel I miss her to this day.''

He stopped, and Mr. Crymes, who was not emotional, returned to the subject.

"If you must pay, you must. And Twigg will do it all in reason. We shall be Little Baptists to a man, I believe—save for you and Tiger. And for my part I hold with a drop of fiery drinking at times like this. It lifts the heart as high as the matter in hand, and gives a bit of a dash to things that they often stand in sore need of. And Gertrude for one—she'll want a thimbleful and a bit over, if she's to see our Minnie drive off without weeping a river.''

"Of course she'll want it, and she shall have it; and if she's got a tap that she's special addicted to, I hope she'll say what 'tis.''

"But keep dark as the grave on the subject, Phil,'' cautioned Mr. Crymes. "You know your boy—boy no more, for a stronger man for his years I never met with. You know him. He thinks 'twill be a water feast—well, better let him think so till he sees the bottles. Then 'twill be too late to make a row. Besides, he'll be married and——''

Philip rejoiced in a conspiracy of this kind.

"Not a another word!'' he said. "Leave it all to me.

and Twigg. And he must be cautioned too, for he's hand-in-glove with the pair of 'em. But he's bound to be our side in this matter. After dark, the evening afore the wedding, the liquor shall arrive to Stannon.''

Quinton nodded.

"Like a thief in the night let it come," he said. "Minnie mustn't know neither—not if it can be hid away from her."

Over this trifle, of which he made much, Philip had his way and was glad. With glee he related his plans to Tiger; and then the younger told him of an event that presently led to more important things. Not the least of Martin's minor anxieties centred on his house. The time was come when the tenants thereof must be asked to depart, that he might improve his property. They were unable to pay a larger rent, but the place was worth more as it stood and would be worth considerably more when the landlord had done all that he proposed. But Martin knew his father's opinion, and was aware that if he turned out old Jane Maine and her daughter Philip would be very angry. Already Ouldsbroom had offered to pay the increased rent; but the futility of this course was not hidden from Martin. To take money out of his father's pocket was to take it out of his own. Chance had now cut this knot.

"Have you heard that ancient creature, Jane Maine, be gone?" asked Tiger. "Went off in her sleep. Mister Martin will be glad, for there'll be no bother now."

And presently Martin himself arrived with the news. He was much relieved and could not conceal his satisfaction.

"I've had a few words with Mercy Maine already," he said. "She's glad that it happened so, for it has saved a long illness and a lot of expense. And she's going at the quarter, so it has fallen out well—as it had to be."

Thus far the passing of Jane Maine fell fairly enough, but on the night before the wedding much evil arose out of it.

Talk ranged over varied subjects, and Philip and Mar-

tin were both excited The latter, despite his press of
business, had found leisure for some strenuous private
thinking, and his ideas now led him into danger. The
present paramount ambition of his mind sprang full-
fledged from the death of his tenant. While debating on
a host of problems, which would clamour for solution
when Minnie arrived to begin her married life at Hartland, there had flashed upon him the possibility of a
grand arrangement by which, at one stroke, the whole
situation might be eased and accommodated.

At another time, with a mind more free to ponder the
project in all its bearings, Martin must have seen the
folly of his new inspiration. But for the moment, much
let and hindered as he was on every hand, with his bride
waiting and a honeymoon to be taken, he did a thing
that might have been guessed impossible and acted ab-
surdly. The absurdity, however, was only apparent to
an onlooker. In effect his proposition, now broken upon
his father's ear, was tragical, and, too late, he perceived
it In a dozen words, spoken out of self-absorbed ego-
tism and loosed from a mind too much preoccupied to
do itself justice, Martin committed the grand mistake of
his life. His own stable and established existence sur-
vived the recoil of this blow, but it descended with shat-
tering force in another quarter on shoulders less strong
to sustain it.

On the night before the marriage Philip was drinking
and smoking. At the kitchen fire hung some clothes and
a linen shirt. They represented his wedding garments,
and Martha had fetched them out of their long repose to
air. Tiger sat at hand with his pipe alight, and Martin,
deep in thought, was eating at the table. He had just
returned from Tavistock. Full of his idea and anxious
to break it to Philip before the business of to-morrow,
the young man finished his meal and presently asked
Tiger to leave them.

"I've got some private affairs with my father," he
said; and then, when Tiger had gone, he spoke:

"Everything is at a climax now, father; and I think
the future is all pretty clear."

"Why, who doubts it? Among us we've planned every mortal thing. 'Tis only left for us at home to have all suent afore you come back, and you may trust Martha for that. What soap and water can do—and I've got a surprise or two up my sleeve for Minnie yet, mind! She'll see a few things that will be new to her at old Hartland when she comes to it. And you will too, Martin."

"Don't be too busy, father. And that reminds me. You know how much I want all to go in harmony when we come back; and I've been thinking a lot about it, and my house falling in just at the nick of time gave me the idea. You see—I don't mean that it should happen now —not for six months or more—not, of course, till 'twas all made ready according to your own fancy; but I can't help thinking—and I've prayed on it too, for that matter—I can't help thinking that, presently, you might be a deal more snug and comfortable in my house than you would be here. I can see you there along with Martha. Minnie would be in every day and so should I, and Tiger too. And there you are—free of all the bustle and bother and turmoil up here. What d'you think of it, father? Not just yet, of course, but presently, when I'd made it fit for you?"

A great silence fell; then the speaker looked at Philip and saw the awful extent of his error.

Martin had been walking up and down the kitchen as he spoke; but now he stood still. The other raised his great head like a hound off a trail, and like a hound he gave tongue. Literally he roared. For some moments no syllable was to be distinguished in the wild tympany of sounds that he uttered. Then some order came among them and the first words that Martin could distinguish was a command to be gone.

"Get out of my sight, you unnatural devil! Take yourself away, or I'll——ordered off—turned off—flung out! Not yet, by God! I'm not weak enough to be hustled over my own threshold yet. You've tried it on too soon! Get out of my sight—go—live in your own blasted house on your own blasted money! Clear out,

I say, or I'll do you an injury and send you afore your woman to-morrow with broken bones!''

"Father——''

"Begone! Don't never take that great name on your lips no more, you wretch! Fatherless you shall be and fatherless deserve to be. And God send this—God lift up for you what you sow presently and let your son cut you to the heart's quick and send you crying frantic to the dogs to be kind to you—as I go now. May you feel what you've made me feel this night; may you sink to be friendless as I am friendless; may your children plot to turn you out of your father's home, as you have plotted to turn me out of mine But I'll not go—d'you hear that? Never, never will I go While this arm can bend and these here fingers grip, I'll lay fast hold of my own, and 'tis only when I'm dead you shall thrust me away; and, if I could, I'd come back again after that and curse your pillow till you yourself fled afore me! Ruin seize you, you graceless, stone-hearted image of a son! And me—to think what I've been—me, with my fool's heart this moment brimming over—brimming over with good things to glad your eyes when you came back! Go, I tell you—if you don't want me to fly at you like a raging beast Go, and don't you think I'll come to-morrow now. Not a step will I come. Married!—I'd sooner see you hanged than married!'' He stopped stricken by his own word Then he repented of it.

"No, not that—not that—for your mother's sake I call that back Eat and drink and marry and——''

He had been standing Suddenly he dropped down into his chair and flung his head on his arms upon the table.

Martin went out and hastened to seek Tiger.

"Get to my father, will you?'' he said "I've hurt him. God, He knows I meant no such thing I made a proposal and he took it in a wrong spirit.''

The other was sorry but did not ask for particulars

"Bad luck, sure enough! Coming to-night of all nights too. I hope it won't shake him for to-morrow. And you—have he cut you up very bad?''

Martin nodded.

"It's my own fault, in a way. I was full of an idea to work well all round. And my mind was—well, it looked all right to me—I didn't know—I didn't guess how father would take it."

The young man was much moved.

CHAPTER V

TIGER could obtain no hearing from Philip Ouldsbroom. A horror beyond analysis plunged his soul into stupor. He sat like a log for some time while the younger man talked; then, disregarding him, he rose and went to his bed. For hours his trouble festered in him, and very early in the morning he came downstairs. He had planned terrific counter-strokes through the night. But two hours after the silent breakfast he was drunk. Martin had approached him, contrite, and expressed the deepest regret for his error.

"I don't know what I was dreaming about," he said frankly. "I can't excuse myself, father. I didn't see the monstrous side of it. My mind was so full. But there's nothing to be spoken more. I'm bitterly sorry for my mistake, and I ask you humbly to forgive me. And I've asked my God to forgive me for saying that. I beg you, who are so quick to forgive all men, to forgive me, father, and not cloud the day."

But Philip would not yield.

"Say no more," he answered. "The truth of the heart will often slip when the mind ban't on guard. Words won't alter it. You've told me what you want. Perhaps I'll oblige you after all. What's the odds now? Your young, beautiful girl don't want old bones cumbering her threshold. Go to her and enjoy her. I wish the pair of you nought but well."

"I implore you to come to the feast, father."

"No—not now; I can't now. I can't face the folk now. Put on your wedding garments and be off."

Martin strove in vain and, when he was gone to dress, Tiger endeavoured to change his master's mind. The farmer had drawn himself a quart of beer and was sitting smoking in front of the fire.

"Best you go, master, 'twill mar all and send 'em away awful down in the mouth, if you ban't there."

"No—no. I've had my pleasure of it. Planning things be the pleasure—not the things themselves. 'Tis the same with all our little secrets—yours and mine. How we thought to see 'em laugh when they came back— didn't we? How we fooled ourselves. They'll not laugh from the heart. And if I'd wanted for to plan a real throb of joy for 'em, the way was to creep off and let 'em find my place empty."

He started up and flung his mug on the hearth. The beer hissed and spurted and the peat sparks flew.

"Death and damnation! When I think of it, I could fire the place—burn it to the ground and myself along with it. And he'd come and not turn colour, but just say—'Lucky I made father insure.' Tiger, 'tis too much —I can't bear it. He've torn the heart out of me at last. I'm cast out, I tell you. Job's self was never called to suffer this."

He made Tiger go presently to meet Mary French and attend the wedding. Then he hustled off Martha White and the labourers. It had been decided that Martha should stop at Hartland; but the master's whim was now to bide there alone, while his son was being married. The old woman, protesting, went. Tiger also, in no small fear, did as he was ordered.

A dozen times during the next few hours his anxious eyes turned back to Hartland.

"A column of smoke would not surprise me at any moment," he confessed to Mary.

But no such thing happened. Philip muddled himself with beer. Then he dozed over the fire for some hours. He moved presently, and by accident kicked a sheep-dog that reposed beside him. She howled and woke him. He rose then, rubbed his eyes and returned to himself.

"I wish I was you," he said to the brute. "You be better thought on by my son than me. He'll be gladder to see you again than me."

But his resurgent spirit winged back to itself presently.

"I'll get across," he thought. " 'Twill be a good thing to do. They'll go off the happier."

He put on the black coat still hanging near the kitchen fire. Then he hurried away; but he was too late. When still half a mile from Stannon, he saw a little crowd at the door. As he watched, a carriage jolted away through the valley over a rough farm road. He put his hands to his mouth and shouted out:

"Hold on, Martin! I be coming!"

But they could not hear. He watched the vehicle disappear and saw the flutter of handkerchiefs from the crowd at the door. A faint sound reached him as the company shouted farewell.

Then he turned sadly, and as he went, some substance in his coat-tail attracted his attention. It was an old shoe he had slipped in there on the morning before, that he might fling it after the wedded pair when they departed.

Before he reached home there came Tiger, hastening back to him from Stannon.

Philip welcomed the young man.

"Bear me out," he said, "bear testimony to my son that I meant to be there. I set forth, but 'twas too late."

The other strove to cheer up Ouldsbroom with an account of all that happened, but Philip was sunk in gloom.

"It can never come over again," he said. "All the joy that I'd planned be lost for ever now."

"They sent you very kind messages the last thing. You was in both their minds," declared Tiger.

"It can never come over again," repeated the other "It's lost to me for all time now."

CHAPTER VI

THE inevitable circumstance overtook Philip Ouldsbroom, and with Martin again removed from him, his spirit grew calm again and he began to forget reality and build once more on the relations he desired rather than those that subsisted. The dream of his heart was always banished by the actual; yet his mental irresolution was such that as yet nothing had killed that dream. It glimmered into being again and again, like a rainbow upon the dark sky of his soul; it persisted there, beautiful and bright, till Martin returned to him and the sun of his hopes once more sank storm-foundered.

He dwelt now largely on the mighty differences wrought by marriage and supposed that character was affected thereby. He related his own experiences in this sort to Tiger, and not only declared, but also believed, that wedlock had made a very different man of him.

"You'll know, you'll know when Mary's handled you for a bit, my bold hero! We ban't half men till we are husbands. A bachelor's a selfish, narrow-minded carmudgeon—good for nought—and that ignorant that we, who know, look at 'em and pity 'em But, given the right woman, she's like springtime breaking over the earth In fact, life's all winter to a bachelor, and it ban't till he's larned to love that he knows any other season. But wait till a true woman's breast be pressed up against yours, Tiger—then you'll feel the warmth of it get into your blood; and you'll bud and blossom and bear fruit belike."

Tiger smiled at his poetry.

"You'm a hopeful old wonder, you are," he said.

"And why for not? Don't I know what wedlock did

for me? I tell you I was a man as never thought of anybody but himself afore I took a wife And after—she found the scant good in me, and tended it, and worked at it and made me a different creature. Not many wives like her, I grant; but the pattern of good women ban't lost and never will be. Minnie's just perfect in my opinion; and I will say I've done my little best to help make her so. She understands my nature something marvellous for a green girl My wife's blood be in her veins, you must remember, because she was Unity's niece on her father's side. And you'll find that she'll do for Martin what her aunt did for me. I've figured it out in my mind, and I've very little doubt that 'twill happen so. She'll be the south wind to Martin and temper his fierce justice with her mercy. She'll larn him what pity means and show him how 'tis only the strongest know the meaning of pity, and only the justest know what it is to forgive. I ban't very strong, Tiger I thought I was once, but 'tis borne in upon me since I've come to be a widow-man that I ban't very strong, but I've got a good power of forgiveness in me, and I've come to know this: that to forgive them that ill-use you is the very best thing for your own heart that you can practise. That's where poor Jesus was the greatest man that ever came among men. He larned the world for all time that forgiveness don't stop at the forgiven. It's food and drink and life to them that use it. You'm a better man every time you pardon a wrongdoer. 'Twas Barbara pointed out that to me once, when I went smarting to her under some outrageous wrong as had been thrust upon me; and I thought upon it and proved the truth of it.''

''No doubt all you say is true,'' answered the other, ''and I'm sure none ever talked better sense. 'Tis easy to say these wise things, no doubt, if you've lived in the world so long with your eyes open as what you have, master But 'tis terrible hard to do 'em at the right moment.''

Before the time was come for Martin to return, Ouldsbroom had entered upon a tranquil phase of life One

heavy drinking bout he had and only one. The day
before Minnie and her husband would arrive at Hartland
found the master up betimes. He purposed to catch a
dish of trout for his daughter-in-law, and set off to the
upper reaches of East Dart at dawn.

Sport here proved bad, and presently Philip climbed
the Moor, and, tramping the tumulous lands behind
Broad Down, entered the valley of the river's western
branch and sought certain familiar rivulets that ran
there.

Hard by these plains the fisherman struck Brown's
House, and presently, after a spell of more successful
angling, he returned to it awhile.

Above West Dart this ruin stands, at the top of a little
square fosse, once sharply marked, but now sinking back
into the heath again. A bank, flung up to make a barrier
between the dwelling and the Moor, was scarcely grave-
high now. It stretched grass-clad along to where, upon
the northern side, ran fragments of piled stones. The
fabric of Brown's House was already reduced to stumps
of shattered masonry. The entrance might yet be
marked, and two slant doorposts of granite still stood
there and bowed in upon each other. The space round
about showed no sign of ancient culture, and all that remained of the building revealed fragments of one chamber alone. Three broken walls encompassed it, the fourth
was gone. Far beyond sight of human activity Brown's
House had stood. Absolute wilderness rolled and rose
and sank again to the high horizons on every side of it.
To the north ascended a green hill, and its crest was lost
in fog that crept stealthily along. Now it thinned, now
thickened suddenly, now broke again. Beneath were
great ranges of marsh stretching from the brink of the
river, and over them, set so closely that they whitened
the bog like a thin fleece of snow, spread the silvery
tassels of cotton-grass. Southerly, fronting the ruin,
there swept that great range of hills whose summits as-
cend above Wistman's Wood and culminate at Crokern
nigh Two Bridges; while to the west ascended Rough
Tor, Devil's Tor, and the sweep of the Bear Down hills.

Here came Philip from fishing, sat among the fallen stones and ate his bread and meat. About him fed a little herd of Scotch cattle, shaggy, black, and dun; above him a curlew wheeled and uttered its short alarm bark of three shrill notes.

The sportsman was well pleased. He knew some humble tributaries of Dart where no rod went but his own. They were too small to tempt a fisherman, but the farmer understood them and had taken many a trout from them. He used a natural fly and 'dapped' little pools and backwaters, where none had guessed a fish might harbour. Now a dozen fingerlings and one half-pounder lay on the grass before him, and he had hopes of another dozen at dusk. For the present he ate and emptied his flask; then a great clump of white heather came under his eyes and he thought upon Minnie and gathered it for her.

Presently he returned to the ruin and speculated upon the story told concerning it. Jealousy was an emotion unknown to Philip. He marvelled that any man, for love of his wife and fancied doubt of her faithfulness, should drag her to this pathless place and immure her beyond sight or sound of fellow-creatures; but that a man himself might welcome such a spot—that a heart tormented by life, or broken against some other heart far harder than itself, might seek these solitudes and suffer in them beyond the reach of any eyes—that thought, while foreign enough to his nature, had become possible to Philip's mind of late years. His days had told him that peace in such a sequestered haunt was precious enough under some states of tribulation. The heart that once had found Job a weariness and solitude a state insufferable, now not seldom welcomed both.

Thinking upon the past, his pipe dropped from his mouth; he rolled over and slept. For hours he lay thus, while a mouse-coloured heifer from the herd, deceived by his stillness, approached and smelt at him. Then he flung out his arm and muttered in a dream, and she galloped away to her companions.

Philip woke sad, for his vision had been of Unity, and

again he had moved beside her. Seldom she visited his
sleep, and it was but to colour his waking with cruel
hunger for the past when she did so. His mood changed
now. He fished no more, but took down his rod, shoul-
dered his creel and went homeward. Half a mile from
Brown's House he remembered his bunch of heather and
went back and fetched it.

In the evening he descended from Hartland to Postbridge to make a final small purchase or two for Minnie.
Then he turned into the graveyard and looked at his
wife's green mound. He had set an ugly mass of stone
upon it and many words. A bird had smudged the
marble and he cleansed it, read the record of Unity's
virtues, and went home a little comforted by nearer approach to her dust.

In the evening he was sociable and happy about the
final preparations. He gave Tiger small peace and
heartened Martha White, who felt gloomy in that her
reign must end on the following day.

"Have no fear," he said. "She's not the sort to see
you hurt. She'll lessen your labours, not add to 'em.
A towser for work—and why not? My son would never
have took up with a lazy girl. And her heart be so soft
as curds. Us shall all shake down very happy, without
a doubt."

Letters had reached Philip from the wedded pair, and
he made Tiger read them and utter his opinions upon
them.

"Happy as pigeons, for certain, master," he said, "yet
glad enough to come home—regular looking forward to
it, you might say."

On the morning of the return Philip surveyed his surprises and was well pleased. He had spent nearly twenty
pounds, for the most part upon valueless ornaments.
Some large oil paintings, from a sale at Moretonhampstead, now decorated the parlour, and various ungainly
vases, hung with cut-glass prisms, were perched upon the
mantel-shelf. He had bought a case of stuffed king-
fishers, for which there was no room anywhere save in
the kitchen; he had also purchased some curtains for

Minnie's bedroom windows, a set of lacquer trays, and a great deal of new cutlery and table glass. He knew that she liked sweet cider and had laid in six dozen bottles of it for her. He had bought a wonderful perambulator that he saw exposed in a shop window at Tavistock The secret of this was imparted to Tiger alone. It came in a wooden crate and was carried down to Hartland cellar and hidden away there under a tarpaulin covered with dried fern.

"I shall fetch it out with a gert flourish of trumpets the day their first be born," said Philip. "How they'll laugh!"

The night closed with cheerful peace. Mary French had come over from Teign Head at Philip's bidding, to help with final preparations, and she and Martha joined the men at supper. All was ready for the return of the married pair, and Philip explained how that he should ride out as far as the 'Warren House' to meet them and bring them on their way.

"Tiger have got to come too, on Martin's own hoss," he said; "and us be going to trot along, one each side of the carriage, and make a regular triumphant procession of it!"

CHAPTER VII

Of Martin Ouldsbroom, as life progressed with him and his characteristics hardened under pressure of the years, it might have been said that he 'scorned to trim his lion's skin with lace.' His nature was resolute, steadfast, and self-sufficient among men. He had a good intellect within limitations, and a clear sight of his own aims. Imagination formed no part of his character, yet he possessed a property of mind that could look ahead and see ahead more clearly than can many men of twenty-one. He knew himself unusually well, and he even had wit to estimate the worth of his own ambitions. He lacked power to display much amenity, yet was not indifferent to his kind. He respected sense and strength of character when combined with rectitude, he exhibited increasing impatience against stupidity and sentiment as he grew older. Tiger said of him that he was never uncivil except to a fool, and that he never cringed save to his God.

The home-life of Hartland opened prosperously, and Minnie at first went full of happiness before her new duties and new significance, but her husband swiftly began to impress himself upon her. He curbed here, and there controlled. He was didactic and insistent. Easy men gave way to him; strong men counted him as a force presently to be reckoned with in the affairs of Postbridge. He appealed repeatedly to his father for the control of the farm's finances, and at first Philip refused; but presently, when convinced that Martin was right, he gradually ceded this business to him. Everything, of course, stood in his own name, and he was aware in six months that the future began to promise more hopeful things. Once possessed of this belief, the farmer set out

370

upon some extravagances in the nature of a surprise for
Martin, and he bought a bracelet for Minnie that cost five
pounds. That such a toy did not accord with her state,
and was useless to her, Martin explained with some
warmth. Whereupon Philip fell into anger, and relations grew strained for a while between them.

The young wife of Martin was called upon quickly to
determine her line of conduct at Hartland, and she suffered in the process. But no middle course opened for
her, and she naturally adopted her husband's attitude to
life, though her heart went out to her father-in-law. In
the matter of the bracelet she estranged him for a while,
because he held that she ought to have kept it.

"If 'tis too grand now, it won't be presently," he declared. "Can't I see what's coming? Don't I know
that Martin be born to be rich? By the looks of it, he'll
never be anything else. But cash is his guiding star,
and that he'll come by, so sure as the south wind fetches
rain."

" 'Tis far, far too fine, father," Minnie answered,
"and you oughtn't to say that Martin will be nought but
rich. He's rich already in far more than money or
money's worth. He's rich in goodness and rich in the
respect of men that stand high. And I wish you'd be
patienter with him; and if his hard work and planning
and all the rest of it make for prosperity, don't we all
get the good of it too? In your large moods you are the
first to grant that."

He argued against her, however, and presently reduced
Minnie to tears. Not at his anger did she weep, but at
the hard things he spoke against her husband. Then she
dried her tears and was angry with him, in so far as her
nature could achieve anger.

"I won't hear it, I won't hear it!" she cried. "You
don't know what you're saying, father. 'Tis horrible
that you can even think such terrible things against him;
and him for ever wondering how best to further you and
better life for you. And never a day but he names you,
when him and me kneel morning and night together.
And I ask for you too."

The picture of their united petition softened Philip instantly. It was not the prayer that moved him, but the spectacle of the young things side by side, each actuated by affection for him.

"You silly little fools!" he said. "Pray to Hartland Tor, or the hawk perched atop of it—they'll hear you sooner than your blessed God. Such things be as vain as the noise of the cow that bellows for her dead calf; but the thought in your young minds that forced you to think of this—that's not vain, and I'm the better and happier for hearing tell about it. And for this trinket, I'll take it back and get summat else instead as won't be too tearing fine. All the same, it don't become Martin to think that the queen's crown would be too fine for your little head, and I'm ashamed of him that he could do so."

Light succeeded darkness in the home; then light was swallowed up by darkness again. Martin knew, long before the end, that it could not last, but he desired one sequel and waited in patient hope that the first step might come from his father. Minnie begged that he would leave Hartland and live in his own house hard by, and Gertrude Crymes also favoured this idea; but Martin did not want to go if such a step might be prevented. He had other views for his house and, when the time for Tiger's marriage came, chose Tiger for tenant and felt pleased to get him.

Martin was very patient with Philip Ouldsbroom, but he was also firmer as time passed. His tact increased, and in most directions he did what seemed good to him. Philip now generally agreed to his propositions and alterations, so long as the younger man first consulted him. But any work undertaken, any change effected without his knowledge, served to make him stubborn and angry. Twice he demolished Martin's plans thus set into operation without his sanction, and those particular improvements he never would hear of again, though in each case the thing intended must have proved of value.

There came an hour when Martin and Philip quarrelled about Tiger. The difference was trivial but awoke some fervour between them before Philip had his way. It related to Tiger's work, and Martin raised the question because, on the occasion, Tiger and Mary were coming back to Hartland. Martin's house was ready for them, and their wedded life would begin in it. But young Ouldsbroom held this a good opportunity to reorganise the labour scheme of the farm, and his plans involved certain redistribution of work that Philip refused to sanction. He had indeed relegated this department to Martin, and it was understood that Martin henceforth controlled the men absolutely; but Philip contended that the proposed changes were not reasonable. The younger man yielded now, for reasons that presently appeared, and Ouldsbroom had his way; but the victory did not hearten him. Much had fallen out of late that caused him discomfort, and not the least of his discoveries was this: that Tiger made a very great deal of practical difference to his waning joy in life. Since first he came there, Tiger had never been absent from Hartland for more than a day or two until the occasion of his honeymoon. And during these ten days Philip missed him exceedingly. He went off now to meet him through a still November evening.

The hour was three o'clock when he started, and faint sunlight brought out slant shadows of hedges stretched over the dim and dewy fields. He climbed Merripit Hill and gazed back a moment over the little theatre of his days. Postbridge lay darkling under its grove, and here and there about the vale ascended a feather of blue smoke, bright against the gloom of earth and naked boughs. Some of the newly ploughed fallow was dark as a patch of night spread against the pallor of meadows, whose herbage at this season appeared to have had all green soaked out of it. A spatter of copper still clung to the beeches, but the bulk of their sodden foliage was heaped in the water-tables by the way, or flung out upon the roads and heath. The fens were livid with dead grasses and white with pools of rain; the furze brakes shone bright green in the vigour of the year's growth. Already rows of little agate buds began to round among their thorns for the pageant of another spring. At one spot on the hill spread an exotic splash of wonderful colour amidst the sobriety of local harmonies. Three acres of purple cabbage adorned a sloping croft, and their medley of amethyst and rose, their subtle, glaucous passages of blue-green and grey, made a sheet of sheer splendour seen from afar. Like a jewel the great square of luscious, sprawling foliage shone upon the bosom of the darkness, and caught amid its own opal harmonies no little of the pale blue sky-colour spread above it. Setting sunshine flushed it also, and the mass burnt into a gracious warmth of genial splendour as the light went westerly and developed an evening glow. Even Ouldsbroom marked this rare colour and pulled up a minute to look at it while he filled his pipe.

"My word, how them cabbages do blaze!" he said to a man who passed him driving bullocks.

Presently the farmer drank at 'Warren House,' and waited there for Tiger to arrive. Jonathan French was also present, with a message for his returning sister from her family, and Mr. Twigg sat by the fireside in the bar. His legs had now failed him, and he could wait upon his customers no more.

" 'Tis hard, Greg, as you who have dealt in good liquor all your life should be water-logged yourself at the end," declared Ouldsbroom, alluding to the publican's infirmities.

"It seems hard to you, neighbour, no doubt," answered Gregory. "No doubt it seems hard that activity such as mine should be cut short; but you must remember Who did it. One Who does nothing without His everlasting reason, and only according to His everlasting plan. I'm being moulded for the next world now. The time is near. One sees His work at every turn lately. He seems to be giving a wonderful deal of attention to Dartmoor just at present Take that unruly member, Adam Truscott. The Lord have struck him, and never did I know such a broken and a contrite heart as he be showing since his accident."

But Philip scoffed

"A broken leg, you mean; and a heart only contrite

so long as the leg's no use Wait till he's up on his pins again, and you'll see all about his heart."

Twigg, however, held that Truscott was saved He revealed an uplifted mood, and appeared pleased with himself in an unusual degree.

"I know the signs," he said, "and never did I strike a better blow for the Lord than when—ill as I am—I got in my pony trap and hurried off to Adam's bed of sickness. I won him and talked and talked while I felt my legs swelling to mountains under me 'Twas a brave bit of work and will go to my account, with others like it."

"So it will, so it will, Brother Twigg," said a Little Baptist who was present

"Ah!" declared Philip, "you'll have a grand time reading over your pages in the Good Book, Gregory."

"So he will then, and very pretty reading 'twill be," cried Mr. Twigg's admirer "I wish us common people could be so hopeful."

"Don't say that," answered the publican "Trust me, neighbours, I'm just a man like yourselves."

But he spoke as though he did not expect them to believe it

"And as to you, Ouldsbroom," he continued, "why for should you flout me because I tell truth? And why for must I speak truth of other men and not of myself? Would the Lord think any better of me if I said worse of Mr. Gregory Twigg than I know of Mr. Gregory Twigg? It may ask for a brave mind to tell the world that we are good; but if you walk with your Maker, same as I have done, you catch a bit of your Maker's wisdom, and I'd be doing a poor service to Him Who has made me what I am, if I pretended His trouble had been wasted."

"Well, well," answered Philip, "no doubt you know best. And when the fiery chariot calls to drive you up into heaven, may I be here to help the send-off."

"You're hopeless," answered Mr. Twigg, not ill-pleased at the picture Philip presented. "But don't imagine that I'm——"

He was interrupted, for a trap drew up at the inn and Tiger appeared with his wife.

They were greeted with warmth, and Mr. Twigg insisted on making them take some refreshment. He also produced a bottle of ginger wine for Mary.

"My wedding present to you and Tiger here was an appeal to the Throne," he said. "I hope you'll bring him to Grace, Mary, and that afore many days have passed. But take this bottle too I wish you well, though I don't hide it from you that more than once your husband has said things that were not what they ought to have been, coming from him to me. However, we will let the dead bury their dead."

Tiger was preoccupied and spent but a few minutes at the 'Warren House.' The young man desired to be alone with Philip and hear how he was faring. He also possessed an item of news for Ouldsbroom's ear.

They departed quickly, and Philip rode beside the trap that was conveying the married couple home When they were arrived and the vehicle had gone, Tiger left Mary in her new home and walked awhile with the farmer. Dusk had fallen.

"As for us, all's well by fits and starts—more cloud than sunshine, no doubt. But now that you're back, I shall be home more Martin have bought up they two cottages by Lesser Merripit. You know the ones. He axed me first, of course, and I didn't see no objection. Busy as a bee he is. My darter-in-law's all right So be the people at Stannon And Saul Hext, to the post-office, have lost that ailing child A very good thing the poor scrap be gone, for she'd never have growed straight I seed her and made her laugh the very day before she died "

He related his news; then Tiger spoke

"You'm looking pretty well; and me and Mary be happy as birds But I heard from Mister Martin this morning He wrote very civil—kind, you might say But—well, you'd best to read it. My eternal welfare be bothering him above a bit. He says that he thought solid for the whole ten days I was honeymooning, and he's come to the conclusion that he had to speak—'twas his duty."

Philip looked anxious.

" 'Duty'—eh? When he names the word 'duty,' 'tis generally along with some damned unpleasant talk or act. What's the matter now?"

"Read," answered the other.

Then he handed Philip a letter and struck matches, by which he was able swiftly to decipher Martin's clear business hand.

"He wants for me to go to church or chapel in future, you see. He says that he holds himself responsible for the souls of them he reigns over, and that he can't have no ungodly man or woman at Hartland. He writes it very nice, and he says that a time will come when I shall know he is right and when I shall thank God for it."

"God—God!" cried Ouldsbroom "Little enough that frozen man knows of God! Ungodly—you? Well, well—so he be going to—there I can't do nothing Take your stinking letter and put it in the pigs' house— to sweeten it. What does Mary say?"

Tiger laughed.

"Mary's above a little thing like this."

"A little thing!"

"So she calls it. I was a bit savage myself when I read it first; and then she read it and made light of it 'The question be, shall us go, or shall us bide?' I said to her; but she shook her head. 'That's not the question at all,' says Molly, 'the question don't lie between going or stopping; it lies between church and chapel—that's all. You don't throw up Hartland for a thing like that —not if I've got anything to say ' "

"Never listen to her," answered the other man. "This touches deeper things than she knows about. 'Tis the liberty of the subject 'Tis tyranny He might so soon tell you how to vote as how to pray 'Tis the spirit of the old time come again, when a man couldn't call his soul his own, or his body either. 'Tis the damned old spirit, when parson and squire ran the parish and ex- pected every man, woman, and child to bend the knee to 'em You get up to Hartland to-night and tell my son that—better still—I'll do it I'm master yet—ban't I?"

"Of course, of course you be. But you must remember
that with the weight of years you, very properly, let him
take this and that off your shoulders. You gave him the
control, and you were right to do it. I'm not angry with
Mister Martin, and I hope you won't be. From his point
of view he's in the right, and, after all—what is it?
Church and chapel be harmless places. 'Tis only a black
coat of a Sunday and a quiet hour or two along with
Mary."

But Ouldsbroom would not hear of it. He argued for
the principle, and such was his rooted hatred of any
recognised dogma or form of worship, that he uttered a
command and bade Tiger at peril of his friendship resist
this despotic order.

Finally Tiger promised that he would ask for a week
in which to decide. His wife had already argued him
into acquiescence; but, for Philip's sake, he undertook
to do nothing immediately. Storms darkened the air of
Hartland, and Philip demanded his rights in the matter.
Martin offered to yield his authority if his father wished
it; then Ouldsbroom, mollified, argued for liberty of
conscience and no more.

Finally, in secret, he decided to get new work for Tiger
and find him a position of improved importance elsewhere. He believed this easy, and for his own part, since
he spent less and less of his days at home, he assured himself that he might see more of Tiger if he was away.
Without revealing his purpose, he scoured the country,
explained to farmers that Tiger of Hartland was in the
market, cried his fame and stated the weekly wages that
he had a right to command. But his efforts to find a
place worthy of his friend were futile. None felt prepared to pay the money that Tiger was supposed to deserve; indeed, Philip's own credit was quite gone now.
His contemporaries had nearly vanished from the fore-
most rank, and the rising generation did not take him
seriously. Some were civil and gave him drink and listened to his speeches; others were too busy to consider
him and sent him off with a short answer. He was grown
shabby and careless of his clothes now: folk who did not

know him guessed that he could be little better than a tramp.

The result of this general canvass on behalf of Tiger did Philip harm, for he found less sympathy and kindness in the world than he had expected, and the lack angered him unreasonably against all men. He made no mention of his failures to Tiger, and he submitted with but a mild explosion of contempt when the young man told him that Martin was to have his way.

One negative comfort arose from the decision: Mary had determined to go to church and not chapel.

As for Tiger himself, his own private plans were long since matured. He meant to stop at Hartland while Philip lived, but knew that he would leave it a month afterwards.

CHAPTER VIII

MARTIN OULDSBROOM'S wife was with child before the winter returned, and, upon that promise, the young husband found himself faced with the weightiest problems that life had yet proposed to him. Anxiety tempered satisfaction. His sober mind looked forward, and even had he been disposed to evade the difficulties that threatened, or postpone solution until their incidence, that was not possible, because already, and daily, from the mouth of Philip he heard the gravity of the danger.

Ouldsbroom was overjoyed. He exalted Minnie above all people, and began his plans and projects for spoiling the future child by spoiling its mother. His activity was boundless, his energy unceasing. He wasted pounds upon surprises for Minnie, and, hidden from him in the exasperated company of her husband, not seldom she wept at the futile follies he committed.

The farmer's altruism, now relieved, by his own impairment, from rational control, ran into excesses; yet such was the fervour of the old heart that planned, that to chide or resent his unsleeping energies had taxed a harder spirit than Martin's. Only he could attempt control, and the result seldom proved successful.

"Master ought to have a keeper, and that's the truth," confessed Tiger. "My wife says that he's like a good fairy gone weak in the head; and there it is in a nutshell."

But not even Tiger could stem the inevitable catastrophe. Martin debated slowly with himself and came to no hasty conclusion. To bring up a child under the same roof with Philip was to ruin a child. Ruin actually waited for the unborn, and he could see nothing ahead but eternal and unthinkable friction from the hour that his offspring came into the world. His duty to the child stood high above any other human obligation in the young man's regard. He, too, had laid his plans and weighed the responsibilities of fatherhood.

The question, reduced to simplest dimensions, soon confronted him. Either his wife and he must leave Hartland, or his father must do so. For the sake of his future property he mourned the necessity of choosing; but greater interests stood at stake, and, since it was impossible again to suggest that Philip depart, Martin, after long thought and pain, determined to leave his home. Minnie begged him to come to no decision until her child was born, and Tiger, to whom he also declared his purpose, foretold that such a step would mean final ruin for Ouldsbroom.

"You're the only drag left on the wheel," he said. "I do what I can, and that's a good bit, but you've got the influence where it's a serious thing. Master knows, when he stops to think, that you be in the right most times. He'll never hear of your going off."

"I shouldn't go far—only to one of my two houses at Lower Merripit. Of course the easy way out of the difficulty—but that's no use, and I won't even mention it. I might be nearer even. I might take your house, Tiger, and you could get over to Merripit or——"

He broke off, inspired by a promising thought.

"How would it be if you and your wife came to Hartland and I and my wife went and lived in your house?"

Tiger offered one objection, but that was final.

"Mary wouldn't do such a thing for all the world," he said.

The other, however, demanded that this point should be left open. It struck him that only so might the problem be solved, and it was not until Tiger pointed out another objection that he abandoned the hope.

"Even if it happened," said the elder, "what good would be served? My house ban't a quarter of a mile from Hartland, and if the old boy can get at your babby here, he can just as easy there. No matter where he is,

to a good mile or two, he'll be running after the child—
unless you was to forbid it. And even you can't do that,
I reckon.''

"I can do it and I shall do it if my child's welfare is
the question A child is more than a parent ''

"Why for worry? Lord knows what may fall out
betwixt now and June, and my wife tells me your little
one ban't due till then.''

"It's not my way to be unprepared. And, for my
father's sake, the sooner he knows my ideas the better.
Then he'll be ready to face changes.''

"Don't deny him the child altogether,'' pleaded Tiger.
"He's building on it something wonderful. It's done
him good a'ready—the bare thought of it. Better us
hope the little thing will work good on him than that he
works harm on it So busy is he that he's forgot to be
drunk for a week, and the nearer comes the time, the
busier he'll get for certain.''

"I know that—only too well. I must have the position
defined I'm not here for your advice, but to tell you
what I propose. But, of course, my father's own wish
must count in the matter—if it happens to be within
reason.''

A few weeks later Martin had speech with Philip, and
explained that he desired changes at Hartland

They rode together on an April day and passed above
Dart on the lofty ridge of Broad Down.

Martin then spoke plainly but patiently. He made
no disguise of his reasons for desiring the change, and
told his elder that the coming child must be brought up
absolutely in his own way, and according to his own
opinions of training and education.

The collision was severe and the result irretrievable.
Philip drew up his horse to listen while Martin spoke.
He did not interrupt him but gazed with dull and scowl-
ing eyes straight into the other's

"In a word, your father ban't fitting company for
your child—is that it?''

"I'm only saying what I think to be right You and
I have different ideas on every subject, and you know

the cruel strain that it is, better than I can tell you. My child's immortal soul is in my keeping; you don't even think he's got an immortal soul. I hate the name of drink; you are under the dominion of it We cannot agree, and I don't judge you, father. But I must judge myself, and I must listen to my conscience, and my conscience tells me that——''

"Didn't I bring you up? Answer that question Didn't I do a thousand, thousand times more for you than a father often does for his son? Didn't I scrimp and starve for you to be fat and prosperous? Didn't I send you to school—fool that I was? Don't you owe all that you are to me?''

"No, father. I owe my education to you, and, in one sense, I owe what I am to you But not in the sense you mean. I don't think as you think, and I don't seek and shun what you seek and shun. I'm not built to be what you like. I'm different from you every way that I can be You make me a sorrowful man, because while it's in my power to do good and be useful to everybody else in my life, I'm powerless—powerless to do good or be useful to you.''

"And why? Because your heart's a stone and you was born without any milk of human kindness in you. I've forgiven and forgotten for twenty years For twenty years, I tell you. But I'll torment myself about you no more You're not a man—or if you are, I'd like to see a devil! I hate you—I hate your shadow. Take all I've got—everything—and my hate in the bargain I'll go, then. I'll go away from Hartland—God's my judge I will. You've fouled the air of my home for ever-more And may your blasted child be a canker and a curse to your age, as you have been to mine. You've worked and plotted for this for years I've known—I've known. I've seen it in your snake's eyes when you've been looking at me. And now you've won and I've lost. I'll go—so soon as I can find a corner for my bones I'll be off. And if the memory of me, wandering friendless and roofless in the world, don't blast your smug life and poison your prayers, then——''

He broke off, listened for no reply, but galloped away as hard as his horse would take him; while Martin stood still and did not attempt to follow.

The furious elder only stopped when a mile of wilderness stretched between them. Then he drew up and found that he had come upon the fragments of Brown's House, where it stood in seclusion. He dismounted and tramped hither and thither, deep-plunged in a phlegethon that burned his soul alive. He cried aloud and raved and stamped upon the earth. For a long time he moved up and down; but presently he sat upon the ruin and slowly grew calmer. His torture abated, his panting bosom stilled.

Then into his mind there flashed a characteristic resolve, and an inspiration, of the extravagant sort peculiar to him, leapt adult from his rocking brain. He would thrust a roof on this wreck of a human home and let the walls shelter yet another miserable man. He would make his dwelling here, and live sequestered evermore as a protest against evil fate.

Nettles and thistles clove to the rack of stone, and, standing shoulder to shoulder, crowned it with their stings and spines. They were seemly company for his heart now. Here, in this immense ring of untrodden hills, with thorns for friends and the foxes for company, he would abide. The standing walls were clothed with stonecrop, lichen, and ferns. Moss clung between their fragments and held them together. They would serve for the short span that he might need them.

Possessed with this sudden resolve, Philip set to work there and then. He dragged out the débris from the remaining chamber, pulled down stone after stone and flung them ready for the builders. He trampled down the nettles, cut away the grass and briars with his knife, and cleared the circumference of the ruin, that its nature might be the better judged. For three hours he toiled here, and the longer he worked the clearer dawned his thought. His labour calmed him; he returned home in peace; a sort of ferocious good humour marked his attitude to Tiger when he met him.

For a week he kept his secret from Hartland, though others already knew it. Meantime he refused to discuss the future with Martin or Minnie. Both strove to propitiate him, but he cut them short.

"My plans be made," he said. "Come the fit time, you shall know 'em. Have no fear that I be going to cast you out. 'Tis the other way round. I know my place. I'm only a bad old man—not proper company for Little Baptists and their babbies. I must be hidden from the wise and prudent, as your Book says. And Martin here don't think 'tis fitting I should be revealed to babes neither. Of course 'twould never do for my grandchild to know his own grandfather—the old man that made Hartland what it is, and was accounted a fair, honest pattern of creature once on a time. Of course such a thing can't be thought upon."

In this spirit Philip persisted for a week; then he told them what he had determined to do.

"And if you think to change me, you think wrong," he said to Martin. "I can very well die there, like the wild beasts die when their time comes. They don't have none to smooth their pillows, no more won't I. Don't pull no faces about it, for though cant be the staple of your life and your thoughts, it be lost on me. You've done what you set out to do; you've drove me from my own door; and may the lightning out of the cloud strike me if, once gone, I ever come back again."

They strove with him, and both Martin and his wife implored the old man to abandon his purpose. Every objection was urged against his scheme; but the more reasonable they sounded, the less he entertained them

" 'Tis done, and you may spare your talk," he said "I've planned all and thought upon all. I shan't trouble Hartland and I shan't trouble Postbridge. I shall take my way by West Dart to the 'Ring o' Bells.' There'll be food and friends for me there For you'll be surprised to know that I've still got one or two people in the world that ban't weary of me."

In private Tiger exercised all his powers of persuasion; and Philip, who hid nothing from him, opened his heart,

25

showed him the mortal wounds of it, and explained that no power would keep him at Hartland longer.

"I ban't fit company for my own grandchild 'Tis all summed up in that," he said. "And since my days are short now, I'll be gone, for I wouldn't turn a dog out of Hartland that loved the place, let alone him as will own Hartland presently. He's robbed me of my own, Tiger. He's snatched away what would have been his soon enough. Well, let him have it. He shan't never say I was hard or unfatherly. Let him have all—money, land —everything. I'll build up Brown's House and take a bit of cash—just enough to keep body and soul together and leave a copper over for a pal That's all I want He can have the rest I don't envy him his fame, or his strength, or Hartland, or any mortal thing. I only want to get out of reach of his eyes and his voice for evermore."

They could not shake him. He had made arrangements with a builder, and the work was quickly set in hand

"Westaway be going to run up a roof and a chimney dog-cheap," explained Ouldsbroom. Method marked his madness. All else faded from his mind He ignored his farm and devoted his energies to making the ruin habitable.

"Till the first day of October," he said, "I be in command here, and after that day you can set the dogs on me if I come inside the gate But, until then, I've a right to bid you all do as I please; and therefore, come Monday next, I order Tiger and Will Rogers to get up over and lend a hand. There's a lot to do, and I'm going to break up a bit of ground and put in a few tons of lime and plant potatoes."

He spoke as little to Martin as possible during these dark hours; but he was kind and solicitous for Minnie Only, after a time, the hard words that he poured out against her husband fired the gentle woman into anger. She knew what her husband was suffering; she knew that Philip was unjust. To her eyes it seemed that the cruelty and unreason lay entirely upon the side of her father-in-law; and this presently she told him.

"Can't you allow for his nature, father? Can't you see that he must do what his conscience tells him? We'll go, and gladly go. We can bide near enough to be useful, and he can be here every day to do your bidding. 'Tis hard and very different to your common way to do what you are doing and let the blame fall on my husband's shoulders. He's fretting about it, and he's asked a score of sensible people what to do for the best."

"No doubt. He'll go to anybody but his own father. How be a proud man to live under a roof where he's despised and hated? You say that he frets. And haven't he got cause to fret? What's his religion worth if he can't keep the Commandments? Ban't he told to honour his father? 'Tis a fine way to honour me to kick me out of my own house. And preaches at his prayer-shop now, I'm told—tells 'em how to run with the hare and hunt with the hounds, no doubt. He's larned that dirty trick, if nothing else. That's what I paid his schooling for A fond fool was I; and now I be finding the price of my folly. She was taken from the evil to come—his mother was I don't mourn for her no more. I did her a good turn when I killed her. 'Tis most enough to make you believe in a watching God to think that she was hurried off out of sight of this. But she'd have stuck to me, mark you He needn't fox himself to think his mother would have bided here when I was thrown out. Grandchild or no grandchild, she would have put me first, as she always did He wouldn't have robbed me of her love and worship, though no doubt he'd have tried his hardest to do it."

Upon that Minnie wept and rebuked him. He answered roughly, left her and henceforth counted her with her husband as an enemy

When Tiger and another came up to Brown's House with their tools on the appointed day, they found that much was already done. Ouldsbroom had arranged with the bailiff of the Duchy to make this solitude his home. He had proceeded in order, and now the walls were up and the timbers had arrived for the roof Two rooms were to be built. The door opened from the east; two windows would look upon the south. But the labourers from Hartland were concerned with Philip's garden Half an acre of ground, outlined by its former enclosures, subtended Brown's House. Philip had already mowed this patch and cleaned it as well as he was able Now Tiger and Rogers lowered down a plough, which they had brought in a cart drawn by two horses. They transferred one horse from cart to plough; then Tiger began to break up the land, while Will returned to Hartland for some bags of brown lime

The spectacle of the plough suggested something to Philip.

"Be damned if I hadn't forgot my hoss!" he cried "And us must have a place for my tools and gear also. So far there's nought planned but the kitchen and my bedroom opening off of it, but, of course, us must have a little lean-to shippon 'pon t'other side."

He hurried off to the masons that he might explain this necessary addition.

CHAPTER IX

THE work of making his new home served to sweeten Philip's mind in some directions. But while cheerful with Tiger, and with friends at Two Bridges or Postbridge, he preserved steadfast animosity against Martin. The latter strained the resources of his character and strove with might and main to moderate this attitude; but for many days he could not. He sought counsel from men, and guidance from Heaven; but no success rewarded his labours. Philip Ouldsbroom would not hear him and would not heed those who came as intercessors for him.

His answer was always the same:

"He's cast me out. I've done with him for evermore. Let them as can stomach such a man be his friends. When I was young he'd have had no friends; but the world's all changed now, and simple hearts and plain dealing be things of the past."

He brought up his few possessions to the hut. He took very little beyond his clothes, his gun, his fishing-rod, and his horse. The place was ready for him by the end of November, and he left Hartland without ceremony and without taking any farewells.

Martin's hope at this period was that the old man would soon weary of his own company. None more sociable and social according to his lights existed, and those best known to Philip foretold that a few weeks in the mournful seclusion of Brown's House would tame the farmer's temper, reduce his spirits, and send him back to civilisation.

He had made no business plans with Martin and left no directions of any sort concerning the conduct and administration of Hartland.

389

Tiger approached the farmer twice upon the subject, but he refused to discuss it

"Plenty of time; plenty of time," he said "I ban't dead yet, and I don't mean to die for a good bit. I shall get peace of mind up here, and that's all a man of my age can hope for. Peace of body's a dream when you'm getting up to seventy year old, or near it. Not but what I'm stout enough. I can go and come by Wistman's Wood to the 'Ring o' Bells'; and there's always a good few of the old sort to give me a welcome there. And as for the money—sink the money—'tis the money have made that snake I called my son what he's come to be. Let him have it. Send lawyer along and I'll put my name to anything and everything. I ax for a pound a week and a fiver added off and on if I'm hard up. And I'll have that down in lawyer's language—else he'd very soon let me starve. The rest be his "

Philip invited none to see him save Tiger, and his visits to Postbridge, when once he had taken leave of it, were few. Occasionally he called on Saul Hext, who now controlled the post-office and Barbara's little shop, but most people avoided him when they could do so without rudeness, and the rising generation held him as a madman. Children were told not to speak to him, and when he came grinning to them with kind words and promises of toys, they ran away and laughed.

For a month after Philip had taken up his new abode, Tiger was sent daily by Martin to see him, and Minnie sometimes wrote a letter begging him to come to Hartland on Sundays and spend the day there But he did not come. Only once, when Martin was from home on business at Exeter, Ouldsbroom returned and spent two days with Minnie. She tried very hard to influence him, but she failed He declared that he was well, and more peaceful than he had been for many years. He talked of Two Bridges and the cheerful company there; he had found a new friend in one Nicholas Edgecombe, a warrener, who dwelt in a house as lonely as his own at Wistman's Wood.

"A very proper red man," he said. "He've befriended me more than once, and gone so far, out of charity, as to see me home now and again when I was bosky-eyed.''

Philip made a very great grievance of his present case. To those who would listen he was never tired of telling the story of his wrongs. Much patience marked the attitude of the elderly to Ouldsbroom, and not until he had wearied the bar of the 'Ring o' Bells' would the kind-hearted publican urge him to desist and go upon his way. Many honestly believed him ill-used; the greater number, knowing both sides, could not see that Martin was to blame. Heated arguments arose upon the question, but none convinced another.

Philip remained unshaken. In the public bar at Two Bridges a labourer declared one night that he had never seen a thief.

"Hast not?" asked Ouldsbroom. "Then cast a good look at my son next time he passes by, and you won't be able to say that again.''

Rumours increased that the master of Hartland had been robbed, and the enemies of Martin gladly believed it. Easy men disliked him much; it was said that he always took and never gave in his dealings. Therefore not a few were pleased to report that Philip had been ill-used and that the stronger will of his son had triumphed when he left his home. Reports became exaggerated and many lies were told, but Philip contradicted none of them.

"The truth's uglier than anything that's said," he declared.

The scandal grew, and Martin found that just men were being influenced against him. It had been reported that his father was starving; that he had cast him out and now only granted him a pittance. In truth, no financial understanding was yet come to, and Martin felt much impeded. Thrice he had endeavoured to see his father, and twice Philip was not at Brown's House when he called there. On the third occasion he refused to admit Martin and bade him be gone. The lawyers had written to Philip, but he had not replied to them.

They had sent messengers to him and failed to find him.

Once more Martin attempted the difficult task of speaking with Ouldsbroom. He rode up to Brown's House in the hour of evening light, when another winter was at hand, and he took with him a china basin containing a pudding of which Philip was very fond. He knocked at the door. Then a voice shouted from a window, and he went round to the front of the house, leading his horse by the bridle.

The old man looked out at him. Philip now shaved no more. His thin hair hung white about his ears, his chin and cheeks were bright with a snowy scrub that shone in the sunshine; his sanguine complexion faded not, but lines and puckers and pouches had wrecked his face His head shook a little on his short neck; only the unconquerable blue of his eyes still sparkled from his countenance, and seemed out of place in that ruined frame.

"You!" he said. "Ban't you weary of coming hither to torment me?"

"I've brought a pudding from Minnie."

"Get back then, and poison a dog with it. 'Twas sweet when it left her hand—'tis foul since it have been in yours"

"Father, I implore you to be reasonable. We'll leave Hartland to-morrow, and thankfully leave it "

"Too late now. Why didn't you go back-along, instead of telling me to go?"

"I never told you to go, or dreamed that you would go. I meant to break it to you that I must go before my child was born D'you think I arrived at that without trouble and grief? D'you think that to stand by and see you killing yourself by inches——?"

"Don't ax me no questions, and don't pretend no lies I've done with you. I sicken at the sound of you; I shut my eyes to get away from the sight of you You're a monster and the snow's welcome afore you, and the east wind and the thunder and lightning I'd sooner be tored limb from limb by savage beasts than home with you again, and I'll never set foot inside Hartland so long

as you're under the roof. And this I'll tell you too: I've
reached a pitch—goaded to it by you—I've reached a
pitch where I'd give the farm away to the first tramp as
would ax me. I'd do anything—anything. I'd burn it
down about your blasted ears, and we'd see then whether
your God would come and put it out. And I offered it
to Tiger—d'you hear that? I offered it to Tiger, but he
wouldn't take it. More fool him!''

His ferocity wore itself out. Then Martin spoke again.

''I beg you to devote just a thought to business,
father.''

''Ah! that's all you think of. Money be the only subject in your mean soul. Money—what's money to me
now? What's anything if you haven't got a friend? I
don't want no money. Take it, keep it, breed it, choke
yourself with it. Share it with your God. Then you'll
be killing two birds with one stone and lining your nest
here and hereafter.''

''The papers they sent you——''

''I lost 'em. They'm out on the Moor somewheres.''

''Could you meet a man if he came to the 'Ring o'
Bells'? They'll make any arrangement you please. I
only want working expenses and to keep up your farm
for you.''

''It ban't my farm. I've forgot it. This here place
is my home, and I ax for enough to keep me and my
hoss, and no more. A pound a week I'll have, and if I'm
hard up and hungry afore the next pound's due, I'll ax
the foxes to lend me a bit, or the criss-hawks to catch me
a rabbit. Have no fear as I'll want your money.''

''Could you be down there on Wednesday next?''

''I'll be there, but see you ban't. Let me have an
honest man and not a rogue to deal with. I only want
a little of my own back—that's all. You can keep the
rest and devour widows' houses and bleat your prayers
and—— Begone, I can't stand the sight of you no more.
Send Tiger if you want me to talk sense. I can't afore
you—you make me mad. Keep away, for I ban't my
own master always now, and I might shoot you in mistake for a wolf. And mark this, Martin Ouldsbroom—

Little Baptist and father-hater—you'll be in hell afore
me yet.''

His bitterness was very terrible He shut the window
of his room and drew down a blind over it to hide the
interior. Martin considered for a few minutes. Then
he left the pudding on a stone in sight of the window
and went away

A sort of understanding was presently arrived at.
Philip signed documents giving control of Hartland into
the hands of his son; and it was arranged that Tiger
should wait upon the old man daily and convey him regular supplies of food and money.

For the time another hand was engaged at Hartland,
and Tiger's duties centred in Philip Martin made these
plans and hoped that they might work with some measure
of completeness and success during such life as remained
to his father.

Many had begged him to have the old man back again;
many assured him that a new-born infant could take no
hurt from the presence of his grandfather, drunk or
sober; but upon this point Martin would not yield. He
hoped only respecting Philip now that Heaven might
busy itself on his behalf. Man was powerless to save
him; and personally young Ouldsbroom saw the outcast
no more. He feared not for his life; but he held it folly
to endanger that life without hope of any benefit therefrom

Tiger did his work well, and sometimes stopped for a
day or two at Brown's House. He reported that Philip
grew quieter and more reasonable. He had asked for his
Bible, and Tiger took it to him, and often read from Job
when the old man had been intoxicated over night and
spent a day in recovering

Philip seldom came to Postbridge, but sometimes he
rode to the crown of the hills and looked upon his home.
The folk would see him perched motionless against the
sky upon Broad Down For an hour at a time he might
gaze into the theatre of his life; and then he would turn
away and disappear

CHAPTER X

MARTIN OULDSBROOM did not permit trouble to ruin his life or come between him and his purposes. Immense native energy was combined in him with an earnest and serious outlook upon affairs. The ruling passion to prosper did not clash with his religious enthusiasm. He was scrupulous, but he was hard, and he lost no chances to succeed and improve his worldly position, while preserving his standard of justice and morality. Unswerving rectitude was natural to him; his sole human weakness centred in the desire to be rich; but it could not be said to come between him and the letter of justice in all his dealings. He had a little money of his father's to handle now, and he effected considerable changes in the old securities. He held that mortgages were the most desirable form of investment, and effected several in the immediate neighbourhood of Hartland. He perceived possibilities as yet unguessed in the vicinage of his home, and dreamed dreams of prosperous lodging-houses at Postbridge. Dartmoor had of late been proved a valuable sanatorium, and Martin, after some speech with a physician upon the subject, saw that money was certainly to be made if good accommodation for lung-sick patients could be established upon the waste. As a Little Baptist, the young man stood high, and bestowed more than a tithe of his energies in advancing the cause of that sect. He believed his persuasion to be absolutely right and lost no opportunity of assisting it. The Order of the Rechabites also numbered him its ardent friend. Temperance was the only subject that had ever prompted this level-minded young man to intemperance; but upon that subject he could wax fiery. He cast many stones in many directions, but not from any glass house. Many hated him for his elevated aridities; but none could point to errors of commission

So he strove on the side of right and built up a solid holding in matters temporal and eternal. Tiger, whose vocabulary and outlook in general had been enlarged since he went to church on Sundays, declared of young Ouldsbroom that he had learned how to serve God and Mammon both.

"You don't know where to have him," he confessed to his wife. " 'Tis a case of a chap who never does a wrong thing, seemingly And yet, if parson tells us true, there never was but one man who didn't do wrong. I suppose he've got some sins hid. For my part, I feel to him like some dogs feel to some men: I can't abide him, yet can't give no more than a dog's reason why I don't."

Mary understood.

"Ban't what he've got that hurts you 'Tis what he haven't got," she said "There's something left out of the man. He'm like a quince—never grows ripe."

"Time may soften even him, however."

"No," she said "It don't soften his sort. 'Tis the rind of him that's so hard. The sun can't get through him. If his old, doting father couldn't do it when he was young, nothing could Ban't Mister Martin's fault that few run to him in trouble. I dare say he'd list to them ready enough if they did "

"He'd list to them—yes. He's civil and patient to all. But he never mixes no sweet with his medicine—to help it down. It's like to make you sick—so you lose the good of it."

When Dr. Forde had speech with Martin, their meeting related to another topic than Dartmoor as a panacea. Philip had been ill, and Tiger had stopped with him and nursed him for ten days. Now he was recovering from bronchitis, and Martin made inquiries concerning his father when at Princetown

"He oughtn't to be there," declared the doctor. "He's

a bit older than his age now—thanks to hard drinking. He's strong enough still; but he wants watching.''

With spring, however, Philip acquired new strength, and the arrival of the child served greatly to interest and delight him.

A son was born to Martin, and its advent rejoiced the mother and turned her thoughts into happy channels.

For Minnie, marriage had proved different from the vision of marriage. Her husband daily grew into a figure more remarkable and worthy of admiration; but she always crept back in thought, like a guilty thing, to the day in the byre when he asked her to marry him, and glowed and adored her with voice and eyes. She had thought that moment was the first of many like it; she had supposed that each caress would be closer than the last, that each kiss would be warmer, each act of love more glorious than the preceding. She had dreamed that love was a deathless thing, lighted from clash of two hearts, whose flames leapt together to burn, with double brightness and double strength, for ever. She had pictured their life; she had seen herself his guiding star, yet felt his strong hand in hers, to help at every crooked turn and steep place in the work-a-day journey. And now her head told her that truth was better far than her hopes; that reality exceeded any girl's guess of what reality might be. But her heart cried out loud while Martin slept; it cried out loud when he rose and dressed without putting his arm round her or pressing his face to hers; it cried out loud when he talked about the coming child and not the coming mother, when he was busy with preparations and counting the cost to himself, never to her.

He was always right, always ahead of need, always ready. He anticipated everything, and omitted nothing that those who understood told him should be done. But she yearned for the food he did not give her; for the worship and wonder and encouragement; for the pride at the glorious thing she was going to do for him; for the praise before this return that she was bringing to his love.

And when the child was born, and Martin came to see

her, he did not stop one fraction of one second after the nurse told him to go again. They were alone together for five minutes, and through four of them he knelt and prayed, with a voice steady and controlled, that the boy who had come into the world might prove a true and faithful soldier in the armies of the Lord. She said 'Amen' when he had done. It was all he wanted her to say. He kissed her then and told her the boy was very beautiful. And that heartened her a great deal.

Philip won the liveliest satisfaction from this advent, and it was clear that the event improved his physical condition through the channels of the mind. He called for an increase of money and spent it at Tavistock upon the child and his mother. But he would not come to see it until Minnie was well and business had taken her husband from home. Then he received the child into his arms and, with his eyes, fed hungrily. He traced imaginary likenesses, and declared that the infant resembled Unity.

Almost his first question was the boy's name.

"I suppose you had no hand in that?" he asked of Minnie.

She shook her head

"There was a lot of talk. My father wanted for him to be called Quinton, after him; and I wanted him to be called Martin, of course, and Tiger thought 'twould please you if he was called after you, father. But Martin had his own opinions. 'I'll give him the mighty name of a mighty leader,' he said, 'and I hope that he'll never live to be unworthy of it.' Baby's called Wesley—just that and no more.''

"I hope as he'll live it down, then," answered the old man grimly. Then his face softened and he handed the child back to his mother. He asked after her health and rummaged in his pockets for gifts that he had brought her.

He shared the midday meal with her, and Minnie made him eat as well as drink.

In the evening Tiger walked back to Brown's House with him and marked the deep magic of this experience.

"There's nought like a babe to soften the heart," said Philip. "And when 'tis the fruit of your own loins, who can resist it? I'm very hopeful about this, Tiger, and out of my experience of life I must be Have you marked how my son bears himself to the child?"

"He cares a lot about it already."

"And well he may do. 'Twill change my son! I swore I'd never call him son again; but there 'tis—'twill out—blood's thicker than water. I've held his child in these arms, and if it can make an old, savage man like me more gentle to the world, surely to God 'twill soften its own father's heart?"

"He's that gentle with it, you wouldn't believe "

"Yes, yes, I would believe. Us have got to be gentle with the little ones, and so us may larn through them to be gentle with their elders. I have seen my grandchild, and my hand be ready to meet my son's I know— I understand how 'twill be. The sight of that poor, blinking little thing took me back, back nigh a quarter of a century, to the day they brought Martin to me from his mother. I know what I felt then, and shall my son——? It must come I've great faith in the power of nature, Tiger 'Tis stronger than religion—stronger than Little Baptists, or Rechabites, or anything. It will be heard, and where Martin stands now, mark me, 'tis hammering at his heart He'll do a deed presently—there will come a great call to him and he'll not resist it The child be crying out and speaking to him a'ready."

"He's a wonder in his way. All through this job he's not let slip one minute from the time he gives to work. The machine goes on just the same. Such a time-saver I never heard tell upon 'Tis because time's money, no doubt."

"So much the worse. If a man's firstborn coming can't jerk him out of the rut of life for a bit, 'tis no credit or vartue to him But wait—wait and see what that babe does Wesley or no Wesley, 'twill bring me back to Hartland. Yes, Tiger, you doubt; but I feel that be coming 'Twill ask for me afore it can speak. You should have seen how it snuggled to me! It knowed

who I was! I must get back. And Martin will come
to feel, afore he's a year older, that I must. He'll grow
wiser every hour he spends along with that child. I tell
you there's nothing like them for showing the proper
worth of things. Till he was four year old Martin would
fling a penny from him and cleave to an old brown pine-
cone, as he loved better'n anything else in the world.
The child will take him back and teach him, with all the
cleverness that every baby's got in it, till the world kills
it out of 'em. And then he'll ask me—leastways——''

Philip faltered and looked at his friend full of questioning.

"Won't he? Won't he, Tiger? You seem doubtful
about it I was that positive a moment agone, but at
my age we grow shaky of our own opinions—except when
we'm drunk. Won't he offer for me to come back,
Tiger?''

"I can't tell you, master. I don't think so. You'd
best not to hope it. Of course you'd be dearly welcome
back to-morrow, and God knows none but would be the
better for it; but Mister Martin—I don't think he'd stop
if you did.''

"Not now he knows what 'tis to be a father himself?
I'll not believe it. I'll stake my last hope on it. Tell
him how the child came to me. Order Minnie to tell
him that from me.''

"You may lay your life she'll tell him and make much
of it.''

"I'd love to mind the child for 'em. I understand
childer very well. I've spent a lot of my time along with
them. You can remember what I was to you when you
was a nipper—can't you?''

"Yes, I can, and never shall forget it ''

"Very well then. I must be there I must be there.
The child must have a little bit of my wisdom along with
the rest. 'Twill help his mind, Tiger. I'll warm his
young, opening bud of a heart just a bit—to temper the
east wind of his father. It must happen like that. And
he'll keep me out of mischief, Tiger—don't you see?
He'll do as much for me as ever I'll do for him. If you

was to put that to my son, it might carry a terrible lot of weight with him.''

But time passed and Martin made no such overture. Once, indeed, a few months later, he desired to speak with his father, and Ouldsbroom readily consented to a meeting, because he supposed that the great question would be asked and that Martin desired to bring him back to Hartland. Such an idea, however, was far from the younger man's mind. Tiger and Minnie had both pleaded, and others represented the reasonableness of the change. But nothing could modify Martin in that particular. He was determined that his child and his father should never dwell under the same roof. The interview he desired related to affairs of business, and when Philip found that for this, and this alone, he had come to Brown's House, he drove the young man from him with reviling.

He continued to see the child as opportunity offered, but only when Martin was from home.

CHAPTER XI

Two years passed by and left Ouldsbroom but little changed. Activity and life in the open air served to counteract his intemperance. It might have been said concerning him, as of the Homeric hero, that he dwelt by the wayside and loved all the world. Like Achilles, he craved only to walk under the golden sun, and had rather lived as a man in a peasant's hut than reign—a ghost among the shades. Yet a ghost he was. The shadow of himself, he haunted the land of his birth, and had already passed from the knowledge of all but a few. Martin Ouldsbroom and the notorious evil endured at his hands continued to be his topic. While the younger did what he might for the old man, and spared no care in reason to preserve him, Philip was set for ever against Martin, and cried out in any ear that would listen concerning the wrongs that he had suffered.

There came a day of summer when Philip proceeded from Brown's House to his favourite haunt upon Crow Tor. There, in the cushion amid the granite rocks, nodded a dozen bluebells, and the time had come to gather them. Martin was to be from home, and the wanderer's purpose might therefore be accomplished. He intended to visit Hartland and take the flowers to his grandson.

With the little bunch in hand he went first to Two Bridges, drank at 'The Ring o' Bells,' and then trudged upon the high road to his old home. Upon the way he observed Martin Ouldsbroom riding towards him. He crept out of sight, therefore, and hid behind a store wall until the other had passed. Martin saw the action, and it was not the first time that he had seen it. No word passed between them now, and no recognition, for the younger knew that it was useless to make an overture.

Another had also marked the incident. Nigh the spot where Philip supposed himself hidden, there sat a vagrant: a shabby, bearded man, unclean and uncombed. He ate food from a piece of paper and basked in the sun. His hat was off, and his long, reddish hair began to grow thin upon his crown. With this sort of spirit the farmer now claimed natural kinship. He saw one who, like himself, had fallen out with the world. Therefore he approached on equal terms.

"Have 'e got a bite to spare, mate?" he asked, and the other pointed to his parcel of broken meat.

"Help yourself," he said.

"Don't think I'll rob you," answered the elder, sitting down. "I've got a shilling in my pocket, and you're welcome to it; but for the moment I'm a thought hungry."

"Not a common complaint with you, I reckon?" said the stranger, regarding his face.

"No—t'other thing be more in my line."

"Fine thirsty weather this. Why did you avoid that dapper young chap on the brown horse?"

"Because he's my son, and the meanest dog that ever went on two legs. Only one failing he has—and that's a hatred of the man that got him. I go out of his way like that, so as I shan't be driven to breathe the same air with him."

"Tell me."

Philip needed no second bidding. His eyes flashed; his head shook; he stopped eating.

"I'm a terrible ill-used old man. My only child hates me and plots to end my days. 'Tis true as the light above us. I starved to send him to school, and then he came back and drove me out of my home; he drove me out; and if I was to fall dead this minute he'd shout for joy. I tried all that mortal could do. I met him in everything, yielded up everything, but he was wolf to my lamb; I couldn't do right with him. And even at that I'd have forgiven him—yes, I would. I'd forgive everything in the world but meanness—that I won't forgive.''

"Quite right. 'Tis a filthy vice, and leads to all that's bad.''

"It has done so with that man. Yet so different he was—so different—till larning and lust for money got hold on him.''

"Never mind Eat and forget him.''

The last speaker brought a little flask out of his pocket.

"You're like me," he said. "You take it neat. We mostly reach that stage before the end. Here's luck·—

> "To our grand patron, call'd Good-fellowship;
> Whose livery all our people hereabout
> Are clad in.''

He drank and handed the vessel to Philip.

"Forget yesterday, old chap," he said, "and remember 'you can't buy to-morrow'; so just live in the present and feel the sun on your old nose and don't worry.''

Philip, however, was not to be driven from his theme. He failed to perceive that here was one fallen from a higher estate than his.

"Let be," he answered "Don't make fun but listen. I was a very jolly man once myself, and lived on laughter; but life has long silenced that.''

"Go on then. Yet I know all you've got to tell. I've met the like of you, master. Heart to heart we are I understand. There's no place for us in this world nowadays. We're born too late by the whole length of the Christian era The joyful, lazy old world was our oyster —not this busy, money-grubbing, snivelling, canting one.''

Philip took a pocket-book from his breast. It was of battered leather, much worn at the edges. A frayed piece of paper appeared in it. The book contained nothing else.

"To show how time will rot a living man, who began well—read that. When Martin was a young youth a snake bit him—and the poison of the snake be in him still. It never worked out. And I wish—I wish to God as he had died then and left me a child's name to love—

not a man's to hate and curse for ever. He lived, and
that was the first letter ever my child wrote me; and
I'd be a happier man to-day, and a better man, if it had
been the last."

The tramp read a child's letter—now grown yellow
and tattered and dirty from perusal under many hands.
Presently he returned it and his voice had changed.

"Can't you show this to him and ask him to go back
and start again?"

"He'd say that he never wrote it; and he'd be right.
His mother lived in them days—as good and grand a
woman as ever trod the earth. But there was nothing
of her in him. Or if there was, it worked out long ago.
I stand as a witness against him, and when I'm dead my
gravestone will."

"Perhaps he won't put one up. But come, come,
you're not tired of the joy of living—else you wouldn't
be carrying that bunch of bluebells with you."

"It ban't life," declared Ouldsbroom. "It ban't the
world, but the damned people in it that have wrecked
me. I'm not wishful to go, though go I must afore very
long. My heart have got a bit of a crack in it, they tell
me. 'Small wonder!' said I when they did. But I'll
trample earth for a bit yet, afore it tramples me. I've
got two creatures to live for—you might say three."

"Then you're rich. A man with three friends is one
picked out of a thousand. I've got none."

"I'll be your friend!" answered Philip instantly.
"You've got sense and you ban't above breaking bread
with a poor old man. If you come to Brown's House,
where I live up over, you can have as good as I've got."

"No, master. But thank you for the offer. Four
friends would be too many for any man. And these
flowers?"

"For my grandchild I've got 'em. I can tell you that
Phil knows a thing or two yet! 'Tisn't many men can
fetch you bluebells off middle of Dartymoor, I reckon!
But I can—out of the very midst of the place. And
more than that I know—more than that. A grandchild
I've got—the son of that mounted highwayman as rode

past a bit ago—but no more like him, thank God, than
he be like me.   'Tis my child, you might say, and I'm
going to fetch him up on my own pattern, and make him
a credit to the family instead of a blight on it.   He'm
in his third year—a very brave li'l boy—and I'll astonish
them in that quarter yet.''

He nodded sententiously.

"The child's your friend, I'll wager?"

"I should just think so.   He'll come to me afore his
mother!   But I never go nigh him while that man's home
He likes me better than his father.   His father whips
him—whips a child not three years old—the cowardly
dog!   If I'd seen him doing it, I'd have torn his throat
out, old as I am   Sometimes I've thought in my cups
as I'd lay behind a hedge for him and rid the world of
him.   But I wouldn't do that.   I'm all open and above
board, I am—and always have been.''

"Leave him.   And your other two friends?"

"There's Tiger.   He's a labouring man as I've brought
up and made, you might say   Rare stuff he's built of.
He understands.   There's no call to fear for the world
if it was full of the likes of him.   He looks after me up
to Brown's House   He keeps clothes on my back now.
I should have been a good friend to him and paid him a
thousandfold, if he'd let me.   But that's all one now.
Three friends, you say?   You'm but a frosty pattern
of man if that's good measure to you   Why, poor chap,
I had five hundred of 'em once!   Five hundred, I'm
sure 'twas.   Not a door but hid a friend once—and now
—But what do I care?   Let me be hungry—let me be
forgot   I've given all—all I had to give—and if there's
none left who want the brave pleasure of giving to me,
I can go without   I ban't very vexed about it when I'm
sober.   I'm a wise old man in my way.   People must
die, and them I've helped be mostly gone.   Us have got
to be thankful for very small mercies in sight of
seventy.''

The other looked at his great round back and bibulous
face.

"Yes, you're wise yet.   There's a good streak of

wisdom in taking flowers to a child. I never did that.''

Philip was elated.

"There's sense in me, I tell you; and if they'd only go the right way about it, the people would find it out. But they'm all too busy about their own affairs. My work's done—or nearly. There's nothing calling to do but to save that child against its father. I've got my ideas; but 'tis a secret yet. Don't you name it to nobody.''

He nodded at his thoughts, while the other took out a pipe and loaded it.

"Here's your shilling; now I must get on my way,'' declared Philip.

"Have you got plenty of money? I don't want it unless you can spare it, though I confess it would be useful. I must get to Plymouth to-night.''

"Take it, man. I've got money. He can't rob me of that. 'Twasn't his earning, mind you. 'Twas gathered by me and father afore me, long before his shadow made my world wintry.''

"Well, well. Carry your bluebells to the child and hear him thank you Ovid says 'The best weapon's an undaunted heart.' You've got that. Life is all a search, master, and very few find anything in the rubbish heap after they've picked it over But sometimes, while you are seeking one thing, you'll come across what's better, like a man shooting snipe and flushing a cock. We'll be hopeful still. Good-bye. I'm glad to have met you, and I thank you heartily for your shilling.''

Philip shook his hand.

"If you like to drop into Brown's House up over, you'll be welcome,'' he declared.

And then he went his way.

The educated wastrel looked after him.

"Turned on the wheel of the world, and not turned true''; he thought; "and if that wheel can't turn us true, it breaks us.''

CHAPTER XII

At the time of hay harvest Philip broke his long silence
and accosted Martin. Indeed, he sought him. At first
the younger supposed this renewal of friendship but
an accident, prompted by Philip's momentary need; but
time seemed to show the elder was changing. Not until
long afterwards did the reason for his renewed amity
appear.

Martin, and the rest, were hard at work in a forenoon
of August upon the crofts of Hartland. The hay fell in
deep swathes where Tiger rode a machine and drove two
horses. He was perched on a shell of iron above the
wheels, and beneath him knives played and purred, glittering in the sweet heart of the crop. Here the mixed
pasture of clover and sorrel and many grasses fell and
stretched withering to silver green upon the verdant,
close-shorn face of the meadow. Behind the grass-cutter
there came men with rakes; and in the next field Martin
and some others, hired for the special work, were turning
and shaking out the drying hay with forks. The sun
smiled upon the proceedings, but before nightfall the
fallen grass would all be piled in little mounds upon the
bosoms of the fields, to protect it against any change of
weather

A battered hat, a red face, and a short stubble of white
beard suddenly rose nigh Martin where he worked He
had seen the familiar bent figure of Philip half a mile
off on the hill some time before, and now the old man
lifted himself from behind a wall on the side of the
field.

Martin was working fifty yards off and did not intend
to take any notice But presently, to his surprise, he
found himself called.

"Come hither, my son!" shouted Ouldsbroom, as though nothing but friendship dwelt between them.

Martin flung down his fork and ran to the wall.

"Good morning, father. I'm so very glad you called to me. Won't you step through the gate and sit down and rest for a bit out of the sun?"

"Rest? No. Why for should I rest? Have 'e got a bit of work for me, Martin? That's what I want. Plenty of time for resting when the sun's down. To be plain with you, along of this thirsty weather, I've used up my money a bit too soon. I be here to earn five shillings tossing hay. I can do it as well as them chaps. Then, having come by the money honestly, I can be off and get drunk in good company with an easy conscience."

The younger was very patient. He turned down his sleeves, wiped his face and got over the wall

"Let us talk," he said "I'm thankful that you could find it in you to come to me. Never stint yourself or borrow money, father. Why should you borrow it? Every penny is yours, and I'm making money for you faster and faster. You mustn't think I touch it. I keep mine and yours quite separate. Would you like to talk about it—or something else?"

"Anything else—anything else on God's earth but that I want to be friends with you again. I'm getting old at last—slowly but surely. I don't want to go back an hour into what's gone. Let all that sleep. But I want to be friends for the future. I want to be free of Hartland."

"Well you know the master is free of his own."

"Not when you're there. For two years I've hated you worse than hunger or thirst or pain And now I've forgiven you. Hate wears itself out I'll make a bargain with you, and if you let me see my grandchild when I please, I'll be friends and say no more against you. Not alone will I see him, if you can't trust me; but when you are by, or when his mother is by."

"Yes, father I agree to that. I'm told that Wesley is very fond of you and will always go to you."

"Why not? Don't he know I'm his grandfather?"

"I'm thankful for this—thankful above measure. I must get back to work now. There's a lot to do. 'Tis hard nowadays to find men who know how to work. I've turned off two haymakers because they only played at work. Here's half a sovereign. Will you come and have a bit of food with us under the hedge after noon?"

He took a ten-shilling piece from a little purse and handed it to Philip.

"No, I'll go in and have a bite with Minnie and the boy presently. But I thank you for asking me. I'm glad you did so. Here! Let me have the fork a minute. I'll show 'em!"

He came through a gate into the field, took off his coat and began to turn hay. Tiger, from his perch not far off, stared and laughed. Then he stopped his horses and spoke to the man, Will Rogers, who was close by.

"A good day's work all round by the look of it," he said. "If that old wonder ban't come down to pitch hay! And they've made it up, seemingly."

"Who would ever have thought of that happening?"

"Well, I can't say I'm so much surprised as some might be. I see most of Mr. Ouldsbroom now, and I've marked a weakening off of his anger for a good bit. He's got something hid, though. He gets that sly and deep sometimes. Nods and winks very wisely to himself and be full of secret plans. He's past mischief now—dear old blid. I ban't feared that he'll do any harm now. 'Tis for the sake of the child that he's made it up, without a doubt. Strange to see 'em together again. 'Tis the difference between sitting on the green grass and a stone-heap between them two men. Leastways, it used so to be when farmer was here."

But Rogers would not allow this.

"Things have changed. Mister Martin's frosty, but you can depend upon him. He'll have the last ounce, but he'll return you a pennyweight that's over. As we get up in years, we find that peace of mind depends on working with them that are trustworthy and won't fool us at any point. I dare say 'tis small in me to feel so; but us can't stand care so light-hearted as time goes by.

He was never the same to me as to you, remember. Us turn to a certainty in middle age, and don't welcome adventure and ups and downs like the boys do."

Tiger admitted this.

"Phil have tried me a thought these last two years, and I don't mind confessing it. I care for him more than ever I cared for him. I'd do anything that a mortal could do for him; but for a humble married man like me, who have found religion—for me to live with that amazing old whirlwind so much as I do, and feel for the most part powerless as the leaf in the river afore him —it have its hard side, Will."

"It can't last so very much longer."

"No, and that's the hardest side of all. The thing must end, and when I think of it ended, I don't know how to——"

A shout stopped him.

"Is there anything the matter? Why are you standing still, Tiger?"

The machine went on again.

Philip had soon done with the hayfork. He returned it to Martin and went off down to Postbridge. The action seemed pregnant and indicative of the changed relations. It was long since he had been at the hamlet, and not a few of the old people there hailed him as one risen from the dead.

" 'Tis Mr Ouldsbroom, surely!" cried Peter Culme, who now had ceased from his labours and, grown to be a very ancient man, drowsed away his end of days beside the river.

"So it is then, and I'm glad to see you're middling clever, too. But you be—what?—a hundred year old, Peter, by the look of you."

"Eighty-one, mister. You've heard tell that Charlie Coombes have gone?"

"Yes, yes. And Gregory Twigg be so full of water that they can't save him, I'm told. I must try and get up over to see him this afternoon. No doubt my son will lend me a hoss. Can't ax you to drink, Peter, for this place still be all behind the age and haven't no licensed house from one end to t'other. But if you travel over to 'Warren House' a bit later, I shall be very pleased to stand treat for the sake of the old days."

Peter thanked him and shook his head Then Philip went on to the shop of Saul Hext and sat down there in the familiar place.

"Let me have a drop out of your private bottle," he said. "Don't grudge it I've got ten bob in my pocket, and I'm going to spend every blessed penny of it in your shop afore I go."

This promise made Saul generous. He brought out a bottle of whisky three parts full, and Philip began to drink.

"Four fingers," he said; "then four more on top of that, and I shall feel a bit better. I've been working in the hay for my son. Did a day's work in half an hour, I assure you! At least, what the young men call a day's work now The way we worked is forgot by this slack-twisted generation. Have a drink along of me, Saul?"

Suddenly Philip felt in his pocket and drew out the half-sovereign.

"Here, you'd best to lay hold of this afore I forget it. I'll have the toys presently. They'm for my grand-child. I'm to go up over to have a bite with Minnie. I'm free of the house, you must know. I've forgiven my son."

He laughed to himself

"Little they guess; little they guess. But I'm that crafty!"

He broke off and looked at Hext suspiciously.

"Be you straight and above board? Can I trust you?"

"I should hope so, Mr. Ouldsbroom," answered Saul.

But the other shook his head.

"Some day—some day. You'll hear it when the time comes. You'll be the first to say 'Well done, Phil!' But I'm a bit too artful to name it yet. I wouldn't even tell Tiger "

He drank and began to grow bellicose. Mr. Hext became anxious and wished the old man away.

"Wouldn't even tell Tiger—not even Tiger. So if you think I'd tell you, you be very much mistaken Tiger's worth ten of you. I say he's worth ten of you, Saul Hext! And though he crept to church at my son's command—'tis humbug and nonsense, and if you think I don't see through it—why, there's nothing I don't see—nothing I don't see. I tell you there's nothing I don't see, Saul Hext I'm like the old hawk aloft. The creatures crawling about below may not mark him, but he sees them, and what they be good for—and then—swoop! —he's on 'em!"

"I think you'd best to come and buy what you want now," suggested Saul. "I shouldn't drink no more just at present, if I was you."

Philip laughed and thumped the table.

"You funny dog," he cried. "Never heard a better joke. But all the same, if you was me—I say if you was me, you white-faced fellow, you'd drain the bottle— same as I be going to do now!"

He was as good as his word.

"Now I want some toys for my brave boy up the hill," he said. He began to fumble for his money, and Hext reminded him that he had already found it.

"Then why don't you give me my toys? Why for don't you give me my boy's toys? I want the toys When I used to come for toys for Martin, they wasn't withheld from me. I say they wasn't withheld..."

Hext presently tied up a bundle of the things that Philip chose; but the old man had sense left to know that he could not get to Hartland at present.

"You hang on to them things till afternoon," he said. "I be going across the road to sit in thicky broken house and have a pipe and think over one or two deep schemes —one or two deep schemes as I be turning over, Saul Hext. I'll come back presently."

He lurched across to where a ruin stood beside Dart, and there, having sat blinking in the sun for a while, he went into the shade. He took off his coat, folded it up with meticulous care, and put it on a stone—one of the ancient tin moulds of mediæval miners, cut into this granite block when Elizabeth reigned Then he laid his head down upon it and soon slept.

It was evening before he woke and came back into life again His nebulous mind slowly cleared, and he remembered where he was and what had brought him hither. He rose, shook himself and went for the parcel of toys Then he tramped the familiar path to Hartland and found Martin, Minnie, and the baby at tea.

Wesley, a sturdy brown boy in whom his parents met, loved Philip well and was soon in his arms. Presently they sat on the kitchen floor together with the toys.

A new era seemed to . ave opened, and the mother's heart was full of thankfulness That the old man could come again to Hartland while Martin was also there, promised possibilities of peace.

Philip was cheerful now ; he ate a little and drank a great deal of tea. It was characteristic of him that he never looked back. The past entered not at all into his conversation, and he spoke as though he and Martin were on the best of terms.

Young Ouldsbroom was content to take it so. He avoided all subjects that could bring a shadow to the other's mind, and strove to speak with hope and cheerfulness. He had not seen Philip at these close quarters for more than two years, and was startled to mark the changes in him. But the old man seemed happy enough and even spoke of business. They talked vaguely, and presently a shout from the boy took Philip back to the floor Here he was at home ; here he was very thoroughly understood The brown eyes of the little child looked into his blue ones and found another child there, ready and willing to do his pleasure and share his joy.

Philip relapsed into gloom when Wesley went to bed. He became silent and declared himself very weary Martin offered to see him home , Minnie hinted that she would make up a bed for him if he desired it; but he declined both suggestions

He called for Tiger; and Tiger it was who presently brought him to Brown's House through the dewy night

The young man much rejoiced at such a turn of affairs; but Philip's mood had changed His head ached, and he grumbled at the length of the way.

"She offered to make up a bed for me, but he said nought If he'd but so much as looked the same offer, without a word, I'd have agreed to bide. But he didn't want it to be so. There's only one in Postbridge as will ever make up a bed for me, Tiger—and that's sexton."

He would not be cheered, and his friend presently got him home and helped him to bed. He fell asleep instantly, and Tiger, before he shut the door and departed, set a loaf and some butter on the table, laid a fire, filled a kettle with water, put some tea in the teapot and made the kitchen as tidy as he knew how.

CHAPTER XIII

Now Philip Ouldsbroom entered upon the twilight of his age, and only a last ambition held him much to life

There came to him a sort of longing to be self-conscious no more, to escape the curse of memory, to awake daily, as the beast, and go his way unlinked by one torturing thought to yesterday, by one cruel fear with to-morrow. In a clear hour he calculated the gains and losses, and believed that to be a fox or a coney would advance his welfare. There was not much he wanted to remember. Unity and Barbara and what they meant; Tiger and his lifelong devotion—that was all. He approached the coveted annihilation often enough through drink, and returned to consciousness with less and less of gratitude.

The renewed amenities waned slowly, for Philip always felt discomfort with Martin, and enjoyed better to be at Hartland when he was not by. He spoke less bitterly against him, but his presence invariably hurt him, and he avoided it. His secret hope centred in Wesley, and he endured what was not little to him on the child's account. Now, with reason staggering, he had matured a secret scheme for the boy's welfare. The time was near when he designed to put this idea into practice; but though in all its fantastic unreality it dwelt full-fledged within his head, none guessed that he dreamed of any such thing. Cunningly he concealed it, because he knew that to hint of the plan was to be frustrated.

Another winter had passed, and on the day when fishing began, there came Tiger to make whole holiday with his master.

A great storm had raged on the first night of March. A red, humpbacked moon went down over the Moor edge and some keen, clear hours followed. The wind freshened hourly and, after midnight, veered south of west and blew a whole gale. The homesteads shook from the thrust of it, a dozen trees fell at Postbridge. Torrents from a black sky heralded dawn and morning came on a shouting wind under grey sheets of rain. Already floods thundered to the valley at the first return of light; but Tiger knew Philip too well to break the appointment.

The sky blew clear by seven o'clock, and before eight he was off to the head-waters of South Teign, there to meet the old man. He carried ample food provided by Minnie, together with his own rod and creel.

They fished with natural bait, and Tiger marked that Philip had lost his cunning. His line fell feebly and was always running foul of rocks and banks. He began cheerfully, but presently relapsed into impatience and disappointment. He emptied his flask long before the time had come for food, and soon afterwards his good humour departed. He threw down his rod, cursed the fish, and bade Tiger come and sit beside him in a sheltered nook and smoke.

"Let the water go down a bit," he said; " 'twill run finer in an hour or so. Us'll sit and have a tell out o' this raging wind. You can't keep the line in the river for it."

They found an overhanging stone by streamside and talked together. The younger had an item of news.

"You'll be glad to know that chap as fired our rick, back-along before Christmas, have been found over to Chagford. He was catched stealing Perrott's poultry, and he confessed to a few other crimes. He knowed all about these parts and said the Hartland rick was an accident along of knocking out his pipe there afore he started off from it."

"I suppose Martin won't say that 'twas his father done it any more now, then," answered Philip moodily.

"Don't you tell that or think that, master. He never, never—— There, whatever can you be about to get such

27

wicked thoughts in your mind—you, as never would hear
or speak a word against any mortal man or woman in the
old days? When you was more in the world, you took
bigger ideas. And I wish you was back in it again for
your own peace."

"I've done with the world—very near; and the world
have done with me. The world knows its own. It don't
know me no more. It don't want my sort now. My son's
the new pattern that the world axes for now."

Tiger laughed at a recollection.

"Mister Martin's a rum un in some ways. You mind
that big barn of Webber's as he got a mortgage over three
year back? Well, now Webber's in a tight place for a
minute and he haven't been able to pay a halfpenny for
two year, and Martin's foreclosed, and Webber's going
bankrupt. Well, and what d'you think? Martin means
to hand the barn over to the Order of Rechabites and
they be going to have a tent there!"

"Water-drinkers and Little Baptists—'tis a choking
air for that poor child to be fetched up in. But we shall
see as to him. Wesley have got a clean-minded grandfather yet."

"And he'll have a brother or sister afore long."

Philip pursued his own thoughts awhile; then he broke
out into a storm of invective against religion. Tiger
strove to still him.

"You mustn't say these things. What's the good of
'em and what's the sense? Live and let live did use
to be your motto. And none ever had a better. I can't
go all the way with you like I used to do, Phil, my old
dear, because I've larned a bit since them days. There's
a good side and a bad side to all things. And there's a
good side to church-going. I tell you 'tis a good thing
for a man like me. There's wonnerful matters in the
Book—more wonnerful matters than you've read out
of it yet. And I do wish, for a change from Job,
you'd let me read out a bit about one or two other
heroes."

"Never!" cried Philip. "What was good enough for
Barbara be good enough for me. And you mind that

when I go under, Martin don't have his way. I'll be buried same as Barbara—or, if not that, then like a dog But no trash and lies and twaddle, no 'eternal life,' or any of that mess over me.''

''The dead live again, however,'' asserted Tiger. ''I've got to a pitch now when I'm bound to believe that the dead live again ''

''They do—in worms ''

''Us have soaring souls, master.''

''No more of that! Dust is dust, and God knows my load of it have got heavy to bear of late. But one more bit of serious work—but one more—and I shall be glad enough to be done. Life's no great loss to me now, Tiger. I've lost worse than that in my time. I've lost pretty well everything worth living for—but you. You'll see me out; you'll close my eyes. You're the only friend as I've got left—you and my grandson. He's all right. My duty—what's left of it—lies there. And then—why, I tell you that death may be the only prize in a life of blanks; and 'twill come as a prize to me afore very long. I thought different once, though—how different I thought once!''

''And must again You'm good for a lot of usefulness and fun yet.''

''I shall hand the child on as a legacy to you. But that's all a secret yet You'll see—come presently I'm full of fight—full of fight till that's off my mind ''

Tiger paid no heed He had recollected another item of news.

''Greg's going,'' he said. ''Can't last another week, they say I was past there two days ago and 'twas mentioned in the bar that Mr. Twigg had begun to take leave of his friends. He's quite happy. He invited old Peter Culme and a few others to come and see a good man die presently; and Peter hopes to be able to do so, if he's well enough, and can get a lift up the hill ''

Philip looked about him and considered

''Let's see,'' he said. ''If us was to travel up over

Hurston Ridge, us could reach to 'Warren House' at my gait in three parts of an hour. It ban't above two miles from here, I reckon.''

''Would you like to do it?''

''Yes, I would. I'm dry as a kiln. 'Tis the nearest drink from this place. And I've no objection to taking leave of the man. We've knowed each other for fifty year and more, and I've often had a good laugh at him.''

''Us'll take down our rods then and fish another time.''

Philip agreed.

''I'm a bit rusty after the winter. I ban't getting out my line very clever to-day.''

They climbed out of the valley presently, and in an hour reached Furnum Regis, on the boundaries of the Forest's eastern quarter. From this ancient place of tin-smelting the distance to Mr. Twigg's public-house was trifling, and after quenching his thirst and resting awhile, Philip sent a message to the sick man.

''Tell him that I've come up from the river special for to see him,'' he said. ''Because I hear he's soon like to be off, and I should wish to take my farewell afore 'tis too late.''

Gregory invited the other to his couch, and Philip went up, but Tiger remained in the bar.

A faithful follower of the publican was sitting beside him while he improved the fleeting hours. Mr. Twigg had nearly reached his tether, but his mind was clear and his body at rest. There seemed to be a shadow of unfamiliar humility in his reflections, and Philip was quick to mark it.

''Blessed if you ban't singing small for once, Greg!''

''We must all sing small when we get to the waters of Jordan, neighbour. But small though we may sing, the Everlasting ear will hear, and be very quick to help us through the river. I'm face to face with it now. I'm on the bank, but I ain't shivering. I'm quite ready for the plunge, and I know Whose holy Hand will be under my chin to help me across.''

"Life's treated you pretty well, taking it all round,'' said Philip. "It's gived you some good childer, above all else, and a cast-iron conceit of yourself that be worth everything for getting a man on in the world.''

"I wouldn't say that. I was blessed with rare intellects and took care to use them. But I never went beyond a fair and reasonable self-esteem. At least I hope not. I've had my trials too—dark and deep, I assure you. The larger you stake in the world, the larger your troubles; and if you play a big game, as I have, and keep in the eye of God and man, same as what I've done for more than half a century, be sure there's many have tried to pull you down, and the Lord have let the devil tempt you and torment you too. You, who know such a lot about the Book of Job—surely you can understand that?''

"I don't understand,'' answered Ouldsbroom. "May I be plagued, worse than I have been, if I understand your precious God and His ways. Look at me. Everything took—one after another—everything took but my pluck and will to go on against all odds. And what have I done to deserve such wrongs?''

"They'm only wrongs because your eyes be blinded to the truths of 'em. And even if your case was as dark as you fancy it is, what's that but the unknown way of the Almighty? God's got a nasty trick of coming back upon us, like a thunderstorm. He'll strike and you'll go on your knees and suffer and moan; and then you'll think 'tis over and lift up and try to settle down once more and count the cost and make the best of it. But, while you'm just creeping out cautiously and hoping for better things, He's on the watch and strikes again, perhaps, and takes all that's left.''

"The very image of His ways!'' cried Philip. "And be that a God to worship?''

"In your ignorance you might think He wasn't,''

answered Mr. Twigg, "but the Lord of Light haven't any use for our little, paltry ideas of what be sporting and what be not. He knows the physic that every sick soul stands in need of, and He sends the physic. He don't mess about and talk to hide His ignorance, and try you a bottle of the wrong stuff and then pass it off and pretend 'twas the right one—like a young doctor I've suffered from of late, who shall be nameless. He understands every case and sends the right remedy, whether 'tis nice or nasty, easy or harsh. I've had many a pill and potion from the Surgery of Grace, Philip Ouldsbroom; and I've let 'em all down without a murmur. We've got to take 'em, whether we want to or not; and 'tis a man's part to swallow 'em in a manly spirit. But you, you're for ever screaming and kicking, like a naughty child as have to be forced."

"And will to the end! Your God's too hard, Gregory, and if I believed in Him, I'd hate, but I'd not love. And we'll see who's right in the long run. You'll know first."

"And it ban't likely that you will be long behind me, Philip. To my eye there's a look about you that says the goal is in sight. I hope as we shall meet again—some day. No doubt there's a lot for us both to learn yet. Eternity won't be spent in idleness. No unemployed there."

"Don't you think I'm going this longful time," said the other. He had passed from his morning despondency into a spirit of hope.

"My work's far short of finished yet, though it pleases the people to think it is. I've got ten years more to go, in my opinion, and plenty to do with them. There's something very important calling for my hand and head —the management of an immortal soul, in fact. At least, if you're right, and we shall all live for ever. And my Tiger believes that now."

"I hope 'tis your own soul you speak of. The mills of God grind slow, but they miss nought. If you are to be caught up at the eleventh hour, Phil, I should go the happier to my own rest. I admit that. The Light have been long withheld from you; but if you begin to see a twinkle of it——''

"No such thing," answered the other. "I'm dealing with—however, I can't let out much about it yet—even to you. If you're spared another few months, I lay you'll hear about it.''

"I shan't be," answered Twigg. "My home is ready and I'm ready for it. A week or two is all that I can expect But where I'm going there'll be news of earth, if I read my Bible aright, and along with other things I hope it may come to my ear that you are on the strait road at last and going along it quick—to make up for lost time.''

"You won't hear that; but you'll find that I'm not played out, and busy taking a hand with the rising generation They be crying for a bit of the old spirit, I reckon; and 'tis their grandfathers, and not their fathers, can best show 'em what that old spirit was like.''

A woman came in, and Ouldsbroom took his eternal farewell of the fellow-man now about to vanish.

"Good-bye," he said; "and may you go easy as a sleeping babe when the moment comes, Greg. You've been a good, useful man according to your lights, and if there's a wakening, as such as you believe, and even such as me ban't too forlorn to wish, though vainly—then you'll be there with the best. Nought would give me greater pleasure than to find out some day that you was right and I was wrong.''

"You'll find it out," answered the other; "and for my part, though dim-eyed now, I can see that the heavenly folds be larger than I thought 'em once. There's no knowing who will be drove in, with Christ for sheepdog. I lived in a deal of doubt on that point; but I die hoping, Philip My mind be getting so big as my swollen body, I do believe. 'Tis like a balloon for largeness now. And if we worms can picture such a power of mercy in the Lord, what must the real thing be?''

"You'll enlarge His mind a lot, I shouldn't wonder,''

said the other cheerfully. "If ever you find Him, Greg, just tell Him to look all round things a bit more Tell Him to try and put Hisself in our places, if He can. I'll get going now, but I'll drink to your good health in the next world afore I leave the bar—as I've often and often drunk to your good health in this one "

CHAPTER XIV

Not even Tiger knew of the grassy resting-place on Crow Tor, but Ouldsbroom, as his natural fire abated, spent much time here, and drowsed and slept away many hours when the weather allowed of it.

He clambered here on a July day, stretched his limbs, and cursed the sun for lacking warmth. It was cold for the season. The wind had gone north after some days of heavy rain, but the clouds were broken at last, and a general improvement marked the weather There came, however, an added sadness to this sad heart from the chill breath of the wind and the lifelessness of what he saw from his uplifted place. Little heather grew hereabout, and only splashes of sphagnum at a mountain spring lightened the waste and welcomed the sun's offer of friendship. The grey granite and green integument of the hills suffered a sort of extinction under this light, and the colour, though fine enough, was too subtle, too reserved for Philip's eyes to mark it. To him the world stretched lifeless and hopeless The reflection of his own spirit turned back to him unbroken from it. He smoked, strove to put away recent discouragements, and occupied himself with his supreme project. The time was nearly come for it. With childish cunning he had matured his plans, and now waited only for a pending event to carry them forward.

He had a milch cow in his little croft at Brown's House, and had laid in great store of biscuits and rusks, sweetmeats and such things as children love Some poultry—safe in a fox-proof run—were also there. He had taken lessons in cooking from Minnie, who little guessed his purpose.

425

Events at Hartland conspired to increase Philip's determination, while its fatuity and folly were quite obscured from his failing intellect. He poured out his whole hopes and energies upon this enterprise. The thought was never long out of his mind, and he prided himself mightily on his skill in having kept it such a secret. But it was the craft of a madman. The idea and its execution alone obsessed him; he did not look beyond it. The thing should be done in defiance of all obstacle, and once done he trusted himself to defend it against the might of the world in arms. He told himself that duty demanded this performance. Each time he met Martin, he came from the interview with increasing fixity of purpose.

Martin was very busy and the renewed amenity had perished. High words had passed, because the younger strove to control Philip's credit, and had grumbled at some large waste of money. He desired Ouldsbroom to inspect the accounts of the farm, and had expected some commendation for his brilliant stewardship. But the old man would look at nothing. Philip asked for increasing sums of money, and when Martin found the purpose to which these payments were put, he withheld them. Once Philip gave a five-pound note to a blind woman on the road; once he marched into the 'Ring o' Bells' with a party of eight gipsies, and spent thirty shillings upon food and drink for them.

He had sworn now never to see Martin again; he had openly threatened in hearing of moor-men to lie in his path some night and shoot him.

The younger man did not fear assault; but he calculated the probable length of Philip's life, and heartily trusted that his end was near.

"We know that they'll do something with him in the world to come," he said to Minnie. " 'Tis beyond human power or human prayer to help him in this one. God made him for His own good purposes; but what those purposes were we shall never know till we hear in another life than this."

Tiger was still told off to the task of watching Philip

and waiting upon him. He met the wanderer now on the way home from Crow Tor.

"Been looking round about for you everywhere, master."

"No matter for that. Come in and us'll have a drop of drink. The baggering sun don't seem to have a blink o' fire in it nowadays. Not for my bones, any way. I can't catch heat."

" 'Tis the cold wind Come and have a bite. I've fetched over a fine shepherd's pie from missis. I'll make a fire and hot it up for you."

"How do she go on?"

"The child's due. But she's very well and cheerful. My Mary's up along with her."

"I'll ride over to-morrow morning. Try and get him out of the way, if you can."

"Twigg's gone," said Tiger. "Last night he died, and very comfortable, by all accounts. His old woman's going to stop and his second son-in-law's to take over 'Warren House.' "

"Even that man was better at the finish than my boy will ever be. Life soaked a little of the cursed starch out of Greg the last year or two But not Martin He'll never bate an inch, or pity weakness, or pardon sin. Never did wrong in the little sense, and never did right in the large one. Born with a flint for a heart; and it's broke everybody but you. Not only me, mind you; but his wife and many another here and there. She may stick up for him; she may say her prayers to him, for all I know; but you look in her poor eyes and remember how once they shined, and read 'em now. Pity—that's the word the world cries out to my son; but his ear ban't built to let it in. He would have ruined that chap over thicky barn but for me. The poor man came to me crying—crying, mind you. Think what a hell of hardness it takes to make a grown man cry. 'I'm alive still,' I said to him. And I've commanded that thirty pounds be given to him. And he's had it. And if Martin had refused to let me handle my own in that matter, I'd nave burned down the barn and let him and his blasted

Rechabites howl in the ruins of it, like the water-drinking jackals they be. And many such-like tales I've heard. When he's driven 'em to their marrow-bones, or devoured a widow's house, or some such knavish trick, then the people find me out and remember I ban't dead yet. 'I was the first to go,' I tell 'em. 'Don't expect nothing from me. Here am I, living here in this here ruin, waiting for death to release me.' But still they come for succour, and I give it if I can.''

''I thought you was feeling better ''

''I'm all right, I'm all right I don't want to die, Tiger, and I ban't going to die, for that matter. My work's not done yet——''

He broke off, and looked at the other. Tiger's back was turned and he knelt and blew on the fire.

Philip shook his head.

''No, I can't tell you—not even you; though well I know you're my side ''

''And always have been ''

''You'll know soon enough. 'Tis a thing calling for some manhood in me 'Twill surprise the pack of 'em when it comes about I've got to live for fifteen year yet—fifteen year. I was never known to drop a job in the middle, and I shan't begin now. And, if need be, I'll fight——''

''Don't you go and do anything rash, Phil Not at your time of life I wish you'd tell me what 'tis. I might help you.''

''I'm not so sure. I'm not so sure; but—leave that. You'll know soon enough. It may happen to-morrow, for all I can tell.''

He drank, and presently Tiger made him eat Long familiarity with Philip's surprises caused anxiety to the younger now. There were things hidden—not only in the old man's mind, but in his dwelling There was a great box locked up in a corner, and he refused to tell Tiger of its contents He had been meddling in financial matters also, and Tiger knew that henceforth refusal would meet his increasing and unreasonable demands in the direction of money. Ouldsbroom had long ago signed control into the hands of Martin. but thus far Unity's son had not exercised it when Philip called for cash.

Suddenly impressed with the importance of keeping well and strong, the old man ate heartily, and presently rose to a more cheerful mood. But Tiger felt unusually anxious for him. He was listless, and his voice sounded weakly. Again and again he came to the brink of his enterprise and trembled to impart it, but abstained.

Presently he grew drowsy and declared that he wished to sleep. Then Tiger left him.

"I'll ride over in the morn," promised Philip, "and I hope as another grandchild's little pipe will be tuning up to welcome me afore long now."

CHAPTER XV

On the following day Philip was in the saddle early. He rode to the top of Broad Down, made fast his horse there, then descended into the valley of the river, and presently reached Hartland.

Tiger was the first to meet him.

"Doctor's come," he said. " 'Tis going on all right—so Mary tells me Mr. Martin's in the house."

"Where's Wesley to?"

"Up under the tor along with the girl"

The old man's heart beat hard. Even as he had hoped, so things fell out. The day was fine; the minds of all at Hartland were preoccupied

"I'll go up and have a game along with him for a bit"

"You can't do better. No doubt Mr Martin will bring you the news himself come presently."

Philip went off, and soon found the little boy with a maiden to watch him.

"You be off home," he said "They'll want you to run messages. I'll take charge of the child and bring him back along presently."

The girl disappeared, and Philip heaved a mighty sigh of satisfaction. His road lay all clear before him now. Wesley expressed the most active delight at change of nurses and was soon playing tyrant.

"Us be going to be men, to-day—you and me," said Ouldsbroom. "Us have got to ride on gran'father's 'oss, and you shall hold the reins, if you mind to. But we mustn't bide caddling about here. We've got to go

430

farther than ever you've been in your life yet, my grand chap—right away up over yonder hill. And there we shall find 'Samuel' waiting for us. Do 'e want to come and see grandfather's house and all the fine things he've got for you there?"

"Ess, I do," declared Wesley.

"Then away we go; and when you'm tired, I'll carry you."

He talked of the sugared biscuits and sweetmeats, and told Wesley to go faster. But the child's short legs could make but slow progress, and the impatient old man picked him up at last and panted up the great slope of Broad Down with him.

Often he looked back, but as yet no sign of life appeared at Hartland, and none had come to seek him on the tor. Now that hill had shrunk to nothing, seen from the mightier mound beyond, and Hartland was hidden

They rested presently, and Philip picked a handful of whortleberries for the boy. Then, full of a sudden fear that he might be pursued and overtaken before he reached his stronghold, he took the child on his back and climbed on.

He was giddy before the summit had been reached; but his excitement kept him alert and fortified his strength.

They turned the ridge of the hill and came to certain neolithic hut circles spread, grey and ragged, in the heath.

Philip's horse was tethered here, and soon he had mounted and lifted the child up before him.

"That's the style! Now I be going to take you all the way to gran'father's house. And you shall steer 'Samuel' and I shall hold you."

The eager infant spraddled out his little legs and held the reins one in each hand. They hung loose, and the old horse went on his familiar way. Philip kept a tight arm round the child and talked to him.

"And will Wesley like to come to gran'father? Will he like to keep house along with me and bide there, and see me shoot birds and catch fish?"

"Ess, I will then."

"And so you shall; and the devil and all his angels shan't take you away from me no more."

Presently he spoke again.

"You must know, Wesley, that me and father ban't quite the same, but I'm older and wiser than him, and I want for you to be a proper man, like me—not half a man, like him. I want for you to be kind to everybody, and large-hearted and gentle to the poor, and all that. But father can't teach you them things, because he's never larned 'em I tried terrible hard to get it into him; but I couldn't. Perhaps I didn't try hard enough. He never understood me—not like you do. But we understand one another something wonnerful—you and me —and a quick-witted boy, like you, will soon larn all I can teach you."

The horse stumbled and recovered himself. Philip's arm gripped the child and Wesley shouted with laughter at the mishap. His grandfather laughed too.

"Whoa! What be 'Samuel' up to? Ha, ha, ha! The rascal! That's right—you laugh like that. You and me will always be laughing. That's what we'm here for—to laugh and make others laugh. But nobody laughs nowadays. But we'll teach 'em. You'm that wise a'ready—you know 'tis better to laugh than cry. Your father never laughed much at your age But you and me will And you'll grow so quick as a larch up-along with me. And I'll bide as I am. Not a day older will I get till you'm a big boy and full of my sense."

The child was excited and joyful. He chattered awhile and pointed to sheep and cattle dotted over the Moor.

"They be all father's things," said Ouldsbroom. "His and mine. You mustn't forget him, Wesley. Ill though he's used me, I won't set you against him. Too wise for that I be going to make such a man of you that, some day, you'll go along to your father and lift him up and do for him what his father could never do. I be going to fashion your little budding mind into such a pattern that you'll teach your father to be a better chap and draw the poison out of him. All that I'm going to do; and though I shan't be here to see it, I shall die easier for knowing about it. Life's a dark thing, Wesley—dark and difficult, because we can't make people see with our eyes. But you must be patient with everybody. You must larn to bend early, else you'll be broke late. They've never broke me, never, though God He knows they've plotted and planned to do it. But you and me ban't built to break.''

He bent over the little boy and lifted his chin and kissed him

''You mustn't think life's all fun. It did ought to be, but it never falls out like that. The world's got into such a mess now that it have to work terrible hard to keep going at all. There's too much work in it now. I see the change even in my time. Less joy than there was, and more care. Folk be like the birds and beasts now. They've no time in life for anything but earning a living. There's more hungry people than there was—more folk and less money for 'em I see a lot of them now—wanderers that don't know what they be seeking. But I can't tell what have brought it about. Nobody demands the right to be joyful now. The highest they rise to is for leave to work their fingers to the bone. 'Tis a very rotten fashion of world, Wesley, where joy's forgot. The boys don't even marry the girls now but in fear and trembling of the future.''

A fox slipped away over the heath ahead of them. The child was all excitement and wanted to follow.

''Beat 'Samuel!' Make him run!'' he cried

''No, no! Mister Fox be safe for the present He'm going to his wife and family, maybe. I lay he was out here to think a bit and turn life over in his mind and get away from the noise to home. So must all we married men, and married foxes too sometimes. Or maybe he was after a rabbit for dinner. You'll see a fine rally of foxes up to Brown's House. They want my chickens. the rascals, but 'No, no,' I say, 'they chickens be here for my brave boy to eat their eggs!' ''

''I do love a naked egg,'' said Wesley, and the old man laughed.

28

"Was ever such a funny fellow? And you shall have many a naked egg, as you call it—hard-boiled wi' the shell off. And many another good thing you shall have— sweeties to make you happy and broth to make you fat! When us come over yonder ridge, you'll see gran'father's house an' gran'father's cow in the croft. And you shall have your own garden, if you mind to, an' I'll come and dig in it for 'e.''

They jogged on and the child said he was hungry.

"And right to be, and soon shall you have your fill "

Philip looked round sometimes, but there was no sign that any followed. His muddled intellect apprehended pursuit and attack. But he was resolved that once within the stronghold of his home, no powers of persuasion or violence should make him yield up Wesley. He had planned this abduction long ago, and with a child's indifference to reality, proposed to bring up the little boy at Brown's House on his own model of what a boy should be.

"You ban't the first as I've trained, my young shaver. There's Tiger—you love Tiger, don't 'e?"

"Ess, I do love Tiger."

"And Tiger was my boy. I made Tiger, and you and him be my only friends now. And I'll make you like him. Tiger's a good man, framed to bring nought but kindness in the world. And your father might be the very same this minute, if he'd but given heed to me. But we'll win round him yet. I'm never beat, and I'll strike at him through you now, and see if that will fetch out the heart of him "

They reached the dwelling, and the child rejoiced at it. He ran about on a voyage of discovery, and presently came in very wet, when Philip called him from the door.

"Here's your meat ready," he said. "Ah, you rogue, you've been in the water I see!"

He locked the door and barred the window after the child entered; then he took off Wesley's shoes, socks and frock and put them by the fire. Next he wrapped a blanket round the boy, sat him on his lap, and fed him with biscuits in hot milk. The old man had drunk heavily on returning home; and now he was refreshed, cheerful, and garrulous.

He talked to Wesley and planned their future together.

"I've forgot your clothes, my bold hero, and that's the only thing as I have forgot. And if they won't see sense and meet me half way and send 'em by Tiger, then you and me will ride to Tavistock some fine morning and get more for 'e. Drink it up, then I'll give 'e a sugar-plum."

The child was happy, wearied out, and ready to sleep. He wanted nothing else. He smiled at Philip now, sighed comfortably and yawned. Philip finished the pap himself with a gulp or two. Then he went to the fire and sat down in an easy chair with his treasure on his lap. He wiped a little rim of milk off Wesley's mouth; and soon the youngster nestling close to him, drooped and slept. In half an hour the man also slumbered.

Elsewhere Martin Ouldsbroom had waited for a child to be born to him. He worked in a little room where he kept his books and accounts. He was making calculations and pondering upon a problem. He gave a tithe of all that he earned to his God; and now he speculated as to whether that sum should be subtracted from his gross earnings, before he paid rates and taxes out of them, or afterwards. The difference was not considerable, for his farm was freehold and the land his own. He decided, however, that the amount of his fellow-man's claim should pay tribute.

Presently a daughter appeared at Hartland, and Martin was told that his father waited on Hartland Tor to hear the news. But when Tiger hastened hither to bring it, and ask the old man back that he might eat with his son and see the baby, he did not find him. Neither was there any sign of the boy. Martin felt some anxiety, and his care deepened as noon passed and the day waned. Minnie was not told, and presently, when she called aloud for Wesley, Martin saddled his horse and rode to seek him.

He guessed that Ouldsbroom had taken him up to Brown's House, and doubted not that he would meet his father and child returning home again.

But he did not meet them, and it was five o'clock before he reached the lonely dwelling, fastened his horse at the gate, and hammered at the portal. Smoke rose from the chimney, but his knock was not answered, and he tried the door, to find it fast.

The summons had, however, wakened Philip, and he made ready. He roused himself, gathered Wesley to him, carried the child, still sound asleep, into his bedroom, and there left him on his bed. Next he peeped from his window and saw Martin's horse. By this time the visitor had knocked again.

Philip opened the window a small space.

"Who's out there?" he asked. "And what do you want?"

" 'Tis I, father. Tiger tells me that you took charge of the boy this morning. But I never thought you'd have brought him all the way up here. You must be tired out, I'm fearing. Bring him along and he shall ride home with me."

Martin had come round from the door. He looked up and saw the old man peering out.

"You guessed where he was—your conscience told you, belike—if you've got a conscience left in you. Yes, he's here; and here he'll stop. I've meant to do this thing these many days, and I've plotted and schemed for it and made all ready. There's everything here as he wants for his body and his mind. And he came gladly, and he's going to bide and be my child, till I've larned him to take his part in the world and undo a bit of the mischief that you've done."

"My dear father, you must not be so foolish. Can't you see this is absurd—impossible?"

"Is it? Well, I don't think so. And don't you 'dear father' me, because you're long cast off and I won't have no hypocrisy. You can carry that to them that trust you, if such there are."

"Let me come in and we'll talk it over," said the

young man. He gave a sigh and prepared to return to the door, but the other laughed aloud.

"You think to come round me like that, do you? I've been such a poor innocent all these years that I can't see through your hookem-snivey ways even yet—eh? No, you don't come in here—never while an iron padlock can keep you out. I've had a brace of extra bolts put up against to-day. And they be close shot home, I promise you. You'll never come in this house while I'm living. And if you did, you'd find your child strangled. He's got loose from you, and never shall you lay a finger on him; never more shall you rob him of his little joys or flog his tender hide. Go back to your newborn child and torture that and hear it scream. Your boy be my boy now—safe from you while this arm can hold him."

"Think, father; think what you are doing. Such things can't be. There's no room in the world for them. I've never denied you your grandson. But you can't have him here. Do be reasonable and see how this must look to any impartial person. Think of his mother, if not of his father."

"I'm his father, I tell you—father and grandfather both. The child's content and at peace. He's thankful to God to be out of Hartland and up here along with me. He wouldn't go back if you was to pray him. He knows what's best. And his mother knows too. No need to name her name. You tell her that he's safe and joyous and full of meat, and that I've bought a shipload of proper food for him—that's all you've got to do."

"I must have my child, father. You can't come between him and me. The law won't allow it."

"Damn the law! I've got him and I'm in the right, and let's see the law as will be strong enough to break my padlocks and take him from me. Be off and get out of my sight. Haven't my eyes ached oft enough at you? And, law or no law, I ban't going to hand the lamb to the wolf for any man's pleasure. No call to prowl round this fold, for you'll never get in. And, mark me: if you use might and think to pull down my walls and steal what's within, then you'll find yourself

cheated for once, as you've cheated the world too often.
You'll find dead folk and nought else. So if you think
to use force, bring two coffins with you—a big one and a
little one!''

Philip felt a hand in his. The child had wakened at
his noise, arisen and come to him.

"Wesley's hungry," he murmured.

The old man picked him up and held him to the window.

"There he is—look at him!" he cried; "ax him if
he wants to go home to be whipped and starved. Tell
that man as you've got no use for him, my pretty. Say
you be going to bide along with grandfather."

"Ess, I be."

"For ever and ever," said Philip.

"For ever an' ever," echoed Wesley.

Martin spoke for some time, and mentioned the fact
that his wife had got a daughter. But Philip only regretted that the babe was born alive, and soon the
younger perceived that nothing could be gained by further speech. His son appeared to be perfectly happy,
and there seemed no immediate fear that he would grow
either frightened or forlorn.

"I'll go," he said. "But I warn you that this cannot
be. Suppose anything was to happen to you——"

"Much you'd care for that. All the ill that has happed
to me in this world be of your heaping. And if my
heart's cracked, don't you ever pretend you don't know
who cracked it. You've murdered me, remember that,
when you hear I'm gone. But it won't be yet. Here's
my work. Night and day I'll be busy for this dinky boy.
I shan't go till he's big enough to stand alone. I shan't
go till I've taught him how to face you. He's made me
young again a'ready. I'm well. I'm strong as a lion.
He'll mend your work yet and help to heal the bloody
wounds you've dealt me."

Philip shut the window and made it fast. Two bars
had been screwed upon the inside, so that none might
force an entrance.

Martin turned and went back to his horse and Ouldsbroom watched him ride away. Then he rubbed his hands and laughed to the child.

"So much for him—soon sent him off with his tail between his legs! 'Twill be a long time afore he troubles us again. You'll be growed big enough and bold enough to fire my gun afore he comes here any more. And then you can shoot him for grandfather—and a good day's work 'twill be."

"Wesley's hungry," repeated the child.

"Come on, then, and stuff; and if you'm hungry, I swear I'm thirsty along of such a lot of talk. But 'tis deeds, not words for us in future. You eat your fill of these here goodies and I'll drink a drop; and then us'll walk out a little way and I'll show 'e the chickens and fetch in an egg for your supper. But I must keep my weather eye lifting—else they'll go and kidnap you from me. And God help the creature as tries to do that!"

CHAPTER XVI

WITH something of the fearful pleasure of a child making believe, Philip kept guard over Wesley when night came. He fed him, washed him, and put him to bed. Then he loaded his gun and shut up his house with a great padlock and two bolts.

For some hours he preserved a keen watch and was alert for every sound. Once he crept out into the summer night and prowled about to see that none lay in wait. But only the voices of darkness fell on his ear. The weather had grown warmer and mist hung drowsily under the stars. Philip was about to retire himself and had already thrown off his coat, when there came quick footsteps at last. The conflict was at hand and his heart leapt.

"Steady! Steady!" he said to himself. "Keep your wits about 'e, Phil; you be going to need 'em now!"

But he heard no speech, and it was clear that only a solitary man approached. The feet did not stop at the door, but came round the house to the window. A dog jumped out, barking furiously. Then Tiger's voice stilled it. Presently there fell a gentle tap upon the glass. Philip stood irresolute, but at a second summons he pulled up the white blind and looked out. Holding the candle above his head, the old man presently recognised Tiger, whereupon he opened the window.

"Be you come as a friend?" he asked.

"A friend always, and you know it, master."

"There's nobody else out there?"

"Nobody else. I've walked up alone."

"Swear it then "

"I swear it. Let me come in and we'll have a tell about things."

"If any other man thrusts through my door, I'll shoot him."

"And welcome. Would I deceive you, Phil?"

" 'Tis hard to trust nowadays. I've been bit very bad in my time. Haven't the blood of my own veins deceived me? 'Tis as if your right hand could lie to your left."

He went round and let Tiger into the house The younger man had come for Wesley, but he felt small hope that he would succeed in his mission. Martin had desired to go also, but when this most difficult of tasks was put upon him, Tiger, while promising little, yet bargained to carry out the attempt in his own way.

"I must go to him empty-handed and alone. and may come back so," he said "There'll be no fighting or struggling with him. I'd rather do away with myself than hurt a hair of his head. If, please God, I can get him to see sense, then I will do. But I'll use nought but gentle words to him."

And now he entered upon his unlikely errand. Philip bolted the door behind him and drew the blind again.

"Mark this," he said. "You and that sleeping boy yonder are the only two fellow-creatures I've got left in the wide world now. And if you're here as a friend, I welcome you, as I have done since first I set eyes on you, when you came to Hartland a hungry, weary lad."

"As a friend, sure enough. I needn't tell you that."

"Drink then—drink away the sharpness of your eyes and the clearness of your voice a bit. I can't trust an empty man. Have a good go at the whisky—then we'll meet on even ground. I was just going to bed with the gun by my pillow. To tell you the truth, my heart's been on the rack too long, Tiger. It have had to fight against more than one human's fair load of trouble. But I shall mend very quick now. Life's got very simple and straightforward at last I see the way as clear as the way of the bird in the air."

"So much the better then. I'll have a drink, and gladly "

The other poured whisky into two tumblers.

"I be running rather short," he said. "I've thought more on milk for the boy than whisky for myself the last few days. But I'll broach another bottle."

"This is enough, Phil—more than enough. I don't want you to get muddled to-night. I want you to listen to me."

But Ouldsbroom fetched another bottle, opened it, and began to laugh.

"I triumphed over him, I warn you! Up he came on his hoss as big as bull's beef. Must have his child that instant moment! 'Did I know what I was doing?' 'The law was against me,' and all the rest of his nonsense. But I soon had him away. He'd have seen the muzzle of my gun if he'd stopped much longer. 'I'll suffer no wolf prowling round my fold,' I said to the villain. And off he went."

"He don't understand you like I do. He came in a wrong spirit, no doubt. But 'tis very different when you and me get together. 'Twasn't very often, after you'd once larned me sense, that I ever catched myself not thinking same as you think."

"No, because you'd got a brain to work upon—a brain and a heart. But my son—— Here, fetch out this cork, will 'e? My strength's a thought low to-night along of carrying Wesley up the hill. Such a fine, solid lump of a child! He's going to be like me in body so well as mind."

"Happy as a lark along with you, no doubt?"

"I should think he was. A noble child at his victuals. So full as a little barrel he be. He'll keep my old bones warm come the winter nights!"

"What did he tell about? Didn't he whimper a bit for his mother when night came down?"

"'Whimper'! Not him. Jolly as a badger, and didn't want to go to bed. Thought to be playing all night along o' me. But of course he went off after his supper. And I washed him and dried him wi' a towel bought a-purpose; and no woman could have done it better. He don't want his mother."

"She wants him, however."

"You can tell her this," said Philip, holding his glass between the table and his mouth: "I've got nothing against Minnie—never had, and never shall have She's a good girl, and if he's broke her and cast the tenderness out of her a bit, that's not her fault. When the frost falls the still water's got to freeze. She's what he's made her now, not what nature made her So I'm too wise to blame her. She's the child's mother, and I've no wish to lift up any bar between her and her own. She can come up along to see him when she pleases; and she'll be welcome, so long as she comes alone. But we shan't always be at home, mind. I'm not going to bring up my boy like an owlet on a rock. He'll travel afield with me and sit astride on my saddle-bow, and see the world and the people in it. He'll go down along to Two Bridges; he'll meet my friend Nick, the warrener to Wistman's Wood; and he shall fall in with other fine men and larn their ways And money he shall never see—never. You tell his father that. So long as he bides under my roof he shall not handle a halfpenny, or hear the cursed devil's chatter of coin with coin. Not a pinch of that poison shall ever touch his hand till he's old enough to know that it is poison. Then he'll use the filth in its proper place—as manure where the land be poor and cries for enrichment. Money's manure, I tell you, and a very respectable thing regarded as such. But once get to lust for it, like my son, and you might so soon roll with the pigs in it. It drips off Martin, and my eyes see it. I mark the stain of it on him; I smell the evil smell of it when he passes by."

"All so wise as can be—like yourself But now, as a friend and as one proud to be your friend, I've got to ax you to listen to me a bit. Have a smoke. I've brought a full pouch "

The other loaded and lighted his pipe. Then Tiger spoke.

"You see, Phil, a clever old man like you must look all around the subject afore you take such a bold step as this; and I make no doubt that you have done, but 'tis often worth while having a talk with another, because two heads are better than one. And though I ban't very clever, yet I think very much the same as you most times.''

"Natural you should—seeing as I taught you to think.''

"That's it, of course. I'm a long way behind you—most of us be, for that matter. But I think same as you, and so the things that I be thinking now be much the same as your thoughts.''

Philip shook his head.

"You'm getting mixed, Tiger. Talking ban't in your line,'' he declared very wisely.

"Right again! But, touching this boy, I've thought a lot, and no doubt what I think you'll think too, if I can set it afore you. In a word, 'tis the mother of him. You must know that she's had rather a bad time of it, and be terrible weak to-night.''

"What's that to me? That snake told me he'd got a daughter. 'So much the worse,' I said to him. 'I wish for her own sake as she'd been born dead.' ''

"Missis be very fond of you, and she puts a large faith and trust in you, same as I do.''

"And every reason to. Haven't I done what I could for her against him? Haven't I withstood him for her? Wouldn't her life have been a better and a brighter thing if she'd took you, for instance, or any other man on earth but him? But him she took, and had to abide by it, and feel the slow frostbite of him creeping through her veins and reaching to her heart. I saw it—I saw it all, and she knew well that I did ''

"She thinks the world of your great kindness. Well she knows that you never brought a pang to a living thing, or a tear to any cheek.''

"If she'd trusted me more and stood my side more, 'twould have been better for her.''

"She looked to you all she could, and she did for you all she could; you don't forget that. But you know how 'tis. No woman was born that could have bided in her maiden mind after she was married to Mister Martin. That strong and stubborn is his nature, that all must bend or break afore it. And so she bent to him."

"And never will she come straight again. But this here child—he ban't built to bend and he shan't be broke neither—not while I'm above ground. Let him break his dogs and his newborn daughter—not my grandson."

"You've no word against the child's mother, however?"

"None. She'd do right, if she was let alone. She's got a gentle spirit and a feeling heart. I'm very well content with her."

"There's none knows you better than she does," declared Tiger. "There's none—not I myself—has more perfect trust and love for you than what she has. I'm come with a message hot from her this minute. And she wouldn't give it to no second person neither. Wouldn't trust it to any other ear but mine, master. Nought would do but I went up in her room and, after she gave the message, she spoke to me again and said, 'Tell father that. Tell him as you heard it straight from my lips, with no go-between.'"

" 'Twill add to her peace, if she's all I think her, to know her brave child be safe while she's laid by," declared Ouldsbroom. "She's no cause whatever to fret for him; she'll not strain her ear to hear him screaming under his father's whip, while she's too feeble to come and fight for him. Safe—safe he is; and presently, when she's strong enough to do it, she can ride up and see him, and mark how he's growed in size and sense. But to Hartland he shall not go. I won't trust him among 'em more."

"Don't say that. There's one stronger call than yours —a call that must be heard and heeded. And you've got to see it the same as I see it. You know me. I'm your side, thick or thin. I've fought for you since I was a child myself. But a mother's a mother, and given a real, right down good mother...."

"Tell me her message and take back mine," interrupted the old man.

"I will then. I mind every word. I've altered nought.

She said 'Beg dear father, for the true love he has for me, to let me have Wesley back, or I shall not close my eyes this night.' And then she said a word to me 'I've had a cruel day, Tiger,' she said; 'for God's sake touch father's heart for me. I've never yet gone to sleep without my boy in my room. I can't do it. 'Twill kill me, Tiger.' There, Phil, you didn't know that In your love for this here boy, you thought only of him and his good; you forgot belike that his mother's heartstrings was wrapped round and round him. She've been torn enough to-day. 'Tisn't in your big spirit to add one grief to her. You couldn't—not if they came and prayed you to do it. You'll see it same as I do now. Don't we always see alike? Be us ever on different sides of a question? So well I know it that I said to her—I said, 'Fear nothing. You'm in the power of one who never yet——''

Philip held up his hand. Great anxiety and tribulation marked his face.

"Say no more," he answered. "Suffer me to think upon this."

He rose and walked about the kitchen. Presently he took a candle and went into the adjoining room.

"Come in here," he said to Tiger. Then the two men looked at the sleeping child.

"That's the answer to his mother's message," said Philip. "Tell her that you've seen the boy sleeping like a cherub—warm, happy, and so comfortable as only a babby can be. Mark down that picture in your mind; feel the soft stuff he's got over him—bought for him, so as my rough covering shouldn't chafe his flesh And now look in this here box and see what I've laid in for him."

Tiger obeyed.

"A wonderful man! Who would have thought, now, your mind could reach down even to a babby's need! Well, well, nought will be wasted. They want for you to come to Hartland and bide there a bit The missis be terrible anxious to see you and ax for your opinion on a score o' questions. And you know how me and Rogers and t'others will welcome you back."

"I shan't see Hartland no more."

"You mustn't talk like that. Now, because his mother wants the child so bad, and because holding of it away from her may be dangering her health, of course the boy must go back. That's your own thought, Phil—I swear to God it is—for you and me always think alike. And I wouldn't believe you if you said it wasn't your thought. He must go. If she'd been different now, then you and me would have felt different. If she'd been a bad sort of mother, and you had anything against her—but it isn't so. She's a rare good mother, and the boy's her life, and it ban't for a brace of wise men like you and me to come between her and her life."

Philip sat down again, stared at Tiger and panted. His head drooped forward and his skin grew grey. Tiger made him drink a little. Then he rose and mended the fire.

"I knew you'd see it," he went on. "What don't you see where another person's good is the matter? A suffering, longing mother—crying for her young and can't reach it! Good God, Phil, I've seen you sore put about for a bitch or ewe when she's unhappy. I spoke to your daughter-in-law afore I left her too. I said, 'You know the master. You know if ever he's come between any creature and their own.' I said, 'He's wise as Solomon in the matter of the happiness of the people and how to add to it.' I said, 'Don't shed a tear, missis; don't feel one thought of fear that you shan't have your li'l boy in reach of your hand this night.' That's what I said to her, because I know you better than all the world knows you. Ess fay! And I've seen deeper in your grand old heart than living man or woman ever will. I ax you—I pray of you, Phil. I——"

Tiger's own eloquence had touched him. He broke off, bent forward, put his hand on Ouldsbroom's and held it tightly. Philip did not move or speak.

The younger rose presently and walked up and down. Philip remained humped up by the table. He emptied his glass and clasped his hands on his chest. At length he spoke, and his voice was weak.

"You was the last—my sheet anchor against any storm.
I never thought that you'd go over to them."

"And never do you think it. I'm but the ghost of
yourself, and when I speak to you 'tis yourself speaking.
And if you'd heard her speak, as I did, you'd think now
as I do and you'd do what I must do. We're not against
you—never you dream that. But 'tis the mother in her
—yearning for her own. You know how it feels better
than I can tell you."

The old man's mind wandered.

"You'm childless yet, Tiger; but you must hope. I
waited long, remember. 'Twill come; and when it do,
you'll never keep it away from me, will you? You'll let
me help to fashion your son, same as I fashioned you?"

"By God, you shall!"

"In bringing up the childer——" began Philip.

He wandered on, and the younger man, greatly daring,
went to the sleeping-room, lifted Wesley gently and
brought him back to the fire. The child still wore his
smock.

Philip started up when he saw what Tiger had done.
He swayed on his legs a little; then he sat down again.

"He'll be shouting out with all his might for you in
the morn," declared Tiger. "You'll be the first word
on his lips, I warrant! And you mustn't keep him waiting, master. I shall tell 'em that you'll come down along
very quick."

The old man seemed stricken in mind and body. He
kept putting his hand out and drawing it back; but he
did not move from his chair.

"Can you take him from me? Have you got the heart
to do it? He's all that's left for me to help—all—out of
the whole earth."

"You'd do the same, Phil—the very same, if we was
to change places."

"You're strong, and I'm weak."

"Don't say that—you shan't say it!" cried the other.
" 'Tis I'm weak afore you, and always have been. The
world's weak afore the likes of you—all that's best in it.
Hold him in your arms, and keep him in your arms—

keep him there so long as you will. And not a regiment of sojers shall take him out of 'em while I can see to fight.''

He put Wesley on Philip's lap. The child turned, half woke, opened his eyes, then shut them again.

''There he is, and there he shall bide, master Only you shall give him up to his mother. None shall take him—none.''

Philip leant back His hand listlessly fingered the child's hair

''I'll give him back, then,'' he said. ''And along with him you can take the last pinch of life I've got left I'd have lived for him—years and years—but now it's all done Tell him, when he grows, how hard I fought for him; but what's one old man against——?''

'' 'Tis your wish I take him?''

Philip nodded.

''To his mother—from me.''

. Presently he spoke to the slumbering child.

''Good-bye, boy; and if ever you hear tell of this night——''

He broke off, then resumed:

''Pick him up and begone. There's a little blanket as I bought for him—wait a minute.''

He fetched the wrap and Wesley's other clothes that hung by the fire. The child was fretful at being wakened and dressed.

''I shall be back so soon as ever I can,'' declared Tiger. ''I'm coming to spend the rest of the night with you But 'twill be morning a 'most before I can be up again. You get off to bed, and I lay I'll bring some joyful words from his mother presently.''

They were at the entrance now.

''No call for you to come back. None need ever come back to me no more. It's all ended now.''

''Don't you say that. Lie down and get a bit of rest. You'll see 'em to-morrow.''

Tiger went away.

''Keep him warm!''

''That I will,'' shouted back the other from the dark-

29

ness. " 'Tis as mild as milk to-night. He'll take no hurt."

Dawn had broken before the weary Tiger returned to Brown's House and found the door wide open and the place empty. Thin white light struggled through the window, but there was not enough to show the interior. The candle had guttered out and gone, so Tiger lighted matches and looked about him. On the table was an empty glass and a bottle of whisky that had been knocked over. Part of its contents had flooded an open Bible. A pencil lay in the book, and a broken clay pipe was upon the floor.

Tiger entered the bedroom, then he looked round the house. A dog came from its kennel, but there was no sign of Philip Ouldsbroom. It seemed that some impulse had called him forth suddenly.

Tiger walked round about and shouted until the hills cried back faint echoes; but no answer came.

Morning broke crystalline over the hills and a cock crew.

CHAPTER XVII

For two days great hue-and-cry was made after Philip Ouldsbroom, and then it chanced that Martin discovered him.

Many had scoured the Moor, persisting in their quest from early dawn to twilight of evening; but it remained for the new master of Hartland to find the old master, and then it was by an accident that he did so.

Riding at sunset of the second day, Martin came aloft to the steep valley of West Dart At hand stood Crow Tor, and he dismounted and approached it. His purpose was to climb the rocks, if possible, and survey the hills round about with a telescope, which he had borrowed for this search.

Upon the crown of the tor an evening wind played faint music and touched the stones to melody, even as a dawn wind, at the morning of days, woke Memnon's granite lips to welcome the ascending sun. But this stone breathed an elegy through the gloaming and made a lamentation for the dead. Beneath it, stretched along, lay Ouldsbroom on his face. He had sought his haunt, climbed to his familiar eyrie unde. the rampire of the tor, and lain down and died there. His hair was dabbled with the falling dew,

> . . . his bowed head seemed listening to the Earth,
> His ancient mother, for some comfort yet.

Martin carefully drew the dead man's watch out of his pocket. It was an heirloom of gold.

At dayspring they came and carried the body away to Hartland.

A shining bed in the whortleberry and green grass
persisted for some hours to mark the place of passing;
but leaf and herbage were restored anon. They lifted
themselves again and sprang up to the call of the life
within them   Then that silvery depression disappeared,
as the sleeping lairs of flocks and herds vanish when they
rise up at dawn and go upon their way.

Unmarked, a scrap of dirty paper remained upon the
little plateau after Philip was borne from it. Now this
fragment, touched by the wind, moved to the edge of the
rocks and presently lifted into air   It hovered, fluttered,
fell into the peaty pool beneath and floated there.

The dead man had fingered it a thousand times and
never parted from it   Once he tore it in half, then
changed his mind and mended the pages again. It was
Martin's first letter, but upon it now might have been
read more than the child had set down. A faltering
scrawl ran over the last empty page, where Philip had
copied words from Job before he entered upon his
journey.

*"He shall be driven from light into darkness and
chased out of the world..."*

Presently the paper sank beneath the surface of the
pool and vanished.

THE END

Lightning Source UK Ltd.
Milton Keynes UK
UKHW020927150822
407319UK00007B/1282